DATE DUE

OCT 27 2005		
MAY 17 2006		
DEC 10 2006		
APR 13 2007		
NOV 26 2007		
NOV 26 2007		

GAYLORD PRINTED IN U.S.A.

DEATH, GRIEF, AND CARING RELATIONSHIPS

DEATH, GRIEF, AND CARING RELATIONSHIPS

Richard A. Kalish

Theodore Lownik Library
Illinois Benedictine College
Lisle, Illinois 60532

Brooks/Cole Publishing Company
Monterey, California

155.937
K14d

Brooks/Cole Publishing Company
A Division of Wadsworth, Inc.

© 1981 by Wadsworth, Inc., Belmont, California 94002.
All rights reserved. No part of this book may be reproduced,
stored in a retrieval system, or transcribed,
in any form or by any means—electronic, mechanical,
photocopying, recording, or otherwise—without
the prior written permission of the publisher,
Brooks/Cole Publishing Company,
Monterey, California 93940, a division of Wadsworth, Inc.

Printed in the United States of America

10 9 8 7 6 5 4 3 2

Library of Congress Cataloging in Publication Data

Kalish, Richard A.
Death, grief, and caring relationships.

Bibliography: p.
Includes index.
1. Death. 2. Bereavement. 3. Grief.
4. Helping behavior. I. Title.
HQ1073.K34 155.9'37 80–18938
ISBN 0–8185–0417–X

Acquisition Editor: Todd Lueders
Manuscript Editor: Merle Stern
Production Editor: Sally Schuman
Interior Design: Ruth Scott
Cover Design: Stan Rice
Typesetting: Holmes Typography, Inc.

This book is dedicated to Suzanne,
who told me that I would learn from her
about death, and instead I learned
to become more open to life.
Which is the same thing.

PREFACE

Death is both universal and personal. It is always a part of our future and is frequently effectively denied. It pervades our arts, our sciences, our politics, our educational systems, our technologies, our philosophies. As a boundary to life that is always present, it serves to organize our lives, yet if death is constantly dwelt upon, life is never lived.

It was over a dozen years ago that I decided I wanted to write this book, which I felt would be both personal and informational, but I knew that I wasn't ready to do so. I felt I didn't know enough. Three years ago, I realized that I would never know enough, and so I began to write. Before I began, however, I needed to know why I was writing the book. Royalties, professional stature, desire for recognition, the enjoyment of writing—all these were factors, but they weren't the cogent issues. What were?

First, there was a great deal that I wished to say, and I wanted as wide an audience as possible. For over 20 years, my professional life has focused on the themes of death and dying. I wanted to integrate what I had learned in those years in the hope that what was of value to me would also be of value to others.

Second, my own professional involvement with death and loss has obviously affected my personal life, and I strongly believe that the influence has been very positive. I am enjoying life and, as long as I do, the prospect of my death is very unwelcome. Someday when I realize that I am facing my own imminent death, I am certain that I will respond with many of the feelings about which I have written. However, I have often thought about what death will be for me, and I believe that these reflections will enable me to better use the time during which I know my death is imminent and enable me to confront my own death with less fear and anxiety. I believe that others who contemplate death, in general, and their own death and dying, in particular, before these become imminent realities can also benefit.

Third, I had the conceit to believe that I could write a book that would be better than other books about death. I believed that I could use what others had written, what people had told me, and what I had observed and experienced myself to write a book that would say it all better.

As I wrote this book, I felt as if I were talking to people rather than writing. Sometimes it seemed as if I were in a workshop, other times in a classroom, and still other times as if I were sitting around with friends at home. And so my audience developed generically from my writing, rather than having my writing specifically geared to an audience.

I am writing for people who want "one book to give me the most understanding of death, the process of dying, and grief." It may be that these people work with the dying in professional or volunteer settings; they may be students in a class on death; they may be individuals in the community who suddenly find that death has become an important part of their lives; or they may simply be people who wish to learn and understand more about death and dying.

The book is intended for people who are just beginning their inquiry as well as for those who have experienced or worked with death, dying, and grief and wish to supplement their practical knowledge. It is for academics who do not resent a book that includes personal observations and for non-academics who are not antagonistic to research and theory.

I wish to acknowledge, first of all, those individuals whose writings have served as a basis for much of my thinking and whose friendship has served as encouragement. I know I am omitting many when I acknowledge Jacques Choron, Herman Feifel, Bob Fulton, John Hinton, Bob Kastenbaum, Colin Parkes, Bob Veatch, and Avery Weisman.

I also want to acknowledge those experts to whom we turned to review the manuscript. Here we tried to select persons to represent a broad spectrum of views and backgrounds: Herb Archibald (clinical medicine), Hank Basayne (humanistic psychology), John Evans (psychology and the ministry), John W. Riley, Jr. (sociology), Ida Martinson (nursing), Vic Marshall (sociology), and Mansell Pattison (psychiatry).

Others who read or helped in developing briefer sections of the book include Marcy Adamski, John Bergez, Cindy Bouman, Stan Friedman, John Enright, Charlie Garfield, Howard Raether, Amy Schenone, and Martin Sicker.

Richard A. Kalish

CONTENTS

DEATH, GRIEF, AND CARING RELATIONSHIPS

PART

1
THE MEANING OF DEATH

The Horse on the Dining-Room Table

I struggled up the slope of Mount Evmandu to meet the famous guru of Nepsim, an ancient sage whose name I was forbidden to place in print. I was much younger then, but the long and arduous hike exhausted me, and, despite the cold, I was perspiring heavily when I reached the plateau where he made his home. He viewed me with a patient, almost amused, look, and I smiled wanly at him between attempts to gulp the thin air into my lungs. I made my way across the remaining hundred meters and slowly sat down on the ground—propping myself up against a large rock just outside his abode.

We were both silent for several minutes, and I felt the tension in me rise, then subside until I was calm. Perspiration prickled my skin, but the slight breeze was pleasantly cool, and soon I was relaxed. Finally I turned my head to look directly into the clear brown eyes, which were bright within his lined face. I realized that I would need to speak.

"Father," I said "I need to understand something about what it means to die, before I can continue my studies." He continued to gaze at me with his open, bemused expression. "Father," I went on "I want to know what a dying person feels when no one will speak with him, nor be open enough to permit him to speak, about his dying."

He was silent for three, perhaps four, minutes. I felt at peace because I knew he would answer. Finally, as though in the middle of a sentence, he said "It is the horse on the dining-room table." We continued to gaze at each other for several minutes. I began to feel sleepy after my long journey, and I must have dozed off. When I woke up, he was gone, and the only activity was my own breathing.

I retraced my steps down the mountain—still feeling calm, knowing that his answer made me feel good, but not knowing why. I returned to my studies and gave no further thought to the event, not wishing to dwell upon it, yet secure that someday I should understand.

Many years later I was invited to the home of a casual friend for dinner. It was a modest house in a typical California development. The eight or ten other guests, people I did not know well, and I sat in the living

"The Horse on the Dining Room Table," by Richard Kalish. Copyright © 1980 by Richard A. Kalish. Reprinted by permission.

room—drinking Safeway Scotch and bourbon and dipping celery sticks and raw cauliflower into a watery cheese dip. The conversation, initially halting, became more animated as we got to know each other and developed points of contact. The drinks undoubtedly also affected us.

Eventually the hostess appeared and invited us into the dining room for a buffet dinner. As I entered the room, I noticed with astonishment that a brown horse was sitting quietly on the dining-room table. Although it was small for a horse, it filled much of the large table. I caught my breath, but didn't say anything. I was the first one to enter, so I was able to turn to watch the other guests. They responded much as I did—they entered, saw the horse, gasped or stared, but said nothing.

The host was the last to enter. He let out a silent shriek—looking rapidly from the horse to each of his guests with a wild stare. His mouth formed soundless words. Then in a voice choked with confusion he invited us to fill our plates from the buffet. His wife, equally disconcerted by what was clearly an unexpected horse, pointed to the name cards, which indicated where each of us was to sit.

The hostess led me to the buffet and handed me a plate. Others lined up behind me—each of us quiet. I filled my plate with rice and chicken and sat in my place. The others followed suit.

It was cramped, sitting there, trying to avoid getting too close to the horse, while pretending that no horse was there. My dish overlapped the edge of the table. Others found other ways to avoid physical contact with the horse. The host and hostess seemed as ill-at-ease as the rest of us. The conversation lagged. Every once in a while, someone would say something in an attempt to revive the earlier pleasant and innocuous discussion, but the overwhelming presence of the horse so filled our thoughts that talk of taxes or politics or the lack of rain seemed inconsequential.

Dinner ended, and the hostess brought coffee. I can recall everything on my plate and yet have no memory of having eaten. We drank in silence—all of us trying not to look at the horse, yet unable to keep our eyes or thoughts anywhere else.

I thought several times of saying "Hey, there's a horse on the dining-room table." But I hardly knew the host, and I didn't wish to embarrass him by mentioning something that obviously discomforted him at least as much as it discomforted me. After all, it was his house. And what do you say to a man with a horse on his dining-room table? I could have said that I did not mind, but that was not true—its presence upset me so much that I enjoyed neither the dinner nor the company. I could have said that I knew how difficult it was to have a horse on one's dining-room table, but that wasn't true either; I had no idea. I could have said something like "How do you feel about having a horse on your dining-room table?" but I didn't want to sound like a psychologist. Perhaps, I thought, if I ignore it, it will go away. Of course I knew that it wouldn't. It didn't.

I later learned that the host and hostess were hoping the dinner would be a success in spite of the horse. They felt that to mention it would make us so uncomfortable that we wouldn't enjoy our visit—of course we didn't enjoy the evening anyway. They were fearful that we would try to offer them sympathy, which they didn't want, or understanding, which they needed but could not accept. They wanted the party to be a success, so they decided to try to make the evening as enjoyable as possible. But it was apparent that they—like their guests—could think of little else than the horse.

I excused myself shortly after dinner and went home. The evening had been terrible. I never wanted to see the host and hostess again, although I was eager to seek out the other guests and learn what they felt about the occasion. I felt confused about what had happened and extremely tense. The evening had been grotesque. I was careful to avoid the host and hostess after that, and I did my best to stay away altogether from the neighborhood.

Recently I visited Nepsim again. I decided to seek out the guru once more. He was still alive, although nearing death, and he would speak only to a few. I repeated my journey and eventually found myself sitting across from him.

Once again I asked "Father, I want to know what a dying person feels when no one will speak with him, nor be open enough to permit him to speak, about his dying."

The old man was quiet, and we sat without speaking for nearly an hour. Since he did not bid me leave, I remained. Although I was content, I feared he would not share his wisdom, but he finally spoke. The words came slowly.

"My son, it is the horse on the dining-room table. It is a horse that visits every house and sits on every dining-room table—the tables of the rich and of the poor, of the simple and of the wise. This horse just sits there, but its presence makes you wish to leave without speaking of it. If you leave, you will always fear the presence of the horse. When it sits on your table, you will wish to speak of it, but you may not be able to.

"However, if you speak about the horse, then you will find that others can also speak about the horse—most others, at least, if you are gentle and kind as you speak. The horse will remain on the dining-room table, but you will not be so distraught. You will enjoy your repast, and you will enjoy the company of the host and hostess. Or, if it is your table, you will enjoy the presence of your guests. You cannot make magic to have the horse disappear, but you can speak of the horse and thereby render it less powerful."

The old man then rose and, motioning me to follow, walked slowly to his hut. "Now we shall eat," he said quietly. I entered the hut and had difficulty adjusting to the dark. The guru walked to a cupboard in the corner and took out some bread and some cheese, which he placed on a mat. He motioned to me to sit and share his food. I saw a small horse sitting quietly in the center of the mat. He noticed this and said "That horse need not disturb us." I thoroughly enjoyed the meal. Our discussion lasted far into the night, while the horse sat there quietly throughout our time together.

1

BECOMING AWARE

Dying.
Death.
Dead.

Three words so easy to pronounce and so difficult to say. And because they are so difficult to say, we often say them in very strange ways. Sometimes we use euphemisms: passed on, terminal, gone west, no longer here, expired, in heaven, in a better place, beyond help, with the angels. Sometimes we restrict our thinking to large numbers: 2 million deaths a year, over 50,000 killed annually in automobile accidents, 1000 dead in Chilean earthquake. Sometimes we fall back on platitudes: it's better that way; she's at peace now; we all have to go sometime; he was old anyway.

Death is the ultimate touchstone for human endeavors. It is the ultimate organizer of time. It is the ultimate enemy of self. It is the ultimate leveler of all persons. It is the ultimate uncertainty and the ultimate certainty, the ultimate chance event, the ultimate negator of passions and plans and power and personal growth.

We are the only members of the animal kingdom able to anticipate personal death and potential extinction, although other animals obviously fight for survival, and some appear to know when death is impending. Nonetheless, only we can plan our lives and our individual actions with our future deaths as one determinant. This very ability to anticipate death is a source of anxiety, planning, denial, love, achievement and lack of achievement, and feelings of meaningfulness and meaninglessness. Awareness of death leads to poetry and visual art and music, to building and conquest, as well as to deceit and whining and pain and pettiness.

The significance of personal death is so immense, so overwhelming, that, in order to escape its contemplation, we use many devices: humor, alcohol and drugs, denial and overt anger. We immerse ourselves in activities in order to avoid thinking of death and risk our lives in order to challenge and symbolically overcome death. Even reading a book on death or taking a course—or writing a book or teaching a course—may be a device to shift death and dying from the personal into the academic, from the emotional to the intellectualized.

There are times when we want to talk about dying or death or the dead; the words form in our minds and on our tongues, but they will not come out of our mouths, so we just giggle or pass on to another topic or pluck a euphemism from the air.

LaRochefoucauld, a philosopher writing over 300 years ago, said that "the human mind is as little capable to contemplate death for any length of time as the eye is able to look at the sun" (Choron, 1964, p. 107). When we need to or wish to look at the sun, we wear special smoked glasses and protect ourselves from danger and pain; when we need to or want to look at death, we also find ways to protect ourselves from danger and pain.

In the past decade, people have begun "to look at the sun" in increasing numbers. The words—*dying, death, dead*—are becoming easier to say, at least for many people. Your foremost concern may be with your own eventual death, with the death of one other person, with the deaths of many people, with the deaths of innumerable others whom you presently don't know—or with all of these. Whatever your individual circumstances, you are now reading this book and, therefore, "looking at the sun." I obviously don't agree with LaRochefoucauld—I wouldn't or couldn't have written this book if I did. I do fully believe that, by the time you have read about 100 pages, you will find yourself able to look at the sun. Doing so will not make you a hero or mean you are supernaturally strong. It will indicate that you live in an era when looking at the sun has been made somewhat easier.

For a few people, the sun will still be painfully blinding, and I would encourage them to find some way to avoid the sun. Even those of us who have been studying, writing about, talking about, and working with death and the dying for many years find there are times when it shines too brightly, and we retreat for a while. You too may find such times. Or you may find that you need to retreat completely. If so, please do. This book should be read for enlightenment, learning, ideas, perhaps enjoyment; reading it is not an endurance test or a symbol of personal worth.

THE HORSE ON THE DINING-ROOM TABLE

Recall the parable about a horse on the dining-room table. When the guests came in for dinner, there it was, quietly sitting and munching. The host, not wishing to upset his guests, made no reference to the horse; the guests, not wishing to upset the host, made no reference to the horse. Consequently, they ate their dinner in silence—so overwhelmed by the presence of the horse that they could neither carry on a conversation nor enjoy the dinner and so imbued with their notion of politeness that they dared not mention the horse. The horse, of course, was death.

We do not have the luxury of ignoring the horse on the dining-room table. Death makes an impact on all of us. Some of us encounter death through our academic programs; some of us meet death in our work; all of us experience death and its multiple meanings in our personal lives and day-to-day actions.

ACADEMIC PROGRAMS

Perhaps you have assumed that only student funeral directors deal with death in their academic programs, but this definitely is not the case. The subject matter of many academic fields includes death: medicine, nursing, anthropology, history, religion and theology, philosophy, criminal justice and law, and demography are only the most obvious examples.

The fact that death and dying are part of an academic program says little about their treatment in the program. Although death often guides the course of history, historians rarely become emotional about deaths; although anthropologists and archeologists study funeral rituals, tombs and burial sites, and death-related practices, they seldom become personally concerned about the death of one individual; and not only demographers, who study death rates, but medical students, who study the etiology and treatment of death-causing diseases, frequently become more involved in numbers or in tissues than in people.

What I am contending is not that student historians, anthropologists, and physicians ought to mourn each death they read about but that colleges and universities have long taught about death and dying in contexts that often depersonalized this extremely personal event.

DEATH-RELATED VOCATIONS

For centuries, a special caste in Japan, the *eta*, was discriminated against because its members slaughtered animals for food and leather. The caste was hereditary; outsiders were reluctant to marry into the *eta* or otherwise join a group that was ostracized from most of the rest of society (Dore, 1958). Although the strict sanctions of decades ago no longer prevail, the *eta* today still are victims of discrimination.

Work with the dying and dead has also been taboo in much of modern day Western culture. Funeral directors, for example, serve as the butts of jokes and as lightning rods for guilt and anger. Grave diggers and other cemetery workers, although avoiding the attacks that are made on funeral directors, are frequently considered persons to be avoided. Deputy coroners also feel that they share this taboo by virtue of their work in investigating causes of death. The wife of one deputy coroner told friends that her husband "worked for the county," in order to be vague about the kind of work he did; many deputy coroners admit that they prefer to socialize with each other to avoid the embarrassment of discussing their vocations with outsiders who would not understand (Reynolds & Kalish, 1976). This sounds a great deal like the plight of the *eta* in Japan today—not officially segregated or isolated, but kept apart by the responses of others and their own discomfort.

Not all vocations concerned with death and dying elicit avoidance. Physicians and nurses are constantly involved with death, and the association does not appear to affect their social status; of course, only a small portion of their work is with the dying, and virtually none is with the dead. Other hospital workers also encounter death: licensed vocational nurses, aides, orderlies, social workers, administrators, record keepers—even the janitorial staff and volunteers occasionally find themselves relating to the dying, the dead, or the survivors.

Consider some of the other vocations that lead to working with the dying, the dead, or matters concerned with death and dying:

- Florists, a large proportion of whose business depends on funerals and cemetery visits;
- Police, who rarely kill—or even shoot anyone—but who often arrive at the scene of a death, decide what to do with a body, and inform family members of the death;
- Life insurance salespersons, who, if properly named, would be called "death insurance salespersons" because they spend their time persuading people to hedge their bets on living and to bet on dying. That is, the sooner a person dies, the more the insurance company has to pay off; if a person lives a long time, the relative payoff is much less;
- Estate planners, who, like life insurance salespersons, are primarily involved with people who are concerned that after their own deaths their money, property, children, spouses, and /or businesses are properly cared for;
- Politicians, whose legislation in the areas of crime punishment, health funding, wars, and the physical and psychological environments frequently determines who lives and who dies;
- Actuaries and demographers, who predict and tabulate deaths by the tens, hundreds, thousands, and millions;
- The military and military planners, who are sometimes ordered to kill and other times required to decide how many millions of deaths a particular country can suffer and still have a military capability;
- The neophyte journalists who write the obituaries;
- The chemists who provide the embalming fluids, makeup, and other chemicals for the funeral industry; the hair stylists and makeup artists who work on those bodies that will have open-casket ceremonies or otherwise be viewed; the casket manufacturers; the automotive industry that manufactures hearses;

- The clergy: those who have congregations, those who serve as chaplains in hospitals and nursing homes, those who provide pastoral counseling;
- Writers, artists, and musicians, who are sufficiently moved by death, dying, and suffering to create words or visual representations or music to communicate their insights and feelings.

There are others you may wish to mention: judges, ambulance drivers, and fire fighters, for example. Some of the professions in our list allow their practitioners to remain isolated from the emotional impact of actual dying and death. Actuaries and chemists, for example, never have any contact in their work with individuals who are dying. Their professional relationship with the dying is impersonal, and they seldom—from what we know—even think very much about individual deaths, except when their personal circumstances evoke such thoughts.

Others cannot remain so isolated. Life insurance salespersons often must call on the survivors; police officers may find themselves leading a funeral procession along a freeway or informing a young woman that her husband has been killed in an automobile accident; clergy and health professionals frequently minister to the dying and their survivors, although both their areas of specialization and personal preferences determine how frequent and how extensive this care is.

It would be reasonable to assume that persons in these last-named vocations might have background training in the meaning of death and in working in the death-related setting. As is often the case, however, the reasonable course is not the one followed. Only very recently have health professionals and clergy begun to develop educational programs that focus on the dying; only in very unusual settings will police or life insurance salespersons attend any formal program on death and dying. If my personal observations are accurate, nurses, clergy, and funeral directors have done more than other vocational groups to advance their knowledge of how to care for dying persons and their survivors; however, even their training sometimes consists of no more than a brief one-day program every two or three years. In the final analysis, of course, it is personal reactions and social attitudes, not vocational identity, that matter most, and many people, using just common sense and intuition, do very well without training or experience.

DEATH AND DYING IN PERSONAL EXPERIENCES

For a very few people, death and dying are a significant, even a major, part of their vocation, and they must confront these events on a personal level every day; for many more people, death and dying are a modest or minor part of their vocation, and they confront these phenomena on occasion or at considerable psychological distance.

What about you?

You are alive and over the age of 10. Therefore, the event of death most likely has or will soon become part of your experience; perhaps the event has already occurred. A grandparent, a neighbor, a family friend, sometimes a pet dies. Each of us faces about five or six major deaths in our lifetimes. Maybe you were first on the scene after a fatal traffic accident or a neighbor's heart attack. The person who died might have been someone to whom you were very much attached or perhaps someone you never saw. The deaths of John and Robert Kennedy and Martin Luther King affected millions of people as strongly as deaths of friends or family members.

If you are under 30, it is possible—not probable but possible—that you have not yet encountered a death that has seriously affected you. You never really knew your two grandparents who died recently, and the other two died before you were 18 months old; you were out of town when the man who lived in the apartment below you died, and you never had much to do with him anyway; you were attached to your dog, but it was really much more your brother's pet than yours.

If you are over 40, it is very likely that you have lost someone close through death. Even if you did a good job of anticipatory bereavement—that is, worked through your feelings about an impending death before the death occurred—or you disengaged from a strong attachment some time before the person died, the impact of the death would not have disappeared altogether.

And then there is your confrontation with your own death. Based on what people have told me over the years, I would estimate that the odds are about one in five or one in six that you have already experienced a situation in which you expected to die: you almost drowned; you were in a serious automobile accident; you were lying in a hospital bed when you overheard the physician tell someone that you were not likely to pull through; you were trapped by a forest fire. The older you are and the more risks you like to take with your life, the more probable it is that you have had the kind of experience to which I am referring.

There is another kind of death confrontation, and that can happen to anyone at any time. For example: one morning, as you were driving home from work, the automobile radio announced the death of a close friend in a motorcycle accident. While you were stuck in traffic, you began to think about this death, and your thoughts drifted to your own eventual death. Suddenly it struck you: someday I'm going to die. Me. *I* am going to die. This too shall pass—and I am part of *this*. *I* will be a statistic, an obituary in the newspaper, a death notice, a body prettified in a casket around which those I love will weep, a decaying body in the desert/on a snow-covered mountain/in the ocean. . . .

You came several degrees closer to acknowledging your own mortality, your own finitude, your own humanness. You experienced your own death in fantasy, and the experience was distressingly real.

Death and dying are not at all foreign to your experience. You encounter reminders of your death in your aging process. You have read about death, seen dying portrayed in the media, visited people who were dying or who had recently lost someone they loved through death; spent several minutes studying a crucifix, wondered about the meaning of "Now I lay me down to sleep," which you first heard as a child, spent several seconds watching a heavy truck coming straight at your VW at 45 miles per hour. You have done these things, and you have survived, sometimes a little worse for the experience, more often a little better for the experience. This may or may not be the first book you have ever read about death and dying, but it is most definitely not your first significant experience.

THE WORDS ARE THERE

Maybe you are young or fortunate enough not to have lost anyone close. Or perhaps, although the death of others has been part of your life from time to time, you feel these events have never played a meaningful role in what you do or what you think about. Although you may have been untouched in either way, perhaps you still find that death and dying are on your mind, indirectly or symbolically, much of the time. How close death and dying are to our consciousnesses is shown by the extent to which death-related words and expressions appear in everyday vocabulary. For example:

- sudden death overtime
- talk a subject to death
- drop dead
- a dead issue
- dead right
- dead ahead
- dead reckoning
- deadhead
- dead from the neck up
- dead weight
- graveyard shift
- killing time
- dead personality
- crucified a speaker
- killed legislation
- political suicide
- deadbeat
- dead end
- dying to meet you

None of these words and idioms refers to literal death, but—with two or three exceptions—you have little difficulty in knowing what is meant, even if you had never heard the expressions before. And with relatively little effort, you could add another six or eight phrases yourself in a few minutes.

Many of these expressions have become so much a part of normal conversation that their reference to death is not even noticed. So have some other kinds of language:

> Ring around the rosy,
> Pockets full of posy,
> Ashes, ashes,
> All fall down.

A familiar rhyme. Children holding hands, moving in a circle, then sprawling in many directions with many poses. Did you ever wonder what the familar rhyme originally meant? Probably not—I never did until someone called it to my attention.

"Ring around the rosy": The infections of bubonic plague, which devastated Europe during the Middle Ages, erupted as rose-colored pox with a ring around each.

"Pockets full of posy": Death was so common that people carried flowers with them to cover the stench; flowers for the dead were also carried.

"Ashes, Ashes": Cremation was necessary to get rid of the bodies that no one wished to touch.

"All fall down": Often "All fall dead" is substituted.

Children in one century developed a rhyme game to cope with death—a rhyme that children in a later century continue to find fun. Although today's children are not aware of the original meaning of the rhyme, it appears that in some unconscious fashion they respond with excitement to its message—perhaps as a way to handle their own death anxieties.

We have become so deeply concerned about the role of media like television and comic books in portraying death to children that we tend to ignore the importance the theme has always had in children's "media." In *Snow White and the Seven Dwarfs* and *Sleeping Beauty*, the apparently dead return to life; in *Jack and the Beanstalk* and *The Wizard of Oz*, good children kill the perpetrators of evil; in the tales of *King Arthur* and *Robin Hood*, the villains die, but the heroes also eventually die. And most of the deaths in the above stories are violent.

The vocabulary of death is always around us, and the themes of death and dying permeate our folk history and legends. Their symbolic, mythic treatment of death allows us to experience our death-related anxieties in such a way that we remain defended against feeling too much anxiety.

AND THE WORDS ARE NOT THERE

Sometimes just the opposite happens. We use the words *death* and *dead* when we mean something else, but we use other words to talk about death and the dead. A number of years ago I spent well over an hour with a lawyer discussing my will and the disposition of my estate. Underlying all that we were talking about was the *fact*—not the assumption or premise or hypothesis, but the fact—that I was eventually going to die. Yet at no point in the conversation did the lawyer ever use the words that referred most directly to what we were discussing.

What did he say? "When you are no longer here. . . ." "After you've gone. . . ." "In the event of your inability to provide. . . ." Finally I asked him where I was going to be "when I was no longer here," but the question so disconcerted him that I decided to leave the issue alone.

The number of euphemisms for death-related words is legion: passed over, went west, across the Great Divide, expired, is with God, went to her Maker, is sleeping with the angels, gone to a well-deserved rest, went to his reward, and so on. There are some situations in which we can easily say "He died" or "How do you feel about dying?" In other situations, the words stick—they just won't come out—and so we shift to other words that have the same meaning but express it in ways that seem gentler. What makes these words "gentler" is that they mask the painful reality of what has occurred.

Thus, while our vocabulary is filled with *dead* and *die* and *death*, the literal meanings of these words are often not used and frequently are avoided. And the closer the reality of death is to us or those we are talking to, the less likely we are to use the words.

THE ARTS AND DEATH

All of the arts have something to say about death and the process of dying. The most immediately obvious, perhaps, are those that use language: fiction, drama, poetry, film, and the lyrics of songs. The novel of James Agee, *A Death in the Family*, expresses the anguish of a dying person and his survivors more vividly than any lecture on the topic. In the novel *Cancer Ward*, Alexander Solzhenitsyn uses death as both reality and metaphor. The death of Don Quixote in Cervantes' novel is accompanied by his decision to halt his bizarre behavior. *Memento Mori*, by Muriel Sparks, is a profound novel of older persons' encounters with death. And Tolstoy's famous short story, *The Death of Ivan Illych*, is probably the best-known piece of fiction that describes the feelings of a man who is condemned to death by illness. The list is endless.

In some plays of Shakespeare like *Hamlet, Macbeth, King Lear,* and *Romeo and Juliet* death is eloquently examined through plot, character, and language. Willy Loman, the salesman in Arthur Miller's *Death of a Salesman*, represents many feelings about the meaning of life and about leaving life. Thornton Wilder's *Our Town* has a poignant scene in which a young woman who has died is permitted to relive one day of her life—but the pain of how much the living take life for granted is too great, and she begs for an early return to the grave.

Popular songs, including rock, country-and-Western, and musical show tunes, often have messages about death; their lyrics frequently describe the death of a beloved person. Although I need not enumerate how often death figures in operas, I will note that even comic strips and television shows occasionally touch on the serious side of life through a comment on death.

Paintings and other graphic art forms often depict either scenes or symbols of death. Sometimes, of course, the scene is obvious: a man before a firing squad, a battlefield strewn with corpses, a family surrounding a sick woman. Visual symbols frequently include an hourglass or some other timepiece (Ingmar Bergman's films have also used this device), a scythe, a skull, bones, a closed book (in some contexts), coffins, a figure representing death, knives, guns, the ruins of buildings, a cemetery (Gottlieb, 1959). Both the content and the mood are relevant in examining the message of the artist.

Through the centuries artists have also applied their talent to "designing for death." As British artist Barbara Jones examines in her excellent book, artists have designed coffins, gravestones, cemeteries, memorial monuments, and death announcements (Jones, 1967).

Because music is abstract, the theme of death may be harder to identify in this art. Nevertheless, some music has been composed specifically for death: traditional and Black funeral marches, requiems, and spirituals, for example. Other music has death and dying as its theme: think of Richard Strauss' *Death and Transfiguration* and Saint-Saen's *Danse Macabre*.

This topic deserves far more attention than I have given it here. The arts are the expression of our deepest feelings—frequently of feelings and experiences of which we are only partly, or not at all, aware. Even during the time that death and dying were not much discussed around hospitals and homes, creative artists continued to represent their feelings in their work. Observations of children have shown that, even at an early age, they can both respond to death themes in the arts, especially fiction and paintings, and create their own artistic productions for comfort and insight (Bertman, 1979–80).

DEATH AWARENESS: FAD, FASHION, OR SOCIAL CHANGE?

Since the beginning of the 1970s, the popularity of death and dying as subjects of conversation has grown immensely. Rather than being taboo, the topic has become appropriate for cocktail party conversation; instead of receiving furtive mention only in medical and behavioral journals, the subject receives constant exposure in newspapers and magazines, on television and call-in radio shows, and in numerous books. No longer discussed only among the "faithful"—and then in whispers—death has become so familiar a topic that the expression "death and dying" is virtually in danger of becoming *d* 'n' *d*. What has happened to produce this change? Is it just a fad, which will soon disappear, or is it a meaningful social change, effectively built into the fabric of our society?

I firmly believe that the recent interest in death and concern for the dying are not merely fads but the consequences of a variety of social changes. These may include: the atomic bomb with its potential for worldwide annihilation, the possibility of ecological disaster, increased life expectancy and the possibility of still greater increases, and the ability of television to bring pictures of war and death vividly into our homes. I would like to explore some of the causes which I believe have been particularly instrumental.

THE SEARCH FOR THE UNDERSERVICED AND UNDERPRIVILEGED

During the 1960s, students and nonstudents who wished to be socially active were readily able to find causes, such as the civil rights movement and the antiwar movement. By the early 1970s, the war in Vietnam had ended, and the civil rights movement had been taken over by those ethnic communities whose rights were at stake. The women's movement, the gay liberation movement, and other later movements did not recruit active advocates from outside their own ranks. This left many young people (and some not-so-young) who wished to serve others but were not certain whom to serve. The elderly and the dying (as well as the physically handicapped) welcomed the attention. Not only was a social/political cause presented but also the equally important opportunity to offer direct human services to needful persons.

At the same time, with the increased conservatism of the later 1970s, the old and the dying did not offer the political and economic threat posed by Third World ethnic communities. Young people could offer their time and energy without angering their parents; indeed, their parents, having older parents to care for, were likely to be highly supportive of their children's activities. Thus, the elderly and, therefore, the dying were "found" by activists. Although these paragraphs are highly speculative, I believe the idea merits attention.

INCREASED POLITICAL POWER OF THE ELDERLY

Older people were not only "found" by the young and middle-aged; they also found themselves. Not so much by increasing numbers, but by increasing education and political sophistication, the elderly began to have a considerable impact on the political scene during the mid-1970s. As a result, new service programs, new training programs for workers in the field, and new rewards for being older began to develop. The money and the jobs attracted more people to work with the elderly, and one of the inevitable outcomes was an intensified concern for working with the dying. If the search for the underserviced, mentioned above, attracted primarily the young, this social change attracted people of all ages to working with the elderly and the dying.

THE POTENTIAL FOR DESTRUCTION

"The atomic bomb does not merely destroy; it destroys the boundaries of destruction" (Lifton & Olson, 1974, p. 8). These authors state that, although we can conceptualize the death of a single person or even of many people, we cannot conceive of the enormity of the annihilation of humanity. Does the existence of this potential for total destruction actually affect the way an individual perceives his or her own death and dying? Very likely so. When asked whether they had "ever seriously considered that all human life might be eliminated from the earth," nearly 60% of a carefully selected sample of adults said that they had. Most commonly they imagined this would happen from a nuclear explosion, although cosmic supernatural events—for example, God's bringing the world to an end—and ecological disaster were also mentioned frequently (Kalish & Reynolds, 1976).

ADVANCES IN MEDICAL AND BIOMEDICAL TECHNOLOGY AND RESEARCH

As the health sciences advance in their knowledge of illness and continue to succeed in extending life expectancy, people expect still more of them. In effect, success breeds expectations of more success. Many reputable scientists are now discussing a quantum leap in life expectancy from biomedical research—not just an increase of a year or so per decade, but an increase of ten or 30 years. This would require more than the curing of illnesses or the improvement of the environment: it would require interference with the normal processes of human aging.

The possibility of significant increases in life expectancy has, ironically, brought people's attention to death and dying. The meaning of death changes in light of the possibility that it may be postponed for extended periods. At the same time, the fact that technology is already available to keep dying people alive for extended periods also brings attention to death and dying. Medical technology does not only extend healthy life; it also extends unhealthy life and the dying process. Many stories of persons whose death has been postponed only to permit an arduous and often painful dying process have been recounted. These cases elicit both sympathy and attention.

Thus, although we are told by knowledgeable persons that medical technology may bring about a significant extension of healthy life, we observe that medical technology can also bring about modest extensions of unhealthy life. We now discuss the right to die and the right to reject life prolongation. These possibilities cause us to consider the meaning of death and, therefore, of life.

LOOKING TO THE INNER SELF

In the 1950s and 1960s, science and technology seemed to foretell wonderful advances. They had virtually replaced traditional religion as the hope of the future. During these same decades, social and political activists were eagerly moving about the country—and the world—trying to change social conditions. Optimism, especially among the young, was high both for the future of science and technology and for the outcomes of energetic activism. Perhaps, at least to most, death seemed unimportant when it was possible to focus on social change.

By the end of the 1960s, the social climate had changed. Social activism was waning, and many of the early activists turned to an inner life—frequently studying with spiritual leaders or gurus. At the same time, optimism for science and technology had soured. Many food additives were found to be not life enhancing, but life diminishing; the factories that supplied consumer needs also dumped pollutants into the air and water; energy was no longer seen as infinitely expandable, and shortages became chronic.

Realizing the limits of social activism, distressed by the failure of the gods of science and technology to effect the good life, and perhaps also made cynical by the Vietnamese War, Watergate, and the increasing conservatism of trade unions, many people moved from seeking satisfaction in changing the world outside themselves to seeking fulfillment within themselves.

There had been previous portents. Beginning in the early 1950s, people became interested in Eastern religions and the inner-directed content of existentialism. At the same time, the use of hallucinogenic drugs began to increase dramatically. Drug "trips" and meditation both focused on the inner self, and both so encouraged a suspension of the familiar kinds of consciousness that they were sometimes referred to as "mini-deaths."

In addition, the human potential, or growth, movement increased in popularity— again a movement that encouraged looking within instead of without. This movement reversed a previous intellectual trend that held society responsible for the ills perpetrated by and upon individuals; once again you and I were being told that we were responsible for our behavior and for what happens to us. Even psychologists moved away from the position that parents influence their children as a kind of one-way street and began to ask how children, including infants, affected their parents.

In effect, the emphasis was shifting from considering the social milieu as the only really significant molding force to examining the individual self. The trend was not to seek change in the individual by manipulating the environment; instead, the potential for individual change was seen to reside within the individual. People began to ask questions about their own being, and this led them to ask about the meaning of their being and, therefore, the meaning of their not-being.

The consequence of all these social changes coinciding at this time in history was to enable people to examine the meaning of their lives, the meaning of life in general, and, thereby, the meaning of their deaths and the meaning of death in general.

So, to return to the beginning of this section: the recent interest in death and in caring for the dying is not an isolated occurrence but is embedded in the social fabric. It has developed because of a variety of social, political, economic, psychological, and religious forces, and its future will depend largely on what happens to those forces. However, in its development, this interest in death has produced its own followers (death educators, death counselors, hospice staff members, workshop leaders, writers), its own industries where its followers work, and its own access to the media. Given the extensive network of people who depend on it for income or personal satisfaction, the interest in death and dying is not likely to wane quickly.

SOURCES OF INFORMATION

Learning about death, dying, and loss, like learning about anything else, should combine personal experience and the knowledge, insights, and experiences of others. These "others" include not only behavioral and health scientists but also philosophers, artists, and persons who are most experienced in being with and working with the dying, the dead, and the bereaved.

Because most of the material in this book is drawn from the literature and comments of behavioral and health scientists, it is worth a few moments to consider the adequacy of these sources. The sources include personal observations, clinical cases, controlled observations, interviews and questionnaires, experiments, program evaluations, demographic data, and a variety of more unusual procedures, such as content analysis or the psychological autopsy. Also used are the personal experiences of people who are particularly sensitive to what is happening not only outside them but within them and who are capable of communicating their insights to others.

PERSONAL OBSERVATIONS

"I once knew a woman who. . . ." "Last year a student of mine. . . ." "A friend telephoned me just the other day to. . . . " "When my uncle died, I. . . ." "At the funeral in Minneapolis, the minister. . . ."

Part of learning in life is to make effective use of personal observations; it is also part of learning to avoid making too much of these observations. Sometimes a personal observation rings so true and seems to typify so many other experiences that it remains vivid. For example, some 15 years ago, a student told me that, when his mother was dying, the physician and his father and sister would talk about his mother's condition in whispers at the foot of the bed, then come to the head of the bed and tell her how well she looked. His mother finally said to him "They must think I'm either stupid or deaf not to know what they're talking about."

Personal observations can alert you to kinds of behavior and situations of which you may not previously have been aware, and then you can determine whether subsequent observations confirm your impressions or indicate that they were atypical. Also, when you observe or are told that the same event has happened to different people in various settings, you obviously begin to develop a principle from your observations.

There are serious limitations to placing too much faith in personal observations. First, because you bring your own biases to a situation, you are likely to attend to and recall only what fits them. A negative bias toward physicians or clergy may lead to your focusing on stories in which such persons are unfeeling or inept. Second, your life brings you into contact with a limited range of people; what they tell you represents, for example, only college graduates or only people who have ceased going to church or only young couples in a suburban community. Third, most of us don't have very many experiences from which to draw, so that one or two observations may lead us to our conclusions, or else a particularly dramatic event may cause us to ignore a larger number of contrary events.

When events concern death and dying, the chance for distortion in personal observation is particularly great, since the topic is so emotionally charged. Feelings are so intense that they may interfere with an accurate perception of what is going on. When, for example, the person dying is your mother or father, you may not be in a position to provide an objective evaluation of the behavior of the physician or the chaplain.

On the other hand, a lack of objectivity should not lead you to reject information altogether, since in some respects it is invaluable. In fact, throughout this book I have made use of personal anecdotes to illustrate various points. It is rare that a personal observation or experience can prove something to be the case, but such examples provide excellent illustrations that permit a better understanding of the significance of an issue. In the same fashion, I would encourage you to draw from your own experiences and observations to increase the depth of your understanding of these materials.

CLINICAL CASES

Physicians, psychotherapists, lawyers, and other professionals, all of whom have intensive interaction with a number of individuals sharing specified characteristics, are able to report their observations and document them with case descriptions. Sometimes they will report on one case in depth. One example of this is the description of a single case of a man in therapy for whom fear of death was an extremely important symptom (Segal, 1958); two sociologists wrote an entire book discussing one case of the dying process of a woman (Strauss & Glaser, 1970). At other times these people will review several cases at once. For example, six cases described in some detail plus allusions to others permitted two psychiatrists to describe the phenomenon of predilection to death (Weisman & Hackett, 1961).

The limitations of small numbers of clinical cases as a source of information are the same as those described in the previous section, with the exception that a person collecting cases is likely to be more accurate and objective than a person making unsystematic observations of what is going on around him or her. When a more substantial number of consecutive cases is studied, more definitive statements may be made.

CONTROLLED OBSERVATIONS

In the middle 1960s, a doctoral student at the University of California, Berkeley, spent several months carefully observing and recording behavior related to death and dying at two hospitals (Sudnow, 1967). He described how bodies are prepared for removal from the bed where the person died: "The body is generally handled nonreverently by aides and orderlies. In turning it around to wrap the sheet, it is grabbed roughly and rolled over with none of the gentility which one observes in the rolling of live persons" (p. 72). And a little later: "One aide, in demonstrating how bodies are wrapped to a new employee, took the young girl into a room where a patient had just been wrapped, and as she pointed to those features of the completed product which marked a good job, she made a point of ostensively showing what she meant, almost hitting the body at each point to demonstrate how tightly the sheet fit" (p. 22).

Sudnow's first statement is a generalization from a large number of observations; his second statement describes one particular event. His book provides a clear picture of how he conducted his observations and the theory behind his procedures. We assume that his generalizations are accurate and unbiased and that his examples are representative and not merely dramatic. However, we don't have to depend fully on the author's word—we also can evaluate what he says in terms of whether it is generally in accord with our own experience.

Controlled observations like these are qualitatively scientific but are not quantitative and will not satisfy persons who wish numbers to support statements. For example, Sudnow does not say what proportion of occasions "the body is . . . handled nonreverently." Is it 100% of the time? Or 90% or 51% or 27%? Some people will find the missing information important, while others will be relieved to read descriptive materials unhindered by charts and tables.

However, controlled observations can be quantified. Sudnow could have set up a careful program of rating the "reverence" with which bodies are handled and emerged with an average and a measure of variability, but that would have been inconsistent with his theories of optimum research procedures.

INTERVIEWS AND QUESTIONNAIRES

The academic journals are filled with studies based on interviews and questionnaires and concerned with death anxiety or fear of death or of dying. A recent critical review by sociologist Victor Marshall (in press) outlines and evaluates many of the instruments. Although matters have improved since an earlier review (Lester, 1967), there is still a long way to go. Developing a reliable and valid measure of feelings about death is extremely difficult, and it might be argued that all those available fall short of adequacy. One difficulty is that many studies are conducted with college students exclusively, who represent only a small segment of the population.

Although most of the studies using interviews and questionnaires have been limited to small groups, such as students in introductory psychology classes or nurses at a large hospital, some have had massive samples. Psychologist Edwin Shneidman developed a lengthy questionnaire asking about attitudes, beliefs, and experiences involving death, dying, and suicide and distributed it through *Psychology Today*. It received 30,000 responses through the mail (Shneidman, 1970, 1971).

A little earlier Daniel Cappon, a Canadian psychiatrist, distributed questionnaires to people visiting the Montreal Exposition, and about 10,000 persons returned their questionnaires to his staff. John Riley, Jr., a sociologist with a long-term interest in the topic, added a handful of questions about various aspects of death to a carefully conducted national survey that was administered to 2000 persons (1970). And Kalish and Reynolds (1976), a psychologist and an anthropologist working together, had interviewers spend a little over an hour each with 434 carefully selected adults, divided among four ethnic communities and three adult age groups, from the Greater Los Angeles area. Although the latter two studies surveyed fewer people, their use of better sampling techniques make their results more trustworthy. Despite this fact, the results from the Shneidman, Riley, and Kalish and Reynolds projects were all fairly similar. I'll refer to the results of these studies at various points in the book, but they are mentioned here to provide some idea of the scope of the research projects that have been conducted on death-related matters.

Not all interviews and questionnaires are used with people in the general community. As a matter of fact, special groups of people are more likely to be studied. Over the years these have included the elderly, patients in mental hospitals, the physically ill, cancer patients, widows and widowers, physicians, nurses, and other health professionals, and the ubiquitous college or university student.

Such studies operate in a variety of ways. Some ask open-ended questions that encourage the participants to talk about anything that comes to mind, while others employ questionnaires that require one-word or multiple-choice answers. Some questionnaires are sent through the mail; others are distributed door to door; and still others are handed out in school—for example, at the beginning of the first class meeting and again at the end of the last class meeting.

Not only the procedures but the kinds of information elicited also vary. Although questionnaires typically ask for attitudes, beliefs, and values, they may also request information concerning experiences, expectations, and knowledge. Studies have been conducted with children of various ages to investigate how the cognitive understanding of death and dying differs with age during childhood (Nagy, 1948).

The limitations of these kinds of research are well known. Since researchers can get answers only to the questions they do ask, unless the preliminary groundwork is very thorough, the important questions might be omitted. Also, there is obvious concern that people won't respond honestly when asked, for example, if they are afraid of death, whether they have ever "heard" or "seen" a dead person, or how long they would avoid going out on dates following the death of a spouse. Sometimes the difficulty is that the situation actually encourages faking a response; other times, because a person hasn't thought about a question, he or she gives an impressionistic, spur-of-the-moment response; still other times people reinterpret a question and respond in terms of the new interpretation.

Some problems arise because of the wording of questions. How afraid do you have to be to check *strongly agree* to a statement about fear of death? How do you respond if you are afraid of the dying process but not of death itself? What is death anyway? What if you really loathe the thought of dying and of being dead, but you don't think you are afraid?

Neither interviews nor questionnaires are restricted to direct questions with direct answers. More subtle approaches, like projective techniques, can be used. People can be asked to tell stories from cards depicting scenes that have some relationship to death or to complete sentence fragments involving the theme of death in some fashion. It is even possible to use the technique of word association. While all these methods are less susceptible to conscious or unconscious faking and distortion, their responses are more difficult to interpret, and conflicting interpretations are common.

Despite the inadequacies of studying attitudes toward death through interviews and questionnaires, I will frequently use information obtained through these methods. While it is important to recognize the limitations of a procedure, it is equally important to recognize the insights to which the procedure can lead.

EXPERIMENTS

Although initially the idea of conducting an "experiment" about death might seem strange or even somewhat macabre, none of the experiments with which I am familiar have partaken of those qualities. Probably the best known series of studies (and among the very earliest) was conducted by Professor Irving Alexander. Working primarily with young people, Alexander and his associates in one study selected 27 words that had previously been shown to be similar in frequency of usage in English. Eighteen words were considered neutral in meaning, but the remaining nine were equally divided among "sex" words, "school" words, and "death" words. A student was presented with each word separately and asked to respond with the first word that came to mind; at the same time, the student's galvanic skin response (perspiration change usually measured on the palm and assumed to be an indication of stress) was also measured. It took students significantly longer to respond to death-related words than to the neutral words; similarly, the death-related words produced a much greater change in galvanic skin response than did the neutral words. However, there was no difference between the death-related words and either the sex or school words (Alexander, Colley, & Alderstein, 1957).

A more recent version compared the responses to death-related stimuli of graduate students in psychology and religion, Zen meditators, and the users of hallucinogenic drugs. The graduate students showed not only greater galvanic-skin-response rates but also higher heart-rate responses. However, when the responses of the two pairs of groups were compared on the basis of stimuli not related to death or on a questionnaire asking about fear of death, the differences were minimal or nonexistent (Garfield, 1977). Perhaps the training of the nonstudent groups, or perhaps the qualities that drew people to these groups initially, did enable them to cope with death with less fear.

You can probably think of other kinds of experiments that would shed light on death and loss. For example, the effects of marijuana and LSD on the dying have been examined (Grof & Halifax, 1977; Pahnke, 1969). Comparing the effectiveness of two kinds of training programs for chaplains who will work with the dying would offer another possibility for introducing a modification of the experimental method into research on death and loss.

PROGRAM EVALUATION

Programs related to death, dying, and loss are becoming increasingly familiar—the hospice movement, counseling the dying, widow-to-widow outreach, and death education, for example. As these programs are planned, developed, and conducted, the people involved have the opportunity to learn a great deal about death and dying. Sometimes, through either the requirements of funding organizations or the wishes of program directors, the programs are evaluated in written reports.

This is the place not to debate the pros and cons of program evaluation but to underscore the fact that a good evaluation report can provide a variety of kinds of valuable information. These include (1) a description of the program itself— its purposes and goals, its procedures, and the people it serves; (2) the outcome of the program—the ways in which it was successful or not and the reasons for both; and (3) ideas and recommendations for similar programs in other communities.

ETHNOGRAPHIC AND PARTICIPANT-OBSERVER METHODS

Living with people—becoming immersed in their social milieu and their daily lives—is a very important method for learning about them. Although this approach has traditionally been used by anthropologists to study foreign cultures, today others have applied this method to various problems of social research. For example, one anthropologist, posing as a depressed, suicidal patient, entered a psychiatric hospital. Prior to entering, he used sophisticated psychological procedures to enable him to feel depressed and highly suicidal, so that he was not acting or pretending so much as functioning as an actual participant (Reynolds & Farberow, 1976). Many studies of funeral rituals and other ceremonies have been written by people who were active participants.

Although this method sometimes lacks the objectivity that can be obtained in statistical studies, it has the advantage of probing a topic in greater depth and with a fuller view of the total context. Carefully planned ethnographic studies of dying persons and their family members are not, to my knowledge, presently available in the professional literature.

DEMOGRAPHIC DATA

Who dies each year and of what causes? What percentage of all deaths are children between the ages of 6 and 10? What percentage of children between 6 and 10 die each year? What percentage of women over the age of 75 are in nursing homes or other long-term care institutions when they die? What percentage of men are married when they die? What percentage of women are married when they die? What percentage of all deaths are from some form of cancer? What percentage of all deaths of persons under 45 years of age are from cancer? What were the comparable figures in 1930? in 1870?

Statistics like these provide help in planning social programs, in understanding what is occurring in a community, in preparing for future trends, and in interpreting observations. For example, many more men than women die at home—most probably because husbands are older than their wives, have a briefer life expectancy, and are cared for at home by their wives. The fact that widows are more numerous and generally younger than widowers has implications for program planning and development and for understanding the marriage role of the surviving spouse. We find that women are more likely to anticipate becoming the surviving spouse, even when they are still young (Kalish, 1971), an accurate statistical projection and one that may well influence their perceptions of the institution of marriage itself.

OTHER PROCEDURES

Numerous other procedures have been used to study death, dying, and loss. One study asked people to describe what "death" looks like as a person (Kastenbaum & Aisenberg, 1972). A second analyzed the content of newspaper articles about death (Reynolds & Kalish, 1976). A third evaluated artistic production of a painter for whom death was a particularly salient theme (Cutter, 1971). Numerous psychological autopsies have been conducted (Weisman & Kastenbaum, 1968). This procedure examines the last months, weeks, and especially days and hours of a person's life through interviews with those who knew the individual and through analysis of medical, education, and work records. When enough psychological autopsies have been conducted, general principles and relationships can be extracted.

No one method is without flaws, nor is any method lacking in value. One in-depth interview conducted by a skilled and knowledgeable interviewer can offer insights that 500 questionnaires cannot uncover; conversely, 500 well-constructed questionnaires, administrated to a carefully selected sample of individuals, can provide an understanding of diverse views and feelings that one or a handful of in-depth interviews cannot reveal.

THE REST OF THE BOOK

A book on death, the dying process, grief and caring relationships can have any of several goals or any combination of the same goals. Those that come immediately to mind are:

- to help people think more about death so that they can better prepare for their own deaths,
- to help people know more about the dying process so that their own may be less distressing,
- to help people understand their feelings about the deaths of others so that they can be both more effective in relating to others who are dying and more capable of doing their own grieving later,
- to help people who wish to work in a professional or paraprofessional capacity with the dying and the bereaved,

- to help people who work in the innumerable fields that touch on death, dying, or grief to know a little more and think a little more about their roles,
- to help people grapple with one of the major philosophical problems that exists—the meaning of death.

The remainder of this book aims to accomplish all these goals—some directly and some indirectly. My intent is to open up many ideas for thought, provide some basic information on the theme, present my own views on the matter, and then leave the final resolution to you.

Since death and the process of dying are not studied by only one discipline, this book is both multidisciplinary and interdisciplinary. Since I am both teacher and human being, this book will move from a teaching stance to a human and personal stance. Your reading will, therefore, take you from the reporting of research data to intense personal experiences, from the psychological to the sociological to the theological to the medical and then back to the psychological, from attempts to get you to examine your own values and feelings to attempts to have you look at the topic from an impersonal distance.

In some instances, I have provided information, based on research, clinical observations and experience, or rigorously developed theory. In other instances I have become speculative and impressionistic. You can easily determine when each of these modes occurs and adjust your reading accordingly.

The next 16 chapters are divided into four sections. The first section examines the occurrence of death, its meanings, people's attitudes and feelings about death, and beliefs about transcending death. The section closes with a chapter that examines differences and similarities in the ways people of different ages experience and perceive death.

The second section focuses on the process of dying. It begins with some information on the causes of death, then describes the process of dying or the living-dying interval and discusses preparation for death. Again the final chapter provides a life-span perspective on the process of dying.

Section 3, which studies grief and bereavement, and Section 4, which examines caring relationships, are briefer than the previous sections. In some sense, of course, the discussion of grief has been anticipated in the discussion of the meaning of death, and implications for caring relationships and caring organizations are scattered throughout the book. The last sections of the last chapter, which are deeply personal, offer thoughts about the kinds of caring for others and for ourselves that are relevant for all of us—not just for those people professionally involved with the dying.

2

WHAT IS DEATH?

You know what death is, of course. Well, what is it?

It's a biological event that occurs naturally to all living things. It's a passage from this existence into the next. It's the transition from somethingness to nothingness. It's a consequence of original sin. It's the absence of life. It's an evolutionary necessity to keep the earth from overflowing with whatever form of life is under discussion. It's a transition into wholeness—becoming one with God. And there are other possibilities, each of which describes someone's definition.

A simple way to define death is ". . . the transition from the state of being alive to the state of being dead" (Kass, 1971, p. 699). Although that definition differentiates *death* from *dying* and from *being dead,* it doesn't help with the broader, more philosophic, and more personal understandings of the meaning of death. For the moment, let's examine the simpler and more limited definition; we will explore the more profound meanings at a later time.

If death is a transition and being dead is a state, we can describe dying as a process. It precedes most, but not necessarily all, deaths. We can observe this process, and we can assume that it is dying that we are observing, although we cannot be absolutely certain that we are watching dying until death has occurred. We may be watching apparent-dying or not-quite-dying instead.

A MORE CAREFUL LOOK

Do you strongly agree, agree, feel uncertain, disagree, or strongly disagree with this statement: I am afraid of death.

Think about the statement and mark your answer down in some way. More people would indicate that they disagree or strongly disagree than that they agree or strongly agree—a phenomenon I will discuss in a later chapter. What I want to know right now is, when you responded to the question, exactly what was it that you were afraid of or unafraid of or uncertain about? What were you conceptualizing as *death*? What images did you develop? Were you really thinking of the process of dying rather than of death—of leaving your family, of being in a hospital, of being helpless and in pain, of losing your ability to experience? Were you thinking of *being dead*—that is, for example, of existing in a nirvana-like state, of being in heaven or hell, of your relationship with a Supreme Being (however you conceptualize that), of total extinction? Or were you thinking of *death,* that moment of transition when you will finally know what death means—or, if death is extinction, when you will know nothing at all ever again.

It's possible that you had a fairly clear idea of what death meant when you answered the question, but it is also very possible that you had only the haziest idea. Perhaps you combined the concepts of death, the process of dying, and being dead and then reacted to a vague concept, which produced feelings of unease and discomfort, rather than to a sharp image that you could readily define.

The more we look at these three concepts, the more obvious it becomes that they cannot be given precise, non-overlapping definitions, but we can develop some basic distinctions. First of all, if we define *death,* as I did before, as a transition, then there is ready agreement, and the issue of definition is simple. However, if our definition of death also requires some statement about when death occurs or what criteria must be met for the term to be properly used, ready agreement disappears.

DYING

When do you begin to die? The simplest answer is "when you are born." Although I've used that response also, it strikes me as a glib and essentially meaningless explanation. Why not consider it the moment of conception or the time when your parents decided to conceive you or the moment when your parents were conceived? By saying that living is dying, we imply that there is no separation between living and dying. That may be poetically true, but I find it irrelevant. Although it is important to keep in mind that everything that lives also dies, I find it more useful to view the process of dying as only one phase of living.

We can examine the process of dying in two ways that are related but still distinct: as it is perceived by a dying person or by any other concerned person and as would be perceived by some objective person who was privy to all possible information.

Objectively, therefore, *my* dying begins when the condition that will cause my death becomes obvious enough to be noticed by someone who had access to all relevant data. Subjectively, for *me*, my dying begins when *I* learn that I have a condition that will eventually cause my death. Subjectively, for *you*, my dying begins when *you* learn that I have this condition.

For example, I consider myself healthy until one day when I have a routine physical examination. Concerned with symptoms that I described, my physician requests additional tests, which reveal that I have advanced stomach cancer. Now, instead of assuming that I will live at least ten or 20 or 30 years more, I can assume I have only one or two years; I can also assume that I am most likely to die from the stomach cancer. I must confront "the crisis of knowledge of death" and enter what Pattison (1977) calls the "living-dying interval."

Objectively, without knowing it, I have gone through several phases. I have passed through a period when the cancer was probably treatable, to a period when it was probably untreatable, to the present period when it is definitely untreatable. When did my dying begin? I would say at the beginning of the last-mentioned period, but you may prefer another time boundary.

Subjectively, the living-dying interval begins when I learn about it, when I have knowledge of it, but we all know that denial of the knowledge of death is powerful. The physician tells me that I have stomach cancer and that I will die of this illness within two years, but I do not "hear" him; I deny to myself that I am dying; I repress or reinterpret what he said. Subjectively, then, am I dying? Yes, because at some level I know that I am dying.

If, instead of dying from stomach cancer, I die from drowning, the crisis of knowledge of death may never arrive or it may last only a minute or two before I die. The objective dying period is then very brief, and the subjective living-dying interval lasts only a moment or does not exist at all.

But what of the case when a man thinks he is dying, and his physician and everyone else thinks he is dying, but he recovers and lives for another 20 years? In retrospect, was that person dying? My personal opinion is that the person was dying. You may take a different position; I doubt that it is possible to find a definition of *dying* that would cover every ambiguous circumstance.

Leon Kass says it well: dying can be defined as "the process leading from the incidence of the . . . cause of death to and beyond some border, however ill-defined, after which the organism (or its body) may be said to be dead" (1971, p. 699). This is the living-dying interval.

When Pattison uses the expression *living-dying interval* he is making an extremely significant point: we are alive until we are dead; we are living until we die. As obvious as that may seem, it is often forgotten or ignored. As soon as I am categorized as dying, people begin to respond to me in a different fashion. It is almost as though I were already dead. I become a non-person, as others not only plan what remains of my life—often without including me in the planning—but also begin to plan both the present and the future for themselves as though I were not still among them.

This disengagement need not and, of course, does not always happen, but it can occur very easily. Many years ago, having decided to leave one teaching position for another, I announced my resignation several months before the end of the year, and my replacement was appointed about six weeks later. Shortly after his appointment, I noticed that people who had previously consulted with me were telephoning him, that plans not only for the following year, when I would be gone, but for the academic year when I was still there were being developed without me. My colleagues remained cordial and were, I felt, truly sorry that I was leaving, but they had already begun the process of disengaging from me and re-engaging with my replacement.

A similar process of disengagement occurs with a dying person; unfortunately, she is much less capable of coping with it than I was. For my departure leaving was equated with having left; for the dying person, dying is thought to equal dead. We need to remain aware that, during the living-dying interval, an individual is *living*—although under different conditions than previously.

BEING DEAD

We can all agree on some aspects of the nature of being dead: the body ceases to function and begins to decay. Not only has the body ceased to function, but the various body parts and organs also cease to function and begin to decay, not necessarily immediately and not necessarily at the same moment, but within a very short period of time. Being dead must, by definition, follow the process of dying and the transitional moment of death. Some of you will believe in an eventual resurrection that permits the spirit to reassume bodily form, perhaps through reconstituting the original body, but more probably in a "body of a new order, the perfect instrument of the spirit" (Cross, 1971, p. 1158). Others believe that the body becomes dust and will never be reconstituted.

What happens to *you* when you are dead? At this point the disagreements will increase rapidly. By you, I mean that unique and never-again-to-be-found entity that is locked within your body (and even that statement may be debated). It is what you mean when you say "I." What happens to that *you* when your body—every part of it—ceases to function?

Do *you* cease completely? Are you extinguished? Annihilated? Never more? Do *you* inhabit another physical body? A person? Another animal form? A vegetable or mineral? Do *you* exist in nonphysical form? In heaven? In nirvana? As a ghost?

What dying is not/*what being dead is* not. Aging does *not* equal dying; aging does *not* equal being dead. To the extent that aging produces decrement (and much aging produces gains, not losses), it is a process that makes us more susceptible to a variety of conditions that can cause our death; with age, our resistance to disease and our ability to recover from illnesses and accidents diminish. Newborn infants share with the elderly a low resistance to disease and a slow recovery rate from some illnesses and accidents, and their death rate is quite high, compared to that of older infants and children, although much lower than it was 70 years ago. But being old is not dying any more than being newborn is dying.

What is unique about dying? What is unique about being dead? The only quality in the dying process that is unique is its eventual end in death. When you imagine dying, you are likely to think about physical pain, psychological stress, discomfort, the loss of other people, unpleasant medical and hospital (or at-home) routines, and the arrangements necessary for after your death. But none of these circumstances is unique to the dying process.

People suffer pain on many occasions, and the pain of the dying process depends upon the cause of your dying, the medical treatments you receive, the psychological care you get, and probably your own attitudes as well. Similarly, you can suffer discomfort and psychological stress on many occasions; you can encounter unpleasant medical and hospital routines without being a dying person; you can suffer the loss of others or arrange for what will occur after your death at almost any time in your life.

But after you die, you will be dead. That situation is very different from others you may have faced. Being dead, actually dead, is irreversible. (See Chapter 6 for an alternative position.) Furthermore, we have no empirical evidence of what being dead is. You may feel you have various kinds of evidence about the nature of being dead—from religious teachings, from logic, from other kinds of experiences, from feeling "it has to be like this"—but only a very few of you would contend that this evidence is empirical (related to observable facts or experiences). Therefore, being dead is a state with empirically unknown (and probably unknowable) characteristics, and this is unique in a way. Third, being dead is forever; at the very least, your present body and earthly existence will be dead forever. Nothing else is forever.

For me, however, the most significant unique quality about being dead is that I will be unable to experience—unable to think or perceive or behave or have feelings. Obviously those of you who believe that there is another existence after this one in which you will be able to think, perceive, and have feelings will not share my opinion about what is most unique about death. For you, what is most unique about being dead may be the opportunity to experience the presence or wholeness of God and/or Jesus Christ, Buddha, or Mohammed personally, to experience another body, to bask in the loving oneness of the universe, or to have your being recreated in another body, in keeping with your karma, or deeds, from this life, while your essences (for example, body, thought, feelings) cease.

These, however, are all theological concepts; although they exert a strong influence upon your behavior and feelings, they cannot be judged psychologically or socially. As a psychologist, emphasizing psychological variables, I need to return to my previous point: in being dead, you/I will not be able to experience.

DEATH

I had been asked to talk at a mountain retreat where about 40 students and a handful of other people had come to spend a weekend discussing death and dying. After dinner a circle of chairs was drawn up around a low-burning fire in a large fireplace, but it was clear that no one was much in the mood for a presentation or even a discussion about death; I was introduced and asked to begin. When I sensed the mood of the group prior to the introduction, I bit almost all the way through a rather long fingernail—leaving only one end of the loosened piece still attached. Following the introduction, I quietly put my finger to my mouth, bit quickly through the remaining nail, and threw the piece across the room. The startled students gasped and gave me their full attention. "You have just experienced the death of one part of me," I said. I never tried that device again, and I am not certain that it would ever work in another context, but the rest of the discussion turned out to be one of the most animated and exciting in my experience.

In retrospect, I am not even certain that the fingernail was alive in the first place, but that is of no account. What matters is that pieces of me and parts of me can die, but *I* don't have to die with them; conversely, when *I* die, pieces of me and parts of me may go on living—if incorporated into another human body, for example—long after *I* am dead.

Earlier I defined death as the period of transition between the process of dying and the state of being dead. The transition may last a moment or a few minutes, but the determination of that period has immense practical and philosophical consequences. Why? After all, we talk about people being "more dead than alive," about people being "as good as dead," about the possibility of returning to life after death. Why is it important to define the moment of death? Why not be a little more relaxed about it?

The answer is simple. Because a train of events follows death, and this train of events does not follow "being more dead than alive" or "being as good as dead." Nor can it occur if the dead person is going to return to life. When *I* die, if it is in a hospital, I will be encased in sheets and removed by a gurney or cart to the hospital morgue, where eventually the funeral home vehicle will pick me (is it "me"?) up for delivery to the mortuary, where, depending upon whether I am to be buried or cremated, I may undergo further processing. If I am not dead, this will not happen.

My survivors will contact insurance companies, the Social Security office, and the office that handles my retirement program, and a variety of business procedures will be set in motion that will eventually lead to payments to my heirs. The funeral home will call either a cemetery or crematorium and set another process in operation (Veatch, 1976).

Close family members will contact distant family members, who will need to decide whether they will make the trip to attend the funeral; the clergy may be contacted to officiate at the funeral; local relatives will prepare both for the funeral and for the visits of out-of-town family members. The local newspaper will be notified, and some friends may decide to miss a few hours of work to attend the funeral, offer condolences to my survivors, and probably eat and drink a little. I will be buried, or perhaps, cremated—but only if I am dead.

There may be some form of religious ritual; close family members and friends will mourn—each in his or her own fashion. These people will now plan a future that is somewhat different from what they had planned before I died—even though each of them had undoubtedly already begun to anticipate my death and plan for that contingency. (A sudden and unexpected death, of course, gives rise to somewhat different dynamics.)

None of these things can happen until I am dead. Not as good as dead, not more dead than alive, not dead but capable of returning, but *dead!* As Veatch puts it "Most types of death behavior (religious ritual, will reading, succession to the presidency) either happen or they do not. A point must be established at which the individual is no longer treated as living" (1976, p. 29). For many reasons, we require accurate knowledge of when (and if) death occurs.

BEGINNINGS AND ENDINGS

Let's begin at the beginning, with the beginning of human life. We cannot, after all, understand the nature of death without understanding the nature of life, any more than we can understand the nature of women, of communism, or of peace without also understanding the nature of men, of a free market economy, or of war. When does life begin?

Over a decade ago, a group of 92 public health professionals were asked about what they saw as the characteristics of a new human life. One-third of those people believed that the "fact that it has the biological potential for being a human being makes it a human being." Just over one-fifth felt that the time at which the soul or spirit enters the body marks the beginning of humanness. (This view forms the basis for much of the abortion controversy.) Most of the remainder described the time at which the individual human being (1) can be perceived or recognized; (2) is alert and recognizes the environment; or (3) is physiologically self-sufficient and functioning on its own (Knudtson, 1967).

Now let's move rapidly forward in time to the end of life. Logically, life should end when (a) it no longer has the biological potential for being a human being, (b) the soul or spirit has left the body, (c) it can no longer be recognized as human, (d) it is no longer alert or able to recognize the environment, or (e) it is no longer physiologically self-sufficient or able to function on its own. And presumably, in each instance, the condition would be irreversible.

About the same time that Professor Knudtson was asking public health professionals when human life began, I was asking a group of university students when they felt human life ended. More specifically, I asked 105 students to write a very brief essay to answer the following questions: "Under which of the following circumstances might you say the person has—in a sense—died? When is he 'dead' for you? Why do you feel as you do?" There followed six alternative occasions at which death might occur. Table 2-1 shows the percentage of students whose essay was based on each of the indicated responses. Because a number of participants selected more than one alternative, the percentages total over 100%.

Look how close the responses of the students I queried are to those of the public health professionals Knudtson surveyed. For both groups human life is defined primarily by its biological potential; biological self-sufficiency and the ability to function also are considered essential to human life. While 21% of the public health people referred to the importance of the soul or spirit, 18% of the students said that people don't die—at least while their souls exist or their spirits are remembered by others. This response was more remarkable in the student group, because it had not even been listed as an alternative; in order to respond in that fashion, the students had to reject the structure I had imposed on them.

Philosopher Robert Veatch explores the definition of death in another way, which is close to my own thinking. "We use the term *death* to mean the loss of what is essentially significant to an entity—in the case of (a person), the loss of humanness" (1976, p. 26). Thus, when consciousness or the capacity for any social interaction ceases and when this cessation is irreversible, death has occurred. In this definition, we don't need to debate whether "brain death" or "heart death" is the more important, since it is the death of consciousness and of social interactions that concerns us.

This perspective doesn't solve all the problems by any means, since we are still faced with the determination of when the cessation of consciousness is irreversible. A committee established several years ago at Harvard Medical School proposes four criteria: (1) unreceptivity and unresponsitivity, (2) no movements or breathing, (3) no reflexes, and (4) flat

TABLE 2-1. Percentage of Students Who Selected Indicated Definition of *Death* or of *Being Dead* for Them (Kalish, 1966)

Condition	% (N = 105)
When the heart stops beating	52
When person loses self-awareness	35
When person wishes to die or gives up	35
Entering hospital or nursing home, knowing he/she will never leave alive	14
Learning of a terminal diagnosis	4
Becoming senile	4
People never die or don't die at time of physical death	18

electroencephalogram. Furthermore, these tests should be made twice, 24 hours apart, to confirm what has been found (cited in Veatch, 1976).

Many people feel that these criteria are too conservative, because they would permit people to continue to exist long after any meaningful life had ceased. Others claim that only the very most conservative determinations of death should be applied, because any alternative might deprive some people of a portion of their life—even if a very brief portion—and because it can never be known with absolute certainty in advance exactly how much life might be added.

To try to grasp the complexities of these decisions, ask yourself a few questions. Would you sign a paper that would require your physician to cease all medical treatment and care if you were defined dead by the Harvard Medical School criteria—even though your heart and other organs could be kept operative by hospital machinery? Would you require your physician to cease all medical treatment and care if you were defined dead because you would never regain consciousness, although movements, breathing, and reflexes were continuing? Would you wish your physician (or someone else) to hasten your clinical death if you would never again regain consciousness? And finally, think of the person whom you love best in this world: how would you answer the previous three questions if you had to make decisions for that person's life?

WHO DECIDES

Who is entitled to define the end of life? Physicians? Lawyers? Philosophers and theologians? Judges and politicians? Everyone equally? Who is entitled to say whether death should be defined as the end of consciousness or the end of any bodily activity?

My own feelings here may well be in conflict with yours. I think the issue is a philosophical or theological one that must be settled in the social-political arena and not in a medical center. Physicians, of course, must make the determination of what is physically possible to do; they have the technology and the experience to understand whether instruments are available that can accurately evaluate the irreversible end of consciousness or the termination of heart activity. But whether the end of consciousness should be used as the end of life is a moral, not a medical, question (see also Veatch, 1976). The definitions, I believe, need to be developed (or left undeveloped, which is a possible decision) by legislative bodies, with advice from medical, religious, psychological, and other experts, as well as from others who are concerned with the issue.

For any given person, of course, a physician is likely to determine whether life is continuing or not. Thus, although I would like to decide for myself whether I want to have my life declared over when my consciousness stops forever, I must permit a physician to decide whether my condition is, indeed, irreversible.

THE RIGHT TO DIE . . . SOONER

Some people talk about the "right to die" and "the right to die with dignity"—both laudable concepts—without a full understanding of the implications of these issues. A person's death does not only *affect* the individual, and we often must consider the right of an individual to die with the rights of that person's family to have him or her live. More important, I feel, is the right to live a life of quality.

I want to have as much power over my own life as possible and, since my death is just as much a part of my life as my work or my eating, I want to have power over my death. This means I want power over where I die, how I die, and when I die. Since no power is absolute, I know that I cannot have full power over these issues, but I can at least have some influence.

To an appreciable extent, I can have influence over my death by the way I live, the foods I eat, the ways I handle stress and losses, the work that I pursue, and other comparable matters. To some extent, my will to live or desire to die is also a factor. But there are many occasions in which my existence is largely determined by other people, and this is particularly the case when I am very ill and perhaps near death or when, for other reasons, I no longer have control over my physical body or social environment.

The situation could certainly arise when I wanted to die, but was able neither to cause myself to die nor to get anyone else to make me die. At that point, I would lose power over myself—especially the power to cause to happen the one thing that I might most wish to happen: my death. To make matters worse, this loss of power over self is likely to occur when I am ill, in pain, facing imminent death, and running up immense medical costs—all of which combine to bring great distress to my family. All these factors would conspire to make certain that I am not dying with dignity.

Before proceeding, I would like to present a few issues for consideration:

1. Does my "right to die" or "right to die with dignity" depend on what I decide or on what someone else decides?
2. Does it depend on my decision—no matter how I arrived at it—or must I present a persuasive case for it?
3. Must I cause my death directly or will someone do it at my request?
4. Can I cause my death, or have someone cause it, by some active agent (for example, poison, sleeping pills) or am I limited to refusing further treatment, which is always a legal prerogative unless I am stopped by some court action?
5. Does it matter whether someone—spouse, child, employer, clergy—opposes my death?
6. Am I permitted only to hasten my inevitable and predictable death, or am I permitted to determine myself the conditions under which I may choose to cause my life to stop?

SUICIDE AND EUTHANASIA

The issues really under discussion include the right to have euthanasia performed and the right to commit suicide. Euthanasia literally means "good death," a term comparable to "death with dignity." I know that the right to die is a burning issue for many people, since I am asked my opinion about that subject much more often than I am asked about any other issue related to my work. Because so much has been written recently about suicide and euthanasia, I will discuss only a few matters here.

One controversy that often emerges is whether there is a difference between active euthanasia and passive euthanasia. The former occurs when something is done to a patient to cause death; the latter refers to situations in which no action is taken to prolong life under circumstances in which action might have permitted a patient to live longer. Removing a patient from a respirator that was maintaining life would be an example of active euthanasia; an example of passive euthanasia might be withholding treatment for a heart attack victim that might have kept that person alive but probably without adequate brain function. Some people and religious groups argue that active euthanasia is morally wrong, but that passive euthanasia is acceptable; others contend that they are merely two sides of the same coin, and that either—or neither—is acceptable.

Several years ago, the state of California enacted legislation permitting an individual to describe the conditions under which he or she would want life-sustaining procedures withheld or withdrawn. One necessary condition was that the individual already have a terminal, incurable disease. This legislation, termed the "natural death act," was believed to apply to cases like that of Karen Ann Quinlan, a young woman who continued to exist without brain function.

The legislation requires that a document, frequently termed a *living will,* be made out when a person is capable of understanding its implications and that its signing be appropriately witnessed. As a result of the way this bill was written, however, the criteria for withholding or withdrawing treatment are so limited that very few people have been permitted to die under its regulations, and it seems possible that practice may have been less restrictive before the passage of the law. Ironically, the attempt to offer individuals more freedom in controlling their lives may in fact, have restricted their freedom (Meyers, 1977). Other states, considering similar legislation, have attempted to avoid the complexities of California's law.

The right to commit suicide has also undergone change. Once forbidden by law, it is still disapproved by custom and by most religions, but legal sanctions against persons who have attempted or committed suicide are no longer in practice. One exception is the limitations some life insurance companies have on paying beneficiaries of a completed suicide—especially if the suicide occurred shortly after the policy was initiated.

Attitudes toward hastening death. In 1939, an opinion poll reported that nearly half the people interviewed answered yes to the question "Do you favor mercy deaths under government supervision for hopeless invalidids?" Some years later, Professor Thomas Eliot, perhaps the first sociologist to call attention to the paucity of research on death and bereavement, conducted a brief study of military service veterans on the same issue. Among the 118 men and 12 women responding, again about as many expressed willingness for a physician to hasten death as opposed the action (Eliot, 1947).

When we asked people in the Los Angeles area whether they felt people should be allowed to die if they wished, approximately half of the Japanese-American and Black respondents and over 60% of the white respondents said yes; only the Mexican Americans were largely opposed. However, there was considerable sentiment to permit the hastening of death only if the person was dying anyway or in great pain; only one person in about 15 believed that wanting to die is sufficient reason for permitting someone to die without other justifications. The major reasons for opposition to permitting a person to choose his or her death were the views that only God has the right to take a life and that, no matter how bleak matters seem, there is always hope (Kalish & Reynolds, 1976).

A comparable study in the Midwest, conducted several years later, found that 75% of the research participants believed that people in the last stages of terminal illness should be permitted to have their deaths hastened (Haug, 1978). If allowances are made for the differences in the phrasing of the question in the two studies, the two sets of results are amazingly consistent: the right to a more rapid death is generally acceptable under specified conditions.

But when we permit people to hasten their deaths because they are dying anyway, the hazard is that, since we are all going to die someday, any one of us could be a candidate for a hastened death. I know the response to the previous sentence: But these people are in pain and their lives don't have meaning any more, so why not let them die in dignity instead of living in torment?

The answer is simple, but implementation is exceedingly complex. Letting people die can be the most humane approach; it can also be an excuse for not providing optimum medical and human care. Obviously many dying people don't want to hasten their deaths—some because they are afraid of dying but many because life still has some meaning for them. It thus seems important to extend every effort to every patient—whatever the condition of the person's health is—to control pain and to make life meaningful—no matter how brief the potential life is. Otherwise we run the risk of using the concept of death with dignity as a rationalization for our own failure to provide life with dignity. The answers are exceedingly complex.

THE POSSIBILITIES OF LIVING . . . STILL LONGER

Assuming you could retain the capacities of a typical middle-aged person, would you like to live to be 100? How about 150? How long is it possible to live?

The ideal of living a long and healthy life has probably always been pursued by people. The fountain of youth was not just the fantasy of Ponce de Leon but is the wish of many, perhaps most, of us. Perhaps the notion of living forever isn't especially appealing, but 150 years, well. . . .

From time to time, a newspaper or magazine article will report on a society in which amazingly large numbers of people live to be very old. These societies are then inevitably analyzed to determine their characteristics, which often turn out to include a rigorous, physically demanding life, low psychological stress, close family and community relationships, a diet that is very high or very low in something or other, and perhaps moderate use of alcoholic beverages and little or no use of tobacco. Physicians and modern pharmaceuticals are, of course, almost unavailable, and environmental pollutants are virtually nonexistent.

Since so many of us would like to know the secret of long life, we have a strong tendency to accept such information uncritically. And since it seems that our "modern ways of living" appear to stand between us and longevity, we can get angry with our own culture, which pretends to provide us with the good things of life, yet reduces years of life in so doing. The three societies that have received the most attention in the past decade or so are the Vilcabamba in Ecuador, the Georgians in Russia, and the Hunza in the Indian province of Kashmir (Leaf, 1973).

Unfortunately, perhaps, for those of us who do like the idea of seeing the year 2100 A.D., careful inspection of the data for at least the first two of these societies seems to explode the myth of wide-spread longevity. While the people are certainly healthy and apparently do live longer than the number of years we might anticipate, the reports that many centenarians reside in these populations are based on an insufficiently careful perusal of the available information.

In evaluating the data from his home country, Dr. Medvedev (1974) presented a lengthy list of explanations for the misperception of life expectancy in the Soviet Socialist Republic of Georgia. These included the lack of documents establishing birth and other significant dates, the desire of the Soviet government to encourage national pride, the well-established tendency for older persons to exaggerate their age in order to gain attention and local honor, and the falsification of documents to avoid military conscription, among other reasons.

A more recent study of the Vilcabamba concentrated only on official records and discussions with the residents of the area (Mazess & Forman, 1978). The researchers found a "systematic age exaggeration beginning at about 70 years" (p. 97), so that a man who claimed to be 97 years old in 1970 was recorded as 140 when he died in 1971; another, who according to records was 61 in 1944, reported himself to be 70 at that time and 80 in 1949, then 121 in 1970 and 127 in 1974. Part of the confusion arose because previous researchers took age claims at face value and misinterpreted church birth records by failure to understand that many people in that society have the same or similar names.

But dispelling the fantasies of extremely long life does not mean that you, as an individual, cannot extend your own life by appropriate physical, emotional, and social habits. For example, another study of long-lived people in outlying provinces in Turkey did show that they had simple diets with little meat or animal fat, no cigarette smoking, vigorous physical activity, ongoing marriages and sexual activity, satisfying social activity, and a positive view of life. Use of alcoholic beverages didn't seem to make a difference (Beller & Palmore, 1974), although other research has shown that people who drink in moderation live longer than heavy drinkers or non-drinkers (Woodruff, 1977).

Or perhaps you have read one of the many newspaper or magazine articles that provides you with a questionnaire to fill out to determine how long you will live—with the obvious implication that you can live longer if you live right (and, of course, if you picked parents who provided you with the right genes). So many years are subtracted for sedentary work, cigarette smoking, job tension, divorce, and having one parent or grandparent who died of a heart attack; so many years are added for limited intake of animal fat, moderate use of alcoholic beverages, and regular exercise.

CAN LIFE BE EXTENDED?

Of course life can be extended. Over the past 80 years, life expectancy has increased, although much of this extension reflects the elimination of deaths in the early years. How might life be extended even further? This can occur in two basic ways: first, through a continued reduction in the present causes of death, and, second, through intervention in the normal aging process in such a way that this process would slow down without deleterious side effects.

We can, therefore, work to improve our living habits—change our diet, exercise patterns, levels of stress and fatigue, use of tobacco and other drugs, for example. This obviously isn't easy, since all of us have made decisions to do things that we know will, or at least believe possibly may, be destructive to our health. We can also work to develop a behavior pattern and life philosophy that reduces chronic stress and, perhaps, intense acute stress, although some individuals may well find a life lacking in stress to be a life lacking in challenge and, therefore, actually more stressful.

We can also work to eliminate environmental pollutants, certain food additives, and other carcinogenic products. Frequently, however, a solution is problematic: a chemical used to fertilize the soil or destroy insects may at the same time both be carcinogenic and increase the food crop so that more people can eat better and less expensively; reduction in industrial waste may prove so expensive to a company that jobs are lost—thus increasing stress and reducing buying power for those affected. The decisions are not easy ones, and they involve a variety of concerns of which life extension is only one.

Since there may be an outer limit to normal life expectancy—perhaps around 90 or 100 years—eliminating disease as well as accidents, war, homicide, and suicide would permit most of us to live up to this outer limit. The ultimate fantasy of this approach is that we all live a healthy life until we arrive at the age of 97 years, two months, and seven days, at which point we immediately drop dead of a cause that we might term *life-running-out*.

Intervening with the aging process, which some biologists say may well occur sometime during the next 50 years (for example, Comfort, 1969), would have a very different effect. It may be possible to slow down the entire aging process, so that the physical conditions that are typical of age 30 today would then come at age 60, and the normal life expectancy might become 140 years instead of 70 years.

This intervention would require some kind of treatment—perhaps a pill or an injection—and might also include changes in living and health habits. Some interesting speculations develop about this treatment: (1) who would control it; (2) would there be enough to go around or only enough for some people; (3) what would the cost of this program be and who—governments or individuals—would pay for it; (4) would it have side-effects; (5) would it be a one-time treatment or an on-going one; and (6) would it help those who were already middle-aged or elderly or only those who were young?

Any program that successfully increased life expectancy might introduce a host of problems: (1) would changes occur so rapidly that great dislocations in populations would result (that is, all of a sudden we would have a doubling of people over age 70, without time to plan for it); (2) how would the resulting population explosion affect the world's food supply and amount of empty land space; (3) what kinds of relationships will occur when six-generation families are common; (4) how will people feel about the possibility of working for 100 years or being married for 100 years; (5) how will we accommodate workers and people in general to living through so many different eras and changes in social values and technologies; and (6) can our educational institutions adapt to all these changing demands?

One concern that is frequently voiced is whether scientists have the moral right to work to extend life by interfering with the aging process—especially since the social problems that will emerge are obviously going to be considerable. Not only will laws need changing and customs require altering, but the difficulties of handling the population increase that is expected with increased life expectancy are tremendous. How much longer would you want to live? How much longer would you want those whom you love to live? How much, in money and effort, would you be willing to pay for extra years?

A final issue that develops from these speculations is how a substantial life extension will alter our perceptions of death. If the boundary of death is first pushed back 20 years, will we then press to push it back another 20 and another and another? Will death be seen as more distressing when it does come early (which may be at age 80), because we assume a life of 140 years? Or will people become so bored with a long life—even a healthy life—that death will not be unwelcome?

KINDS OF DEATH

What constitutes the beginning of life and the ending of life is apparently seen quite differently by different people. One approach to defining life and death delineates three levels of existence (or non-existence): physical—further divided into biological and clinical; psychological—the state of self-awareness; and social—further divided into self-perceived and other-perceived (Kalish, 1968).

PHYSICAL LIFE/PHYSICAL DEATH

Physical life refers to both the existence of functioning organs and the existence of a functioning organism; in the former case, each organ can have a somewhat independent existence; at the same time the body as an entirety can live or die independently of individual organs. The former has been termed *biological life* and the latter, *clinical life.* Each has a beginning, an existence, and an ending, and while these periods are closely related to each other, they are not necessarily identical.

Clinical life and clinical death, for example, are all-or-none propositions: the organism is either functioning or it is not functioning; it is either clinically alive or clinically dead. When clinical death occurs, the death certificate may be signed.

Persons suffer biological deaths as each organ dies, but the individual himself/herself does not necessarily die. The heart may cease to function at a different moment than the lungs, liver, kidneys, or stomach. The brain can cease to function, or cease certain of its functions, while the heart is still reasonably healthy. The beginnings of biological life also do not necessarily mean that the individual qua individual is living. Most of the organs begin to function during the fetal period, and we have fairly accurate information about when each develops.

The initiation of clinical life is a matter of definition, and the theologian, the philosopher, the physician, you, and I all have an equal right to an opinion. Do we begin our lives at conception? At birth? When we are viable or capable of continued existence outside our mother's womb? How much biological life must there be before we can say of an individual "That person is alive"? How much biological death must occur before we can say "That person is now dead"?

When these questions were asked of public health professionals, 43% answered that human life begins at conception; another 26% selected some time after conception but before birth; 9% believed life began at birth itself; and 22% thought it was some time after birth (Knudtson, 1967). Obviously there is room for disagreement even among those who are most concerned professionally. Your belief about when clinical life begins will influence your feelings about the rights of an unborn child, the prerogatives of a pregnant woman to select abortion over childbirth, or the nature of a crime committed against a fetus (Kalish, 1968).

My tooth dies (biological death) as a part of me when it is pulled from my body; so does my leg if it is amputated, although the skin, blood, tissue, bones, and nerves in the leg do not all die at the moment the leg is severed. As a matter of fact, animal tissues "have been preserved outside the living organism—far exceeding the life-span of the organism from which they were taken". (Choron, 1964, p.4).

So some parts of me may far outlast "that which is me" and some parts of me will die before "that which is me" dies. We don't disagree much about those parts; what we disagree about is when the "me" dies. For this to happen, the organism that is "me" must cease to function as an organism and, given our present state of knowledge, the cessation must be irreversible. When this event occurs, the legal definition of death has been met, and the death certificate can be signed.

PSYCHOLOGICAL LIFE/PSYCHOLOGICAL DEATH

Psychological life refers to being aware of self or the world around; psychological death occurs when this awareness ceases. Deciding the beginning of psychological life is difficult, but it would occur very early—perhaps at the time of the earliest cognitive acts in which purpose is involved. When an infant cries to gain parental attention or makes a conscious effort to move in order to avoid discomfort, that would indicate the earliest phases of psychological life. Or it might be viewed as beginning at or even before birth.

Psychological death, when it occurs, most often affects those who are very old or who have suffered some severe losses in brain function, perhaps through an accident but more commonly through Alzheimer's disease or a similar condition. It is normally not an all-or-none occurrence, since most people move in and out of awareness or function with some level of hazy awareness. Total psychological death comes, most often, at the time of physical death, but in some instances takes place earlier.

In one study, it was noted that only 5% of dying elderly persons in a geriatric facility had consistently and completely ceased to be aware of what was going on, even during the few days prior to their physical death (Kastenbaum, 1967b). Half were in full contact with the world, and the remainder were in partial or periodic contact. For that 5%, however, psychological death had occurred earlier; those people were either hopelessly confused, fully comatose, or so sedated they had lost cognitive function.

People who are psychologically dead not only do not know who they are—they do not know *that* they are. This circumstance is obviously very distressing to family members. You often hear comments like "That isn't really my father—my father died weeks ago," or "I don't know her, and she doesn't know me. Why doesn't her body die also?"

Physical death is irreversible. What about psychological death? We seldom know for certain. An elderly, apparently disoriented, woman suddenly regains a semblance of psychological life when her daughter visits, improves further when she sees her grandchildren, and then lapses into confusion when the family leaves. Psychological death can be accelerated by a hostile or an empty environment or by medications that leave a person in a semi-stuporous condition. It can be postponed by a warm, embracing environment, by sensory stimulation, by avoiding use of the above medications as long as possible, and perhaps by a strong desire to remain psychologically alive.

It is this very possibility of reversibility that adds a significant moral issue to the human and health treatment of persons who are psychologically dying. If we treat such people like non-persons by ignoring them, by talking about them in their presence as though they were not there, by depriving them of social or sensory stimulation, we may very well be increasing their confusion. In so doing, we may actually be hurrying their physical deaths as well. Since these people are sometimes seen as being "as good as dead," the tendency is to treat them as though they were already dead, and family members and health caretakers all withdraw psychologically. The possibility that the condition is reversible, at least in part, is never tested. This means that these people are deprived of whatever remaining psychological life they might otherwise have had.

But ministering to people who are in this condition is not easy for most family members or health professionals. A substantial effort is frequently required to effect relatively little change in responsiveness (although sudden and extreme changes do occur). For the family member the process is difficult and painful; for the health professional the process is frustrating and often regarded as not worth the effort.

SOCIAL LIFE/SOCIAL DEATH

Although you can be socially alive or dead to yourself as well as to others, the term more frequently refers to the ways in which you are perceived by others. When a person perceives you, for all practical purposes, as dead or nonexistent, you are socially dead for that person. For example, your mother enters a nursing home, where the only concrete evidence of her existence is her monthly bills and occasional cards; her role as your mother has ceased, and you and she have not substituted new roles. She may be socially dead to you and to others in your family in varying degrees: totally dead to one sister who lives near the nursing home but never sees her and rarely mentions her, still alive to a brother who lives some distance away but retains his concern and involvement.

Is she socially dead to herself also? That depends, of course, on how she sees herself. If her self-image now is of someone who is as good as dead or, for all practical purposes, dead, then she is socially dead; if she perceives herself as still having at least the vestige of vitality, she is not socially dead to herself.

Social death can lead to psychological and physical death. If your family perceives you as socially dead (although they might feel some anxiety or guilt about so doing), they are likely to isolate themselves from you. You would find this depressing and stressful, and if you were elderly, somewhat confused, and in an institution, the depression and stress might well have significant effects on your interest in living and on your daily habits of eating, exercising, and remaining stimulated. Your physical and social environments would become less stimulating, and, consequently, psychological death might occur more readily.

Being written off as socially dead can lead to feelings of hopelessness. Your need for the strength and supportiveness of others is not met, and your present situation does not permit you to function effectively without these supports.

> Jonas was an elderly man who had lived in the nursing home for four years, ever since his 81st birthday, when his children decided that they could no longer care for him in their homes without disrupting their own families. However, all three of his children, numerous grandchildren, and his aging wife, who was crippled with severe arthritis and living with a somewhat spry sister, came to visit often. Jonas received at least two visits every week, and often more.
>
> Then, within a brief period of time, his wife died, his oldest son became seriously ill with cancer, and his daughter's husband retired and she moved with him to Florida. Although he was somewhat confused, Jonas was alert enough to know what was happening, and his deep concern for his son plus his feeling of being abandoned by his wife and daughter led to a kind of stress that he had great difficulty handling. As visits dropped off and his depression deepened, he became increasingly confused. Then, as the licensed vocational nurse tending his unit said, "When I had to tell him his son had died, I could see the change. He just turned his face to the wall and didn't say a thing. And he hardly ate anything after that. One morning when I went to give him breakfast, I saw that his face was covered with tears. He was unconscious when I returned for the tray and had died by that afternoon."

We find a powerful interaction between psychological death and social death. An elderly person's confusion and disorientation will predispose others to withdraw; when others withdraw, the potential for becoming confused and disoriented increases. And, although rigorous experimental evidence is lacking, these factors undoubtedly work together to hasten physical death.

I have elaborated on the meaning of physical, psychological, and social death, because I have found that, while many people recognize that death is not unidimensional, they are unable to develop a clear picture of what they do mean by death. Legal death, with very few exceptions, coincides with clinical death. We find that an understanding of death as multifaceted is relevant not only to the helping professional but to persons involved in public policy.

Many kinds of death exist—of that there is little doubt. You will occasionally hear someone refer to a "living death"—usually a reference to being in prison, holding a despised job, residing in a community he or she hates, being constantly in severe pain, or being in an intolerable marriage or family situation. You may have called someone "dead from the neck up" to imply that his or her ideas and feelings were stultified and routinized. To each kind of death, certain reactions are appropriate. It seems important to have a clear idea of exactly what kind of death we are confronting so that our reactions are appropriate to the situation. We would not, therefore, respond to a social death as though it were a psychological death or to a psychological death as though it were a clinical death.

Death means different things to different people under different conditions. The term is used literally and metaphorically. It is used in an absolute sense to describe what most of us would agree death is and in relative senses to describe partial deaths or deaths of parts. The more we probe into the meanings of death, the more complex we find the situation.

3

THE MEANINGS OF DEATH AND FACING DEATH

We all confront the possibility of death—our own and that of others—at all times. The only difference between you and the 90-year-old man or woman severely ill in a hospital whose predicted death is an hour away is that the statistical odds are immensely high that your death will come later. The odds are not 100%; indeed, the only time the odds become 100% is when you're betting that you will die eventually.

In other eras, this life was regarded as a brief respite between birth and death, between being conceived and entering the kingdom of heaven. "The man of the late Middle Ages was very acutely conscious that he had merely been granted a stay of execution, that this delay would be a brief one, and that death was always present within him" (Aries, 1974, p. 44). Or, more recently, as the Yaqui mystic Don Juan tells Carlos Castaneda, "The man also realizes that death is the irreplaceable partner that sits next to him on the mat" (Castaneda, 1972, p. 150).

Was this awareness of the proximity of death so distressing that no enjoyment of life was possible? Not according to the French social historian Aries: "And that man felt a love of life which we today can scarcely understand, perhaps because of our increased longevity" (p. 45). Not according to Castaneda, who wrote of Don Juan: "He knows his death is talking to him and won't give him time to cling to anything, so he tries, without craving, all of everything" (p. 151). And certainly not according to the major religious faiths of the world.

Life is precious because it isn't forever, because we don't have more than we want. Thus, in its own strange way, the knowledge of the certainty of eventual death and of the possibility of immediate death enhances the richness of life—at least for those willing to live life in the face of what some have termed the absurdity of death.

WHOSE DEATH?

The meaning for me of facing my own death is quite different from the meaning for me when I face your death or the notion of death in general. The meaning for me in facing death now is quite different from the meaning for me of facing death at a later specific time or indefinitely far off in time.

In the event of your death, I—as an observer—still remain. I can view your death from outside—no matter how much you are a part of my life. If you are my client, patient, parishioner, customer, then I have learned to come close to death and yet to get up and walk away when all is said and done; my world is not untouched by you, but with rare exception it remains very much intact. If you are a casual friend, an acquaintance, a neighbor, my world is touched, perhaps somewhat moved, but except for a brief time the effect of your death on me is slight. If you are someone very close, my world may be disrupted by your death, but at least I remain. My own death "means the total disintegration and dissolution of (my) personal world" (Koestenbaum, 1971, p.6). For all practical purposes, then, when I die, the world ceases to exist.

This doesn't necessarily mean that I prefer your death to mine, although that may well be the case. I may actually prefer that you outlive me, since the loss of you through death might be more difficult for me to face than my own death. The death of a loved one is often perceived as worse than the death of oneself (Geer, 1965).

Sometimes we look at our own death as though we were looking at the death of someone else. We become an observer at our own death instead of a participant. Not only do we plan our funeral and visualize it occurring; we see the sadness of our friends and family members. The truth, of course, is that we can see these scenes only in fantasy, since with our death our ability to experience ceases also (Koestenbaum, 1971).

THE INEVITABILITY OF DEATH/THE IRREVERSIBILITY OF DEATH

Parked in a driveway overlooking San Francisco Bay is a medium-sized truck carrying the legend on its side: Life Extension Through Cryonic Suspension. The cryonics movement advocates freezing persons very rapidly at the moment of death so that their bodies remain as nearly intact as possible for an indefinite period. Cryogenicists believe that sometime in the future the biomedical sciences will discover cures for whatever diseases or injuries caused death; then the bodies can be unfrozen and brought back to life (Ettinger, 1966).

Although it's easy to make fun of the cryogenicists (and they themselves are only too aware of the immense difficulties that form barricades to their success), they represent just one of many movements in history that have attempted to prolong life on earth indefinitely. For example, Ponce de Leon in his search for the fountain of youth pursued a similar path.

Most people in Western societies see death as inevitable and also as irreversible. Once we have been dead, we remain dead. In fact, it is our subjection to fateful limitations that, in part, differentiates us from gods. Humans are finite in all ways—including in the duration of their lives.

However, there are people throughout the world, including some in our culture, who assume the literal reality of ghosts and, therefore, do believe that the dead return to experience this world much as they experienced it before they died. Even then, however, the person returning as a ghost usually does not reside on earth in a familiar earth-bound form but, appearing only on occasion, exists in some special kind of bodily form.

BUT FIRST, MEANINGS IN LIFE

Death is one boundary of life. Conception or birth is another. You may see death as a permeable boundary, through which you will move to another form of existence, or you may see death as an inflexible boundary at which you will cease. In either event, the meaning of death is intimately bound up with the meaning of life. "Since death . . . belongs to life as obviously as the border belongs to a country . . . , the only way to inquire about death is obviously to inquire about life" (Thielicke, 1970, p. 8).

Before we move ahead, we must distinguish two concepts that are so intertwined they may appear to be identical. The first—the meaning *of* life—implies the existence of some ultimate meaning that explains why people exist in the first place. Choron, a foremost philosophical authority on death, proposes that this issue must be considered as follows: (1) whether each individual life is part of a unified plan or process that can be understood as such; (2) whether life can be understood as the expression of a pervasive world spirit; and (3) whether life is a symbol of something else that is "above" or "beyond" an individual life (Choron, 1964).

Although these significant questions are far beyond the scope of this book, how people feel about them does affect their view of death. If, for example, you feel that your life is part of a universal plan, then you are likely to believe that your death is also part of that plan. Rather than being absurd and meaningless, your death will fit into something much grander than you yourself. Does this make your own death easier for you to accept? We certainly don't have any good evidence about that question, but it might well do so.

Meaning *in* life is a totally different matter. It is what is so important to you that it gives your life purpose. The meaning or purpose need not have any significance broader than your own pleasure. Give some thought to what makes your own life meaningful. It need not also make your life meaningful in the future, but it must be something that you would feel very empty without right now.

Is work what gives purpose to your life? Perhaps your present work and your career goals make your life meaningful. (Mandatory retirement is extremely unpopular among some elderly people not only because of loss of income or social contacts but because of participation in the work itself.) Or is it achievement in general that gives your life meaning: the number of books you write, the number of insurance policies you sell, the number of patients you help, the number of awards you receive, the number of people you enable to become better people? What about status and recognition? Is one of your purposes to win awards or to have people know your name—to attain fame (and, if possible, fortune)?

How about personal growth? Is your main purpose in being alive the opportunity to become the "best you that you can possibly become?" Is it to grow in understanding of yourself and of others, to mature in wisdom and knowledge, to make the most of the abilities that you have?

Or do loving and being loved give your life meaning? Do you wish more than anything else to leave your mark by developing loving human relationships? Or even relationships with nature?

What about a cause? Is there a cause to which you are so dedicated that it forms a significant—even the most significant—purpose in your life? The cause might be political or religious or social or creative; it might have a formal organization, an informal organization, or no organization; it might be finite in nature—for example, the next political campaign—or almost infinite in nature—for example, the espousal of world peace.

Does serving God offer you most of what you wish? Perhaps you see both life and death "as part of the gift of being that is given by God, whose love sustains and gives meaning and value to life, while dying is part of the wholeness of life" (John Evans, Ph.D., personal communication). Then do you wish to live in relationship to God? Is this the traditional God of Western religions? Is it some other god?

All of the above offer purposes in living, but none—except possibly for the service or adoration of God—explain the meaning of life. Furthermore, each of the purposes ends with death—either your death or the deaths of persons you have influenced. These are human purposes, and like all that is human, they are finite.

How difficult is it for you to consider the transitory nature of what you have accepted as the most significant meanings in your life? For one friend of mine, it was the source of immense sadness. Fifteen years earlier he had written an extremely fine book, which was more widely quoted and more widely used as a textbook than any other on the topic. He had expected that this book, this achievement, would still be important 10 and 20 years later; he had wanted his achievement to live because only in that way could this accomplishment continue as a source of meaning in his life. Then a year from retirement, past the point of desire to write another book, he realized that more recent students had not even heard of him. He became depressed at the transient quality of his accomplishment and came to feel that his life had been without purpose. Had he been able to accept the time-bound character of his achievement, he might have been satisfied that he had contributed to the knowledge of tens of thousands of people over a ten-year period, but because of the kind of person he was, he needed to extend that contribution to many more tens of thousands of people over a 30- or 40-year period.

To return to our original concern: because death is a boundary to life, it annihilates meaning *in* life for most of us. Your work, your achievements, your status and recognition, your personal growth, your capabilities for loving and being loved, your contribution to causes are all negated by your death or, if not by your death, then eventually by the deaths of others.

MEANINGS OF DEATH

I've just said that one meaning of death is that it negates most meanings *in* life; it does not need to negate meanings *of* life. For example, if life is perceived as part of God's gift—as it is in traditional Judaism and Christianity—death is also understood as part of the same gift. The German theologian, Thielicke (1970), believes death is an expression of God's will that human beings do not forget that they are human and not God. Since God is infinite and people are finite, people cannot effectively aspire to be God.

If death is God's will, as the Old Testament states in Job 1:20, then death has meaning—although any particular death may still be painful for both the dying person and the survivors. Death can also be part of an evolutionary plan that does not depend on a traditional God. For example, death may be perceived as an evolutionary necessity. Older things and people die to make room for the younger, while the selective reproducing processes promote the adaptation of the organism to a changing environment. If all the old of a species lived, the world would soon be overrun with that organism. At the same time, the species would not change since the old would also continue to reproduce. It is only with the deaths of certain organisms (or people) prior to the time at which they reproduce that the species can change genetically. Evolution can be seen as another kind of plan—except that we don't need to assume that God has developed it.

Being part of an evolutionary or religious plan may offer some consolation, but it seems a dubious argument to invoke with someone facing a very intimate and personal event. I'm dying and you want to talk about some absolutes that are never going to affect me in the least. This is much too abstract and impersonal, and it leaves me emotionally untouched.

In both the divine plan and the evolutionary plan, death is seen as necessary—perhaps good, perhaps evil—but necessary. Death may not be so much part of a plan as simply a part of life. If it is part of life, a natural and inevitable part, then there should be no reason to fear death—or so one familiar argument goes. Unfortunately it may not be very persuasive. "Disease, injury, congenital defects are also a part of life, and as well murder, rapine, and pillage" (Ramsey, 1974, p. 82). True, these other events may be preventable in part, but they are certainly part of life today. It is unlikely you would tell an accident victim "That's too bad, but—well—it's part of life." The same explanation is sometimes equally unsatisfying to someone who is dying.

When we contemplate the nature of death and of being dead, we often develop conflicting beliefs. For example, we might view death simultaneously as absurd and meaningful, as beautiful and ugly, as extinction and as transition, as punishment and as reward. These apparent contradictions need not necessarily be real contradictions, however; for example, an event may partake of both beauty and ugliness. Sometimes one aspect is more in evidence and sometimes the other.

DEATH DESTROYS MEANING/DEATH AS MEANING

Consider this apparent conflict. First, because death makes life transient and because anything that does not exist is without meaning, death destroys the meaning of life by destroying the possibility of further life. Second, since death provides an end to life and since the end of life means that time is finite, people are forced into making irreversible decisions concerning the use of time (because once time is spent, it can never be retrieved), and these decisions reflect the meaning people impose upon life.

In the former case, death has no meaning in and of itself. It merely *is*. Death occurs without logic or inspiration; it has been built into a genetic program, which each generation inevitably passes down to its successors. This view proposes that death robs life of meaning.

In the view of Frankl and many others, however, death gives life the potential for meaning. Several centuries ago, the predominant view was that death was a trial conducted by God to determine the worthiness of each dying person (Aries, 1974). Your ability to avoid temptation and die courageously was, in large part, a measure of your entire life. In the extreme case, if you died well, it did not matter how you had lived.

For entirely different reasons, some contemporary writers assign death a meaning. They believe that the knowledge you will die challenges you to do something with the life you have and that the passage of time—the death of each moment—challenges you to do something with each moment (Bulka, 1974; Frankl, 1963).

A further point can be made: the mystery and power of death can be a creative force. "The highest spiritual values of life can originate from the thought and study of death" (Ross, 1975, p. 1). Because death is such a basic matter in both religions and myths, it gives rise to serious thought and creative endeavors. Michelangelo is quoted as stating "No thought exists in me which death has not carved with his chisel" (Ross, 1975, p. 2). I am not contending that death should be welcomed but that there is in death a constructive as well as a destructive force (Ross, 1975)—death both obliterates meaning and creates meaning.

DEATH IS BEAUTIFUL AND TRANQUIL/DEATH IS UGLY AND FIERCE

> Come lovely and soothing death,
> Undulate round the world, serenely arriving, arriving,
> In the day, in the night, to all, to each,
> Sooner or later, delicate death.
> [*Walt Whitman, "When Lilacs Last in the Dooryard Bloom'd"*]

> The last enemy that shall be destroyed is death.
> [*I Corinthians 15:26*]

> Cry woe, destruction, ruin, loss, decay;
> The worst is death, and death will have his day.
> [*Shakespeare, Richard II,* III, *ii, 102–103*]

Is death lovely and soothing? Or is it an enemy to be destroyed? In one of its familiar images in our culture, death is compared to a pastoral scene, where all is calm and contented. After the pain and toil of life, death offers peace and love or else peace and nothingness.

One experienced death counselor has decribed how he encourages dying people to "let go"—to permit themselves to die, to relax and "be taken by death." He paints a picture for them of how easy it is to die and how good it will be to be dead. This technique is used only for individuals who, although near death, hold on to one thread of life because of some unfinished business or fear of dying.

This view of death is supported by reports from people who claim to have died and then returned to life (for example, Moody, 1976). Their descriptions of what it is like to be dead almost always include warm reunions with loving family members or some other very positive experience.

Many years ago I read a science fiction story—I can't recall either the author or the title—in which a man found the secret to truly long life and made himself impervious to death for several hundred years. Then, through an ironic turn, he was incarcerated, and the prison was unexpectedly abandoned. The story ends with his realization that he is doomed to be totally alone—without any human contact or sources of pleasure—for hundreds of years. The Struldburgs in *Gullivers Travels* suffer a similar fate: they continue to age and to endure the problems of aging while unable to die. At first Gulliver believes them the most blessed of people, but he later realizes the horrors of their lives.

Death can be a welcome relief for people who are weary or ill or who see themselves as burdensome to others and useless to themselves. Pneumonia was once called "the old man's friend" because it caused death for many elderly people who were suffering greatly from other illnesses.

It is important to avoid the assumption that contemporary views of death are the same as past ones. For example, our era has been called the period of the non-hero, but in other eras, including our earlier history, the hero was a significant figure. For the early Greeks, the heroic ideal often required that the hero die. First, to be a hero meant that one had to give, or at least offer to give, the one thing that meant the most: one's life. Second, the hero was of such stature that he should not permit himself to deteriorate—better to die early than to age miserably (Bowra, 1957). Another Greek view of that period was that "no man must be counted happy until he is dead, because there is no knowing what disasters may befall him in life" (Bowra, 1957, p. 49). In fact, it has been suggested from writings of Xenaphon and from Plato that Socrates was willing to drink the hemlock, not so much as a virtuous act but, because at 70 years of age he preferred to avoid the indignities of failing health (M. Sicker, personal communication, 1978).

A number of years ago, a psychologist asked people to personify death and describe their personifications. What does death look like? What would death be like? The responses were categorized, and one of the most frequently mentioned categories was termed "the gentle comforter." According to one woman, a registered nurse, "Death would be calm, soothing, and comforting. . . . He would be kind and understanding and yet be very firm and sure of his actions and attitude" (Kastenbaum & Aisenberg, 1972, p. 157). This seems remarkably like the views expressed in Whitman's poem (see p. 53) and certainly represents a significant theme on the nature of death.

The unpleasant side of death, called "the macabre" by the researcher, was also represented in the study. "An extremely thin and emaciated form, scarred, burned, contorted, about twelve feet tall." "The personality is a coldness, hollowness, absolute nothingness." "He's grouchy, cranky, sullen, sarcastic, cynical, mean, evil, disgusting, obnoxious, and nauseating" (Kastenbaum & Aisenberg, 1972, p. 156). These quotations, the responses of three undergraduate students, remind one of Shakespeare's description of death as comparable to woe, destruction, ruin, loss, and decay—and yet still worse than any of these.

Which is death really: beautiful and tranquil or ugly and fierce? The answer, of course, is in the eye of the beholder. The answer also depends upon the kind of dying process that is occurring *and* whether we are considering that dying process or its endpoint, for the process could be fierce and death itself serene.

Shneidman takes a particularly strong position on the question of whether death is beautiful or ugly. He discusses the need to deromanticize death. "Psychologically, our current attitudes toward death are unconsciously sentimental" (1971, p. 11). Since consciousness is all that we have, its loss is the worst thing that could occur. Rather than consider death to be a serene and natural ending to life, Shneidman calls it the "curse to end all curses" (p. 12). He argues that it is about as loving as kidnapping or rape, since like those two acts it violently takes its unwilling victims.

Although these words need to be heeded, they give rise to a serious dilemma. On the one hand, if we advocate that death is beautiful, we may be guilty of trying to avoid dealing with the real emotional difficulties faced by dying persons; we offer them a sedative when what they require is the emotional support to face their own pain. On the other hand, if the romanticization of death seems so widespread and so important in the coping processes of many persons, an iconoclastic, myth-destroying position may be less a matter of being honest than of displaying our own power and self-righteousness.

At a personal level, I tend to agree with Professor Shneidman's position. I believe that too many people, including those involved in counseling the dying, espouse the position that "death can be beautiful" in order to avoid the confrontation with the ugliness and unpleasant passions that can accompany dying and death. If you believe that death is soothing and comforting, or romantic and melancholy, you are entitled to this belief. For myself, I believe that death is unfair and cruel—whatever the dying process may be—since it robs me of me, although I recognize that the time may come when life will be so painful that I will welcome death as an alternative.

DEATH AS EXTINCTION/DEATH AS TRANSITION

Is it possible to think of yourself as being in a state of nothingness? A void? Extinction? Non-being? Perhaps this is impossible; perhaps we can think of others as no longer existing but not of ourselves as such. I can conceptualize a world that exists without me, but I cannot conceptualize a "me" that exists without the world—that is, without consciousness. Certainly the perception of death as the total, irreversible, permanent cessation of consciousness is one of the most familiar ideas of what does occur at the time of clinical death, regardless of the difficulties of applying it to our own consciousness. "It is the prospect of not being any more that makes most men abhor death" (Choron, 1964, p. 10).

Which does death mean to you: extinction or transition? What happens to your consciousness? After clinical death, is there anywhere and any way in which any thing knows it is still you? Will this whatever-it-is continue to know that it is you for only moments or for years or for centuries or forever? If so, death is a transition, a passage from existence in bodily form in this world either to existence in another form in this world or to existence in some form in another world. If, on the other hand, you believe that clinical death marks the complete cessation of all consciousness or you-ness forever, then for you death is extinction.

Two separate issues enter into a decision about whether death is passage or extinction: first, what you believe, and second, what you would like to believe. It is not unusual for someone to believe that death is extinction yet want his or her own soul or existence to continue in some fashion. Many people have forcefully expressed their need to believe in continuation. For example, Bismarck, the great nineteenth-century German leader, said "Without the hope of an afterlife this life is not even worth the effort of getting dressed in the morning." Franz Kafka wrote "Man cannot live without a continuous confidence in something indestructible within himself." According to Emerson "The blazing evidence of immortality is our dissatisfaction with any other solution."

Statistical evidence supports these quotations. When David Reynolds and I asked 434 adults in Los Angeles whether they believed they would live on in some form after death, just over half responded affirmatively. When we returned to the issue with the question "Regardless of your *belief* about life after death, what is your *wish* about it?", fully 70% said they wished there were life after death, while only one respondent in eight wished that there were not (Kalish & Reynolds, 1976).

It is difficult to accept the idea that all consciousness ends forever with clinical death. Indeed, one psychiatrist has claimed that the fear of death and anxiety over being finite is *the* major factor in schizophrenia (Searles, 1961). The schizophrenic symptoms provide an escape from dealing with the anguish of knowing we are not "forever." People diagnosed as schizophrenic sometimes experience themselves as already dead—perhaps the ultimate symptom in avoiding a realistic death encounter. If I am already dead, then I can't be made dead. Even though this is a highly speculative and probably untestable idea, it opens up a provocative area of thought.

Extinction and passage are not, however, the only possibilities. A third is an intermediate state following clinical death and prior to either extinction or passage. Thus a number of African societies recognize a *Sasa* period during which an individual continues to exist after his clinical death. It lasts as long as some living person still recalls the dead person and his or her name from personal contact. The person remains in a *living-dead* state and can continue to appear among the living and be recognized and acknowledged by them. When no one who knew the dead person is still alive, he or she enters a state of *collective immortality,* which is a kind of permanent limbo for spirits or shades of the dead. The dead person may, however, be forced into nonexistence, and this is seen as the worst possible happening (Mbiti, 1970).

Many people I know—I suspect some of you feel similarly—maintain a strange ambivalence concerning extinction and passage. Although they claim to believe in extinction, in nothingness, and assert that their views coincide with their preferences, they maintain a number of values that contradict their verbalized position. Just ask such people how they would feel if their bodies were chopped up and ground down the disposal. A grotesque image? Not if there is no symbolic value to the body. I recall one friend who, after passionately declaring his aversion to any kind of life after death, asked that his ashes be scattered at the top a mountain he had had great pleasure in conquering. I suspect he maintained, at some level of consciousness, an image of himself peering out through his ashes with 20–20 vision at the surrounding countryside.

DEATH AS PUNISHMENT/DEATH AS REWARD

The idea of death as punishment is deeply ingrained in Western culture. In the Old Testament Adam and Eve are punished for their sins by expulsion from the Garden of Eden, where they could have remained immortal (Choron, 1963). Because of their sin, known as Original Sin, they fell from grace and lost God's gift of immortality for themselves and for all their descendents. Consequently, we are all condemned to die. "Once death appeared, the only thing God could do for man was to prolong his life, as a reward for obedience to His Law" (Choron, 1963, p. 82).

Some people believe that the sins they perpetrate as individuals will also shorten their lives. A long life, then, would be one reward for appropriate behavior. Death occurring to large numbers of people may also be seen as a punishment for the sins of a society. God flooded the world—destroying everyone except Noah and his family—in retribution for humankind's evil ways. Through the centuries, people have attempted to propitiate various gods with prayers and gifts in order to avoid catastrophes, and some victims and non-victims of disasters view them as punishments for individual or societal behavior (Wolfenstein, 1957). When a calamity strikes some person, group, organization, or country that you dislike, you assume it is a punishment for their "sins" (or whatever term you might prefer using); when a comparable calamity befalls you or your group, organization, or country, however, you are more likely to ask "Why me?"

Many cultures share the view that one's own sins contribute to a briefer life. The Hopi believed that kindness, good thoughts, and peace of mind led to a long life; according to the Berber, deceit was punished by a shorter life (Simmons, 1945). Among the general population of the United States, over one-third of 434 respondents to a questionnaire agreed with the statement "Most people who live to be 90 years old or older must have been morally good people" (Kalish & Reynolds, 1976); the implication, of course, is that they view long life as a reward for good behavior. Nonetheless, the same people may also believe that "the good die young"—the implication in this statement is that the good are protected in this fashion from the evils of this world—and that the deaths of the elderly are not punishments. These latter deaths are frequently seen as appropriate—these people had lived out their allotted years, and it was time for them to die.

Frequently, when someone who isn't old dies, we seek an explanation for the early death in the person's behavior. At one level, we may look to heavy drinking or smoking, to poor health and eating habits, to working too hard because of greed as reasons for having died "before one's time." Then we can think "Of course that man had a heart attack—smoking two packs a day, drinking like a fish, and working 12 hours a day to pile up the dollars; he was just asking for it." He has been punished for his secular sins, and, since we don't smoke, drink, or work like he did, we won't have to die. Indeed, it even appears that people who survive a heart attack feel morally and psychologically superior to those who have died (Appleton, 1975). If we can blame the dead person for having died, we can escape both our own mortality and our own responsibility.

At a second level, we may literally see "the hand of God" reach out and cause someone's death because they were "bad" people. Nearly two-thirds of the respondents in the Los Angeles study mentioned above agreed with the essentially fundamentalist position that "accidental deaths show the hand of God working among men" (Kalish & Reynolds, 1976).

Death can also be seen as a reward. We have discussed some of the positive aspects of death earlier—the ideas that it gives meaning to life, that it challenges people to do their best, that it is part of a divine plan or of evolutionary necessity, and that it is a release from suffering.

DEATH AS LOSS

Stop and think for a moment. What will *you* lose when you are dying? What will *you* have lost when you are dead? Loss is a constant theme in writings on death and dying. For many people, death is the ultimate loss because it is the loss of consciousness which, as Shneidman has said, is really all that we have.

Of the many losses that accompany the dying process and death, I will discuss only a few here: the loss of experiencing, the loss of people, the loss of control and competence, the loss of the capacity to complete projects and plans, and the loss of body.

LOSS OF EXPERIENCING

Although the loss of the capacity to experience anything seems to strike many philosophers and writers as the most important of all losses, respondents to several questionnaires appeared to feel otherwise. Given seven possible losses caused by death, several hundred to several thousand respondents in each of three studies ranked the loss of the ability to experience first, fourth, and sixth.

Although the differences among the studies initially seemed confusing, they eventually developed into a very sensible picture. The respondents in the study ranking highest concern for this loss were primarily young, introspective, and intellectually sophisticated (Shneidman, 1971); the study in which the loss of experiencing ranked near the bottom was based on participants who were older, more likely to be parents or grandparents, and more likely to believe in traditional religious and social values (Kalish & Reynolds, 1976); the third study was more heterogeneous in its population (Diggory & Rothman, 1961). Furthermore, in both of the latter studies, it was demonstrated that older people were less likely to be concerned with loss of this ability than were younger people; the remaining study did not provide information on age differences.

I will for the present assume that death will lead to the loss of capacity to experience, but what about the process of dying? In some serious and terminal illnesses there is a tendency to become confused (loss of capacity to experience accurately and, perhaps, meaningfully) and to sleep a great deal or to lose consciousness. Moreover, medication for pain often produces drowsiness and other kinds of loss of consciousness. Therefore, most dying persons experience more than usual loss of consciousness during their last hours, days, and weeks.

LOSS OF PEOPLE

When I die, I will lose you. You will lose me. I will lose me. And I will empathize with your losing me. The loss of others begins during the dying process. As my energy diminishes, I cease being willing to make the effort to see people who don't matter a great deal to me. Increasingly as time goes on, I restrict myself to two groups who mean the most to me: first, to those family members and very close friends whom I care for the most and who are themselves capable of being with me in my present state and, second, to the health professionals and hospital staff, who may be very instrumental in keeping me comfortable, free from pain, and in a good mood; who, in effect, have power over my life; and whom I often have come to care for (or despise) with great intensity.

When time becomes very short, I can only bother with those whom I consider highest priority. Even if this means I will hurt a few people's feelings, I can't help it. I really know my priorities now and must serve my own needs, rather than the needs of others. There may be some to whom I am very close whose presence disturbs me—perhaps, because I am upset by their grief or because they play games, irritate me, or talk too much. I can try to get my message across to them because I do want to see them, but I may not have the time for such messages or the energy to figure out how to deliver them.

Theodore Lownik Library
Illinois Benedictine College
Lisle, Illinois 60532

I also know that, when I am dead, I will have lost these people. Therefore, my anticipation of my impending loss forces me to adjust, to cope with what is to come before it has come. I may try to push these losses away from my awareness, but that is almost impossible. Nor do I need to have begun the living-dying process to be upset by knowing these losses will occur. Merely being alive and over the age of nine or ten may be sufficient, and young children do sometimes fantasize the loss of parents.

I also know that you will grieve for me and mourn my death, and that both pleases me and further saddens me. I would hate not being missed, since I want to feel that others care for me; at the same time, I dislike being the source of your upset and sadness. I know how sad I am at losing you, and I assume you are also sad at losing me. Of course, you will—well, you *may*—eventually get over losing me and will—well, *may*—find a replacement, but I will be dead and therefore. . . .

How upset is a dying person that his or her survivors will be bereaved? Apparently it is extremely important, and dying people often go to great lengths to protect their friends and relatives during the dying process. The Los Angeles survey (Kalish & Reynolds, 1976) found that "my death would cause grief to my relatives and friends" was the most important of the seven losses or effects of death listed; the other study involving many older and married participants also had it ranked first (Diggory & Rothman, 1961).

Anticipation of death does not give rise only to the loss of others. It may also bring about the exact opposite: reunion with others. This theme, familiar in Western culture, has recently emerged in conjunction with the search for proof of an afterlife. Numerous books, appearing in the mid-1970s, detailed reunion experiences of people about to die and of those who had presumably been declared dead and subsquently returned to life (Moody, 1976; Osis & Haraldsson, 1977). The literature on suicide also discusses the fantasy many people have that their deaths will reunite them with loved ones who have already died (Moss & Hamilton, 1957). Once again we find apparent opposite meanings in death: loss of others and reunion with others.

LOSS OF CONTROL AND COMPETENCE

As I sit at the typewriter and write these paragraphs, I am in full or reasonable control of much of my life. Within limits, I can eat when and what I want; I can go to bed and get up when I want (work, telephone, and children permitting); I can stay at home or leave the house, turn the television on or leave it off, and walk slowly or run quickly when and if I wish. My body does what I want it to—again within reason. Except for an occasional yawn when I am trying to appear alert, my body follows my conscious and unconscious orders.

What kind of control will I have when I am dead? I know that I will lose some control during the dying process, but I don't know what will happen to me when I am actually dead. In this existence, I have at least some control, some influence, on what happens to me and on what goes on around me. But will any of that remain when I am dead? Some people value control greatly. It is important to them that they not appear foolish to others, that they not become so involved in a relationship that the "power" is turned over to someone else, that they always appear to know what they are doing on the job. Knowing what is happening and what is going to happen next are ways of having at least some control. In death, we don't know what our control, our power, will be. And this can be extremely disturbing to many people.

Competence also matters a great deal. We are presumably awarded in some fashion on earth for our competence, but what about in death? Death, as Kastenbaum (1977) says, is the great leveler. Just as guns became known as equalizers, because they permitted a weak person to be as powerful as a strong person, death levels or equalizes the rich and the poor, the powerful and the powerless, the creative and the pedestrian, the competent and the incompetent, the religious and the irreligious.

Death completes the leveling process. Although a grand monument is built for you and a small stone plaque is placed flat on the ground for me, these symbols acknowledge memories of you and me, not an actually existing you and me. This ancient awareness was well expressed over 2,000 years ago by a contemporary moralist, Publius Syrus, who said "As men, we are all equal in the presence of death." Your power and riches may help you live a little longer, but you and I share the eventual losses of competence and control that are part of death.

LOSS OF CAPACITY TO COMPLETE PROJECTS AND PLANS

Right this moment, as I am writing these sentences, I have innumerable projects and plans that I wish to complete. Most immediately obvious is my wish to finish this book; I also want to see my children grown and independent—not because they need me to accomplish that but because I want to see it. And there are many places I want to visit. You may have comparable projects still incomplete—perhaps some academic program or a sales campaign or a fund-raising campaign for your favorite political or charitable cause.

If you learned that you were going to die before these projects could be finished, you would undoubtedly feel frustrated and angry. I know that I certainly would. One of the first things people do when they begin to realize that they will die fairly soon is try to figure out how to get their projects finished. Sometimes it is possible to complete the project before death occurs; sometimes it is necessary to compromise or permit someone else to help; sometimes it is necessary to realize that the project will never be finished.

Your unfinished business may be less concrete than a sales campaign. Perhaps you had an argument seven years ago with your brother, and you haven't spoken to him since; perhaps you cheated a friend some years ago and you have been meaning to admit your guilt; perhaps you had been postponing a backpacking vacation in the Rockies until you had more time. Often the projects and plans that are uncompleted at the time of our deaths are tasks that have been unfinished for a long time.

LOSS OF THINGS

Death negates all the wonderful things that materialism offers. You have saved for a color television set, a sports car, an expensive stereo with tape recorder, and a vacation home. If only you could live forever, you could continue to accumulate more and more things. Or you could accumulate friends or experiences or store up trips to foreign countries. When you are young, it seems that if you wish hard enough and work hard enough, you shall eventually earn all the good things.

There's an old expression, You can't take it with you. And to that, one person responded "If I can't take it with me, I ain't going." What is the use of having all those expensive things if you can't have them forever? Death certainly puts earning money in a different light. Perhaps the despair that Erikson (1963) discusses in his characterization of the stage-conflict that occurs in late middle age derives to some extent from the realization that life will end and, therefore, will not permit the unending acquisition of things, of people, of places, of experiences.

Since you can't take it with you, what is it that is important to have or to have done by the time you die? Upon what would you like to look back when you are 65 or 70? Can you live today in a manner that allows you to have that kind of life and those kinds of things to look back on?

LOSS OF BODY

What happens to your body when you are dead? Perhaps you believe that it really doesn't matter. All right, but try to imagine yourself without your body. It's very difficult. In spite of the changes in our bodies, in spite of whatever unhappinesses we may have with our bodies, the truth is that we see ourselves in terms of our bodies. With death, the body—at least for some people—becomes a shell that no longer has any meaningful relationship with the essence or spirit of the individual who inhabited it; for others, the body disappears physically but remains in some sort of psychic state in which it waits for a resurrection; for still others, the corporeal body ceases to exist, but its symbolic representation is generated in heaven or in some other kind of existence after death.

As I mentioned earlier, even if we insist that we don't care about our bodies, our behavior often implies that we really do care—very much.

Many people respond with horror to the image of *their* body (or, to make it worse, the body of someone they love) devoured by worms underground, or burned or cremated, or buried without the protection of a casket. The virtual terror that is expressed at the thought of desecration or deterioration of the body strongly suggests that people, in fact, find the body very important.

The theme of mutilation is powerful and familiar in myths, fantasies, and fears of death. In part, the mutilation of the body after death is feared; in part, death is seen as a mutilation or the process of dying is seen as (often justifiably) a mutilating process. This means that dying and death lead to a loss of body integrity or physical wholeness. Not infrequently the medical treatment required to keep people alive—or alive longer—is also harmful to the body (for example, cobalt treatment for cancer). People then must face mutilation of the body in order to live several months longer, and some prefer more rapid death.

Thus, in the dying process, mutilation may be caused by the disease or accident or by the cure. In death, mutilation through decay occurs to the body after the death occurs. And symbolically the entire process of dying-death-dead may be seen as desecration and mutilation. Part of the mortician's task in the United States and Canada is to restore the appearance of the body to eliminate the appearance of mutilation.

DEATH AS A SEXUAL EQUIVALENT OR LOVER

The relationship between death and sex is evident in many ways. Sometimes a similarity is stressed. Orgasms, for example, have been referred to as small deaths. Two decades ago, death was called the new pornography (Gorer, 1959)—a description that has seen frequent use since. Other times death and sex are in opposition. In the tension between Freud's eros and thanatos, the former is life-giving and sensual, the latter death-giving and destructive. Freud also suggested that the fear of death was merely the displacement of some sex-related fear (Freud, 1959a).

Artists have long perceived a relationship between death and sex. It is evident in the paintings and writings from the sixteenth to eighteenth centuries: novels in which a young monk watches over a beautiful woman who has died and paintings in which a person suffering death agony appears to be in a sexual trance (Aries, 1974).

The Harlequin complex is another example of the relationship between sex and death. Harlequin was a lusty, sometimes satanic, fictional character, who has appeared at various times in literary history and was associated with both death and sexuality. The Harlequin complex is found in ". . . a person, usually a woman, who not only does not fear death but actually appears to be looking forward to it with a sense of excitement. The possibility both thrills and attracts her, at the same time that it frightens her" (McClelland, 1963, p. 95). One psychologist used the Thematic Apperception Test (a well-known projective technique in which people are asked to tell stories about pictures they are shown and the stories are then analyzed) to examine the Harlequin theme further. She found that death themes often had sexual overtones, especially among women who were terminally ill (Greenberger, 1965). This perception is reminiscent of another of Kastenbaum's personifications of death: the "Gay Deceiver," who is "a physically attractive and sophisticated person who tempts his victims with veiled promises of pleasure—then delivers them unto death" (1972, p. 166).

Two psychoanalysts, writing about a half century ago, arrived at similar conclusions after interviewing both mentally healthy and mentally ill persons. Among six basic meanings of death, one was "an equivalent for the final sexual union in intercourse" (Bromberg & Schilder, 1933).

DEATH AS AN ORGANIZER OF TIME

Earlier I mentioned that death provided a boundary to life. Without this boundary, it would rarely be necessary to do anything today—it could usually be done as well tomorrow, and we would never run out of tomorrows. In fact, death brings not one but two boundaries: the certainty of eventual death and the uncertainty of the time when it will arrive. Death might appear in five years or five days or five minutes.

Each of us must find a way to balance these two boundaries. How would you live the next five years if you knew five years was all the time you had? How about the next five days? How about living until you are 90? Each of these is possible, and each individual, either by plan or by negligence, develops his or her own life plan. Some bet more on a brief life and give little thought to long-term plans; others bet on long life and expend their time and energy in "building today for a better tomorrow"; some few are fortunate and can do both simultaneously. Most of us develop some kind of balance, and this balance changes as we grow older, marry or establish comparable relationships, assume family responsibilities, and see our friends and relatives die or become seriously ill.

Death places a particularly severe time boundary on the dying. They now must allocate their remaining time, a relatively scarce commodity, among the many things they wish to do. Often the difficulties caused by this—as well as by poor health—prevent the dying from using their time in satisfying ways. This is one of the reasons that I personally shy away from the expression "death with dignity" and try to focus on "living with dignity until death."

The notion of death as a boundary lacks some reality for the person who is not yet in the living-dying period. Nonetheless, all of us can contemplate what we would do with a finite, predictable amount of life ahead. Knowing that you are going to die in the foreseeable future shares many characteristics with leaving a home or community. Many people

TABLE 3-1. Responses of 434 Adults of Four Ethnic Communities in Los Angeles to the Question "If You Were Told That You Had a Terminal Disease and Six Months to Live, How Would You Want to Spend Your Time Until You Died?"

Response category	*Age*			*Sex*	
	20–39	*40–59*	*60+*	*Male*	*Female*
Marked change	24*	15	9	23	11
Withdraw/inner life	14	14	37	17	24
Concern with others	29	25	12	16	29
Complete project	11	10	3	9	8
No change	17	29	31	28	24
Other	5	6	8	7	6

*These figures are percentages.

Note: Coding was done by interviewers in response to unstructured answers (Kalish & Reynolds, 1976).

From *Death and Ethnicity: A Psychocultural Study,* by R. A. Kalish and D. K. Reynolds. Copyright © 1976. Reprinted by permission.

wish to take in as much as possible of life in the time they have left; others prefer to withdraw quickly. When basically healthy people were asked "If you were told that you had a terminal disease and six months to live, how would you want to spend your time until you died?", most people responded that they wanted no change in what they were doing (see Table 3-1). However, almost as many people indicated that they would show their concern for other people by being with them, expressing their love for them, and doing things for them; large numbers also stated that they would withdraw and focus on their inner lives or that they would change their lives markedly (Kalish & Reynolds, 1976).

Note the correlation of sex and age with different responses. Some of the reasons for differences are structural; for example, the elderly, who generally have fewer projects they are working on, are less likely to have projects to complete; similarly, they have fewer people they love who are still alive and in need of their attention. Sex differences seem to reflect traditional role perception differences of men and women.

Statistics, obviously, can only present one part of the picture. The comment made by a middle-aged woman to a similar question deserves, I feel, to become immortal. "If I knew I only had a brief time to live? I'd just buy a better brand of cologne." She went on to explain that she wouldn't change her life-style, but she would afford herself a few luxuries of "the simple things in life." And another statement, perhaps one that epitomizes death for so many people, was made by a 13-year-old who was dying from an accident: "I didn't have time to. . . ." The statement was never finished (from the notes of Amy Schenone).

THE MEANING OF NEAR-DEATH EXPERIENCES

Some people face their own deaths, fully believe they are going to die, and then either recover or find that the situation has so changed that death has been postponed. During that time period—perhaps moments or perhaps weeks—they prepare for death.

> I had been a volunteer fire fighter for three years, but I had never seen anything like this. Six of us had been fighting the fire from a clearing when we realized that the fire had worked all around the clearing, leaving us in the middle. The heat was becoming too intense and I had completely given up hope of escaping when a tank came crashing through the fire and took all of us on board.

> Just as we veered toward shore, a large freak swell toppled us over, and I found myself in the water, nearly a mile from shore, my body aching and exhausted from prolonged strenuous physical activity. I have always been a poor swimmer, but I found a floating life preserver and put it on. However, my body began to go numb, my strokes became slow and weighted. In the midst of this, I had the thought "I wonder if this means I won't have tomorrow's anthropology assignment in?" In a moment I became aware of the absurdity of my concern and began laughing uproariously while swimming. I felt free and opened. [From the notes of Stan Friedman]

> After seeing the other car coming straight at us, the next thing I knew I was in the hospital, and a man dressed in black—a priest—was just behind my head, apparently to administer the last rites. I knew that I was going to die, and I passed out again and didn't learn until some weeks later that the man was not a priest after all, but a policeman who had brought us in to the hospital.

> After the oncologist told me that the cobalt treatment was my only choice and that even with it, I would only live for six or eight months, I decided to go ahead with the procedure. One treatment was enough! The side effects were terrible!! I never returned and, since my oncologist was angry with me for not showing up, I found another physician who would help me. I haven't done anything special since that time, except to live as healthy and full a life as I can. My cancer just stopped spreading, and I'm in about the same shape today that I was in three years ago, before my one cobalt treatment.

> During the fall I experienced absolutely no unpleasant feeling. I clearly recall that I somersaulted in the air three or four times; that made me worry that I might lose the pocketknife that my father had given me as a present. In spite of the severe brain-rattling and several skin cuts, I . . . had not the slightest unpleasant, painful, or anxious feeling. I did not feel the impact at all since already well before that I had become completely unconscious (following a 72-foot fall). [Noyes & Kletti, 1972]

The possible causes of near-death range far. In one study I collected 323 brief descriptions of such events. The largest number of near-death experiences were caused by physical illness and occurred during surgery, although some took place in childbirth. The next largest categories of causes were motor-vehicle accidents, drownings, and war-related events (Kalish, 1969).

Although the procedures for obtaining the descriptions were not well-planned, the results were still suggestive. About half the study's participants described their initial reactions to anticipated death. The two most common responses, expressed with approximately equal frequency, were (1) panic and fear and (2) concern about family and others. Other reactions included anger, prayer, resignation and helplessness, calmness, the recollection of past experiences, and the wish to escape the death-causing circumstances and to live. I found it surprising that, although fear was the most frequent response, it was mentioned by only about 20% of the people who discussed their reactions.

One possible explanation for the lack of fear is that the respondents had forgotten or repressed their actual feelings, but it is more likely that fear during death encounters is not as common as normally believed. Supporting this supposition are several studies based on interviews with persons who had near-death experiences (Moody, 1975; Noyes & Kletti, 1976; Osis & Haraldsson, 1977). It has been proposed that a kind of depersonalization occurring in the face of life-threatening dangers separates the conscious awareness of people from the distressing reality of their impending deaths; this detachment even permits people to watch themselves dying—at least in some circumstances (Noyes & Kletti, 1976).

Another kind of reaction to ongoing death encounters is an out-of-body experience. Two Florida investigators interviewed some 50 patients who had suffered documented near-death experiences, during which they had become unconscious. Of these, seven had "definite recollections, while unconscious, either of viewing their bodies from a detached position of height several feet above the ground . . . or of 'traveling' into another region or dimension" (Sabom & Kreutziger, 1977, p. 196). None of these persons had a psychiatric history nor did they have religious views that would predispose them to such accounts. The causes of the experiences, however, are still very much open to speculation.

The immediate reactions to these experiences are certainly dramatic. What about the long-term effects? Does a near-death experience provide a handicap, or can it be enriching? Although the answer, of course, depends upon the individual personality and the individual circumstances, some patterns were observed in my study. About one out of three persons mentioned increased caution, fear, or avoidance of the cause of near death (for example, a person who escaped drowning would avoid swimming or boating). However, no one described ongoing emotional problems, major somatic changes, or permanently increased anxiety levels, and only a handful indicated any long-term negative consequences. Much more frequent were claims that the experiences caused greater optimism and made the people live each day as it came, feel good about life, and want to live.

TABLE 3-2. Constellations of Experiences of Persons Reporting Near-Death, Based on Factor Analysis

Factor I. *Mystical*	**Factor II.** *Depersonalization*	**Factor III.** *Hyperalertness*
Feeling of great understanding	Loss of emotion	Thoughts sharp and vivid
Images sharp or vivid	Body apart from self	Thoughts speeded
Revival of memories	Self strange or unreal	Vision, hearing sharper
Sense of harmony, unity	Objects small, far away	Altered passage of time
Feeling of joy	Detached from body	Thoughts and movements mechanical
Revelation	World strange or unreal	
Controlled by outside force	Wall between self and emotions	
Colors or visions	Detached from world	
Strange bodily sensations	Body changed in shape or size	
	Strange sounds	
	Altered passage of time	

From "The subjective response to life-threatening danger: An interpretation," by R. Noyes and D. J. Slymen. In *Omega,* 1978-79, *9*. Reprinted by permission.

Many people expressed an increased concern for other individuals and for humanity in general and an increased interest in religion (Kalish, 1969).

In a more recent study, which used greater methodological sophistication, nearly 200 people who had survived life-threatening experiences completed a 40-item questionnaire of possible reactions. A statistical analysis of the items showed that they fell into three constellations: mystical (sense of harmony and unity, colors or vision, feeling of great understanding), depersonalization (loss of emotion, detached from body, altered passage of time), and hyperalertness (thoughts sharp or vivid, thoughts speeded up). The cause of anticipated death influenced the nature of the experience. Thus, feeling detached from one's body was almost twice as common among people who had falling accidents as among those who had drowning accidents; persons with serious illnesses were much more likely than accident victims to report feelings of great understanding (see Table 3-2 [Noyes & Slymen, 1978–79]).

Interestingly, even persons who survived suicide jumps off the Golden Gate and San Francisco Bay bridges were all found to have had transcendent experiences that resulted in increased religious and spiritual feelings. All of the seven persons interviewed were grateful to have survived, and only one subsequently attempted suicide. Several reported feeling they had died and been reborn (Rosen, 1975); this sense of rebirth was described by many of the people interviewed by Raymond Moody (1975) after near-death experiences and also by dying persons who had been administered LSD under careful supervision (Grof & Halifax, 1977).

Confrontations with death seem to give more meaning to life. Many people have told me that, after their near-death experiences, they tended to live and enjoy each day as it came, that they appreciated life much more than they had before, that their various pursuits in life fell into truer perspective. Plato, in the *Apology*, stated that "the life which is unexamined is not worth living." Others have insisted that people cannot fully enjoy and appreciate life until they have confronted the reality of their own death. Aries (1974) contended that life was enjoyed more when there was the chance that death could occur at any time, rather than when people felt assured of a high probability of long life, because enjoyment had to be taken immediately or else be forfeited forever. Near-death experiences cause life to be examined, increase one's feeling of being related both spiritually to the world and personally to others, and can enhance the richness of life. (This section was based, in part, on materials provided by Stan Friedman, Berkeley, California.)

For all of us, then, death has many different meanings. The meanings vary as a function of our age, sex, and religious affiliation. More important, they vary as a function of our life circumstances, such as health and available support systems, our personality characteristics, such as coping abilities and ego strength, and our personal histories and experiences. Developing a coherent concept of what death means is very useful but often not possible. We are entitled to be inconsistent about what death means to us at any given time, since it is so immense and so complex that its meanings are often in flux—changing at the very moments that we try to grasp them. But we continue to think, feel, and behave on the basis of what we assume the meanings of life and death to be.

4

EXPERIENCES, THOUGHTS, AND ATTITUDES TOWARD DEATH

It's all right to not like death. It's even all right to hate death intensely—both the idea of death and the prospect of personal death. I'm not even certain that hating death will make dying more difficult or that being fascinated by death would make dying easier.

Hating death is certainly not a recent phenomenon: "nothing was so hateful to the [early] Greeks as death" (Choron, 1963, p. 31). Historically philosophy itself has its roots in the significance of death and the transitory nature of life. On the other hand, the concept of death as something necessary and good is also very old. Almost contemporary with the Greek negative view of death was a positive one; it held that the soul would continually be cleansed through death and eventual rebirth in another body until it finally attained reunion with the divine (Choron, 1963). So these two themes—death as an evil to be avoided and death as an escape from earthly pain and a means of reunion with the divine—date back to the origins of Western history.

Attitudes toward death antedate ancient Greece, of course. As long ago as 100,000 B.C. the Neanderthal people were burying their dead with food and tools (Noss, 1969). We can't tell what attitudes were reflected by these actions, but they at least suggest beliefs that death was a transition to another existence in which these objects—or the shades of these objects—would be useful.

EXPERIENCE WITH DEATH

Whatever else the burial rituals of prehistoric people meant, they obviously show that death was considered extremely significant by them. We also know that they experienced death much more frequently than we do today. One sociologist has pointed out that while the modern urban citizen might average one day per *decade* participating in funerals, a member of a preliterate society could have spent as much as 100 days per year (Robert Blauner, personal communication). If these data are accurate, our present funeral attendance is 0.1% that of our distant ancestors.

What has been your personal experience with death? How often have you spent time with someone who you knew would die soon? How many funerals have you attended? Has any of your friends committed suicide or been a homicide or accident victim? Have you ever been at a gathering—a party, a political rally, a church affair—where someone unexpectedly died?

If you are typical of others in this society, your answers to these questions will be evidence that your contacts with death have been minimal. I'm referring now not to knowing people who have died but to experiencing the dying process and the deaths of others. A century ago, the chances were that your experiences with death would have been considerably more numerous. Today, death occurs primarily to the elderly; death occurs in the hospital; the physical site of the dying process is off-limits to the young by regulation and custom. All these factors conspire to limit your experience with death. Even if your vocation brings you into frequent contact with death and dying, you have probably developed a very different category for deaths encountered professionally and deaths encountered personally.

In the Los Angeles study, people were asked "How many persons who were dying did you visit or talk with during the past two years?" Over 60% of the people we interviewed hadn't talked to or visited a dying person during that time period; 72% of those under 40 responded in that fashion, compared to only 55% of those 60 and over (Kalish & Reynolds, 1976). Actually, this isn't as great a difference as we had anticipated. Although the older persons undoubtedly had accumulated a much greater lifetime experience than the younger, the experiences didn't vary much during a two-year time interval.

Corresponding to our expectations—younger people (20 to 39 years old) were much more likely than older persons (60 and over) to have experienced no deaths among their friends or family (25% versus 10%); conversely, nearly three times as many people in the older group had known eight or more persons who had died during that interval (22% versus 8%) (Kalish & Reynolds, 1976).

Some evidence exists that people in our society are becoming more willing to face dying and death again. There is a movement to permit people to die at home, and there is some indication that hospitals now provide greater flexibility in the regulations that prohibit children and young people from visiting their relatives, especially dying relatives. But as long as it is older people who die and as long as older people live independently from their children and grandchildren and die in hospitals, our contacts with death will remain minimal.

Try to gain some empathy for people who lived in societies in which death was *not* predictable as a function of age. Consider what it must have been like to have known that the infant death rate was enormously high, that many women would die in childbirth, that plagues were likely to wipe out entire communities, that contagious diseases—tuberculosis, pneumonia, cholera, scarlet fever, and the ever-present smallpox—could infect people and cause their death at any time—no matter how healthy and youthful they were.

Some of you, of course, have had more experience with death than the average, which may be why you are reading this book now. Just the opposite is true for others of you: you may be reading this book because you recognize your lack of experience with death and you wish to develop some kind of practical or emotional preparedness. But the major issue is: how does the well-known lack of experience affect each of us?

First, we tend to be ignorant in the face of death, dying, and relevant rituals. We don't know what to say when we are with a dying person because we have no prior experience; we are uncomfortable at funerals because we have gone to so very few; we don't know how to approach mourners—whether to cry with them or exhort them to be brave—because we have so seldom been with mourners and almost never mourned ourselves.

Second, we end up turning to experts to learn what to do. The experts have traditionally been older family members and friends, the clergy and, more recently, the funeral director. Often there is still an older person around who has experienced death often enough to know what to do. Recently, we can also read a book or attend a workshop or get in touch with the local death educator, but the books, workshops, and educators are more likely to help us with our feelings than to teach us appropriate behavior and ritual. They can make it easier to speak with a dying person, but they rarely direct their efforts at helping us know what to do at a funeral.

Third, we may feel awkward in the situation, and when we feel awkward, we normally wish to get away. So we find reasons to avoid funerals, to postpone visits to the dying, to leave a wake quickly, to mumble something vague to the surviving spouse or child or parent. (Since there are so many other bases for our discomfort in these situations, lack of experience makes a difficult situation much more difficult.)

Fourth, we lack the reminders of the finitude of life. Ministers have, in past generations, used funerals—especially the funerals of the nonelderly—to remind their parishioners that life is fleeting and that faith, charitable works, love, and whatever else they were promulgating had to be expressed without delay. Death could come quickly and unexpectedly, and it was important to be prepared. When we encounter death and death rituals only on rare occasions, we can go for extended periods without stopping to consider our own mortality.

Sometimes an experience that can be shared is useful. Those of you who were at least 5 or 6 years old in 1963 can probably recall what you were doing on November 22 of that year—the day that President Kennedy was assassinated. Whether you were 5, 15, or 55 years old at that time, his death most probably had a significant impact on you. You may well have thought about your own finitude, your own human impermanence. You may have felt very weak and vulnerable, frightened, uncertain of what would happen next. If a powerful, charismatic, protected leader can be struck down, so can any one of us. It's difficult to recall, some two decades later, the feelings and fears that we had at that time; nonetheless, it is amazing how much most people can recall. Ask your friends what they felt and how they spent that day.

THINKING ABOUT DEATH

You probably have trouble recalling what happened November 22, 1973, or November 22 of last year, but it is likely that you do spend some time, perhaps only a little time, thinking about death on November 22. And on Easter, Veterans' Day, and Yom Kippur (if you are Jewish or live in a community with many Jewish people). You may not think of your own death, but you do think about death and its meanings.

How often do you think about death? That's an extremely difficult question to answer, in part because you aren't certain whether I mean all the kinds of death described above (for example, my death, my dying, your death, etc.) or just death in the abstract; nor do you know whether I am including, for example, reading about a homicide in the newspaper or seeing a killing in a television police drama. Furthermore, you aren't exactly certain how often *often* is: if you brood about your own death one hour every two weeks, are you thinking about death occasionally or a great deal?

Despite these problems, however, if I asked you that question, you would probably give me a quick answer that would at least represent your view of how often you think about death. An 1896 article, probably the first to report statistical survey data on this matter, indicated that only 7% of 226 adults never "dwelt on death or suicide," while 60% obviously had given at least moderate thought to the matter (Scott, 1896).

Other studies have reported varying data. One national study with excellent sampling found that almost equal thirds answered "often," "occasionally," and "hardly ever/never" when asked how often they thought about death (Riley, 1970). Another national sample that included more younger and better-educated persons asked the question in more concrete fashion. Just over one-fifth of the thousands of respondents said they never thought about their own death, while 5% did so daily (Shneidman, 1971).

Two recent studies conducted in Los Angeles primarily interviewed racial and ethnic minority group members (in these instances, Blacks, Spanish Americans, and Japanese Americans). Once again the data were not comparable. In one study, a third answered that they thought about their death "not at all," and only 9% did so "frequently" (Bengtson, Cuellar, & Ragan, 1977); in the other study, nearly 60% said they never or hardly ever thought about their own deaths, while 17% had such thoughts every day (Kalish & Reynolds, 1976).

What can we make of this hodgepodge of results? First of all, it would be useful if investigators used the same wording for the questions and the same alternatives for the answers, since none of the above studies are exactly comparable. Second, different groupings within society give very different responses, so that the frequency with which Black and Mexican Americans say they think of their own deaths is considerably greater than that of Japanese and white Americans (Kalish & Reynolds, 1976). What we don't know is whether these statistical differences represent actual differences in frequency of thoughts or differences in willingness to admit such thoughts. This is an inevitable problem in a survey. Since there is no evidence of differential distortion among the ethnic groups, I will accept the results at face value—but with extreme caution.

Perhaps we empathize with Freud who admitted to thinking of death every day; his biographer believed that he was preoccupied by thoughts of death (Jones, 1953, 1957). Or perhaps we agree with one person who commented "One does think of death, but one doesn't remember how often." That's really a very valuable point. For example, although I had been sitting at this typewriter and working on this section for nearly one hour, I hadn't contemplated *my* own death until I wrote the above quotation. At what point in reading this chapter, did you contemplate your own death? Was it just a few moments ago?

So it seems that I can think a great deal about death—your death, death in the abstract, death of all those people over there—without ever thinking seriously of *my* death. That's probably fortunate, since a steady diet of thinking of *my* death is likely to be as counterproductive as a careful vigil to avoid thinking of my death.

What does it mean to think a lot about death in general or about your own death in particular? First and foremost, it means that for some combination of reasons death has a high degree of salience or relevance in your life. Death might be important because of something taking place in your environment—for example, the recent death of a close friend who was several years younger than you, a letter from your physician asking you to come in for extensive blood tests, or your mother's recent diagnosis of breast cancer. Reading this book, participating in an academic program about death, or attending a workshop on death might also increase your awareness of death in general and of your own death.

You might be thinking about death because of disturbing occurrences inside your own body. Perhaps the other evening you had an excruciating pain running down the left side of your body; maybe there's a patch on your face that seems to be spreading; or perhaps you've had your first serious asthma attack since childhood (an asthma attack is not going to cause your death, but, by keeping you from breathing, it may well lead you to think about death).

Or perhaps your thoughts focus on death because of earlier experiences that have made death salient for you over the years. Your mother died when you were 8; you were in an iron lung as a child; your uncle, whom you loved very much, died in a car accident on his way to visit you; your grandmother shared a home with your parents, and they cared for her during the two years she was slowly dying of cancer. If death caused a significant threat or disruption in your early life—even if your parents and other adults assumed that you were too young to be aware of its significance at the time—you might find thoughts of death persevering in your adult years. Not really having understood the meaning of death at the time (if, indeed, we ever truly understand the meaning of death), you never adequately dealt with the feelings the early experiences elicited in you. Or, even if you were old enough to understand something about death, you did not work through the fears and anxieties that the experience evoked. Now, as an adult, thoughts of death seem to press upon you—perhaps representing your unconscious attempts to come to terms with the experiences and feelings of many years earlier.

In fact, your earlier experiences did not necessarily have to be directly with death. Childhood fears of being abandoned or of being mutilated can translate into fears of death. Nor is it necessary for the experiences to have occurred during childhood. Recent experiences, such as the death of a close friend, may have the same effect. One 40-year-old man found himself constantly thinking of death after reading a vivid account of the horrors perpetrated by the Nazis in a World War II German concentration camp.

Finally, death may frequently invade your thoughts as self-inflicted punishment for some real or imagined "sins" you have committed, because you feel immense anger with someone else and have a fantasied fear of retribution for your anger, or because you associate death with an escape from a world that you frequently find very painful.

There are obviously many reasons for death to be salient for you or for any other person. Whether these reasons imply a favorable or a negative reaction to death in general or to your own death, the overall significance is that death is important to you and that you are capable of dealing with thoughts of your own death. (You may not report thinking about death because you are repressing such thoughts, but that is another issue which will be discussed later.) According to one study, people seem to think about death "under three deeply personal circumstances: an accident or 'near-miss,' a serious illness, or the death of someone significant to them" (Riley, 1970, p. 35). Although it was not mentioned in this study, I would assume that people also would think more about death as they grow older. Of course, because older persons are more likely to encounter serious illness and the deaths of others, they have both situational cues to death-thoughts and life-circumstance cues as well.

We have very little information about how much dying people themselves think about their own deaths, although I would assume that most of them do a great deal of thinking, wondering, and fantasizing about what is happening to them. One study provides some information. In his hospital experiences in Great Britain, psychiatrist John Hinton examined the correlation between various aspects of a person's background and his or her willingness to talk about dying. He found only one correlation that occurred with even moderate consistency: dying persons with young children, sadly enough, were more likely to talk of the fact that they might be dying (1972).

Is thinking about death valuable? Or is it detrimental? Those questions cannot be answered in the abstract. Ignace Lepp, a French priest and psychotherapist, has suggested: "Constant meditation on death is paralyzing for both action and life. On the other hand, nothing is accomplished by repressing the thought of death or trying to drown it in a sea of distractions" (1968, p. 134).

THE DENIAL OF DEATH

The term *denial* is used so often and with so many different meanings in discussions of dying and death that it deserves some explication. First, the formal definition: "an unconscious defense mechanism whereby the truth of certain thoughts, feelings, or wishes is disavowed because of its painful or threatening nature" (Goldenberg, 1977, p. 586).

Denial is, therefore, different from avoidance. People may decide to avoid talking about death and dying; they may decide not to visit a cemetery; they may decide not to take a course about death or to read this book. To use the psychological definition—they are not *denying* death; they are avoiding it. Their actions are conscious, and denial is unconscious.

Another distinction is also important. Denying one's own dying is very different from denying death or denying extinction. The denial of death is the denial that I *can* die; the denial of dying is the denial that I am (or you are or he or she is) dying. Although related, the two are still very different.

We are often described as a death-denying culture. This means that our social institutions and social values have developed so that the idea of death is disavowed and excluded. Many authors, myself included, however, don't believe this is the case (Parsons & Lidz, 1967). Although we do deny or exclude death in some instances—by using euphemisms, keeping children from knowledge of death, refusing to exhibit coffins as window displays, removing dead patients from their hospital rooms without telling their roommates why—we accept death in other instances. For example, cemeteries are kept open to public view and newspapers run obituaries.

The individual denies death in many ways. One of these is through participation in activities in which death has a high probability of occurring. A friend of mine who had been seriously injured when his sports car went off the side of the road told me recently "It's just impossible that I should die from a car accident, and I still don't believe it can happen." Although he had used a larger car and driven more carefully for two or three years after his accident, he finally purchased another sports car and resumed his previous driving style.

Much of our behavior suggests we believe we will live forever. The major compromises with good health habits that many of us make in our daily living imply that "it doesn't really matter." Equally significantly, we tend to use time as though we had all the time in the world, rather than a finite—and unknown—amount of time.

Some people who might otherwise not believe in immortality deny death by denying that death will change things very much. These people, by viewing death as a rite of passage to another, often fairly similar existence, deny the concept of death as extinction. (Your personal religious views of what happens after death will determine whether you perceive this as a form of denial or as the truth about immortality.)

Still other people—including many accountants and estate planners—express denial of death by not planning for it; for example, they don't make wills because they feel that as long as they don't acknowledge the inevitability of their death by planning for it, they logically won't die. However, sometimes it's difficult to evaluate if an individual who doesn't make out a will because she or he insists that "I'm just not concerned about death" is, in fact, strongly denying death or basically accepting of it.

Why does denial occur? Because—for some persons and under some conditions—death is too stressful to contemplate. Since we can't fully obliterate the knowledge that death is real, we unconsciously find ways to insulate ourselves from the emotional impact of this knowledge, and these means may require us to avoid contact with or mention of death. If I don't talk about it or read it, then it isn't there, and it can't happen to me.

AN INITIAL LOOK AT ATTITUDES

What is an "attitude toward death"? One definition of *attitude* is "a relatively enduring tendency to think, feel, and behave in a consistently favorable or unfavorable fashion toward a concrete or abstract thing (including person) or idea." Thus, I may be expressing an attitude when I have unpleasant images of what my own dying will be like, when I feel that your death would create immense problems for me, and when I tell a friend that I will not accompany him to his brother's funeral.

The concepts of *attitude* and *feelings* overlap so much that it is virtually impossible to discuss one without the other. In this chapter, I will discuss the feelings and attitudes of what we call the general population—that is, of all of us. (I will focus on the feelings and attitudes of persons who are themselves dying in Chapter 10, on those who care for the dying in Chapter 14, and on the bereaved in Chapter 13. Elsewhere in this book I will describe the death-related experiences of specific groups of people, such as children, churchgoers, the bereaved, and death-related professionals.

Feelings and attitudes toward death, like all feelings and attitudes, vary considerably from person to person—even among individuals who have extremely similar backgrounds. Even if two people share views about some aspects of death—perhaps the importance of funerals—they may well differ on other death-related matters—such as the propriety of children being at funerals. When we discuss the death views of "our society," we must keep firmly in mind that we are generalizing and are constantly running the risk of over-generalizing.

Death attitudes not only vary among individuals or among societies; they also vary across time for a given individual or for a society. Consider yourself for a moment—only yourself. Are your views of death and its various components the same today as they were five years ago? Will they be the same five years from now? The evidence suggests that, depending on your mood, your experiences, and your immediate physical and social environments, they will change from year to year and even perhaps from day to day or from moment to moment. Similarly, the views of your society or of groups within the society change over the years. For example, the death awareness movement has represented social change in the ways we relate to persons who are dying.

Since death and dying mean many things, we cannot talk about *an* attitude toward death. I may have very different feelings about (a) my dying eventually, (b) my dying in the next few days or weeks, (c) your dying eventually, (d) your dying in the next few days or weeks, (e) my being dead, (f) your being dead, and (g) the abstract concept of death. The factors that determine my feelings include (1) what the relationship of the person concerned is to me, (2) how imminent death is, and (3) whether it is the process of dying or the state of being dead that is involved.

Of the several studies made of the relationship of these factors, two are especially important. In one, two psychologists devised four separate scales: fear of death of self, fear of death of others, fear of dying of self, and fear of dying of others (see Figure 4-1). These scales were then administered to two groups of undergraduate women, and the scores were intercorrelated. There was virtually no relationship betweeen fear of death of others and fear of dying of self; similarly, the correlation between fear of death of self and fear of dying of others in the reciprocal relationship was erratic; however, there were significant correlations within the remaining sets of factors—the strongest relationship being between one's own dying and the dying of others (Collett & Lester, 1969). Apparently, two separate

	Fear of own death	Fear of own dying
Fear of Death of Others	Moderately high relationship	Very low relationship
Fear of Dying of Others	Ambiguous relationship	Highest relationship

Figure 4-1. Relationships between selected death attitude variables. (After Collett & Lester, 1969.)

concepts developed: death versus dying and self versus others. Relationships within either concept were significant; relationships between factors not tied together by one of the concepts were weak. Because the number of people in each study was only 25, only women were included, and the age and education ranges were limited, however, generalizing from these data must be done cautiously.

However, another study, discussed more fully in the next chapter, found four factors involved in death anxiety; these are death avoidance, death fear, death denial, and reluctance to interact with the dying (Nelson & Nelson, 1975). The two studies do not contradict each other, and no one to my knowledge has conducted research to integrate the two. It certainly appears that people differentiate between death and dying and that they recognize several different bases for death fear and anxiety. We are mistaken when we describe *the* death attitudes of our society or of an individual as though there were only one set.

ORIGINS OF DEATH ATTITUDES

If I were asked what most influenced my attitudes toward death, I would probably search through early experiences and exposures, many of which are now lost to recall. I can recall—I must have been 5 or 6 years old—the body of a man lying, covered, in the park, while policemen were busy nearby talking to people and writing; I can recall the occasional death of a family friend or elderly grandparent.

But we also have experiences with and exposures to death throughout our lives that influence our values and attitudes, and research has done little to bring these to light. In one study people were asked which of a list of factors influenced their attitudes to death the most. The interview, which did not probe into forgotten memories or repressed experiences and feelings, nevertheless evoked responses that seemed indicative of factors to which people attribute their death attitudes. It appears from Table 4-1 that the most powerful influence on death attitudes is the confrontation with one's own death or the death of someone else, while both religious

TABLE 4-1. Responses of 434 Greater Los Angeles Residents to the Question: "Of the Following, Which One Has Influenced Your Attitudes toward Death the Most?" (Kalish & Reynolds, 1976).

	Ethnicity				*Age*			*Sex*	
INFLUENCE	*Black American*	*Japanese American*	*Mexican American*	*"Anglo"*	*20–39*	*40–59*	*60+*	*Men*	*Women*
Being or thinking you were close to death	10*	22	18	14	19	14	16	18	14
Death of someone else	26	41	39	35	33	42	30	34	37
Religion, mystical experiences	40	15	23	25	15	25	39	23	28
Reading	7	2	5	6	7	6	1	5	5
Conversations	3	4	7	5	7	5	2	4	6
Funerals, other rituals	3	6	0	8	6	3	5	5	4
Media	2	3	4	2	5	1	2	3	2
Other	10	8	4	6	10	4	7	9	4

*These figures are percentages.

From *Death and Ethnicity: A Psychocultural Study,* by R. A. Kalish and D. K. Reynolds. Copyright © 1976. Reprinted by permission.

and mystical experiences and having a personal death encounter are also important. Unfortunately, influences such as the expressed values of parents or childhood discussion with age peers were not included.

WHAT FEELINGS AND ATTITUDES TOWARD DEATH ARE POSSIBLE?

Frequently researchers consider "attitudes toward death" and "fear of death" synonymous. Not being afraid of death, accepting death, being open to one's feelings concerning death, and other possible attitudes toward death, many of which are at the opposite end of the continuum from fear of death, have been relatively ignored in research as well as clinical and theoretical writings (for a thorough discussion see Marshall, 1980).

A person may feel awe and wonder in the face of death. Death is so powerful, so overwhelming, so inevitable, so imposing, so permanent, that it can induce such feelings. The awesomeness and wonder may, in turn, lead to feelings of terror or feelings of peacefulness.

Or someone may be curious about death. What does it mean? Where does it lead? Is it really irreversible? How does it feel? Or does it feel at all?

Perhaps the most ignored attitude toward death is *dislike.* If I like to be healthy and sickness keeps me from being healthy, I will dislike sickness; if I like being wealthy and high taxes keep me from being wealthy, I will dislike high taxes; and if I like being alive and death is going to keep me from being alive, I will dislike death. My dislike may be so intense as to describe it as hate.

Strangely, relatively little has been written in the academic and professional literature about disliking or hating death, although there are numerous references to anger about one's own dying or the death of a loved one. One exception is an early study (Bromberg & Schilder, 1933) that concluded that people are more likely to express sadness, dislike, and regret in considering their own deaths than they are to express fear or anxiety.

Freud contended that we cannot imagine our own deaths, "and whenever we make the attempt to imagine it we can perceive that we really survive as spectators" (Freud, 1959a, p. 305). Although we can consciously talk about our own death, "our unconscious does not believe in its own death; it behaves as if immortal" (Freud, 1959a, p. 313). This, Freud speculates, might be the secret of heroism: that unconsciously we don't believe we will die and, therefore, again unconsciously, heroic and high-risk actions don't lead to fear of death. We do, of course, recognize the reality of the deaths of others, and Freud suggests that the origins of psychology itself might be in the concurrent emotional pain and sense of triumph that we feel at the death of a loved one (Freud, 1959).

While I personally recognize Freud's wisdom when he says that we inevitably see ourselves as surviving our own deaths when we think about death, I don't agree with his assumption that we maintain an unconscious belief that we will never die. However, Freud's position on this issue and his implicit assumption that death fear and anxiety were displaced sexual anxieties most probably were instrumental in delaying examination of the meaning of death.

DEATH ATTITUDES: CONSCIOUS AND UNCONSCIOUS

Both observations and studies have shown that unconscious attitudes toward death may conflict with conscious attitudes. Over two decades ago, a series of studies investigated this conflict. One of the studies had the title "Is Death a Matter of Indifference?"; the authors concluded it definitely was not. First, they asked a small number ($N = 31$) of college students how they felt about death; the students responded with a high level of indifference. Next, they showed the students a series of words flashed briefly on a screen. Then they presented the students with a series of words and, using the word-association technique, they asked for the first word that came to mind. The words fell into four categories: neutral, sex, school, and death. The time it took to respond to the words was measured, as was the students' galvanic skin response (a measure of stress and anxiety usually based on increase in palm perspiration). The results were very clear. Despite the claims of indifference, both measures of response to death-related words showed highly emotional patterns—like the responses to the school and sex words—and were very different from the responses to the neutral terms (Alexander, Colley, & Adlerstein, 1957). Other studies by Alexander and Adlerstein had comparable results (1960).

The conflict between conscious and unconscious death attitudes is apparent not only through research but in our daily observations. A good friend of mine laughs at me for my interest in death, says that I must really be afraid of death to spend so much time worrying about it, then subsequently casually mentions that he is so unafraid of death that he hasn't even bothered making out a will. (I make the opposite assumption—that a man with three children rapidly approaching college age who hasn't made out a will is avoiding the idea of death.)

Why is it, then, that people who say they aren't afraid of dying or of their own death show they are indeed afraid when we measure or observe their fears and anxieties indirectly? One obvious answer is that people are reluctant to admit death fears to others; they may feel it makes them appear weak or unduly vulnerable. An alternative explanation is that people don't normally think about death, and so their almost automatic response when asked is to reply in the negative without giving the matter serious thought—perhaps upset just enough by the question to avoid giving it serious thought.

A third possibility is that people are not aware of how fearful and anxious they are about death. When they say they aren't afraid, they are totally sincere, but their voice or their sweat glands or their eyes say otherwise.

There is a fourth alternative, which is frequently overlooked. When I ask you, whether in a research interview or in a casual conversation, whether you are afraid of death, you think of the abstraction, death, rather than the reality, death. Even if I ask you about *your* death, your response is the same.

If you were encouraged for two or three minutes to dwell on what it means to die or to be dead, the responses might be quite different. If I asked you to think of those you were going to leave behind or of facing the possibility of nothingness, of extinction, then you might become more fearful or anxious. The full impact of the meaning of *your* death to *you* probably cannot be absorbed in response to a simple question. While you are saying that you aren't afraid of dying or of death, you give evidence of general arousal and concern by the increase in the time it takes you to respond, by the change in your tone of voice, by the alterations in the biochemical responses of your body. The habit of displacing this fear and anxiety was instrumental for many decades in keeping Western psychology from recognizing death anxiety as a significant influence on human behavior.

What do people say about the meaning of their own death when they are asked? On the one hand, many people admit that they have difficulty in conceiving of their own deaths or of themselves as dead. On the other hand, the same people have relatively little difficulty in visualizing their funerals and their bodies at the funerals (Bromberg & Schilder, 1933). Because these data are from a study conducted nearly a half century ago, a follow-up investigation of some of its topics would be extremely valuable.

IS DEATH TABOO?

The concept of taboo has two different, almost contrary, meanings. The first meaning is "sacred" or "consecrated;" the second refers to what is dangerous, forbidden, profane, or unclean (Farberow, 1963). Death fulfills both meanings in some ways. Gorer, a British anthropologist, carried this idea even further by writing about death as the new pornography (1967). Children, he pointed out, had once been familiar with the process of dying and were, in fact, urged to think about their own deaths ("Now I lay me down to sleep . . ."), but they were assumed innocent of sex, and an attempt was made to keep them that way. More recently, Gorer points out, children are encouraged to think of sex as natural and can hardly avoid sex-related pictures or words, but they are often assumed innocent of death, and an attempt is often made to keep them that way.

In 1961, Herman Feifel stated that death was a taboo topic, and no one would contradict him (Feifel, 1963). Is death taboo today? Is it pornographic? The answer seems complex. To some extent, death is sacred, and to some extent death is dangerous and unclean—something bringing dire consequences if not avoided.

But that isn't the entire picture. Thus, our newspapers describe many deaths in every issue—some in the news columns and some in the obituaries. Cemeteries are open to the public, and the names of the dead are prominently displayed. Yet morticians and coroners and gravediggers are often embarrassed to tell others what their field of work is. Both health professionals and the general public have developed innumerable euphemisms to replace *death* and *dead.*

Assume that a close friend of yours was extremely ill. Would you telephone her to ask how she was feeling? Probably. What if she told you that she was feeling terrible and that she was "doubtful about the outcome of her illness"—the implication being, of course, that she might die? Would you ask her if she meant that she might die? You probably would not, but you might ask someone else, another close friend, a relative, perhaps even someone who knew her medical condition. Somehow, it would feel like a violation of her personal world or a crude intrusion to ask the possibly-dying woman whether she was dying. Or you might have assumed that she didn't want to discuss her prognosis. However, it would not have the same implications to ask someone else about her. Now assume that your friend has fully recovered from her illness. It is likely that you will be able to talk with her freely about her close call with death, but you may never feel able to ask her how her mother died, since you are under the impression that the death was caused by suicide.

Let's shift from this friend to some other friends. Consider, for example, a close friend whose husband just left her for another woman, or another friend whose business went bankrupt, or a friend whose parents were just sentenced to prison for fraud, or one whose child recently flunked out of college, or someone you have just learned is impotent and desperately wants to become a father. Would you be likely to telephone any one of these individuals to ask about their predicaments? In the event that you did call, would you say something like "I'm sorry to hear that your husband left you," or "That was too bad about your going bankrupt" or "How about getting together to talk about your impotence—I'm really a good listener"?

It is not death alone that is taboo—any more than marriage or business or imprisonment or education or sex is taboo. In our society we are uncomfortable in the face of certain kinds of failure, certain kinds of intimacy, certain kinds of loss, and we are led to believe that others are similarly uncomfortable. Therefore, we avoid topics that we feel would bring discomfort to them or to ourselves. Our attitudes toward death are such that, in certain contexts, we perceive it as failure, as intimacy, and as loss.

Fortunately, the taboo nature of death and dying does appear to have abated somewhat. Does this also mean that people are less afraid of death, less anxious in the face of death? Probably not, although the increased openness concerning death very likely permits us to handle our fears and anxieties better. The next chapter investigates these emotions more fully.

5

FEAR AND ANXIETY

> "The thing of which I have most fear is fear" (*Montaigne*, in 1580).
> "Nothing is so much to be feared as fear" (*Thoreau*, in 1851).
> "The only thing we have to fear is fear itself" (*Franklin Roosevelt*, in 1933).
> "We seem to fear the fear of death" (*Kastenbaum & Aisenberg*, in 1972).

No, this statement by Kastenbaum and Aisenberg is not in agreement with the previous three. In fact, its meaning is just the opposite—that we have an inordinate fear of the fear of death, that we go to unnecessary lengths to help (or even require) people overcome their fear of death, that we are made so uncomfortable by the fear of death that one might question why we protest so much. Kastenbaum and Aisenberg seem to be saying that it is all right, perhaps even desirable, to have some fear of death. As one research participant said "You are *nuts* if you aren't afraid of death" (Kalish & Reynolds, 1976).

However, there is a danger in putting too much faith in comments like the above: we begin to assume that fear of death is inevitable and, thereupon, exclude any basis for contradictory information. So, when people admit to fearing death and their deaths, we surmise that they really fear death. But, if other people insist that they do not fear death or their deaths, we surmise that they are denying their fear of death and really have this fear nonetheless. We know best because our theory tells us so—it doesn't matter what anyone else says. In fact, we may be correct. Perhaps individuals who contend that they have no fear of death are unconsciously or consciously covering for a considerable fear. But the evidence is not yet in, and, I believe, we are usually well-advised to accept what people say at face value rather than attempt to become mind-readers.

There is little doubt that the death attitude that receives the most attention—and deservedly so—is the fear of death. The term *fear* is usually used when there is a specific, identifiable source of the fear; *anxiety* refers to feelings of apprehension and discomfort, similar to those felt in fear, but without a known identifiable source. It is difficult to know, when we consider death, whether the source is known or not, and so *death fear* and *death anxiety* are used almost interchangeably. We also use such terms as *terror* and *dread*.

What causes the fear and anxiety? As early as 1915, G. Stanley Hall stated "We long to be just as well, strong, happy, and vital as possible, and strive against everything that impedes this wish or will. . . . We love life supremely and cannot have too much of it . . . while we dread all that interferes with it" (p. 569). So we dread and, therefore, fear that which deprives us of what we love.

But death has other consequences that we fear—the many losses: loved ones, achievements, purposefulness, the possibility of experiencing, the physical body, control. For many people, the fear of death is the dread of extinction—of becoming nothing, of annihilation and obliteration—while for others it is the dread of entering the unknown and facing the possibility of judgment, punishment, and retribution. It may also involve the fear of separation and abandonment—separation from people, from places, from all that one has ever known. In addition to our fear of our own deaths we fear and are anxious about our dying processes and the deaths and dying processes of those whom we love.

Fear of death has at least two positive outcomes. First, if we did not fear death, we would not exert nearly so much effort in avoiding death. And, if that were the case, many, perhaps most, of us would die at an early age. This would have the effect of eliminating the human species. The fear of death, or, at least, a death avoidance, might even be the outcome of evolution, since presumably those species that did not fear death ceased to exist, and those individuals in our species who did not fear death did not live to reproduce.

The second positive outcome of death fear is less certain. There has been a great deal of speculation that fear of death has led to great creativity (for example, Becker, 1973). Those who hold this view believe that many artists have attempted to express their fear of death through their art; sometimes they express it directly by depicting death and sometimes indirectly by pouring their fear and anxiety into a variety of kinds of artistic endeavors.

STUDIES OF DEATH FEARS AND ANXIETIES

The academic literature is filled with studies of death fear and anxiety; some are based on mail questionnaires and others on interviews or materials distributed through classes and workshops. Although the results of the studies are fairly consistent, some variation occurs as a result of the wording of the questions and the characteristics of the specific groups participating.

One familiar finding is that, in response to direct questions, people seldom indicate a fear of death. In the only national sample ever asked this question, Riley reports that only 4% "gave evidence of fear or emotional anxiety in connection with death" (Riley et al., 1968, p. 332). When asked in a later study what the "worst things" were about being old, less than one person in ten cited fear of death (National Council on the Aging, 1975). Furthermore, Dave Reynolds and I found slightly over one-fourth of the multiethnic respondents we queried admitted that they were afraid of death (Kalish & Reynolds, 1976). Roughly 20% of the Black and "Anglo" respondents acknowledged fear, while slightly over 30% of the Japanese Americans and Mexican Americans did. The Kalish and Reynolds study may have found a higher proportion of fear because the question was asked in the middle of a one-hour personal interview on death and bereavement; the respondents may have felt freer to admit their fears or they may have had previously unknown fears stirred into consciousness by the interview process.

The validity of the results of death anxiety studies has been called into question. Do the findings actually represent what people are thinking and feeling? The truth is that we don't know. We can probably assume that the answers people give are what they *believe* that they believe, although there is probably some conscious distortion that occurs. But we neither know how much unaware distortion occurs nor how often we ask so sophisticated a question that the respondent, never having given serious thought to the question, answers with the first thing that comes to mind. (Of course, the first thing that comes to mind may be the best and most honest response anyway.)

In Chapter 2, I discussed a second problem with these studies: the difficulty in responding on a simple five-point scale to questions like "Are you afraid of death?" Now I want to add another limitation: at the conscious level you may not be afraid, but your unconscious behavior may suggest some degree of fear or anxiety. Perhaps the most significant attempt to resolve this problem was a study of reactions to death at the conscious, fantasy, and below-the-level-of-awareness levels (Feifel & Branscomb, 1973). Although the study's measures of the latter two levels are debatable, its conclusions are still important: "The dominant conscious response to fear of death is one of repudiation [of the *fear*]; that of the fantasy or imagery level, one of ambivalence; and at the nonconscious level, one of outright negativity" (Feifel & Branscomb, 1973, p. 286). The implications are apparent: the deeper we probe into the unconscious, the more death fear and anxiety we find. The implications of this finding for our behavior are more difficult to determine.

A third concern is that researchers do not always differentiate in their studies between fear (having a known cause) and anxiety (having a vague, diffuse cause). They are likely to develop questionnaires that combine the two by including both fear items and anxiety items. And they are not always careful in the title they assign a questionnaire. The fact that a scale consists of both fear items and anxiety items does not mean that the scale is without value, but it does mean that you need to be even more careful in the ways you use it and how you interpret your findings.

Fourth, not only is there a difference between fear and anxiety, but there are undoubtedly numerous components of both fear and anxiety. One study (Nelson & Nelson, 1975), using a statistical technique termed *factor analysis*, determined four dimensions of death fear/anxiety. These were (1) death avoidance ("I could sleep in the room with a dead body."); (2) death fear ("Everyone in his right mind is afraid to die."); (3) death denial ("I would want the best casket available so my body would be well protected."); (4) reluctance to interact with the dying ("I would mind working with dying persons"). These are not unrelated factors—indeed, most of them correlate quite substantially; they are a way, based on statistical analysis, of viewing the dimensions of death anxiety.

We don't need statistics to show that death anxiety is not one simple dimension. Thus, one person is perfectly comfortable attending funerals and visiting the cemetery but becomes upset if a favorite television character is likely to die; another talks freely about dying in a hospital but becomes panicked anytime he fantasies being buried.

A fifth difficulty is to decide whether the scales are measuring death anxiety or general anxiety. I believe that some people who have relatively little general anxiety are anxious about their deaths, while other highly anxious individuals have relatively little death anxiety. However, I must admit that, although I believe that to be the case, I haven't yet found good evidence of it.

In spite of the numerous studies on death fears and anxieties, there is only modest consistency in the findings,whether the factor studied is sex, religion, age, or personality characteristics. The trends that do emerge must still be seen as tentative.

The many limitations to our measures of death fears and anxieties do not mean, however, that the studies should be ignored. In each study it is important to consider (1) the nature of the measuring instrument, (2) the characteristics of the group being questioned, and (3) the conditions under which the study was conducted. If you know these three things, you can evaluate the applicability of the research findings.

SEX DIFFERENCES IN DEATH FEARS AND ANXIETIES

Many studies have found women to be more fearful or anxious about death and dying than men (for example, Kalish, 1963; Templer, Ruff, & Frank, 1971), while others have found no differences (for example, Dickstein, 1972; Handal, 1969; Kalish & Reynolds, 1976). However, women do appear to think more often about their own deaths. And, if they believe they are going to die within six months, women would focus their attention on others and live an inner-centered life; in the same circumstances men would want a marked change in life style and would devote time to completing projects (Kalish & Reynolds, 1976).

As recent research has become increasingly careful in measuring death anxiety and death fear, its results have become more complicated. It appears that our society gives more permission to women to be afraid of death—or to be afraid in general—than it does to men. Perhaps the differences in death fear and anxiety measured between men and women merely reflect a willingness on the part of women to admit fear or to take the time to think about death or a lowered degree of denial of death anxiety—rather than an actual higher level of death concern.

PERSONALITY DIFFERENCES IN DEATH FEARS AND ANXIETIES

Logic suggests that people who display higher levels of death anxiety should also exhibit higher levels of other kinds of anxiety. Research evidence based on the relationship of death anxiety with general anxiety (Templer, 1970) and manifest anxiety (Dickstein, 1972) supports this assumption. It would be interesting to study relationships between various forms of anxiety with procedures that do not depend on attitude scales. For example, one study evaluated death in dream content as a measure of death anxiety (Handal & Rychlak, 1971), but I don't know of any follow-ups.

Logic also suggests that a number of other personality variables should be related to death anxiety. For example, since dying implies losing control, people who are fearful of death might be expected to be fearful of loss of control. Similarly, people with high needs for achievement might fear death more than the average, since their deaths would eliminate all possibilities for achievement. On the other hand people who feel competent in general or who have been successful in self-actualizing might be able to face death with less fear.

The above assumptions are not supported by the data. Two reviews of numerous studies probing these issues emphasize that results are inconsistent, but most findings indicate that relationships fall far short of statistical significance (Pollak, 1979–1980; Schulz, 1978). Perhaps the problem is not that the relationships do not exist but that the scales are not adequate for the task required.

Other variables, however, have been linked to fear of death. A scale of guilt was correlated with scores on a scale of death fear, and the relationship was statistically significant (Siegman, 1961). Perhaps feelings of guilt lead to fears of punishment for this guilt, and both death and what lies after death are seen as potentially punishing. Another interpretation is that the results reflect a general tendency for people who respond with anxiety to certain aspects of their lives—that is, with guilt—to respond also with anxiety to other aspects—namely, death.

A relationship between meaning in life and death anxiety has also been reported in several studies. The more an individual felt that life had no meaning for her or him, the greater the reported feelings of death anxiety (Blazer, 1973; Durlak, 1972a, 1972b).

Numerous studies have investigated the relationships between fear of death, variously measured, and personality difficulties. One respected interpretation of Freud (Fenichel, 1945) proposed that death is likely to arouse anxiety because it reproduces earlier anxiety-causing events, such as the separation from mother. Other early theorists, contrary to Freud, believed that death fears were basic and important fears in their own right and not simply diverted expressions of other fears (Jung, 1959; Klein, 1948; Stekel, 1949).

Given this background, it would logically follow that persons who feared death more would also display various kinds of emotional distress to a greater extent. In fact, one brief review indicates that there is a small but inconsistent relationship between various measures of emotional upset and neuroticism and various measures of death fears and anxieties (Schulz, 1978). And, as might be expected, people who are depressed are more fearful about death (Jeffers, Nichols, & Eisdorfer, 1961; Rhudick & Dibner, 1961).

New studies dealing with death anxiety and personality variables are being conducted and published all the time, and presumably someone will develop a research methodology that will avoid the kinds of distortion that the present measures allow. Paper-and-pencil questionnaires have their place, but the measurement of death anxiety is apparently too complex to be accomplished adequately in this fashion.

There are many other personal characteristics that affect an individual's death fears and anxieties, and some will be discussed in later chapters. These include age, religiousness, and health. As is often the case, however, the more interesting questions have not been studied systematically—perhaps because they are so difficult to investigate. It would be useful, for example, to be able to understand what kind of early childhood training concerning death and dying would reduce later death fears and anxieties. It would be interesting to learn whether taking a course on death and loss would have any effect whatsoever on one's ability to cope with grief two or three years later. Since the content of a course on death can vary so, a researcher might have to ask which course content is most effective. Another interesting question is whether different personality types would profit from different courses. The speculation goes on and on.

EXPRESSING THE FEAR OF DEATH

When you are frightened or anxious, how does your behavior change? How does your internal state change? The obvious response is that there are a variety of possibilities and these depend upon the circumstances. A variety of possible responses is also true of death fears and anxieties.

Avoidance. We often avoid what frightens us, sometimes consciously and sometimes without awareness. The person who says "I am not going to that funeral because funerals depress me," is displaying a conscious avoidance of a symbol of death. The same person may well avoid a hospital visit to a dying friend for the same reason. Society provides many specific safeguards to permit us to avoid contact with death and dying. It provides institutions for the dying, encourages the use of euphemisms in discussing death, makes certain that the death-related aspects of funeral homes are not conspicuously displayed either in advertising or on the building exteriors, and socializes us to be uncomfortable in asking people how they feel about the death of a friend or family member.

Unconscious avoidance of death-related matters is also familiar. Rather than stating explicitly that funerals make us uncomfortable, we may find ourselves "too busy" to attend; rather than admitting that we don't wish to visit a dying friend, we may decide that she or he already has ample visitors or is probably too ill to appreciate our visit. If the topic of death or dying arises at a social gathering, some people are likely to drift away from the conversation fairly quickly, not necessarily from lack of interest (although that can be a motive also) but from strong feelings of vague discomfort (that is, of anxiety).

Another unconscious dynamic to avoid death anxiety is perceptual defense. This is the unconscious use of defense mechanisms so that matters concerning death and dying are not perceived and processed in the ways we usually perceive and process information. Early studies showed that death words took longer to be recognized than neutral words (Alexander & Adlerstein, 1960; Golding, Atwood, & Goodman, 1966). Although not all studies consistently show these results, there is some evidence that people take longer to perceive signs and symbols of death in their social environments; a likely interpretation is that the delay is a perceptual defense.

A very different way of avoiding death is to channel so much energy and time into other activities that there is nothing left for death. So people throw themselves into work, pleasure, the pursuit of fame, study, meditation, or travel, for example. Given this intense involvement, they are too busy when awake and too exhausted when ready for sleep to give thought to death. Their anxieties, however, appear in dreams or are expressed in somatic or psychological symptoms since not even extreme activity and extreme exhaustion are sufficient to keep such anxiety from awareness forever.

When, for whatever reasons, death anxieties do produce too much discomfort as they press into awareness, there are still ways to avoid the feelings of tension. One familiar means is the use of certain mood-changing drugs or alcohol. It isn't unusual for heavy drinkers to admit that they want to drink themselves into oblivion (Lepp, 1968). Sleep is another way to avoid the pain of anxiety. Like drugs and alcohol, it serves as a retreat from the world; it is also a response to the fatigue that can be generated by anxiety-induced feelings of tension. Sleep, in fact, is closely related to death in many ways: it is often a euphemism for death and was regarded by the ancient Greeks as the twin brother of death (Kastenbaum, 1977).

Changing life styles. In our generation, the advice of the health professional is more likely to be heeded than that of any other professional, and health professionals fill us with advice about how we might postpone the time of our deaths. You are familiar with the advice: eat properly; avoid high-cholesterol foods; watch your weight; take vitamins; exercise properly; jog (or don't jog); swim; play tennis (but not too strenuously); follow a yoga regimen; sleep properly; avoid stress; avoid smog; avoid tobacco altogether and avoid abuse of coffee, liquor, and drugs.

I am not finding fault with the advice. In fact, I strongly believe that much of it is useful. My point here is that following such advice is an attempt to remain both healthy and alive. It isn't unusual to read that some respected physician or gerontologist has claimed that there is no reason why we shouldn't routinely live to age 80 or 100 or 130—or virtually forever—except that we eat poorly, exercise inappropriately, or otherwise follow improper life styles. This seems to me to be one way of expressing a fear, or at least an unrealistic avoidance, of death.

Not everyone accepts health professionals' advice as the ultimate authority. Many people still believe that proper moral behavior will be rewarded with long life. This view is not restricted to those following traditional religious philosophies; it is also held by adherents of the holistic health movement, who talk about spiritual well-being, personal growth, and the importance of the whole person. So although one group espouses belief in a traditional God and another group encourages personal growth and self-actualization, both groups are assuming that their notion of holding to proper values will lead to a longer and healthier life.

Dreams and fantasies. Dreams are a representation of our feelings and thoughts in visual form. Some dreams represent feelings and thoughts of which we are not consciously aware; they occur at night, when our "psychological guard" isn't up and we are less defended. These dreams may symbolize wishes, fears, anxieties, needs that are unacceptable to the "critical me" that keeps such notions out of awareness during wakefulness. Other dreams may just represent feelings and thoughts that are impinging so strongly upon our minds that they appear during sleep.

Since death fears and anxieties are both powerful and kept from consciousness most of the time, they do appear in various guises in dreams. Sometimes they produce nightmares; other times, a death dream will not be at all disturbing. One early study found that students who report more concern about death also report more frequent nightmares (Feldman & Hersen, 1967). As is true of all dreaming, death dreaming is usually symbolic and indirect. If you had a dream of yourself lying in a box, you might quickly recognize the box to be a coffin and the dream to be about your death. However, the dream might also be about your feeling restricted or isolated or peaceful or, if you pun in your dreams, boxed in or even being a boxer. Dreams are tricky, but if you find an interpretation that both fits the dream and "feels right," it is likely to be accurate.

How often do people dream about their own deaths? In the Los Angeles study of death attitudes, about one-fourth of the 434 respondents admitted to having dreamt of their deaths on at least one occasion. The older the individual, the more often this experience was reported (Kalish & Reynolds, 1976). Of course, these results have some limitations: most death dreams are not obviously about death, and most dreams in general are not recalled the next morning. Therefore, we need to take these responses with a grain of salt and recognize, first, that only a small minority of persons will acknowledge dreams of their own death and, second, that the fact that this number is small is in itself significant.

Fear of death often is manifested in fantasies. Perhaps you have had death fantasies as you drove along a country road at twilight, when the calm beauty and slight boredom of the drive took your mind from your driving to your inner feelings. You may also have fantasies of death when you are drifting off to sleep at night. Did you ever fantasize being at your own funeral? Tom Sawyer and his friends had this fantasy come true: they were at their own funeral, where they listened to people cry over their deaths and extol their virtues. Have you ever said, either aloud or to yourself "You'll be sorry when I'm dead?"

Death fantasies, like all fantasies, may be under conscious control or may occur when your thoughts appear to go wherever they wish. In either case, it is perfectly normal to have fantasies, including death fantasies, and sometimes fantasies—like dreams—appear frightening, grotesque, and distorted.

When people are very sick, perhaps dying, their fantasies and dreams, reflecting their fears and anxieties, often differ from those of persons who do not face their own imminent death. Frequently a dying person will describe a dream to a friend, family member, or member of a hospital staff in an attempt not only to understand what the dream meant but also to involve the listener in the dreamer's feelings and fears. The dying person is using the dream to make a statement that he or she hopes the listener will interpret correctly and respond to with support and understanding. One dream was described as follows:

> I am at home, but it's nowhere I've been before. I go into the pantry to get some food. The shelves are stacked with seasonings and spice, all the same brand, but there is nothing to eat. I feel I am not alone in the house. It is just turning dawn, or is it brilliant moonlight? I turn on the light, but it comes from another room. Something creaks. I am not alone. I wonder where my dog is. I need more light. I need more light and more courage. I am afraid [Edinger, 1969, p. 104].

The other being in the house is presumably death (Fortier, 1972).

Are dreams of someone else's death ever accurate predictions? Is it possible to dream of someone dying, then to learn several days later that the individual did indeed die at that time? These are controversial issues, which you must answer according to your own experiences and beliefs. My own beliefs are in diametrical opposition to each other. On the one hand, because such ideas are contrary to my concept of the derivation of knowledge, I believe they are always explainable in some logical fashion that does not involve unknown kinds of perception; on the other hand, so many reputable persons have reported these experiences that it becomes impossible to refute the existence of the phenomenon. Obviously, I admit to being totally uncertain about this issue. The longer I have lived, the more things I find unexplainable—and the easier I find it not to worry that they are inexplicable.

Challenging death. Another way to cope with fear of death is to challenge death constantly—and win. The lives of persons who do this resemble a constant game of Russian roulette, except that they express their challenge through dangerous activities (parachute jumping, hang-gliding, car racing) or through dangerous work (combat soldiering, fire-fighting, transporting explosives). Of course, not all persons who participate in these activities or jobs are challenging death, and some who do so claim they are indifferent to death. Are they really indifferent? Are they so in love with death they want to die? Or do they fear death so much that they must continually risk their lives to prove to themselves that they can vanquish death? Perhaps all of the above are valid descriptions of some persons. We have little understanding of this phenomenon.

One study of risk has some intriguing implications, however. Investigators positioned themselves at a busy thoroughfare crossing in Detroit and observed how people crossed the street. They evaluated the crossing behavior of 125 people, 25 at each of five different ages, on the basis of the risks that they took. For example, at one end of their continuum was Type A Pedestrian, who stood on the curb until the light changed in his or her favor, glanced briefly at oncoming traffic, immediately entered the crosswalk, moved across at a moderate-to-brisk pace, and exhibited no erratic behavior. At the other end of the continuum was the Type E Pedestrian, who stepped out from some location other than the corner—for example, from between parked cars—and crossed against the traffic light without looking in either direction.

The researchers, who then interviewed the pedestrians, found that the more cautious street-crossers both expected to and wanted to live longer than the high-risk crossers (even when age was controlled, since the high-risk crossers tended to be younger than the more cautious crossers); the low-risk crossers also reported less stressful lives than did the high-risk crossers (Kastenbaum & Briscoe, 1975). Perhaps, then, people who challenge death do so to handle stress with the knowledge that their challenge may cost them their lives. Possibly death has a certain amount of fascination for them. This is a highly speculative interpretation, but the study opens up a variety of possibilities, among which are thoughts of creative kinds of research methodologies.

Finally, another way of challenging death may be by becoming a physician or other health professional. Although such persons eventually lose to death, they are instrumental in postponing the success of death for others and, perhaps symbolically, for themselves.

And so forth. A list of ways to express fear and anxiety about death could continue almost endlessly. For example:

- resorting to defensive humor—gallows humor—to make fun of death and thus establish superiority to death;
- displacing fears of death onto other matters, such as work or sexuality, which in the long run are less distressing than death;
- becoming death-related professionals, such as death counselors or educators and perhaps writing books about death (like this one);
- expressing feelings creatively in paintings, musical compositions, poetry;
- expressing the anxiety through physical changes in the body—for example, through backaches, stomachaches, headaches, shallow breathing, perspiring.

LEARNING TO FEAR DEATH

A group of infants are removed to a desert island where they are cared for by effectively programmed robots who provide them with survival care, physical affection, and emotional concern. Indeed, the robots do all the "right" parenting, but they know nothing about death, and their programming does not permit them to react in any way to the concept. The children develop their own method for communicating and their own social order. They will eventually experience the death of others on the island and the death of animals and plants. Now: do they develop a fear of death? Given 100 such islands, would individuals on all 100 develop a fear of death?

Several hypotheses are possible:

1. Everyone (or almost everyone) is born with a fear of death.
2. Everyone (or almost everyone) is born with no tendency to fear death, but living in this world makes it inevitable to fear death.
3. Everyone (or almost everyone) has an inevitable tendency to fear death, but this tendency can be overcome by appropriate love and learning.
4. We have no more tendency to fear death than to fear telephone poles, but many of us receive faulty early learning and develop this fear; then it becomes difficult, perhaps impossible, to overcome.

Consider some of the ways in which death fears and death anxieties might develop.

Early socialization. Young children are given ample reinforcement for developing fear of death. Parents and others who socialize them are constantly reminding them when they are in danger or when they do something that might harm their health. They hear death spoken about in hushed voices, tinged with dread. They are often told very directly that certain behavior is expected of them so that they won't die. Fairy tales describe the deaths of evil people as punishment for their evil, while good people live happily ever after. The constant message, both direct and indirect, is that "death is bad." This message is pervasive; it comes from family, friends, school, church, and the media.

Separation. The young child has learned that the absence of his or her mother or other significant figure means the absence of the biological and the social support, so necessary for well-being. Initially the infant is totally dependent upon others for survival and satisfaction. The absence of mother (or father) means no food, no cuddling, no warm blanket, no clean diaper. Separation is always painful and difficult for the infant, especially as it challenges his or her sense of powerfulness and invulnerability—of virtual omnipotence (Becker, 1973).

As the child matures, he or she learns that death is a significant separation—perhaps the ultimate separation—from mother, father, and all significant persons. Given the anxiety and fear elicited by even brief separations, the child finds the possibility of this separation too great to bear. The separation of death is feared as the ultimate separation and the ultimate cause of vulnerability and helplessness. The death of someone else arouses these feelings, while contemplating the death of oneself does so even more dramatically.

Anger and fear of retribution. No relationship is perfect, and this is probably truer of intimate relationships than of more distant ones. No matter how good a parent-child relationship is, there will be ample cause for anger and hostility. Therefore, "no child escapes forming hostile death wishes toward his socializers" (Wahl, 1959, p. 24). However, the world of children is magical (after all, to get fed all they have to do is cry or demand or just be there), and the knowledge that they wish death (which may be understood as *removal*) for their parents suggests to them that their parents might have comparable reciprocal wishes. Furthermore, a parent definitely does have the power to put such wishes into effect, so, if the child directs anger toward the parent, the parent might indeed respond with comparable anger and bring about either death or abandonment. This greatly enhances children's sense of vulnerability, since neither their power nor their magic is as great as that of their parents (Becker, 1973). Consequently, children, fearing their parent's anger and ability to abandon them, fear death, which is associated with these actions.

Entering the unknown. You may feel you "know" what happens after you die so that death does not lead to anything unknown. If you believe this, you are, I suspect, in a minority. Most people have beliefs or assumptions or desires about what happens after death, but they don't claim to "know." Moving to a new community, entering a new college, or traveling abroad by yourself can all be exciting, but they can also be frightening. Sailing on uncharted seas—entering the unknown that is death can be much more frightening because it is so completely unknown.

What are the possibilities? Perhaps there is no unknown, just nothingness. Perhaps there is heaven and hell as described by authors of the Renaissance. Perhaps there is "peace and love everlasting." Perhaps there is judgment. Perhaps there is something that we cannot now possibly imagine. This is the time not to discuss what is after death but to acknowledge that knowing that the future is unknown and perhaps unknowable can make that future very frightening.

There are, of course, other ways in which we learn to fear death—for example, by learning to fear the losses that death causes: of experiencing, of loved ones, of projects, of things.

"HEALTHY-MINDED," "MORBID-MINDED"

If death fears and anxieties arise primarily or completely from the sources mentioned above, we should be able to overcome a large portion of those fears. We would take care to avoid destructive early socialization, to eschew unhappy separation fears, to help children work through their anger and fear of retribution, and to provide an understandable picture of what death is. This is the position that Becker (1973) describes as the "healthy-minded" argument. Given healthy family relationships, security, love, help with anger, and support in the face of the unknown, children need not develop a fear of death. Rather, they will later come to recognize death as a normal part of the life span.

Becker then posits the other side of the coin: the "morbid-minded" argument. In taking this position, he accepts the idea that the social environment and family relationships can modify the fear of death, but he posits that it cannot be altogether eliminated: " . . . the fear of death is natural and is present in everyone, that it is the basic fear that influences all others, a fear from which no one is immune, no matter how disguised it may be" (1973, p. 15). In establishing his point, Becker argues that the fear of retribution occurs inevitably. Since this experience cannot be avoided, the fear of death cannot be avoided.

I don't know whether Becker's healthy-minded position has more or less merit than his morbid-minded position. Both recognize the importance of early learning and later experience. Both allow family relationships and a sense of security to play a significant role. Both take into account the notion of unpredictability and vulnerability; that is, people may feel helpless both in protecting themselves against a punitive attack and in coping with unknown forces. This helplessness reminds them of their mortality, of their vulnerability to death. On the other hand, neither takes adequate note of anthropological studies. The difference is that the morbid-minded stance presupposes that some death fear, even terror, will remain no matter how "healthy" the social environment has been.

Some people contend that since death is normal and inevitable, fear and even avoidance of death are inappropriate. I would question this position. We might say "Cancer is merely a normal part of life; it is natural. What we need are courses, even in elementary school, to help people overcome their fear of cancer, so that when cancer comes, they recognize it as part of the natural flow of life and learn to accept it." Replace *cancer* with *stroke* and reread the sentence. Now try *rabid-dog bite.* Finally, use the word *death.* You probably realized why the passage sounded so familiar: you have seen it before.

I don't mean to deprecate attempts to reduce the fear individuals have of death. Such attempts are normally beneficial. However, my own views are that the fear of death is just as normal as death itself, that such fears are adaptive, and that they need not be viewed as pathological unless they interfere in some significant way with the life of the individual. Indeed, as I stated earlier, fear of death has evolutionary value, since, if no one feared death, most people would die quite young, before they reproduced, and the human species would have ceased to exist long ago. This does not require the existence of a survival or self-preservation instinct, but can arise from the second of the hypotheses presented earlier—namely, that people are not born with a fear of death, but that inevitable life experiences teach them such fears.

OVERCOMING THE FEAR OF DEATH

Although the fear of death is usually appropriate, it can become powerful enough to be disruptive and to interfere with regular life tasks. Even when it is not disruptive, however, it is painful. Since most of us wish to reduce the pain we suffer, it is appropriate to work toward overcoming such fear—even though death fear is normal and even perhaps useful and adaptive.

A great many arguments have been advanced by philosophers and others over the centuries as antidotes to the fear of death. For example, Robert Burton in the seventeenth century urged us to divert our thoughts to other matters; Machiavelli suggested escape in study; Spinoza exhorted us to love God; Montaigne advised that we immerse ourselves in thinking and talking about death; in the second century, Marcus Aurelius argued that when death occurs we will have no sensation and therefore no awareness that death has in fact occurred (Choron, 1964). It has even been pointed out that, since we don't fear our nonexistence prior to our births, we should not fear nonexistence after our deaths (Choron, 1964).

Each of the above arguments is used today to help people overcome their fear of death, and each helps some persons. However, the arguments tend to appeal to the intellect, and fear of death is a feeling that is often not influenced by such appeals.

If intellectual arguments are not particularly useful in overcoming death fear, how do people cope with such fears? Neither throwing oneself into involvements—pleasure, work, fame, sex, or study—to avoid thoughts of death nor challenging death directly will work indefinitely. The fears of death will manifest themselves in some fashion.

Living life fully. In my own experience and certainly in the experience of many others, the people who fear death the least are those who love life the most. This initially seems to be a contradiction, since one kind of logic suggests that you are best able to lose what you like least. I have applied another kind of logic. People who are not living as they want to live have not been able to get what they want from life. Their lives remain incomplete, and they seek for meaning and completion. It is not just that they find life boring; it is rather that although they wish to live life fully, they are not fully living life. When faced with their death, they are frightened. They have less adequate senses of self and are, therefore, generally more readily frightened. More importantly, however, they are frightened because they realize that now they will never have the chance to *really* be alive. In a way, their lives will be over before they began.

Those who live their lives fully have enjoyed what they have had. They may feel cheated and angry, especially if they have unfinished tasks, but they are less afraid, since they have taken from life as much as they were able to take. These individuals still have some fears of death, but these fears don't interfere with their enjoyment of life. They are able to use each day well. Thus, if they die today, they do not regret having spent yesterday as they did. In a way, they "realize that [they] might die at any moment, and yet live as though [they] were never going to die" (Lepp, 1968, p. 77).

This chapter has returned to the theme of the meaning of life, which was discussed first in Chapter 3. In talking about people who are serene when they face old age and death, Lepp writes "Conscious of having lived for something and having been fulfilled in life, they are capable of spontaneously conferring meaning on that ultimate act of their lives which is death" (1968, p. 142). Lepp has no trouble acknowledging that these persons still have some anxiety about death—he points out that even "Christ . . . knew the terrors of agony" (p. 142)—but the meaningfulness of their lives has made their deaths more acceptable to them.

Establishing continuity of life. The most obvious way to overcome the fear of death is to believe that, although physical death may destroy the body, it cannot destroy the spirit, soul, or existence of the individual. This belief permits clinical death to be a rite of passage to another form of existence, rather than an extinction of existence. But this matter deserves a chapter of its own, and that chapter follows.

6

TRANSCENDING DEATH: RELIGION AND IMMORTALITY

> "If immortality be untrue, it matters little whether anything else be true or not" [*Henry Thomas Buckle* (1821–1862)].
> "Without the hope of an afterlife, this life is not even worth the effort of getting dressed in the morning" [*Prince Otto von Bismarck*].
> "Man cannot live without a continuous confidence in something indestructible within himself" [*Franz Kafka*].
> "As for a future life, every man must judge for himself between conflicting vague possibilities" [*Charles Darwin*].
> "Neither can I believe that the individual survives through death of his body, although feeble souls harbor such thoughts through fear or ridiculous egotism" [*Albert Einstein*].

The weight of opinion is certainly that there is an afterlife and, in the event of uncertainty, that there should be one. Choron, from whose book the previous quotations were selected, states "There is no doubt that the denial of the finality of death appears to most people as the most satisfying solution to the problems of death" (1964, p. 14). It seems as though people who have not had a satisfying life look toward subsequent existence as a way of compensating for what did not occur on earth, while those who have found life pleasurable seek for some kind of continuation of consciousness.

Studies confirm the assumption that most people believe in life after death. Thus a national survey in 1936 found that nearly two out of every three adults believed in life after death; this increased in 1944 to 76% and has remained near that figure since (Argyle & Beit-Hallahmi, 1975). While most people believe in an existence of some sort after death, an even larger number desire that such an option exist (Kalish & Reynolds, 1976). Based on our Los Angeles study, I would estimate that fewer than one person in ten in that community preferred extinction following clinical death to some kind of existence.

Nevertheless, conflicting opinions coexist. Thus, well-conducted national study found that over half this country's adults believed that death was like a long sleep (J. Riley, 1970). This suggests to me a kind of non-aware existence, and it seems to contradict the more common notion that death leads to a "life of abiding union with . . . Christ" (Cross, 1958, p. 682). I suspect the truth is that many people have vague and inconsistent images of an afterlife, and that this occurs regardless of a person's religious affiliation. There seem to be several reasons for not wanting any kind of life after death. First, some individuals undoubtedly fear either divine punishment for what they have done during their lives or some other hellish afterlife—with their notions of hell ranging from the physical tortures written of by Dante to the psychological tortures described by Sartre. A second reason for wanting no afterlife would be a simple preference for extinction, for nothingness, for a permanent leave taking of everything. And third, persons may disbelieve in an afterlife because they find it impossible to conceptualize such an existence.

TRANSCENDING DEATH

I am very attached to me. I don't want me to leave everywhere forever. If I must die—and I suppose that I must—it seems unfair for death to mean that nothing more continues. I can accept the thought that I wasn't here before I was born—although you may not share that view—but I have considerable difficulty in coping with the idea that my being is temporary.

Are we really temporary? After all, to believe in life after death or in some kind of immortality is to assume that some part of our existence continues beyond clinical death. Perhaps only life on earth is temporary while existence is forever. In Chapter 2, I discussed three kinds of death—physical death, psychological death, and social death—and I alluded to other forms of death, such as legal death. Here I would like to return to these themes again in a discussion of life after death.

PHYSICAL IMMORTALITY

Physical death has two subcategories: biological death and clinical death. Since we die biologically when parts of us die, we can live on biologically when some physical part of us continues after "we" die. Perhaps this is why having children is so important to many people. Each child carries something physical of each parent. In a very real way, the parent continues through the child, the grandchild, and so on ad infinitum. As long as your descendents continue to have children and as long as humanity exists, some part of you continues. This mystique that a biological part of the parent exists in the child is probably one major reason that many people resist adopting children.

If your children are biological extensions of you, then you are similarly a biological extension of your parents. In recent years people have tried to look back across generations in order to find their origins, their "roots." Similarly, many adopted children have sought their biological parents. Both trends appear to represent an attempt to connect with one's past. To some extent this also means seeking a physical preexistence: who was I before I was born?

Our present life thus becomes one existence in a series of existences, and we are part of a series rather than simply an isolated life. The series stretches far back in time and also will stretch far forward in time. Lifton points out that this kind of immortality is more than just biological and that people can express it through symbolic connections with "one's group, tribe, organization, people, nation, or even species" (1977, p. 278).

In contrast to biological death, clinical death describes the death of the organism. Clinical immortality, therefore, means that the body does not really die, or to state it more cautiously, it means the body does not really cease to be. The history of the world contains many examples of the belief in clinical immortality—ghosts are one—in which the physical body continues to exist although in altered form. That physical body, as I will discuss later, must be inhabited by a "self" or a "soul." Keep in mind the story of Dracula and the other characters on the midnight television horror films. Their bodies, altered perhaps by longer teeth and fingernails, continue to exist; but they are inhabited either by a totally new personality or by the old personality in altered form.

Clinical immortality, to be meaningful, must also involve psychological immortality (see below). Otherwise the body is possessed and becomes, for example, a zombie or the vehicle for creatures from outer space—the stuff of science fiction. Although most people in our culture probably believe that the body becomes an empty shell after clinical death, what happens to that body is still important to them. Many elderly people living alone, for example, are greatly concerned that their bodies may not be found for several days after their death. Funeral establishments sell airtight and watertight vaults to encase airtight and watertight caskets that encase carefully embalmed bodies. Our behavior and our feelings certainly indicate that many of us retain a strong psychological attachment to our bodies.

PSYCHOLOGICAL IMMORTALITY

Psychological death is the cessation of self-awareness or consciousness, and it affects relatively few people in this society. Psychological immortality, which is the continuation of consciousness after death, provides the basis for the traditional Christian concept of afterlife as an existence in which the individual retains awareness of self and experiencing after having suffered clinical death. Those who do not accept this form of immortality are faced either with total extinction at the time of death (Kalish, 1968) or with some form of "being at one with God" or "being unified with the universe," which implicitly, but not explicitly, signifies the loss of self-awareness and conscious experiencing.

Although most people would probably agree that "it is the prospect of not being anymore that makes most men abhor death" (Choron, 1964, p. 10), some would favor the idea that even extinction is "reassuring and more logical than a concept of afterlife that includes perception without organs, memory without brain, and existence without matter" (Parkes, 1967, personal communication).

To become more personally involved, try this fantasy: think of yourself as a body without a brain; then think of yourself as a brain without a body. Under which condition are you more likely to perceive yourself as no longer you?

If you do remain psychologically immortal, what can this mean? First, it might be manifest through an afterlife that replicates much of what exists in this life. That is, you might be with family and friends and perhaps even meet new friends; you might eat and sleep and play; you might even experience challenges and tensions, successes and failures. This is the notion that children seem to develop, along with the presence (or sometimes absence) of a Supreme Being.

Second, psychological immortality may mean that your experiencing is limited to a sense of oneness with a Supreme Being, with nature, or with the universe. Rather than offering the anthropomorphic appeal of the first alternative, this possibility suggests a kind of eternal peace and love, the "peace that surpasses all understanding."

Third, you could remain immortal by staying on earth but not perceivable by any living persons. You would be a ghost. You couldn't interact with any of the living, except under unique circumstances, but you could observe them and perhaps influence their lives in limited ways.

Fourth, you might be reincarnated into another body, but to have psychological immortality this new body with "you" residing in it must be aware that "you" once resided in another body. This is not the Eastern religious concept of transmigration of souls, which assumes that the new entity has no memory of previous existences; it is believed, however, by some persons in the West. The famous case of Bridey Murphy, a nineteenth-century Irish woman who purportedly was a previous existence for a twentieth-century American woman, is an example. Awareness of the prior life occurred to the American woman under hypnosis, and she showed a remarkable, although inconsistent, knowledge of nineteenth-century Ireland. It later turned out that as a child the American woman had had an Irish housemaid who had regaled her with stories and descriptions of Ireland; so this evidence in support of reincarnation is dubious.

A fifth possibility, once again cut from the cloth of science fiction: it is conceivable (perhaps you think it inconceivable) that our consciousness and personality could be transplanted either to another body or to a form that was not like a human body. This would be an earthly immortality and could last at least until science, customs, and natural disasters obliterated your new form.

SPIRITUAL IMMORTALITY

One kind of immortality has no counterpart in the kinds of death discussed in Chapter 2. Some individuals regard life on earth as a lower or less adequate form of life than existence after death. Life on earth requires struggle, pain, upsets, emotions, stress, decay; life after death is filled with peace, love, fulfillment, and a sense of harmony. Leading a spiritual life brings one to this kind of immortality, which signifies that you are "in harmony with a principle extending beyond the limited biological life span" (Lifton, 1977, p. 278).

One example of spiritual immortality is nirvana; this is a state that is undefinable, immeasurable, and infinite and not a state of annihilation (Watts, 1957). In nirvana one is released from the pains of going through continuous incarnations and lives. The issue of consciousness seems to be resolved by the implicit assumption that self-consciousness ceases when nirvana is achieved.

The Western counterpart to the Buddhist nirvana is often expressed as "being at one" with God or with nature or with the universe or with humanity. It is not clearly specified and defined, because it defies specification and definition. The belief generally includes negation of the meaning of time as well as of the meaning of matter. That is, all time is now; all matter is matter and is unity or one single whole. And psychological life ceases. If these ideas strike you as strange or even ridiculous, you have a lot of company. On the other hand, if you can grasp what the words mean—if something in you is attuned to their meaning—you also have a lot of company.

SOCIAL IMMORTALITY

When others perceive you as living, you are socially alive; when others perceive you as dead, you are socially dead. Social immortality is probably as familiar and perhaps as important as psychological immortality. After your clinical death, you will continue to exist for others in symbolic ways. This doesn't mean that *you* will exist clinically or psychologically, but that many symbols of you will exist, and people will relate to these symbols to some extent in the way that they had related to you. Consider some of the kinds of social immortality (Lifton, 1977).

- In memories. Other people will remember you—the kind of person you were, the things you did with them, the meanings you had for them. For example, your grandfather, who died when you were very young, still lives in your memory.
- In oral tradition. We tend to associate the oral tradition with societies that lacked writing or printing, but we all have a kind of oral tradition. The stories that your mother told you about her grandparents are part of your oral tradition. These days we have two useful alternatives to the old form of oral tradition: writing and taping. (Capture your own oral- or written-tradition for yourself and your descendents by interviewing your parents and grandparents.) These extend the duration of social immortality beyond the lifetimes of the persons with the actual memories.
- In groups to which you have belonged. Almost all of us have been part of many groups: family, friendship, school, church, social club, work, political party. Our impact on each of these groups is likely to extend beyond the time of our membership in the groups, and it sometimes extends beyond our own lifetime.
- In your family name. In many traditions maintaining and honoring the family name is significant. The family name provides a kind of continuity for the parents—especially for the male members of the family.
- In ancestor recognition. In some cultures ancestors are acknowledged in rituals and ceremonies long after their deaths and even long after they have been forgotten as individuals. Although members of the Church of the Latter-Day Saints (Mormons) do not worship their ancestors, they do try to learn who their ancestors were since they believe this is the only way these people can be brought into the afterlife. The television series *Roots* inspired many people to search for their origins; their efforts brought about a kind of social immortality to ancestors whose names and identities had previously been lost or ignored.
- In creating or achieving something that will continue to live. In addition to being a form of biological immortality, children are also a means of social immortality. In planting and tending a garden one also creates something living. Helen Burke, a Seattle woman whose integrity and toughness bought her several years of life that her physicians had not anticipated, planted a garden shortly after she learned that she was terminally ill with cancer. "I wanted something of me to grow after I had died," she said. You can also gain social immortality by developing a business, writing a book, patenting an invention, playing college football, acting in theatre productions, or having your name on a tombstone. Your name is already immortalized with insurance companies, schools, colleges and universities, social security, the Internal Revenue Service, hospitals, and other such institutions.
- In entering history books or record books. Those men and women who have expended great effort, perhaps even lost their lives, for a cause that was recognized by history have gained a type of social immortality. Many individuals exert an immense effort to get their names in the *Guinness Book of World Records* for the same reason. Politicians and other well-known figures often become deeply concerned with the ways in which history will record their deeds.

LEGAL AND ECONOMIC IMMORTALITY

Also symbolic, but still different from social immortality, is the extension of self that we can attain through control of property after our death. Through estates, trusts, and wills, the very wealthy endow universities and museums, maintain businesses, and establish foundations, all of which carry their names for years, even centuries, after their deaths.

There are cultures in which the possessions of the dead are buried with them (Shaffer & Rodes, 1977); each new generation begins over with the acquisition of material goods. This is definitely not true of the United States. In spite of inheritance taxes, it is possible to continue to provide support and to control the nature of this support beyond the limits of your own lifetime. Through legal actions, such as creating a will and a trust or estate, you can determine what your children will have money for—college and medical purposes, but not vacations, for example. You can punish or reward your children by respectively giving a large portion of your money to other relatives or to charity, or by bestowing a large proportion of your estate on one child.

You can also set conditions on the dispersal of money: one child will receive a portion of your estate only if she completes college within four years after your death; another child will lose her share if she marries the man with whom she has been living. In fact, the courts may strike down your conditions, but even then you have had a substantial impact after you died—although perhaps not the impact you wished.

And you can will or give material possessions to others that will enhance their memories of you and place a symbolic part of you in their homes and lives. There are many ways you can exert control after your death.

THE LIMITS OF IMMORTALITY

Some immortality is more immortal than others. Obviously, this is a ridiculous statement, but my previous uses of the term *immortality* have not been consistently appropriate. In fact, I have used "immortal" when I should have used a more modest term. *Immortal* means both "escape from death" and "lasting fame." Except for spiritual immortality and infinite psychological immortality, the other examples are temporary.

Let me use myself as an example again.

I have three children. Through them I will gain both biological immortality and social immortality. I have made a substantial impact on the lives of some other people, and they will carry me in their memories. I have an estate and some material possessions, which I shall give to others and thus attain some legal/economic immortality. I have written books and articles, which are in individual and public libraries, including the Library of Congress; my name is in many indexes, abstracts, and library cards. My father was a sculptor, and as a result I have my image at ages 6 months and 18 months in bronze and marble. And the records: birth, school, college, draft, medical, insurance, credit, social security, investments, businesses, home ownership, marriage, ...

But such immortality is not full immortality. Eventually no one left alive will remember me or will remember hearing anyone talking about me. My children will die, and the family name will disappear or change. My material goods will wear out, fall apart, mildew, burn, or get lost. The libraries will crumble—if the books and index cards don't disintegrate first—and the innumerable records will eventually turn to dust. Someday, 500 years from now, an archeologist or farmer will turn up the bronze statue of a small infant, and my social immortality will be in a museum as an anonymous infant of the twentieth century.

Unless you believe in spiritual or psychological immortality, your immortality is likely to be temporary and, therefore, not especially meaningful. Religion traditionally provided the basis for a belief in immortality, but, as one psychiatrist has suggested, lack of faith has undercut a belief in immortality for a large proportion of the population. It may be that modern-day despair has been caused by this lack of faith (Lifton, 1977).

The potential for total annihilation of all human life, which is part of the nuclear age, presents some complications for all concepts of immortality. First and most obvious is the fact that, if the world is destroyed, all forms of secular immortality become impossible (Choron, 1964). That is, there will be no libraries, people with memories, descendents, investments, tombstones, computers, or ghosts on earth to establish immortality. Second, if the earth and humanity cease to exist, the religious concept of the resurrection must change, and virtually all concepts of immortality except spiritual immortality become meaningless or, at the very least, require considerable reconceptualizing (Lifton & Olson, 1974). The development of the nuclear age has required that people reevaluate their traditional views of religion and of the nature of being human.

WHAT DOES IT MEAN?

Some of you may have found the previous few pages extremely abstract. What implications do the various kinds of immortality have for human behavior? What is your idea of what will happen to you after your clinical death? Perhaps you have several contradictory ideas: (1) there is only extinction; (2) you will exist in some form with God or with some universal spirit; and (3) you will be able to watch those on earth whom you love. Believing such contradictory ideas is not unique. The mixture of your views will, of course, affect how you feel about your own death, how you respond to your grandmother when you talk with her about her dying, and what you feel when you read that a casual friend of yours has committed suicide.

If your vocational interests draw you toward working with the dying, the concept of immortality becomes more immediate and relevant for you, since dying persons often talk about what, if anything, they will be after clinical death. You might evaluate your own social immortality, as I did mine above, and, in some instances, find yourself encouraging others to do the same. Even if you don't especially wish to work with dying people, you will inevitably find yourself, if you enter any of the helping professions, in contact with people for whom death and dying are significant, pressing matters. As these people face their own deaths or the deaths of others, their concepts of immortality will become part of their patterns of coping. The more you understand in advance your own concepts and those of others, the more effective you are likely to be in your work.

MOVEMENTS THAT TRANSCEND DEATH

Undoubtedly the most significant movement that encourages belief in immortality is organized religion. Christians are encouraged to believe that they can overcome death through some combination of belief and appropriate behavior; Moslems, Hindus, and Buddhists can achieve the same goal by practicing their religions; for Jews and Confucians, the possibilities of transcending death are more obscure, but, as individuals, many persons from both religions do believe in some form of existence after death.

Do these religions, then, represent a denial of death? In one sense they do. But it becomes very important not to evaluate an entire belief system because one segment of it may be interpreted as a denial of death. First and most importantly, even if we could establish beyond a shadow of a doubt that a belief system was death-denying, we are not thereby saying anything about the larger truth or validity of that system. Second, by applying knowledge of psychology to explain the needs of people to accept certain beliefs, we are showing only why people believe as they do and not whether their beliefs are true. In fact, you could make a strong case for religious transcendence of death as healthy acceptance rather than denial.

People who have religious views that enable them to transcend death are sometimes criticized. The tone of the criticism often suggests that the religious person is a kind of intellectual sissy, who doesn't have the strength or integrity to know *the* truth: that death is extinction. This criticism overlooks two important facts. Although for some people a belief in overcoming death is comforting, for others, a belief in extinction after death is comforting. And whether or not a particular belief is comforting has nothing to do with the test of its truth.

NOT REALLY DYING AT ALL

There are other movements that propose that people can overcome death. For some of these our present bodies would be immortal. One movement, for example, first suggests that the duration of life can be extended by proper health practices and then jumps to the assumption that, if we only used *the* really proper health practices and had *the* really proper beliefs, we could remain alive almost indefinitely. Similarly, some persons who have discovered the importance of the emotions and of ideas in overcoming physical ailments leap to the conclusion that, if our emotions and beliefs were totally what they should be, we could live forever.

I'm obviously very skeptical of these beliefs. Not only do I believe they are inaccurate, but also it seems likely that they will both exacerbate the guilt that sick people already feel and encourage others to avoid those who are sick. That is, if you are sick because you have lived improperly or have thought improper thoughts, then it is your fault that you're ill, and I don't need to take any responsibility for what you are going through. After all, being sick doesn't just happen by itself—it only happens when you want it to happen or when you deserve it.

Let me try to state my own position clearly and succinctly. I definitely believe that the condition of one's health can be drastically changed—for better or for worse—by beliefs, emotions, and health practices. I also definitely believe that sickness and death are still in everyone's future and will always be and that there is a limit to life beyond which beliefs, emotions, and health practices cannot take us. Although research will undoubtedly continue to find ways to slow down the aging process, a major breakthrough in life extension is unlikely.

Another movement that suggests we don't really die at all is cryogenics. The cryogenicists arrange to freeze the bodies of people just at the moment of death—to do so earlier might be considered homicide—and then to maintain these bodies in a state of limbo. When the cures for the causes of death of these people are found, they are to be revived and treated, and, consequently, they will have overcome death (Ettinger, 1966). In the event that the freezing process doesn't work, then the individual is indeed dead, which is no worse than he or she would have been anyway. Although all this sounds like science fiction, a number of people have, in fact, been frozen in the hope of later revival.

The cryogenics movement raises a number of problems that also sound like science fiction. For example, cryogenicists usually assume that the world in which the frozen people will be revived will be a better one. But what if it is worse? What if the revived people are kept captive and used only for strange kinds of medical research? Further, consider the problems of twentieth-century Rip Van Winkles: how would they adjust to the new world? What kinds of work could they do? What would happen to family relationships? There are some highly practical problems also. Can the estates of these people be given to their heirs? Should insurance companies pay the beneficiaries?

DYING AND RETURNING

Do people ever experience death and then return to tell others? According to some writers (Moody, 1976; Osis & Haraldsson, 1977) they do. Not only do they die and return, but their descriptions of what death is like are remarkably similar. And, so the reasoning goes, this similarity is a kind of evidence that the individuals did, indeed, experience their own deaths.

What were dying and death like? For the most part, the experience was very pleasant. The dying/dead person is "overwhelmed by intense feelings of joy, love, and peace" (Moody, 1976, p. 22); he or she may hear beautiful music, may see friends and relatives who have already died, and may experience a beautiful light—usually white although occasionally blue. Not infrequently, the dying person feels himself or herself moving through a dark passage, like a tunnel, with loved ones on the far side. And then comes a pressure, often an unwanted pressure, to return—to move back from these beautiful scenes and reenter the world of the living.

The authors state that many, although not all, of the people involved had been declared clinically dead by their physicians and that their reports were not made until later. Often, thinking they would be considered mentally disturbed, they were fearful of telling others. Not infrequently they reported out-of-body experiences.

> During the operation, I felt that I was awake and leaving my body. Then I realized that I was watching the surgeon operating on me, except that I was above the surgeon, looking down on the whole action. I moved around the room a little, but essentially I was intrigued with the operation, since its success would determine whether I would live or die. As the surgeon came near the end of his operation, I reentered my body and lost consciousness.

Sometimes the out-of-body experience takes the person far from the location of his or her physical body; the person may "visit" a friend or loved one or view a scene taking place at that moment or in the past. On occasion, the dying person, once revived, is reported to have learned something that couldn't have been known under "normal" conditions. Or the friend or relative visited also reports a strange and eerie feeling or a comforting sense of communication and awareness at the same time that the dying person recalls having visited.

So far only one person has studied these altered states of consciousness by talking with a large number of dying persons and determining their experiences (Garfield, 1979). All other researchers have simply followed up on claims of persons who have reported the experience after it occurred—frequently many months or years after its occurrence. Garfield worked with 173 cancer patients who subsequently died of their illness; he spent an average of three to four hours a week with each patient over a time span ranging from a few weeks to nearly two years. Of these persons, 21% mentioned altered-state experiences, and these could be classified in four categories:

In the first category were people who perceived a powerful white light and heard celestial music; they also encountered either a significant religious figure or a relative who had died previously. These individuals invariably described their experiences as "real, peaceful, and beautiful."

The second category of persons reported encountering demonic figures; their experiences also occurred with great clarity and reality.

A third group described dream-like images that were blissful, terrifying, or both. Their images, however, were not nearly as vivid as those of the first two groups.

The fourth group of persons experienced a void or a tunnel or both. In their experiences they drifted in either an uncontrolled or a limited space or they fluctuated between the two.

As you may be aware, these experiences are also reported by people not facing death: women in childbirth, people during a religious experience, meditators, individuals taking mood-enhancing drugs. Therefore, the obvious question is "did these events really happen?"

Your answer will depend upon your personal and religious beliefs and upon what you accept as evidence. Have you or someone you trust had a comparable experience? Are you able to suspend your assumptions about normal reality and become open to new kinds of reality? Whether you believe these experiences were products of fever, imagination, anesthetic, stress, drugs, or fear or actually occurred, it is important to know that they are reported frequently and are not in any sense a necessary sign of pathology. It is equally important to recognize that an individual who has had such an experience is going to be affected by it—certainly in his or her view of death and most probably in other ways as well.

ENCOUNTERING THOSE WHO HAVE DIED AND RETURNED

Virtually all preindustrial societies believed in ghosts (Simmons, 1945). In fact, becoming a ghost or spirit was in many ways considered compensation for being dead, since "the life of a spirit could be, under favorable conditions, more noble and desirable than an earthly existence which had already become burdensome at best" (Simmons, 1945, p. 224). Being a ghost was not at all bad: you could have power over the living and receive deference from them, in the form of services and sacrifices. Ghosts were appeased, since the living wanted their support and feared their anger, through gifts, food, rituals, prayers, lavish funerals, and other means (Blauner, 1966; Simmons, 1945). In exchange, ghosts expected to be called upon to help their survivors by protecting them against enemies, by intervening with other supernatural forces, and by watching over them. Indeed, Blauner (1966) has suggested that the ghosts of people who were the most involved with their community at the time of death were the ghosts most to be feared: they had so much unfinished business they would be restless, unhappy, and possibly punitive.

Among the Anggor, a tribe in New Guinea, death is seen as the final separation of two components of the individual: the *vital spirit* and the consciousness or personality. In life, the personality dominates, but, when the person dies, the life spirit takes control. Since the powers of the vital spirit are great and since these spirits do not behave rationally, they can harm the community, and the Anggor will call upon their guardian spirits for help (Huber, 1972). There are certainly historical parallels in our society: for example, why do we use such heavy tombstones, and what is the meaning of *rest in peace?*

A common fear about ghosts was that the spirits would retaliate. If you feel guilty about your behavior toward someone who has died—especially if you at all think that your actions may have contributed to the person's death—you may express your guilt through fantasies of retaliation. Conversely, have you ever fantasized that you died and returned with increased powers to reward your friends and punish your detractors?

Like preindustrial societies, highly developed nations also have a tradition involving ghosts and returned spirits—although the latter communities do not officially accept their tradition. In fact, one kind of event that might be viewed as involving ghosts is very familiar in this country and in Western Europe. In a national survey of a few years ago, 27% of the respondents admitted to having felt sometime that they were in touch with someone who had died (Greeley, 1975). In my own work with David Reynolds, over 40% of those interviewed answered yes to the question "Have you ever experienced or felt the presence of someone after he had died?" As many younger people as older people had had this experience.

Many of these encounters occur with someone who has died fairly recently. Nearly all of 22 young and middle-aged widows reported experiencing the presence of their dead husbands in some way (Parkes, 1972). "It was like a dream, but it wasn't really a dream," is a typical description of one of these encounters. A familiar statement is "That is the chair that he sat in, everyday when he came home from work, and he smoked his pipe and read. I still see him in that chair, and I smell the pipe tobacco, although I know he isn't really there." Or, "My grandfather. I will feel the room [get] cold, and I'll feel his presence near me." Studies of widows in England (Gorer, 1967) and in Japan (Yamamoto, Okonogi, Iwasaki, & Yoshimura, 1969) yielded similar results and examples.

Experiencing the presence of someone who has just died has been compared to the phantom limb phenomenon, in which a person whose leg or arm has been amputated still feels its presence. "The brain undoubtedly contains a 'working model' of each limb. . . . It is therefore no surprise to find that the amputation of a limb does not abolish our 'working model' of that limb" (Parkes, 1972, p. 348). Perhaps the strong sense of attachment to the person who has died, like attachment to the limb that has been lost, maintains the previous "working model" for a period of time. Because of the intimacy of the relationship, the person who has died has become like a part of the survivor. After the death, the image representing that part continues to exist.

Mystical and transpersonal experiences are frequently reported, but people are often reluctant to discuss them except with trusted friends. Encountering the dead, having an out-of-body experience, and perceiving different realities are all very different kinds of experiences, but they share the problem of being interpreted by others as a sign that you are a "little crazy." Our fiction is filled with such occurrences, some frightening and some comforting (*Hamlet, Carousel, A Christmas Carol, Macbeth, Wuthering Heights*) and often represents actual, desired, or feared experiences.

Although relatively few encounters with the dead are frightening (Kalish & Reynolds, 1976; Moody, 1976), one kind of experience is—that of being possessed. A play of some decades ago depicted the possession of the body of a young girl by a *dybbuk,* a legendary figure in Jewish lore who had some business on earth he wished to transact. In exorcising the dybbuk, the girl was also killed. Much more recent was the extremely popular novel, *The Exorcist,* and the film based on the novel. Again a young girl was inhabited by the spirit of the devil. Supposedly based on factual events, *The Exorcist* confronts us with several questions: first, did these events really occur and, second, if they did not really occur, what are the psychological dynamics that produce the behavior that appears to be caused by the devil? Further, why does the concept continue to re-emerge in both fiction and reported fact? Is it fear or guilt or attachment that leads to such possession? Is it another way to express the "sickness of the soul"? Is it a manifestation of paranoid schizophrenia? No explanation appears entirely satisfactory.

Despite the claims of some people that they have proof of communications with the dead, I believe that the reality of those events will forever remain an unsolved mystery. As I said before, whether you believe in the possibility of such communication depends largely on what you require as evidence. And its significance is two-fold, both what it means if such communication does occur and, perhaps, can be made to occur with greater frequency *and* what the entire issue implies for our views of death and the transcendence of death.

RELIGION AND DEATH

One significant task for almost any religion is enabling its adherents to cope with their own deaths and with the deaths of others. Another significant task for almost any religion is ascertaining that its adherents are behaving in accordance with the tenets of the religion. Given the immense power of death and of the hope of an existence after death, I would hypothesize that many organized religions have used people's beliefs in their capacity to determine what happens to people after death to control the behavior of people in life. I'm not suggesting that a group of religious leaders sat down to discuss this issue, then decided to do so; rather, these were the values that developed, virtually inevitably, through the histories of religions.

Therefore, if you behave well in this life (however your faith defines proper behavior), your next life will be a reward. If you behave badly in this life, your next life will be (1) hell, (2) lack of oneness with God, lack of eternal peace and love, or limbo, (3) a return to earth in another, and less desirable, form, (4) more accumulated bad karma.

RELIGION AND MEANING

Based on informal interviews with a number of physicians, nurses, and hospital chaplains, it was found that one of the three most important factors contributing toward an "appropriate death" was finding meaning in the life that had been lived, as well as finding meaning in the relatively brief life that was to come. This meaning was often expressed in terms of religion, relatedness to God, and a sense of continuity or immortality (Augustine & Kalish, 1975).

Before I can discuss the relationship between religion, meaning, and death, we need to have a common understanding of the definition of religiousness. Religion can be defined in terms of denominational affiliation, church attendance, or the performance of prayers and other rituals; it can be understood as the adherence to a set of beliefs or having had feelings or experiences that people will agree are "religious"; knowing about religion or behaving according to religious principles are other ways of defining religion (Glock & Stark, 1965).

If we probe for the meaning of religion by using the concepts of *peak experience* (Maslow, 1970), *ultimate concern* (Tillich, 1959), or *transcendent experience* (Bellah, 1969), "religion is seen more and more as a level of consciousness rather than a particular conceptual manner of expressing intellectual convictions" (Augustine & Kalish, 1975, p. 7). The nature of religious feelings, then, becomes "the ability to experience awe, wonder, and even terror through a kind of cosmic, non-ego-centered awareness of the mysterious depths of life and reality" (Augustine & Kalish, 1975, p. 10).

In order to understand the effect of religion on a person's feelings about death and dying, we need to learn how to help people communicate these religious feelings; for when this communication is possible, it is the essence of the feelings and experiences that are communicated and not merely broad empty symbols. That is, if you and I have both experienced the death of someone we loved deeply, and if we have both been open to the full force of the experience and haven't diluted it with meaningless words, then we have shared a religious experience and we can understand, within limits, each other's feelings. There is deep meaning in what we have experienced and shared, and our religiousness has been expanded by grasping this meaning.

STUDIES OF RELIGION AND DEATH

Unfortunately, the studies of religion and death ignore the sophisticated kinds of definitions discussed by Augustine and Glock. Instead, religiousness is frequently measured by a combination of belief in God, church attendance, and fear of hell. Nevertheless, some studies have yielded interesting results.

The debate about whether religious beliefs and affiliations increase or diminish fear of death goes on. One side claims that the punitive aspect of religion, encouraging fears of hell and judgment, is so strong that belonging to and believing in one of the major organized religions would increase death anxiety. Or, differently stated: since religious beliefs help people cope with death, those individuals who are more afraid of dying are more likely to become religious (Feifel, 1959). The opposite side states that religion comforts the dying by making them feel loved by God and certain they will experience life after death. Religion, therefore, reduces fear of death.

Although neither position is entirely correct, available research does seem to indicate that religion diminishes the fear of death. Several studies do show that the more religious an individual is, the less that person shows fear of death (for example, Jeffers, Nichols, & Eisdorfer, 1961; Martin & Wrightsman, 1965; Swenson, 1961; Templer, 1972).

Four different studies, however, have approached the task in a more unusual fashion. Although the specific questionnaires and definitions were not at all the same in these studies, all found that fear of death was least strong among *both* the deeply religious and the deeply irreligious; persons intermediate or undecided showed the greatest anxiety (Gorer, 1967; Hinton, 1963; Kalish, 1963; Nelson & Nelson, 1973).

Elisabeth Kübler-Ross expressed the situation nicely: "Those few [truly religious persons] have been helped by their faith and are best comparable with those patients who were true atheists. The majority of patients were in between, with some form of religious belief but not enough to relieve them of conflict and fear" (1969, p. 237). Like Augustine (see previous section), Kübler-Ross emphasizes the difficulty of knowing who is "truly religious" and who not.

Although much more could be said about religion, meaning, and death, one point seems particularly important to make. It is not religion per se—not simply going to church or claiming to believe in God—that influences death anxieties and fears. Rather, it is the particular beliefs that one holds and the intensity with which they are held that have significance. Persons with strong inner beliefs—in a traditional God and afterlife or not—most probably find more meaning in life. Whether they see their death as occurring because of divine or natural causes, whether their meaning comes from traditional religion or personal philosophy, whether death means continuity or annihilation, these people are secure in their beliefs and can better contend with death. One excellent example of the influence of religious beliefs in conjunction with supportive family and community is found among the Amish people, a community of conservative Protestants living primarily in Indiana, Pennsylvania, Ohio, and neighboring states. These people believe strongly in their religious teachings, which include the concepts that death is a natural part of a life that is itself temporary, and that only eternal life with God transcends this life. Both preparing for one's own death and caring for those who are dying seem to be comfortably accepted. "One Amish woman related that each month her aged grandmother carefully washed, starched, and ironed her own funeral clothing so that it would be in readiness for her death" (Bryer, 1979, p. 257). Another woman described her appreciation for being able to help care for both her parents and her husband's parents in their dying processes. "In their intensive caring they had the opportunity to work through their grief. . . . In the same process, they were moving toward the personal reorganization . . . needed . . . to return to the tasks of living that follow the death of a loved one" (Bryer, 1979, p. 258).

As Amish religious beliefs encourage acceptance of death and the dying process, their close and supportive families and communities provide personal care that is often unavailable in less cohesive communities. Communication among family members about an impending death is common and not especially tense; a dying person is provided with as much autonomy as possible, which may include encouragement to make plans for his or her own death and death ceremonies; and both a dying person and the bereaved are given effective community and family support (Bryer, 1979).

Because Bryer's study focuses attention on the relationships among religious beliefs, personal interactions among community members, and the social structure of the family and the community, it's impossible to determine how much of the effectiveness of the Amish approach comes directly from religious beliefs and how much from personal relationships or community and family structure. However, community studies of this sort can do a great deal to shed light on the meaning of both religion and of community on death and the process of dying.

The relationship between religious beliefs and practices, beliefs concerning immortality, and feelings about death is a complex one, which has not yet been effectively integrated and understood. It would appear that both the content of a system of beliefs and the extent to which an individual incorporates these beliefs influence the person's perceptions of death. Unfortunately, there has been relatively little evidence that a coordinated effort has been made by religious scholars and behavioral and social scientists to work on this task and even less evidence that individuals who combine knowledge of both areas are pursuing these matters.

7

THE PSYCHOLOGY OF DEATH: A LIFE-SPAN PERSPECTIVE

According to legend, Gautama Buddha's father attempted to protect his son from learning of the pain that exists in the world by discouraging him from leaving the grounds of his several palaces and by keeping the roadways clear of any signs of worldly suffering. Eventually the gods, determining that Buddha should have such exposure, arranged that he view old age, disease, and death. Gautama found these experiences so upsetting and his subsequent encounter with a calm ascetic so inspiring that he left his household to venture into the world (Noss, 1969).

For my purpose, this legend says two things: first, we cannot protect people from knowledge of pain in the world, and, second, when we do attempt to protect people from knowledge of such suffering, their distress, when they eventually—and inevitably—encounter this pain, is even greater. On the other hand, the encounter with suffering can produce a richer understanding of the world. Early Buddhist writings quote Gautama Buddha as saying "I also am subject to decay and am not free from the power of old age, sickness, and death. Is it right that I should feel horror, repulsion, and disgust when I see another in such plight?" (Noss, 1969, p. 126).

We seem to work very diligently in our culture to maintain the innocence of children. Much of society's early rejection of Freud came from his emphasis on the sexuality and sexual awareness of young children, which contradicted the assumed contemporary knowledge of their innocence. Although today we have largely come to accept the validity of Freud's interpretation of childhood sexuality, we now maintain that children are innocent of death. We more than maintain this notion—we often insist on it and then do whatever we can to make our prophecy self-fulfilling.

CHILDREN VIEW DEATH

No matter how much we protest that children are, in fact, ignorant of death or that children should be kept ignorant of death, children are no more ignorant of death than they are of sexuality. They may lack an adult understanding of the phenomenon, but they know it exists. My daughter at age 2½ came in from the backyard, where she had been playing by herself, with a dried leaf that had fallen from a tree. She solemnly deposited it on the kitchen table, announced "Leaf dead," and went about with her play. Of course, she might have heard neighborhood children talk about dead leaves, but I believe she had already picked up the concept of "dead" and applied it to the leaf.

Children in our society often do not encounter a personally significant death until they are at least well into their teens. They may read about thousands of people being killed in an earthquake or hear about a suicide of someone in their community, but these events normally have no emotional impact on their lives: they are impersonal deaths. A hundred years ago, the deaths of children and young adults occurred frequently, but today very few children experience the death of brothers, sisters, parents, aunts, uncles, or cousins. Grandparents, of course, do die, but even most grandparents are not in their 60s until their grandchildren are in their teens; also, with geographical mobility, some children are isolated from close relationships with grandparents.

In other times and other places, very young children were exposed to death in a very personal and meaningful way. A family member would die at home, and the child would be involved with this person throughout the dying process; children in rural communities would experience both the births and deaths of animals—including the slaughter of animals for food; in wartime and during natural disasters, children often saw the dying and the dead all around them. There was no way to hide death from these children, and the deaths had to be explained to the children, who needed to incorporate them into their own cognitive framework. Today, when death is the province of the elderly and takes place in hospitals, these experiences are no longer familiar. At most, the child will be told that a grandparent is dying; later, he or she may attend the funeral and, perhaps, view the body in an open casket.

Many children are first exposed to personal, meaningful death when a pet dies. The deaths of goldfish or turtles may elicit little other than curiosity: why did the animal stop moving, and what will happen to it? The deterioration of the body intrigued one young child who buried and dug up his lizard on several occasions (Zeligs, 1974). A young child may become deeply involved in the mysteries of death and what happens after death, but great sadness is not common following the death of a turtle or fish.

When the dead animal is a pet bird or, more importantly, a dog or cat or horse, children's responses are much more intense. These are animals that have more of the characteristics of human beings, and they not only react but act upon. That is, a cat, horse, or dog is responsive to a person and can become very much attached to a child; they can develop a two-way relationship. The death of a beloved pet is a real tragedy for a child, and well-meaning adults who try to assuage the child's feelings by promising to buy an immediate replacement or by insisting that "it was only a dog" are denying the reality of the child's feelings. If a boy's younger sister had died, would his parents have said "Don't cry—we'll get you another sister"?

The death of a pet offers an excellent opportunity to teach children about life and death, about grief and surviving grief, and about whatever religious beliefs the parents hold. The children will survive this death, and they will almost always be able to relate to another animal—but only after they have completed grieving for the animal that died.

DEVELOPMENTAL STAGES

Very young children, 2 or 3 years old, probably have little understanding of death. They live in the present and do not comprehend the nature of passing time (Jackson, 1965). I once asked my son, when he was about 3, where he was before he was born. He had learned his lesson well, and he told me that he was in his mother's "tummy." When I asked him where he was before his older sister was born, he appeared to recognize the unlikelihood that both of them occupied the same stomach at the same time. Then, he began to talk of other matters: either the notion of his own nonexistence seemed irrelevant or he found the idea too confusing.

The idea of nonexistence—either not yet having been conceived or no longer being after death—is incomprehensible to very young children. However, it is possible that even at an earlier age, they do have an awareness of not-being. Several authors have proposed that the game of peek-a-boo in an initial attempt to test the possibility of going into a void and returning to the familiar environment. What is not accessible to the infant through his or her senses often does not exist for that child. The fact that peek-a-boo can engage even an infant for several minutes at a time, a long period to maintain attention, attests to the compelling nature of the activity. The shrieks of pleasure upon her or his return to the known world offer supporting evidence (Maurer, 1961).

That children develop conceptual awareness in stages is at the core of the theories of the famous psychologist Jean Piaget. The best-known stage approach of concepts of death was developed by a follower of his, from written compositions and drawings by and discussions with 378 children living in Hungary (Nagy, 1948). The author constructed three age-related stages from the children's responses.

Stage one. Before the age of 5, children do not perceive death as irreversible. Rather, they view it as a departure or a sleep—in effect denying the permanence and irreversibility of death. Life continues in spite of death. The dead person continues to think, to grow bigger (if the dead person is a child), to remain aware of what goes on in the world. One young child commented as the family car drove past the cemetery "That's where the dead people live."

At the same time, the child recognizes that the dead person is gone. The pain of loss through death for these children is the result of separation. They may ask where the dead person is now, how she feels, whether she is ever going to return. Since death is departure or sleep, the child may become fearful of sleep—a condition that may be exacerbated if she recites the familiar prayer "Now I lay me down to sleep . . . " and contemplates its meaning—or become anxious when a parent leaves for a business trip.

Children at this age take much of what they are told very literally, and this includes the platitudes they are offered as explanations for death or the present whereabouts of a dead person. One young child, told "God has taken your baby sister to be with Him," was subsequently overheard talking with God—asking for his sister to be returned and begging God not to take him also. The boy's tone was one of extreme anger mixed with fear. Another child, told his father had been taken to heaven, became intensely interested in birds and their flight patterns; he later explained he was interested because they could be with his father while he could not.

Stage two. From the age of 5 or 6 to about 9, children tend to personify death. Death is a skeleton, a bogeyman (often an unconscious euphemism for death), a wicked person, a killer. Death "has big eyes and white clothes. It has long legs, long arms" (Nagy, 1948, 1959, p. 91); "[i]t takes [people] up in some kind of carriage" (p. 91); "Death angels are great enemies of people" (p. 92). Death has a personality, may be invisible, and literally carries people away. Now, instead of denying the permanence of death, the child places death as an entity outside of her or his own self.

Stage three. After age 9, children recognize that death marks the cessation of life, and that it operates from within the body. It is now inevitable, irreversible, and results in the end of bodily life.

A later study confirmed the general sequences suggested by Nagy. Children at each of three age levels (3-4, 5-6, 8-9) were interviewed, and their responses were coded and scored. The two younger groups were significantly more likely to view death as reversible; they also tended to personify death and to believe their personification could think and have feelings. The youngest group perceived death as primarily a "going away"; slightly older children viewed death as drastic personal change; and the oldest group saw death as a loss of life (Portz, 1972).

It also seems that a strongly expressed affective response to death is unlikely to occur until age 9 or so. In one study, children were encouraged to discuss experiences in narrative fashion; the project was set up so that they would talk about their experiences with death during the process. Those children younger than 9, described deaths of strangers, pets, and even family members in objective, unemotional terms. Only the older group discussed feelings and emotional attachments (Menig-Peterson & McCabe, 1977-78). This did not mean that the younger children were unfeeling but that their expressions of emotions were limited.

Other investigators have reached conclusions at variance with Nagy's. There has been considerable criticism of the stages for ignoring differences in the children's social, economic, and cultural backgrounds (Bluebond-Langner, 1977). One author, having analyzed available studies, concluded that a truly mature grasp of death occurs later than age 9 (Kastenbaum, 1977); other writings propose somewhat different stages, such as finding relatively little personification among 5-to-9-year-olds (Bluebond-Langner, 1977; Kastenbaum, 1977). The most challenging attack on the accepted stage theory was based on research with terminally ill children that showed them to be aware of the significance of death at much earlier ages [Bluebond-Langner, 1977 (see Chapter 11)]. It may be that younger children have an immature understanding of death because they lack experience with the phenomenon and not because they are unable to comprehend its meaning (Bluebond-Langner, 1977). Any final decision must be held in reserve.

SEPARATION AND ABANDONMENT

Children's feelings and attitudes about death reflect numerous factors: the children's level of development and cognitive understanding, their personal experiences with death and with separation, the knowledge they have acquired from their parents, peers, and others in their environment.

The theme of separation occurs again and again. Even very young children have experienced a variety of kinds of separation, ranging from being apart from their parents to having a favorite toy fall apart and disappear into the rubbish. They learn that some kinds of separation are not permanent (parents return) and some kinds of separation are permanent (the toy does not return). If their basic life is stable and they feel loved and cared for, separations may be mildly disturbing but probably are not upsetting or disruptive. Conversely, if the fabric of the child's life is not stable and if the child is anxious and uncertain about what is going to happen next, separation may add to feelings of anxiety and concern.

As children come to understand that death means permanent separation, they are likely to become afraid of death. As they learn that death is inevitable and that they are powerless to prevent it, they will feel helpless, which is a very unpleasant kind of feeling to have. Very young children believe themselves to be all-powerful, and learning of their impotence in the face of death is a direct challenge to their assumptions of omnipotence. Becker (1973) contends that these feelings are inevitable and occur to all of us, that they are part of our recognition that we are human and temporary and vulnerable, and that the dread of death is therefore universal. This dread obviously begins in childhood and would be especially strong in children who do not feel cared for and protected by their parents or other adults.

Since death is often described by adults as a kind of sleep and since children may make a similar interpretation, some children come to fear going to sleep. Their powerlessness and vulnerability while asleep may contribute to their fear. Death-related nightmares are not unusual, although it is difficult to determine the extent to which these represent separation fears more than specific death fears.

When children become intensely afraid of separation, they may be fantasizing that their parents will abandon them. One group of children received word-association tests to evaluate their associations with death. Nearly half of the 91 7-year-olds mentioned "death" in response to "very sad," and the death of mother was especially prominent (Mitchell, 1967). Mother's death is certainly a legitimate cause for both sadness and fear of abandonment.

With the increasing number of divorces and single-parent families, I would hypothesize that the fear of abandonment may be increasing in children, although an alternative hypothesis is that children will come to realize that separation does not mean abandonment. Viewed rationally, the fact that two parents live apart reduces the likelihood of both parents dying at the same time through an accident or catastrophe. This rational view becomes virtually irrelevent, however, in the face of two other circumstances. First, the children have already experienced the partial loss of one parent—most frequently the father; even if he is still accessible and has ongoing contact with the children, he is no longer in the household. Second, with one parent gone, the loss of the second parent would leave the child without any protection. And, of course, to make matters worse, in single-parent families, the remaining parent is often extremely busy and likely to be away from home much more often than in the case of two-parent families. Remarriage of the single custodial parent may reduce anxieties; however, if a child feels that the parent is taking love and affection away from him or her and offering it to the new spouse (and that person's children), the sense of abandonment may actually increase.

GUILT AND RESPONSIBILITY

It was 3:00 P.M. Friday afternoon, and four students were talking outside their high school. Their physics teacher, noted as the most demanding teacher at the school, had given another of his lengthy assignments, and Alice wasn't at all happy that her weekend was going to be spent on writing up an experiment rather than playing tennis. "I wish he'd drop dead!" And the other three agreed. Sunday's newspaper carried a notice that the teacher had had a serious heart attack, and Alice came down with a severe stomach ache that kept her home for the entire week. Although she knew that her fervent statement had nothing to do with the teacher's coronary, she admitted that she couldn't shake off her strong feelings of being responsible.

Alice, an intelligent girl, was not given to superstition, but she still couldn't absolve herself of guilt. How much more powerful similar feelings and statements are when made by children whose cognitive awareness of cause-and-effect is based much more on omnipotence and magic.

We all find ourselves wishing to be rid of someone else, and these wishes can become powerful enough to think of that person's death. A familiar cartoon depicts a man standing at the edge of a steep cliff and posing for a photograph being taken by his wife. The caption reads "Just one more step back, dear." The hostile humor is funny because it expresses what so many of us feel at one time or another.

Children often become angry enough with their parents, their siblings, or their friends to wish them spirited away. "To think of a thing is the same as doing that thing" (Zeligs, 1974, p. 34) for many children, and if that "thing" occurs, they may—like Alice—see themselves as responsible. One mother who often said to her children "Oh, you'll be the death of me yet," died when they were still young, and one son couldn't help feeling that he had caused her death. Another child was living with an elderly grandparent who was extremely ill; her mother told her not to let the screen door slam because it would disturb her grandmother. One day, when she let the door slam, her mother shouted out the usual irritated complaint; that evening her grandmother died, and for years the girl felt she had caused her grandmother's death.

Not only do children feel that their thoughts and words can have lethal effects, but they may also fear reprisal. Since, for young children, death is reversible and dead people still exist in some altered form, it stands to reason that, if the child has the power to wish someone to death, that person is going to wish the child to death (Zeligs, 1974). If slamming the screen door can cause grandmother's death, the grandmother, in whatever earthly or ghostly form she wishes to assume, can slam the screen door right back. To undo this possibility, the child may perform a ritual—for example, a prayer that blesses all people he or she loves (Zeligs, 1974).

Much of this behavior fits with the concept of the Oedipus complex, the personality dynamic, discussed by Freud, that describes the desire of children to rid themselves of competition with the same-sex parent in order to possess the opposite-sex parent. Eventually children resolve the Oedipus complex by identifying with the more powerful same-sex parent and possessing the opposite-sex parent indirectly through this identification process. However, if the competing parent dies before the identification process is completed, the death wishes against that parent may lead to guilt and fear of retribution.

EXPRESSIONS OF DEATH AWARENESS

Children, like everyone else, can discuss death directly and indicate their feelings about death indirectly through play, metaphors, and puns. Since children's use of language and their ability to apply abstract symbols are still limited, indirect communication may be more important for them than for adolescents or adults.

In Chapter 1, I pointed out that the centuries-old game, ring-around-the-rosy, was originally a device children used to express their feelings about death. It isn't the only one. When children play cops-and-robbers or cowboys-and-Indians, they act out a death, which is always reversible. However, the richest play media for expressive feelings about death are dolls, puppets, and other kinds of unstructured imaginative play. Wishes, fears, and experiences all emerge projected onto the dolls or through characters in creative play. The doll representing baby sister dies a horrible death, then is returned to life by a kindly and all-powerful big brother doll; a fantasized bogeyman comes to take two children, who successfully fend off the spectre; a father doll dies, is buried, becomes a baby, and returns. The representation of perceived reality occurs in play.

Children's misunderstanding of adult language can lead them to express their feelings about death in ways that the adults, in turn, cannot understand. One boy, age 2½, who had been weaned from his bottle for many months began to demand the bottle again, with a real urgency in his voice. "It was . . . the fear of death that I heard in his voice" (Brent, 1977–78, p. 286). The basis for the child's fear, it turned out, was that, when the family car had run out of gas three times, he had picked up the comment that the motor had died because of lack of fuel. In addition, the boy had heard that his baby sister had been having gas because of her bottle. You can put the rest together easily enough.

Sometimes it isn't that the child doesn't understand adult language but that adults don't listen hard enough to what the child is saying. A young girl whose sister was dying told a psychiatrist that she wanted a "crying doll" for Christmas. When the psychiatrist pursued the issue, the girl said that she was unable to cry because her mother wouldn't cry with her, and they couldn't cry together; therefore, the girl felt she had to restrain her own tears. The crying doll, of course, could give the girl the tears that she was not being permitted to display. The psychiatrist enabled the mother and daughter to share their sorrow, and, as she left the room, the child told her that she didn't need a crying doll anymore (Kübler-Ross, 1974). All of us speak of our deepest concerns in indirect ways—children perhaps more than adults—and death-related issues are so powerful that direct language is often difficult. Nevertheless, most people working with the dying would agree with Kastenbaum that "in speaking with children about death, simple and direct language is much to be preferred over fanciful, sentimental, and symbolic meanderings . . . . Try to provide them with accurate information. . . . See if they understand what you have said . . . and if that is really what they wanted to know in the first place" (1977, p. 132).

THE ADOLESCENT AND DEATH

As children grow older, their cognitive capacities and emotional maturity change, so that, almost inevitably, they become more like those of adults. Adolescents are more aware of themselves, more concerned with their identities than they had been as children and, perhaps, more concerned than they will be as adults. They are much more likely to think about and plan the future, and, since death is part of their future, their awareness of death in general and of their own death also increases.

In early adolescence, death seems very remote; intellectually it's recognized that it will occur someday, but that day is placed in a far-off and vague future. Younger teenagers probably do not integrate into themselves the idea that death will someday cut them off from a meaningful life. By age 14 or 15, adolescents have become somewhat more independent in their thinking and are more able to contemplate their own deaths. Now is the time for philosophizing and daydreaming about the future. The idea that death will someday put an end to that future can be very upsetting. Adolescents probably think more about death at 14 or 15 than they have at anytime before (Kastenbaum, 1967; Zeligs, 1974).

When a friend or acquaintance does die, the prematureness of the death and, I suspect, the suddenness and unexpectedness of it make it especially difficult and upsetting. People are caught totally unprepared, in part because the death has occurred out of time sequence. I know of several instances when the death of a high-school student has disrupted the entire school: students, teachers, and staff. Sometimes the death is handled openly, even if caused by suicide, which has been increasing as a cause of adolescent death, and everyone can mourn together. On other occasions, the school does not officially acknowledge the death and the administration and staff insist that everything must proceed as though nothing had happened. I believe that the denial required by the latter circumstance is normally much more difficult for teenagers to handle.

A great many studies of college-student attitudes toward death have been conducted, but very little published research is available on people between the ages of 12 and 18. Nevertheless, we do know some things: we know that their death rate is the lowest of any age group and that accidents and suicides account for a large proportion of the deaths that do occur; we also know that many high school students have attended courses, written term papers, and worked in values clarification programs involving death and dying.

Furthermore, we know that in many ways adolescents' perceptions of death resemble those of adults. I was very much impressed when I was asked to discuss death with a seventh-grade English class just after they had finished studying *Romeo and Juliet*. The pupils asked very many of the same questions and brought up the same issues normally discussed by college students and adults. They had obviously done a great deal of thinking about death, and I believe their reflections preceded their reading of the Shakespeare play. But these were particularly intelligent students, who were in an accelerated class. One author has suggested that it is generally the brighter teenagers who think a great deal about death (Kastenbaum, 1967); another found in her research—not surprisingly—that higher achieving high school seniors had more mature concepts of death (Maurer, 1964). And although I have no specific data to prove my contention, I assume that the individual differences among adolescents in viewing death are greater than the individual differences among children.

Obviously this area is largely unexplored. It would be particularly useful to know (1) the developmental changes in concepts of and feelings about death from ages 12 through 18, (2) the extent to which adolescents are vulnerable to death fear and anxiety (Zeligs [1974] has hypothesized they are especially vulnerable), (3) the differences, if any, in death fear between adolescents whose parents have divorced and those who reside with both parents, and (4) the changes in adolescent views of death which the increasing adolescent suicide rate may signal.

YOUTH AND MIDDLE AGE

Sometimes we treat the years from about ages 21 to 60 as a transition from youth to old age rather than as a part of the life-span developmental process. In very recent years, books like *The Seasons of a Man's Life* (Levinson, 1978) and *Passages* (Sheehy, 1976) remind us that growth and change are as much a part of these years as of the years of childhood or old age. The study of death and dying, like the rest of the behavioral sciences, lacks knowledge about the changes in attitudes toward death that occur during these years.

It isn't that there are no studies of the meaning of death for people during these years—there are substantial numbers. The difficulty rather is the paucity of attention focused upon the adult development of concepts and feelings about death and loss. Some research has established correlations of one or another variable with age; for example, it has been shown that fear of death diminishes with age, but nothing has been said about the development of this reduced fear of death. Most studies look only at the endpoint, the later years, and discuss only how the older person developed his or her views, and not how these views were expressed at various adult ages. There is to my knowledge *no* study that has accomplished for people between 18–60 what Nagy (1948) accomplished for children.

Nevertheless, there is still a great deal that we can observe about the changing involvement with death of people in this age group, and there is one study that compares responses of three adult age groups (20–39, 40–59, and 60+) on a large variety of death-related issues.

First, each year, as we grow older, an increasing number of our age peers die. At 30, I rarely heard of a friend dying from any cause other than accident or suicide—and even those occurrences were rare. Each death was unique and remembered. By the time I was 40, this was no longer the case. Not only did I learn of the occasional death of a friend my age, but obituaries frequently informed me of the deaths of celebrities my age or younger. Such accounts are commonplace for me at 50. A statistical analysis performed in Scotland provided interesting substantiation of my experiences. This investigator assumed that a man had 32 friends of exactly the same age and that, as soon as one died, that person was replaced by another. Given these circumstances, a person between the ages of 35 and 44 would suffer the death of a friend at least once during that time period; during the next decade, he would lose 2.6 friends by death; and between ages 55 and 65, 5.6 friends would die (Bytheway, 1970). Because of the way I have interpreted the data, these figures are slight underestimates.

Additional data confirm this study. In the youngest of the adult age groups in the Los Angeles study, 25% of those interviewed did not know personally anyone who had died during the previous two years; only 8% knew eight or more such persons. For those in their 40s and 50s, the figures were 17% and 14%, respectively; for those over 60, it was 10% and 22%. Other responses support these data: among the youngest adults 42% had not attended any funerals during the previous two years and 70% had not visited anyone's grave except during a burial service; in the two older age groups, 29% (40–59) and 27% (60+), respectively, had not attended funerals, and 50% (40–59) and 43% (60+) had not visited graves (Kalish & Reynolds, 1976).

One more question is relevant. Only 1% of the youngest group of adults had ever told someone that he or she was going to die; 7% of the middle-aged respondents had performed that task (Kalish & Reynolds, 1976). The data suggest that each year we are more often reminded of our own finitude, since death rates rise geometrically and, presumably, the deaths of our friends and age peers rise accordingly.

Second, as I get older—from 30 to 40 and then to 50—my parents also get older, and I increasingly find my friends concerned about their elderly, ill, and dying parents. Stan's mother dies a few years after his father's death, and he at 55 and Suzanne at 47 talk about becoming middle-aged orphans. What does this mean? When at least one parent is alive, death "feels" less probable, because we "know" that parents die before their children can die. The death of our parents means not only the loss of a loved person but also the elimination of one psychological barricade protecting us from death.

Third, time left to accomplish things begins to run out. At 30, there is ample time to do everything I want; at 40, I still have 25 or 30 years of work left ahead, but I become aware that not all my friends are going to live that long, and I have a tinge of wondering about whether or not I will make it; by 50, I know that well over half my life has been lived, and that I need to sort out what I want to do with the remaining time. One author views age 40 as the time when "a man knows more deeply than ever before that he is going to die" (Levinson, 1978, p. 205). By and large, during the following few years, a person will come to terms with mortality and will give increasing thought to how he or she as an individual will achieve immortality (Levinson, 1978).

Fourth, my obligations to others change. When my children are young, not only do I feel an obligation to help them along their beginnings of life, but I also want to enjoy being involved in the process. As they and I get older, the urgency of these feelings diminishes. When they are grown and have established themselves in whatever way they have chosen, I can feel one part of my work has been accomplished. Three times as many older persons as young adults stated that they were *not* concerned that death would mean they could no longer care for their dependents (Kalish & Reynolds, 1976). Other obligations may, of course, develop through work, community participation, or caring for an ill spouse, but these also may seem less demanding as I reach 50 and then 60.

Fifth, research does show that the middle-aged adults are less fearful of death and dying—including their own death and dying—than are younger adults. Just over one-fourth of the middle-aged study participants stated that they were afraid of death; just over one-half stated that they were not afraid. The comparable figures for young adults were 40% and 36%; half again as many younger adults are afraid and half again as many middle-aged adults are unafraid (Kalish & Reynolds, 1976). Another study compared three generations of women in the same families: mothers (average age 46) were significantly less afraid of death than their daughters (average age 21) (Kalish & Johnson, 1972).

Responses to two other questions supported the idea that younger adults are more afraid of death than the middle-aged. Fewer younger adults (62%) than middle-aged people (75%) stated that they never dreamed about their own death, and fewer younger adults (53%) than middle-aged adults (65%) would accept death peacefully than fight it actively (Kalish & Reynolds, 1976).

All these findings suggest to me that younger people have more difficulty with and feel more anxiety about death—especially their *own* deaths—than do older persons. However, at the same time, because death seems much less imminent, it is much less salient in their lives. That younger people view their own deaths as many more years off than do older people (Reynolds & Kalish, 1974) is neither surprising nor "bad." Young adults have more to lose than do older adults: they have not yet received the number of years of life, the experiences, and the relationships to which they feel entitled. They are less likely to die soon, but, if they did, they would be deprived of more.

An obvious question that arises is whether the study respondents were honest. My own assumption is that they responded as honestly as they could; if there was any distortion, it was the same for each age group.

DEATH IN THE LATER YEARS

Many of the trends that I described in the previous section continue into the later years. The inevitability of death comes closer and probably impinges more on day-to-day activities; it certainly impinges on future plans. Yet, there are considerable individual differences in the reactions of older persons to death.

Older people are constantly reminded of death. It is difficult to ignore death when not only age peers but much younger persons die. The elderly are, of course, much more likely than the young to have lost a spouse, brother, or sister through death; they almost always have experienced the death of at least one parent; they have had more friends die; they attend more funerals; and they are more likely to visit gravesites (Kalish & Reynolds, 1976).

COPING WITH DEATH

Erik Erikson has proposed the two ego conflicts of the second half of life as *generativity versus stagnation* and *ego integrity versus despair* (1963). In earlier years, because time seems unlimited, it is possible to use time freely and to plan a future. The meaningfulness of an activity, a relationship, education, work—all appear to extend into an indefinite future. As years pass and the indefinite future becomes less infinite, meaningfulness must be generated increasingly in terms of the present. The middle-aged person needs to remain capable of generating involvements and avoiding stagnation—especially in view of her or his diminishing fantasies about what the future can be. In the later years, it is equally necessary to retain a good sense of self in the face of increased potential for despair: despair that so many things are still not done; so many hopes still unrealized—and so many things done that cannot be undone. Time may now seem too brief to begin again.

In some ways, this new awareness provides freedom rather than despair, but the older individual must be able to see it as freedom for it in fact to be freedom. Since long-range plans must sometimes be curtailed because of death, ill health, or diminishing access to power through work and relationships, the older person may devote himself or herself to more immediate concerns. When you can no longer build a new service program, increase your hardware-store sales, or put into effect your idea for increased office efficiency, you can focus on enjoying the sun, taking a walk, watching grandchildren and great-grandchildren grow up. Perhaps these things are as important anyway. Since everything we do will eventually not matter very much, we might as well do what brings us enjoyment and pleasure at the moment we do it. Our "immortality" will not endure very long by establishing a better sales program, so why not watch a flower grow?

These matters, obviously, are philosophic, and there is no wand we can wave magically to make an older person see them as I have proposed. But at least the potential is there. Death, then, simultaneously gives freedom and takes freedom away.

Another way older people cope with death is by preparing for it. More older people than younger people have (1) made out a will, (2) made funeral arrangements, (3) paid for a cemetery plot, and (4) arranged for someone to handle their affairs (Kalish & Reynolds, 1976; J. Riley, 1963). The elderly are less likely to have life insurance than late middle aged persons. This is consistent with what we know about the realities they face: many older persons no longer have dependents who will require support after their death. Again, it is important to draw attention to the differences not only between age groups but within age groups. Thus, the extent of a person's education also influences the preparations she or he makes for death; the better-educated elderly are more likely to make such plans (Riley, 1963).

Belief in some form of continuity after death is undoubtedly another method of coping with death. In a Florida study, 61% of older persons strongly believed in a life after death, and another 11% tended to believe (Wass, Christian, Myers, & Murphey, 1978–79); 64% of those over 60 in the Los Angeles study also believed in some sort of life after death (Kalish & Reynolds, 1976); even higher numbers have been found in earlier studies (Cantril, 1951). However, a larger proportion of older people wish there were life after death than believe there is (Wass et al., 1978–79).

ATTITUDES TOWARD DEATH

As I mentioned earlier, one of the more consistent research results in the area of death is that fear of death diminishes with age. Studies of diminishing fear of death with age have been conducted with a variety of populations and utilized a variety of instruments (Bengtson, Cuellar, & Ragan, 1977; Feifel & Branscomb, 1973; Kalish & Johnson, 1972; Kalish & Reynolds, 1976; Kogan & Wallach, 1961; Martin & Wrightsman, 1965). And the proportion of older persons who state that they fear death remains amazingly similar from study to study. Even a study in India confirmed the findings (Sharma & Jain, 1969). As an example, in a group of alert, institutionalized elderly, 16% stated that they feared death (Kimsey, Roberts, & Logan, 1972). Five percent of one multiethnic population in Los Angeles County indicated that they were "very afraid" (Bengtson, Cuellar, & Ragan, 1977); the figure from a totally different multiethnic group in the same community was 10% who were either "afraid" or "terrified" (Kalish &

Reynolds, 1976); 10% of a group of older community volunteers admitted that they feared death (Jeffers, Nichols, & Eisdorfer, 1961). Depending on the particular group surveyed, the wording of the questions, and the context, specific percentages will obviously vary, but the numbers are normally not far from those cited.

A well-known longitudinal study of older men, begun when the participants were in their early 70s and completed a decade later, provides additional substantiation. Among these men, who were studied intensely, "few were found to be overtly afraid of death, and those who were seemed to have attitudes formed early which were deeply characteristic of their entire lives" (Rosenfeld, 1978, p. 16). Many of these healthy older men were able to accept their own future death. Among those who did not wish to confront the idea of their own mortality, most used defense mechanisms such as humor and appropriate denial, and most had made concrete plans for their own death—for example, wills had been written, burial arrangements made. Perhaps the most significant finding of this study was that, at least for many of these men, the greatest challenge was not that of facing death but that of using the "bonus years," the years after retirement and after most of their age peers had died, to their own good advantage (Rosenfeld, 1978).

At the same time that older persons are less fearful and more accepting of their own deaths, they think more about death than younger persons (Kalish & Reynolds, 1976; Riley, 1963). At first appearance it may seem that these two results are contradictory, but I don't believe they are. First, older people recognize that they have relatively little futurity. The deaths of age peers and younger people and the awareness that their lives are coming to a close, make them think more about death. In turn, having had more death experiences and having been forced to think about death, they have also been required to work through some of their fears and anxieties.

Second, their futures are not as attractive as those of younger persons. Many older people have some chronic disease or physical handicap that they know is likely to worsen; the loss of friends, of work possibilities, and of perceived social value all conspire to reduce the value of life for them. This can lead to a disengagement from life and a greater willingness to accept death.

Third, most people in industrialized nations anticipate a life expectancy of 65 to 70 years. I believe that people accept this fact as a given: if they face their deaths in advance of those ages, they feel deprived, but if they live longer, they feel they have received their just measure.

Fourth, some older people are ready to stop coping with the demands of the world. One 92-year-old man, functioning with minimum impairment and enjoying life, said that he was ready to die whenever his time came—although he denied that he was eager to die. He feared the changing social and political arena, and he was suspicious of his new neighbors; he felt no more meaning in life and was no longer interested in seeking new experiences, which finances and health made difficult anyway. For the next three years, he pursued only familiar routines, which he appeared to enjoy in a quiet way. Then he died easily and quietly.

This fourth point may find additional confirmation in the results of the study, mentioned earlier, that asked people of various ages whether they felt that death came too soon. Middle-aged persons were more likely than younger people to feel that death comes too soon. The number of people over 60 who agreed with this statement was small as was the number of younger people who agreed (Riley, 1963). The wear and tear of life becomes too much, and death, while not actively sought, is essentially accepted when it occurs.

In some ways, death has very much the same meaning over the entire life span. But, because views and feelings are inevitably influenced by situation and context, older people look at death from a different position than middle-aged or younger persons do; children and young adolescents are in still a different position. And historical situations also affect age differences. People who were socialized to those views of death that prevailed in 1910 are likely to be different in their feelings and attitudes than those who were socialized in 1980.

Thus, while the ultimate meaning of death remains the same, perceptions of the meaning of death change as the individual grows older. It is possible, of course, that older people simply deny their fear of death more frequently than do the nonelderly. I don't believe this is the case, but it is a hypothesis that I cannot test adequately at this time. You will need to judge this for yourself.

Both attitudes toward death and the meaning of death change across the life span. In part, this change represents the differing life experiences and life situations of each age group, and, in part, it represents the specific historical time and the specific cultural context in which we live. Although the changes are well documented, the reasons for the changes are far from understood.

PART

2
THE PROCESS OF DYING

*Notes On Robert**

These extracts are from the journal of Marcella Adamski, written when she was a volunteer with Shanti, an organization that provides free psychological and social services to dying persons. Ms. Adamski is presently a counselor and consultant working in adult transitions.

October 27

I introduced myself to Robert as a member of the Shanti Project, which arranges for visits to people who are seriously ill. He immediately responded that he was indeed seriously ill. "I'm not going to get better." Then, without any prompting he gave a detailed account of his illness. At one point in the diagnostic process, the physician had handed him a pile of x-rays to take to another physician. Written across the top in red ink was "Cancer?" His doctor had never even told him that he might have cancer. "Maybe that was his way of telling me."

His first reaction to learning about the cancer was "No, not me. It must be some mistake. The reports are wrong." In fact he didn't feel he even needed to be concerned right away since he understood his treatment as being only for his emphysema. He was on morphine every four hours, which reduced the discomfort and permitted him to be lucid. His greatest fear was pain, not death.

At one point his left lung collapsed, and his family thought he was going to die. At that time he felt he wanted to give up. "It was then I accepted my death, but I chose to continue living."

"I didn't go to church much, but I do believe in God. I feel there must be a reason why I am still living. I don't know what it is. But I knew many people who had cancer. They are all gone. I am still here. There must be a reason."

His wife is fully aware of his illness. She visits every day. His greatest concern is that she must now take care of the bills and business that he once handled. They have a small pension, and the bills are enormous. He

*"Notes on Robert," by M. Adamski. Copyright © 1980 by Marcella Adamski. Reprinted by permission of author.

wept then, feeling that he was such a burden. "If I was gone, she could make it on the money we have." But he wants to live. There was much guilt around this issue.

His daughter visits sporadically. "She doesn't admit I'm sick. She can't accept it. We talk, but not about my sickness. She only likes to see me when I am up and dressed."

(Later) *Marcy*: "What's it like to be here in this nursing home?"

Robert: "Well, I know they are good and will be there—but I'm afraid if I need help in the middle of the night, they won't know what to do. Also, too many of the others are old and senile, and I'm not 60 yet—I'm different than the rest. I'd rather be somewhere where the other people have the same problem I have."

(Later) *Marcy*: "Are you tired now? Would it be better if I left?"

Robert: "No, I like to have visitors and I enjoy talking with you. The medical staff is so busy. My doctor comes to see me after work, but I know he is on his way home. He does stay to talk a little though."

Then Robert spoke more about his own death, saying he had accepted it but felt he could only go on as long as the pain was not severe and he had the use of his mind.

After I left the interview, I noted the following reactions. Before going in to see Robert, I felt my usual stage fright. However, he turned out to be very easy to talk to. At times he cried, and I could both accept and understand that. I had no need to "cheer him up" or give him solutions. I was especially struck when he said "I know I have terminal cancer. I know I am going to die. But I don't know when. That makes me still like everyone else. They don't know when either. He seemed especially pleased when I said I wanted to learn from him so I could be of help to others who were in the same condition. He gave me a big squeeze and said he would be delighted if I could come again. I realized after I left that we had been together for 90 minutes.

October 30

I spent 30 minutes with Robert today. He looked weary and told me he had slept well, but was experiencing a lot of pain. We talked about the pain. Later he spoke of looking forward to doing certain things, like visiting his brother in Portland, but he realizes he won't be able to do them. "However, these hopes are the only things that keep me going."

Then he spoke of his wife. They had been very close, and he wondered if it would have been better if they hadn't been so close. She has told him that she can speak more easily to strangers than to him about his illness. He worries about her being alone.

I was in a low mood and didn't feel as effective or "there." Or perhaps his pain and loneliness and dreaming aroused my own anxieties. I wanted to do something to help him relax, but I didn't and I felt inadequate.

November 6

Was with Robert for an hour today. After general amenities, Robert asked to know more about me because he felt he had talked so much about himself. I gave him a brief outline of my life.

(Later) I asked if he had seen his doctor. It had been two weeks. "He lives nearby and could visit me more often. But I'm glad he doesn't, because I would have to pay $15.00 a visit. All he does is come in and say 'Hi, how are you feeling?' I'm paying over $1000 a month to be here and I can't afford extra costs. Soon Medicare will help out, and my insurance company will pick up some of the costs."

He then told me about his recent treatment. "But I don't give up hope. I was so sick one time and everyone thought I would die, but I lived. I don't know what it is but I think God has some special plan for me."

Marcy: "So you feel like you might not die?"

Robert: "Yes! People do recover. There *are* miracles. My wife doesn't like it when I talk like this. But I need some hope to be able to go on."

We talked more, and I began to weep. He seemed moved and wanted to comfort me. I'm glad he saw some of my vulnerability.

November 14

Robert was not in the nursing home, but had been transferred to the local hospital. I went there. He told me how intense the pain had been during the tests they had taken. He had had a whole day of tests and was exhausted. He told me a lot about his life and background, and I felt he was avoiding dealing with why he had been moved to the hospital. He didn't like being there, since he looked at the nursing home as a home.

November 24

I hadn't seen Robert in a long time. I had an extremely busy schedule, and I didn't want to see him out of obligation when I was exhausted. We talked about his visit to the hospital.

Robert: "Those doctors are just noncommittal. They just stand there and say 'ummhmm' and you talk and when they leave, you realize they haven't told you anything."

Marcy: "Did you ask the doctor what the test results showed?"

Robert: "No, I was afraid to ask."

Marcy: "That's understandable."

Afterwards I wondered why I hadn't pursued the issue. Probably two reasons: first, I finally began to realize how frightened Robert was, in spite of his brave front; second, I wanted to share Robert's fear with him, to be in the same "space" that he is in. Perhaps I was afraid also.

December 4

This time Robert brought up his daughter. "I want to mend the fence between my daughter and me" (interesting metaphor). "She's bringing a friend because she doesn't know how to face me alone. But I don't want her to feel bad, like I would have if I had gone to Reno instead of visiting my sister when it turned out she was dying. Sometimes people are sick over a period of time so that you don't realize they can take a turn for the worse—you think they will always be around" (a premonition?).

January 8

No dramatic changes in him. He had read *Living with Cancer* and wanted his wife to read it. He wept when telling how a cousin had died and the children hadn't ever been able to say they loved him.

January 16

Robert's wife had just been visiting, and he told me about it. (Later) He turned and showed me a welt like a water boil that had appeared on his thigh. He was worried, since he had not had anything like it before. He speculated that it might be the beginning of a bedsore, but he couldn't imagine it was because there was no pressure on that part of his body. Then he did show me a bedsore that was healing.

I was pleased that I was able to look at his sores and not be repulsed. I always want to be able to look at a person's physical problems with sympathy and understanding, acknowledging them for the terrible things they are without making the person feel ugly and repulsive because of them.

January 22

Robert told me that his wife had read *Living with Cancer,* and he wanted me to read it next. His wife had told him how she had read a book on widows, but had kept it covered so he wouldn't see it. Previously, when she would ask him what he was thinking, he would joke and say nothing about his thoughts and feelings. Now that has all changed. They can share a lot.

I began to talk about my women's group, and he asked me some questions. The matter of sexual fantasies came up, and he looked thoughtful. I asked him what it was like not having the intimacy of his marriage. "It's hard because we were so close. That was a real part of our lives. Now we have to express it differently. You have to talk a lot more about what you are feeling, and use touch and looks. It's a different kind of love."

He talked again of how he *chose* to live when his future was precarious. His wife had said she would not have done the same thing if she knew she would have had to suffer as long as he has. He didn't feel that she wished he were dead but that she wouldn't have the courage to go on. I remarked that sometimes it is difficult to see people suffer, especially those we love. I also stated that I sensed this part of his life was somehow needed for his growth and that was why he didn't choose to die at that time. "After an experience like this one, you are different. You are more open, tolerant, and can accept people better."

He spoke of depression. "It's a cycle. The pain gets bad. I cry. I get angry for crying. Then I get depressed." I told him that it was not only okay to cry but at times the very best thing he could do.

It was a good visit, funny at times.

February 11

Robert died early this morning. Slowly and with much difficulty. For some strange reason, I stopped by the hospital much earlier than usual. His bed was empty and freshly made. I went to the nurse's station. His wife had been with him. I wished they had called me. I wished it had been easier for him. I wished I had come just two hours sooner. I wept.

8

CAUSES OF DEATH

Men die sooner than women, but not in all societies; the poor die sooner than the wealthy, but not in all instances; those who smoke die sooner than those who abstain, but not in all cases. We are all entitled to one life—and one death. When we die, what we die from and how we die vary; what is invariable is that we die.

WHAT CAUSES DEATH?

What influences your life expectancy? Is it your genetic inheritance? Your mother's health and nutritional habits when she was carrying you *in utero*? Your own early and subsequent health and nutrition? The psychological stresses that you encounter and your methods of coping with them? Your medical care? Your inclination to overeat and put on weight? To smoke? To drink heavily? To lead a sedentary life with minimal exercise? Is it the air and water contaminants where you live? The risks required of you in your work? The risks in the leisure activities you pursue? Your use of preventive medical facilities? Your exposure to unsanitary conditions? Your access to and utilization of a good health-care system? Chance factors?

All of the above—and more than the above—contribute to the determination of how long you will live. To some extent, you can affect how long you will live. You can make certain decisions about your diet, your health care, the risks you take when you work or drive or play, your visits to physicians. You can make important changes in your life: reduce your stress at work by changing jobs, move out of a community where air pollution is high. But to some extent, you have nothing to say about how long you live: your genetic inheritance and your mother's health during her pregnancy, for example, are beyond your control.

Although most persons would agree that the conditions listed above influence life expectancy, other influences are considerably more controversial. Would a hex placed on you shorten your life? Even if you didn't know it? Would good behavior lengthen your life or evil behavior shorten it? If so, by whom or what? Your own psychological forces or some outside entity?

In some cultures today, it is believed that disease is incurred through the ill wishes of enemies and that cure must be brought about either by propitiating those enemies or by rallying one's own gods on one's behalf. Among Africans " . . . the commonest cause [of death] is believed to be magic, sorcery, and witchcraft" (Mbiti, 1970, pp. 203-4). Among 47 cultures for which Simmons (1945) could find data, 17 regarded death as unnatural (for example, the result of hexes, witchcraft, supernatural interventions), and 26 others only partially accepted the idea that death was a natural event. For example, the Anggor tribe of New Guinea perceive death *only* as resulting from active aggression of specific persons. An anthropologist, investigating 177 deaths in this area, found that 72% were unequivocally attributed to sorcery; another 15% were attributed to homicide, which is interpreted there as a kind of sorcery; the remaining deaths were considered to result from epidemics, intervention of spirits, and old age, which is itself believed to be the result of a kind of sorcery (Huber, 1972).

Nor are we, in North America, immune to this kind of thinking. Among some individuals today, length of life is seen as caused in part by rewards or punishments for good or evil behavior. When asked whether "most people who live to be 90 years old or older must have been morally good people" just over one-third of a carefully selected mixed ethnic sample answered affirmatively (Kalish & Reynolds, 1976).

Your beliefs about what factors influence your life expectancy are going to influence your behavior, and your willingness to alter your behavior in directions that will increase your life expectancy says a great deal about how much you value long life in comparison to other satisfactions.

DEATH RATES AND CAUSES HERE, THERE, AND THEN

Life expectancy of white infant girls born in 1976 in the United States was 77 years; white boys were expected to live to age 70 (*Information Please Almanac*, 1979). These figures are substantially higher than the 51 years girls and 48 years boys who were born in 1900 were expected to live. Not only has general life expectancy increased substantially over this period, but the differential between males and females has also increased. Much of the increase in life expectancy, however, has occurred because of reductions in infant mortality, childhood deaths, and maternal deaths in childbirth. Thus, the increased life expectancy during the same period for white men age 40 was less than five years and for 40-year-old white women, just over ten. In other words, in 1900, a 40-year-old white man could anticipate living until he was about 68; by 1976, this had increased only to 73 (*Metropolitan Life Insurance Statistical Bulletin*, July-Sept., 1978). For white women, the comparable figures went from 69 to nearly 80. Data for non-whites are compiled separately; although they are lower at each point, they are increasing more rapidly (*Information Please Almanac,* 1979).

If we continue back as far as prehistoric times, we find that the best estimate of life expectancy is about 18 years, with many and perhaps most deaths caused by violence (Dublin, 1951). In early Greece and Rome, people probably lived into their early 20s; by the Middle Ages this had extended in England into the early 30s (Lerner, 1970). As the age of anticipated death changed and as the common causes of death changed, the meaning of death and the appropriate care of the dying also changed.

The reduction in infant mortality, mentioned above, is considerable. One recent study states that, of every 1000 infants born alive in eighteenth-century London, between 300 and 400 had died before their second birthdays; a century later, deaths per 1000 during the first year (note the shift in data base) were around 150. In 1900, in the United States, the infant mortality rate was 100 per 1000; by 1970, it was only two per 1000 (Marshall, 1980). The large number of infant deaths was one reason families in 1900 tended to have many more pregnancies than families do today. As a result, the typical married couple who lived to their early 40s were very likely to have lost at least one child by epidemic, accident, or illness, and the deaths of two or three children were not at all unusual. This means that very few people reached adulthood without having lost a brother or sister. Most certainly the exposure to death at a personal level was immensely greater than today.

There is considerable variation in death rates among countries: the statistics of less developed nations are comparable to those of other countries at the turn of the century. Rates and causes of death are influenced by climate, health-care availability, public-health practices, food supply, sewage facilities, and so forth.

Social class also influences death rates. Among low-income persons, deaths occur more commonly during infancy, childhood, and young-adult years; many of these deaths are caused by gastrointestinal disease, the communicable diseases of childhood, influenza, and pneumonia—even though these illnesses have been virtually eliminated among persons with higher incomes (Lerner, 1970). The lack of access to health services and the lack of awareness of preventive measures probably contribute to these data. On the other hand, members of the more affluent middle class are more susceptible to deaths from heart attack, stroke, and cancer in their middle and late years. The blue-collar working class appears to escape both the early deaths of the low-income groups and the mid-life deaths of the higher-income groups. Overall, it has the best mortality record (Lerner, 1970).

The contribution of ethnic background to life expectancy is also well-known. In the United States, Blacks have a higher death rate at all ages until 70 than non-Blacks. At about 70, a reversal occurs, and Blacks, especially Black women, have a longer life expectancy than do their non-Black age peers (Myers & Soldo, 1977).

Just as death rates have changed with the decades, so has the predominancy of causes of death. In 1900, influenza and pneumonia were the major causes of death (just under 12% of all deaths), followed by tuberculosis (11%), gastritis and related diseases (8%), and heart disease (8%). Cancer was ranked eighth with under 4%. By the mid-1960s, however, heart disease accounted for 39% of all deaths, cancer for 16%, and vascular lesions affecting the nervous system for 11%. Influenza and pneumonia accounted for only 3% of all deaths, and tuberculosis caused virtually no deaths at all (Lerner, 1970).

As health problems are eliminated by medical research and treatment and improved care, life expectancy increases and the major causes of death change in nature. Thus, cancer was not a major cause of death a century ago because cancer is largely an illness of the elderly, and most people didn't live long enough to be susceptible to cancer—they died earlier from smallpox or tuberculosis or pneumonia. At the same time, there were probably fewer carcinogens created by human endeavors a century ago, although we do not know that for certain. This brings up an intriguing speculation: what will people die from when cancer and cardiovascular disease are eliminated?

Heavy smoking, working on a high-stress job, or living in a smoggy city is never listed as a cause of death, although numerous studies have investigated their effect on life expectancy (see Woodruff, 1977, for review). The destructive effects of long-term exposure to low levels of radiation are not attributed to "human error" or "mechanical error" but are hidden away among the tens of thousands of cancer deaths. Obviously, what we consider to be a recordable cause of death is the result of our cultural values; we tend, for example, to look to an illness or medical model.

SUICIDES, ACCIDENTS, DISASTERS

Execution and capital punishment, suicide, combat death, civilian death in war, industrial accidents, automobile accidents, home accidents, medical errors, burning, drowning, homicide, euthanasia. Of the numerous causes of death, the way in which an individual dies affects that individual, the family and close friends, and the health caretakers; sometimes it also affects observers or, in the event of a powerful or well-known person, many acquaintances and strangers.

> An airplane crash in San Diego killed all the passengers. Since the flight did not stop in San Francisco or Oakland, I didn't look at the passenger list.

> About six months later I received a letter from a close friend that discussed various personal matters. One sentence caught my immediate attention: "I read about Len Wright in that San Diego crash—how awful."

Len Wright was never a close friend of mine, although we did work together for a while, and I hadn't seen him in some five or six years. Yet his death from the airplane crash set a whole series of thoughts and feelings into motion for me. How much more it would have affected me had our recent involvements been substantial. And how much more I would have been affected had he been a homicide victim or executed for some crime. Is dying in an airplane crash any better or worse than dying of a sudden coronary? Or a slow cancer? That's a question you need to answer for yourself. Sudden deaths from accidents, homicide, or war have a powerful effect on the survivors—even if there is no living-dying interval. This may be even truer if the body is mutilated, if great pain is experienced or if the dead person was in the middle of important projects or had significant family responsibilities.

SUICIDE

Suicide has held a fascination for poets and psychologists, for philosophers and physicians. Some people romanticize suicide by viewing it as the one way in which a person can exercise ultimate control over his or her life; others see suicide only as an insane act. Argument rages over the moral right of a person to take his or her own life. On the one hand, if I am not in charge of my own life, I am not in charge of anything: it is my life and I should be able to take it if and when I want. On the other hand, because death by suicide affects not only the person committing suicide but many others as well, the family and even society in general deserve protection from suicides; another argument against suicide is that, while it is irreversible, it often arises from stresses that can be alleviated with help or simply with time.

On one matter, there is little disagreement: suicide is one of the leading causes of death in the United States and Canada; it ranks in or near the ten most frequent causes of death for all ages after childhood. Adolescent suicide, in particular, is rapidly increasing; its rate for residents of the United States between 15 and 24 years of age is three times higher today than it was 25 years ago. It ranks as the third most frequent cause of death for boys and the fourth most frequent cause of death for girls in this age range (Saltus, 1979). Suicide rates vary greatly from country to country and even from group to group within each country. Some of the variability, however, arises not from actual suicides but from differing methods of defining and reporting deaths as suicides.

Not only are completed suicides a matter of considerable concern, but those suicide attempts that do not result in death are also a major concern. Since suicide is frequently seen as a cry for help, resulting from feelings of helplessness and hopelessness, the first response of mental-health professionals is to try to help the individual cope with the life situation that produces these feelings. We tend not to think any longer about "suicidal personality types" but about situations that lead persons to contemplate suicide. The person who is still alive after a suicide attempt virtually always needs some kind of help or support. The help may be emotional support, psychotherapy, financial aid, a job, or, on rare occasions, institutionalization.

Often the suicide attempt itself is sufficient to produce change. People become aware that death can really occur, and they realize that being dead will, while solving their immediate difficulties, also cause significant losses for them. Most persons who were kept from jumping from one of the San Francisco area bridges did *not* subsequently make another suicide attempt.

In many ways, suicide is a social act, meant to influence others. It is one type of communication, and it might be meant to say:

> I am angry and I am going to punish you in the worst way possible. You will feel guilty long after I kill myself.
>
> You never paid any attention to me—no one ever paid any attention to me—but you will pay attention to me if I attempt to kill myself.
>
> I need help but I am not able to ask for help; I don't know how to ask for help. This is a way to ask for help.
>
> The pain of my life is too great, and I can't stand it any longer. Either someone has to help me out of this pain or I will help myself out by dying.
>
> I want to control you, and I can do that by attempting suicide. I will be victim and you will be rescuer.

The frequent assumption today is that people who attempt or commit suicide are either mentally ill or under great psychological stress; physical illness, financial problems, work and love losses, and other factors are rarely mentioned as causes. Nevertheless, persons who commit suicide are still sometimes viewed as cowardly, inconsiderate, or even evil (Kalish, Reynolds, & Farberow, 1974).

Some people are more likely to commit suicide than others: men (although women make many more attempts, men commit many more suicides), older people, unmarried persons, individuals living alone, those who are in poor physical health, mentally ill persons, unemployed and retired individuals (Dorpat & Ripley, 1967). But these are statistical trends, and many suicides do not fit these patterns at all. Also, except for sex, all the above high-suicide conditions are found more often among persons of lower socioeconomic status.

Not all suicides are obvious ones. For example, a man who has been very depressed for some weeks has been talking a little with friends about "getting away from it all." While traveling 70 miles per hour on the way to work one morning, his car hits a freeway abutment and he dies immediately. Did he knowingly commit suicide? Were his stresses so great that he wasn't aware of how fast he was driving or where his car was heading? One approach, called the *psychological autopsy*, has been used to try to determine whether such an act was overtly suicidal or not (Weisman & Kastenbaum, 1968). Persons conducting a psychological autopsy review the dead person's life, especially the history of events immediately preceding the death, very carefully, and they put together a comprehensive chronology. Through extensive experience and research, moderately accurate predictors have been developed that appear to differentiate suicidal deaths from deaths by other causes.

Often, the person attempting suicide doesn't really want to die. He may be consciously aware that the suicide attempt is not supposed to cause death, or he may be unaware. So he swallows a bottle of sleeping pills in a motel room three miles from his family, then telephones them to say "I won't bother you any more. I'm going to die peacefully right in this room." He hangs up. Is he consciously aware that his car is parked right outside the door of the room with the license plate facing the street?

Or she engages a close friend in an ostensibly intellectual argument about the right to commit suicide—becoming increasingly emotional as the discussion progresses. The friend she selects to talk to is a clinical social worker. Has she consciously selected the one person she knows who would quickly understand the hidden message?

Sometimes the desire for the attempt to fail is even more obvious: he barely cuts his wrists enough to draw blood or she not only makes a call from a motel room after taking pills, but asks her friend for help. One familiar pattern is to use a suicide attempt to bring a separated spouse back into the household; it is not unheard of for a woman or a man to make suicide attempts every time a frightening breakup occurs. And there are some husbands or wives who act out their part of this serious game by returning to "save" the person attempting suicide.

The impact of suicide on the survivors is, indeed, immense. Not only is a close family member removed, often at a time when that person was still important to others, but the survivors often feel responsible for not having intervened to stop the death from occurring. In fact, they feel responsible for having encouraged the death through their actions.

Edwin Shneidman, a leading figure in the suicide prevention movement, has encouraged *postvention* to reduce the emotional damage done to those who are close to suicide victims. Postvention refers to "those activities that serve to reduce the aftereffects of a traumatic event in the lives of the survivors" (Shneidman, 1973, p. 33). There is a need for such activities because "survivor-victims of such deaths are invaded by an unhealthy complex of disturbing emotions: shame, guilt, hatred, perplexity. They are obsessed with thoughts about the death, seeking reasons, casting blame, and often punishing themselves" (Shneidman, 1973, p. 34).

If all suicides are self-destructive acts (although you might wish to debate this point), are all self-destructive acts attempted suicides? How about cigarette smoking, reckless driving, heavy drinking, or consciously living a highly stressful existence? Are these indirect ways of committing suicide? Or are they conscious decisions in which the individual establishes priorities, even though the risk is there?

A totally different kind of issue emerges in some discussions of suicide: is there such an act as a justifiable suicide? Are there times when remaining alive makes less sense than ceasing to live? Too often the responses to these questions are made too quickly, without adequate thought. Frequently lives that seem hopeless are not hopeless; the availability of one truly caring individual might cause a suicidal person to decide to live. My first reaction to the question of justifiable suicide is to ask about specific situations: is there any change that anyone can provide that would enable the person to wish to live? There may be. There may not be. I do become concerned that too many of us allow the idea of a justifiable suicide to absolve us of responsibility for providing another person with reasons to live.

Conversely, there are people for whom the pain of living and the total hopelessness of the future clearly outweigh any potential for life. In many instances, these individuals are already terminally ill, and their future is a matter of weeks or, at the most, months (although the differences in life expectancy between them and the rest of us are quantitative, not qualitative). In other instances, a physically ill or depressed person feels that he or she is using up too many resources or is causing too much distress for loved ones. Death is seen as liberating the ill person or liberating those they love.

Is there such an act as a justifiable suicide? I can only answer for my own value system.

The literature on suicide is voluminous. All I have done is touch on a very few issues. Some others include causes of suicide, the relationship of depression to suicide, methods of committing suicide, treatment programs for persons involved with suicides, the role of suicide-prevention centers, and the significance of suicide notes.

ACCIDENTS

Of the three kinds of death examined in this section, accidents are by far the most familiar. Accidents, especially automobile accidents, are the major cause of death of younger persons. As people grow older, they are more likely to die of other causes than accidents. Among the elderly, accidents, although lower on the list, still cause many deaths; however, their accidental deaths are attributed to automobiles relatively less often; many are caused by a fall, which, in turn, is often caused by dizziness resulting from cardiovascular problems or from medication.

Since accidental deaths frequently occur to the young and are sudden and unexpected, family members are caught unaware. The feeling of responsibility evoked by the death is not the same as that from deaths from illness. For example, an industrial accident may result from faulty machinery or from carelessness; a hunting gun that accidentally discharges may kill the person who handles the gun or someone else; an automobile accident may result in the death of the driver, the passenger, someone in the other car, or a pedestrian. And the factory worker, the hunter, or the driver may have been drinking, taken some drug or medication, or been daydreaming about his or her recent divorce.

It is sometimes helpful to believe that the person who died in some way deserved to die. That makes "sense" of what is otherwise perceived as an absurd or meaningless death. If the factory worker had been using "speed," if the hunter had been drinking, if the driver had been daydreaming, they "deserved" to die from their stupidity; we have a place to direct our anger. Conversely, if the dead person was not the "deserving" one, then the anger is directed at the person who caused the accident and did not die. In the latter situation, the death just "doesn't make sense," and it is often much more difficult to accept.

DISASTERS

A special kind of accidental death is the death from a disaster. Although disasters don't account for a high proportion of the deaths in a nation, a disaster can have a tremendous impact on one particular community. An airplane crash is likely to wipe out entire families or an entire basketball team or the top management of a small business; an earthquake, tidal wave, or volcanic eruption can be even more devastating.

We can all be struck by disaster: earthquake, tornado, radioactivity from a nuclear plant or carrier vehicle, explosion, fire, crippling snowstorm, volcano. But an individual tends to ignore warnings, perhaps because he or she feels "I am immune—it can't happen here, but if it does, I will survive."After the disaster has occurred, we may blame the carelessness of others, the cynicism of bureaucrats, the lack of good warning systems, the cost-cutting of industrial executives, payoffs to inspectors. But this is all after the fact. "The failure of the warning-predicting-preventing system often is associated with the most common and ordinary attitudes and practices of our society" (Kastenbaum, 1977, p. 102).

During a disaster, some people emerge as true heroes: they devote their time and energy and risk their lives to help others. Other people are consumed by fear for their own lives or property or by anxiety for the well-being of those they love. Some disasters cause so much death and destruction that immense stress and anxiety are generated.

One author, who is both a professional sociologist and a professional funeral director, describes eight practical matters that must be attended to in disasters (Pine, 1974):

1. The victims who survived the disaster need to be cared for, fed, given medical attention, housed, and so forth.

2. Persons who are not directly involved usually need to be kept away from the area (the problems of helping disaster victims when surrounded by sightseers or scavengers is a familiar one).
3. The disaster area should be left as undisturbed as possible, in order to facilitate subsequent investigations.
4. When people have died, the locations of their deaths are usually marked and recorded before removing the bodies.
5. When possible, the bodies of the dead are identified, and their deaths are legally certified.
6. The next of kin need to be notified.
7. The final disposition of the dead is accomplished.
8. The psychological and social needs of the family members of the dead should be considered and given attention.

The final item, caring for the needs of the family members, is often overlooked because of the stresses of the disaster, the numbers of persons who must be notified, and the usual lack of an effective system for handling such matters. We cannot anticipate and plan for all disasters, and frequently the cost and the time required to take even modest precautions are considered too high.

Perhaps the greatest disaster of modern times—certainly the disaster that has had the greatest impact on the modern world—was the dropping of atomic bombs on Hiroshima and Nagasaki. Although you may not wish to consider this a disaster since it was the consequence of a human act and not a natural disaster, its impact was like a disaster's all the same. Probably the best psychological book about Hiroshima was written by psychiatrist Robert Lifton (1967). Based on hundreds of interviews and many months of observations and discussions, the book describes the first experiences of the bombing as involving an initial *immersion in death* and subsequent psychic closing-off, during which people "simply ceased to feel. They had a clear sense of what was happening around them, but their emotional reactions were unconsciously turned off" (1967, p. 31). The next reaction, which Lifton termed *survival priority*, was the guilt that the *hibakusha** felt about having survived, while so many others died. The dead, the dying, the disabled were so numerous as to be overwhelming; so many people cried out for help that no survivors were immune from the feeling that they had failed to help at least one person who needed it. In most, perhaps all, instances, guilt and shame grew over the years, as more deaths resulted from the radiation. And, of course, the survivors experienced anger and fear, as it became apparent that all those who were affected by the radiation had to deal with illnesses and disabilities, which they hadn't originally anticipated.

There seems little doubt that surviving any disaster leaves an indelible mark on the survivor; surviving the atomic blasts at Hiroshima and Nagasaki caused psychological changes that no amount of psychotherapy and no duration of time can erase.

*Survivors of the atomic explosions at Hiroshima and Nagasaki.

THE DEATH INSTINCT

One explanation of why we all die is that there is a basic psychological drive toward death, which is comparable to the drive for food or sleep. Choron (1964) traces the concept back 2000 years to Seneca, who spoke of *libido moriendi*, but it was Freud's description of *Todestrieb*, virtually a literal translation of Seneca's term, that brought contemporary attention. The death instinct, or drive toward death, has been one of Freud's most controversial contributions to psychoanalytic theory (Choron, 1964). Freud perceived the sexual drives as leading to life and self-preservation. To produce a kind of counterpoint, he hypothesized a death drive, which has the task of leading organic matter back to an inorganic state (Freud, 1920, 1950). Freud and some of his followers used the death drive to explain sadism, anorexia (an illness in which the individual does not eat and may eventually starve to death), suicide, and a variety of forms of self-destructive behavior. It would also explain daredevil behavior, in which risks are taken so frequently that death is a likely eventual outcome.

Since sexual instincts and pleasure are normally sufficient to counter the power of the death instinct, most of us are not self-destructive to any significant degree. However, we all do display signs of hastening our deaths—perhaps we desire to return to the peace of non-action—and this could best be explained as resulting from a drive toward death.

I happen to be among those who believe that the evidence for the death instinct or drive is so limited that it is not a useful concept. Since the notion of instinct or drive indicates that the feelings or reactions are unlearned and occur virtually inevitably, I find it easier to believe that the various kinds of self-destructive behavior are learned, that they arise from the social and psychological environments.

There is, nevertheless, some support for a death drive. Perhaps you have had the experience of thinking, as you rode home after a particularly satisfying and enriching evening, that that would be a good time to die, then, when everything was going well and everything seemed right. You were at peace with yourself, and you felt that you might retain that sense of peace if you could only die right then. You could explain these feelings as a death drive, but you could also explain them, as you could explain the desire to commit suicide or to risk your life, as something that you learned as the result of your years of being alive.

It has been suggested that Freud postulated *Todestrieb* because of his own great fear of death (Choron, 1964). If a death drive exists, then perhaps death is as natural or even desirable for the individual as it is for the effective operation of the evolutionary process.

All this is, of course, totally speculative, and it is unfair to question a theory by attacking the motives of the theorist. The death drive is not a core concept of psychoanalytical theory, and it is not normally assumed in other theories. However, some psychoanalytically oriented people find it useful in explaining behavior that otherwise is exceedingly difficult to explain.

UNEXPLAINABLE DEATHS

Can you wish yourself to death? If so, does your wishing or your willing make itself felt through reduced appetite, poor digestion, reduced circulation, and other direct influences on your physical organism, or does it operate in some other fashion? Is there such an event as a voodoo death? If so, what is it that causes the death? Conversely, can you wish or will yourself to remain alive, long past the time at which any knowledgeable physician would have predicted your death? If so, what are you doing to make it happen?

No question exists that competent medical, nutritional, and other health-related care can extend life expectancy. Similarly, poor medical and nutritional practices and care will reduce the life span unnecessarily. More speculative, however, is the possibility that social and psychological means can successfully influence the physical health and, therefore, the life expectancy of an individual.

PREDILECTIONS TO DEATH

We know that some people wish to die. The more formidable question is whether some people hasten their own deaths through means that are not normally termed suicides. Most people seem to accept this possibility. In our Los Angeles attitude study, we found that well over three-fourths of the 434 adult respondents agreed that "people can hasten or slow their own death through a will-to-live or a will-to-die" (Kalish & Reynolds, 1976).

Many physicians have described incidents in which patients appeared predisposed to die. One article described six persons who died during or shortly after being operated on, although each had had a good prognosis and none was considered suicidal, depressed, or anxious. Yet prior to their deaths, they were all convinced that they would die and fully accepted their impending deaths. In each instance, the death was viewed by the authors as being appropriate; that is, death appeared understandable as a solution to medical and personal problems. Such persons are said to have predilections to death (Weisman & Hackett, 1961).

Some years ago, a professor of education told me of an extremely dramatic "unexplainable" death that he felt he had inadvertently caused:

> In the early 1920s, he was a young high-school English teacher in a small rural community, whose population represented a variety of ethnic backgrounds. As a class assignment, he asked his students to write a story based on a folk legend of their particular ethnic group. One student, a girl of Portuguese background, mentioned that she knew a folk story she thought would interest him, but that she had been told a great calamity would occur to anyone who divulged the legend outside her ethnic community. The teacher finally persuaded the girl to write that story as her assignment.

> Within a very few days, the girl's fiance was brutally killed in an industrial accident. Within two months, following a lengthy period during which she steadily weakened, although she did eat fairly regularly, the girl died of no medically recognized cause.

Shneidman (1963) labels persons like this girl *Psyde-facilitators*—one of his numerous classifications of orientations to death. The Psyde-facilitator is a person who is "more-than-passively unresisting" to death when illness occurs and both psychic and physical energy is low. This definition accords with the following description, quoted from the coroner of a large city: "Every year men die after suicidal attempts when the skin has scarcely been scratched or only a few aspirin tablets have been ingested" (Richter, 1959, p. 311).

The desire to die is not always as obvious as in the above cases, and other kinds of unexplainable deaths have also been described. Reports from North Korean prisoner-of-war camps in the early 1950s told of American prisoners who died much more rapidly than the physical conditions alone warranted (Strassman, Thaler, & Schein, 1956). Viktor Frankl (1963), the existentialist writer, has pointed out that apathy, signifying perhaps a lack of meaning in life, was often predictive of death among inmates of Nazi concentration camps. Equally dramatic are the well-known descriptions of infants who died from marasmus (Ribble, 1943), a wasting illness associated with young children and not attributable to any particular known disease. The children who died had been institutionalized and not given proper loving care, although their physical needs were often met. Both the POW deaths and the marasmus deaths can be understood in the context of hopelessness and helplessness (the two frequent criteria for explicit suicides); the will to live is lost.

A psychiatrist, interested in the possible connection between intense emotional upset and sudden, unexpected death, collected 275 newspaper clippings describing such occurrences. He developed four major categories: first, the extremely traumatic disruption of an intimate relationship or the anniversary of such a loss (135 deaths); second, situations involving danger, struggle, or attack (103 deaths); third, loss of something very important, such as status, self-esteem, or highly valued property, or defeat, disappointment, or failure (21 deaths); and, fourth, a moment of triumph, public recognition, or reunion—what the author terms "happy endings" (Engel, 1977). Presumably, these persons encountered highly stressful experiences, some continuous and others sudden and unexpected, that produced physiological changes that were too great for the person's system to handle. Dr. Engel's own determination from the data he collected is that the sudden, unexpected deaths were primarily due to cardiac problems.

Perhaps the elderly are even more susceptible to death from despair and helplessness than persons in other age groups. It isn't unusual to hear an aide at a nursing home say something like "When his children didn't visit him that Christmas, he turned his face to the wall; two days later he died." Living in an institution with few pleasures makes visits and maintaining old relationships even more important than they otherwise would be; when other people no longer seem to care, the institutionalized older person just gives up on life. I don't believe that there are any good research data to prove this assumption, but people who work in these facilities frequently report such events.

VOODOO DEATHS

Voodoo deaths, hexing, and bone-pointing offer a journey into the exotic for the individual who wearies of the more mundane world in which she or he lives. In voodoo death, the person who desires the death is not the person who is to die, but someone else, perhaps an individual paid to place the hex or perhaps an individual who has cause to wish the death to occur.

Authorities are not in agreement about the effectiveness of voodoo death. One study by two psychiatrists indicated that medical authorities in communities where voodoo was freely practiced were in essential agreement that voodoo deaths did occur (Hackett & Weisman, 1961). Another physician makes the case that voodoo deaths are not psychological, but occur because the hexer actually murders the victim, often by poison, in order to collect his fee; however, he makes it appear that a spirit power caused the death (Barber, 1961).

Not all voodoo stories have unhappy endings. A professor of psychiatry observed a fascinating series of events while he was a visiting professor in a foreign country:

> A man was brought to the hospital, obviously near death and also extremely frightened. Once we ascertained that his fear was not because he was dying, but because of a curse placed on him, the head physician decided to try an experiment. He went to the medicine man and threatened him with homicide charges in the event that the patient died. Of course, this was against local law and also had no chance of succeeding in court, but the medicine man didn't know that. Although he denied any responsibility for the hex, he did agree to visit the patient in the hospital where we observed him give some message to the dying man. Within one day, the patient's condition began to improve, and within a week he was completely recovered and returned home. [M.E. Wright, personal communication].

EXPLAINING THE INEXPLICABLE

What causes unexplainable deaths? One possible answer depends upon mystical, extrasensory, or supernatural interventions. People who desire to die just . . . go ahead and die; the curse from a voodoo hex is sufficient by itself to cause death.

Another possibility, which is certainly more in keeping with most modern thinking, is that changes in living patterns lead to death. People under a curse learn about the curse and, believing in its efficacy, they become frightened; their fear then changes their eating patterns, so that their nutritional intake is reduced or they can no longer adequately digest what they do eat. At the same time, their sleep patterns are disturbed, and they become fatigued. Between the lack of adequate nutrition and the increasing fatigue, their resistance to a variety of illnesses is reduced; they easily become ill and die. The same explanation could be applied to the prison-camp deaths and even the post-operative deaths. Furthermore, many of these people have already suffered social deaths: they are isolated from persons who matter to them, and they receive no cognitive stimulation, since they do not attend to the stimulation that is available. This social pattern exacerbates their increasingly precarious health condition, and the result is organic breakdown (Kalish, 1970). Hackett and Weisman (1961) suggest that truth and mutual trust might provide a counterhex.

Another tack is to look at the studies of stress. The more stress a person encounters, the more likely that person is to suffer illness; resistance seems to reduce with stress. Certainly, prison camps and voodoo curses will cause immense stress for everyone, and certain persons perhaps are particularly susceptible to this kind of stress.

Another possibility, which does not really contradict the previous ones, is that voodoo and hex deaths are produced by strong fears that cause intense action of the sympathetic-adrenal system and a rapid fall of blood pressure (Cannon, 1942). However, one well-known study described rats that had their whiskers clipped and were then put in jars filled with water. The rats died, but their lungs contained virtually no water; rather, they apparently died of slowing of the heart (Richter, 1959). This suggests they died of despair rather than of fear. The general consensus among those who have written on this topic is that the unexplainable deaths are caused by depression, which arises from despair and helplessness.

MAGICAL NUMBERS

- I am a 42-year-old woman with two children. My parents and their parents all died before the age of 45; my older brother died at the age of 45; my father's two brothers were killed in the War, and my mother's brother died as a child; the only cousin I have who was born before I was born died at 44. The deaths in my family resulted from a variety of illnesses and accidents, so there is no particular pattern in that regard. Will I be alive for my 46th birthday?
- I am the father of three sons, the oldest of whom has just had his twelfth birthday. My father died when I was 13. Will I die when my oldest son is 13?
- Both my parents were physicians, and all my life I heard them called Dr. Albans. I always felt that if I could be Dr. Albans also, I could die happy.

> Finally, when my youngest child went into third grade, I was able to get into medical school. Next month, I will also be Dr. Albans. Will I then die?

Some of you will understand these magical numbers, while others of you will have little feeling for why they are important. It is not unusual to feel that one's life script calls for death at a particular age, based on family history or some fantasy. Do people die according to these scripts? From time to time, I have been told of someone who has, yet I also know that many people live past the age or situation they imagine calls for their death. No research has been done on this topic, and research would be extremely difficult to conduct—although investigations of the effects of anniversary reactions on other events, such as mental illness and suicide, do suggest significant influences.

Magical numbers can also work in the opposite direction.

- I was born in 1925, and I always wanted to see the new century in. I used to think that was the year 2000, but I learned some years ago that next century doesn't begin until 2001. I *must* live to see that year.
- My youngest child has always been troublesome, but I know he will settle down when he is older. I *must* live to see him settled down.
- All my life I have been fascinated by China; I have read everything possible on China, and I probably know more about it than most State Department experts. I *must* live to see China.

None of us knows how these magical numbers and events work or even if they have any effect at all. Nevertheless, they are part of our feelings and beliefs about ourselves, and if you believe—as I do—that we do have some control over how we live and when we die, then you can at least consider them as possible influences in our futures. One psychotherapist frequently asks clients in family therapy to tell her about how they see their deaths, and she states that very few adults are unable to respond. Their magical numbers influence not only the possibility of their dying, but also how they plan their lives. Those whose magical numbers call for an early death may press for early success or may decide to spend a lot of time with their families. Those who anticipate a late death or have never considered the possibility of dying (however unrealistic the latter is, many people fit the description) may plan a very different kind of life for themselves.

BENEATH THE STATISTICS

Beneath each statistic on causes of death are real people who have died in real ways. Somehow large numbers of deaths can turn the human reality of death into an abstraction. One death of one person, especially of one person who has made some impact on your own life, is very real.

Similarly, the vast arrays of numbers about causes of death can also become very real by giving some thought to what each cause of death means to the person who is dying, to the family and friends of that person, and to those who are caring for the dying person.

First, the cause of death says a great deal about the extent to which dying takes place with pain and suffering. This is not simply a matter of sudden death versus non-sudden death. It is a question of what hurts and how much it hurts, of what discomforts there may be—such as difficulty breathing, reduced ability to walk or talk, incontinence—and how long and with what intensity these discomforts endure.

Second, the probable health-care program develops directly from the cause of death. What kinds of medications are necessary, and what kinds are encouraged? What side effects, both physical and psychological, do these medications have? What kinds of care can occur at home, and what kinds require hospitalization?

Third, what is the person capable of doing during the living/dying interval? With some terminal illnesses, the individual can pursue normal tasks for an extended period of time. With other conditions, normal tasks are slowly or, sometimes, suddenly dropped behind.

Fourth, the dying person's self-concept depends to an appreciable extent on the nature of the terminal condition. With some kinds of treatment, secondary effects, such as loss of hair, chronic fatigue, or vomiting and extreme stomach upset, are common. Besides affecting behavior in the obvious ways, these affect a person's self-concept—for example, the willingness to enter into social activities and the ability to continue to view himself or herself as a normal person with normal difficulties.

Fifth, the cause of death influences the ways in which others perceive the dying person. Some people, because of their health, are immediately recognized as being very sick; others can be very sick but not have their sickness visible. Some forms of death are frightening to others: cancer is still perceived, although not always consciously, as contagious, and many people will avoid cancer patients; stroke victims who cannot speak or whose bodies are no longer under their cognitive control are also distressing to their friends and family.

And, of course, there is great variability in what happens within any single cause of death. There are many kinds of cancer, each with its own range of possible medical and psychological occurrences. The same can be said of each kind of illness or other death-causing condition.

Thus, all deaths, regardless of cause, have certain qualities in common; deaths from the same cause have additional qualities in common. And, at the same time, among persons dying from a particular cause, there is a great range of possible health-related and behavioral kinds of responses, feelings, and events.

9

BEGINNINGS AND AWARENESS

The concept of dying differs considerably from the concept of death, but, because they share so many concerns, neither can be discussed for any length without reference to the other. Previous chapters in this book have dealt with aspects of dying, although the chapters may have been focused on death: *dying* was defined and the "living-dying interval" discussed in Chapter 2; the fears and anxieties associated with death, described in Chapter 5, inevitably touched on the fears and anxieties of dying; the meanings of death and of facing death examined in Chapter 3, are inextricably bound up with the meanings of dying.

Therefore, as I discuss the process of dying, some of the words may be familiar because you have read them before, but it seems appropriate to reintroduce the ideas in this context.

HOW DYING OCCURS

"While we can readily claim that dying is a process that is fully as complicated as living, because it *is* a part of living, to say that people die as they have lived is from a psychological viewpoint wholly meaningless" (Weisman, 1972, p. 122). Throughout our lives, our behavior shows reasonable consistency so that it is moderately predictable; and throughout our lives, our behavior shows reasonable inconsistency, so that it is moderately unpredictable. As with any kind of behavior, our dying process is both consistent and inconsistent with our previous behavior.

One factor that influences how we die is often ignored, although it is overwhelmingly important: what we die from. Death can occur through a lengthy illness or a sudden illness, through a condition that enables us to continue to function or one that reduces our functioning greatly, through so-called "natural causes" or through accidents or suicide, through a painful condition or through a relatively painless condition. I might fare amazingly well after a sudden coronary—pick up the pieces of my life when I leave the hospital and reengage in my previous activities until a subsequent heart attack causes my death two years later—but I might fall apart in the face of a disease that is progressively crippling. You, on the other hand, show tremendous spirit with your crippling illness, but you could not handle the anxiety of knowing that a sudden second heart attack could strike without warning. The truth is, perhaps surprisingly, that we have almost no information on how or even whether different kinds of people cope with some kinds of deaths better or less well than with other kinds. However, there are numerous writings concerning the psychosocial factors that surround the specific conditions that cause death. These range from a description of the fourteenth-century plague, the Black Death, that wiped out at least one-fourth of the population of Europe (Langer, 1964), to a brief paper describing the conditions under which 51 infants were dying from hyaline membrane disease (Morgan, Buchanan, & Abram, 1976), to a sophisticated study on the psychosocial components of cancer deaths (Weisman & Worden, 1975).

THE DYING TRAJECTORY

Claudia Teder was diagnosed as having terminal cancer when she was 48 years old; her prognosis, assuming that she underwent radiation treatment, was for a probable life expectancy of eight to ten months, and she was told that she would probably spend the last three or four weeks in the hospital. After two treatments, she decided to discontinue the program; she returned to work, remained home with her husband and son, and was found dead one Sunday morning about a year later after a party.

Ed Briscoe had a heart attack at 41 and another at 51; following each of these, he returned to almost full activity. His third attack, at age 58, came without additional warning, and he died before the ambulance arrived.

Harvey Muller, a 33-year-old policeman, was called to break up a fight between a husband and wife. As he arrived at the scene, the wife yelled at him to leave; he didn't, and she shot him through the head. He died immediately.

Laurene Marks reached her 80th birthday in good health, but shortly thereafter she complained about not feeling well. The subsequent diagnosis was cancer; because of her age, she and the physician agreed not to attempt an operation. She then accepted a modified treatment program. Her health deteriorated very slowly, and she remained active for two more years, then house-bound for another six months. Finally, just before her 83rd birthday, she died in the hospital.

The dying process of each of these four persons could be charted across time. Set up a graph with *time* along the horizontal axis, and *nearness to death* along the vertical axis. Then chart each of these person's conditions across time. This is known as the dying trajectory (Glaser & Strauss, 1968).

The purpose of understanding the dying trajectory is most certainly not that of playing statistical games with people's lives. Glaser and Strauss point out that people who are dying, their family members and friends, and the relevant health professionals anticipate the dying trajectory of the ill and make their plans around it. Work associates, political supporters, or more casual friends might also wish to understand the death trajectory: how long will the dying person remain alive, in reasonable health, able to care for himself or herself; how is the death most likely to occur; how probable is the death to occur as predicted?

When the trajectory is as anticipated, the various participants in the process are prepared, both psychologically and in terms of providing care, for what occurs. When the assumed trajectory does not take place, people, left unprepared, experience additional dismay and stress—even though the dying person might be living a longer and healthier life than was anticipated (Glaser & Strauss, 1968). There is also the possibility that either a patient's acceptance of a physician's projected dying trajectory or a patient's own fantasized trajectory will become a self-fulfilling prophecy. The expectations that others have of us are powerful forces in molding our behavior and attitudes; perhaps these expectations can influence the duration of the living-dying interval as well.

Sometimes, of course, the dying person and those in her or his environment will anticipate differing trajectories. For example, the terminal patient may assume that death will come in about two or three years after a lengthy period of mild discomfort; the medical staff may believe that death is much more imminent and that the discomfort will be much more acute. These differing perceptions can lead to a range of problems: the patient may be unwilling to follow a particular treatment program or he or she may feel betrayed by and angry with the health professionals when (and if) they are found to be correct. Ironically, when the patient far outlives the prognosis of the physicians, it is not unusual for the latter to be upset, irritated, or embarrassed, even though they may be pleased for the patient's sake. After all, none of us likes to be in substantial error in matters that involve our presumed competence.

Since most deaths in the United States and Canada are not caused by those respiratory ailments that used to affect people of all ages, but by chronic degenerative diseases which affect primarily the elderly, the nature of the dying process and, therefore, the care of the dying have changed over the decades. For example, some forms of cancer lead to a living-dying interval of several years, during much of which time the patient can go about his or her everyday tasks as before; dying from a stroke may also permit a lengthy living-dying interval, although many stroke deaths occur very quickly. However, dying from influenza or pneumonia normally describes a dying trajectory of two or three weeks to six or eight weeks, during which time the patient remains too sick to participate in normal activities.

DEATHS SUDDEN AND NOT SUDDEN, EXPECTED AND NOT EXPECTED

The commonly accepted ideal death, if there is one, would be a healthy 85-year-old's dying suddenly of a heart attack that has occurred without causing pain. The trajectory is like half a rectangle: a straight line across time drops immediately to the baseline at age 85. When asked which was more tragic, a sudden death or a slow death, half again as many people thought the latter was worse, although the differences diminished greatly with the age of the respondent (Kalish & Reynolds, 1976).

Believing that a sudden death is preferable is partly based on the assumption that there is less pain in a sudden death. Also, because sudden deaths are often unexpected, a person is spared most of the anxiety and stress that develop from anticipating death. Even when sudden death can be anticipated—for example by a coronary patient—the elimination of a long living-dying interval is often desired.

Deaths that are slow need not also be painful, either for the dying person or for family members. Sometimes, of course, the pain, both physical and emotional, is immense, and there is no real escape. "There is the slow, inexorable debilitation of a chronic illness or traumatic injury. . . . [The process] is worsened by . . . being forced to watch the disintegration and loss of the image of the loved one as he slowly dies" (Paulay, 1977–78, p. 173). This is the kind of death that we all fear.

The sudden-death trajectory, however, has many problems that are often ignored. It may be a cruel death for the survivors. Although they are spared the anguish of caring for the dying person, they are also prevented from preparing themselves for the death. The shock can be immense, since there has been no opportunity to become accustomed to the idea that the person is going to die. Denial is probably greater for the survivors of a sudden, unexpected death.

Also, frequently there is unfinished business, especially if the dead person is not yet elderly. Perhaps arrangements for dying have not been made: there is no will; no one knows where the key to the safe deposit box is; bank books are scattered about the house and office; many tasks related to business or family or household matters are still up in the air. And, even more important, there is often unfinished personal business: good-byes are not possible, old angers cannot be salved, unexpressed feelings can never be expressed. The survivors also have been cut off from doing the things they had planned to do and saying the things they had always planned to say.

Deaths from accidents, suicides, homicides, and natural disasters are often sudden and unexpected, although sometimes the victim holds onto life for weeks, months, or even longer. Although these deaths usually are sudden, they are frequently regarded as particularly tragic or unpleasant for several reasons: they are mutilating; they often occur to people who are young or who are seen as dying prematurely; and they are often seemingly unnecessary or absurd.

The family members of these victims are frequently concerned with the possibility that they have some kind of responsibility for the death. "I knew she was depressed, but I didn't think she would do this!" "I tried to tell him not to drive home when he was tired." "I did my best to keep him away from those people." "I just had the feeling that she shouldn't have gone to work—there was something in the air."

INFLUENCING THE TRAJECTORY

Many factors besides the nature of the health condition itself influence the course of the dying trajectory. Moreover, even the "nature" of the health condition itself isn't inevitable and unchangeable—a condition forced upon a passive organism by some all-powerful, external source.

Some of the influences are obvious: the previous health of the individual, the extent of medical care, the nutrition—the usual considerations that facilitate good health in some individuals and less adequate health in others. In addition, misdiagnosis and inappropriate health care and personal care can shorten the life expectancy and, therefore, change the shape of the trajectory.

Undoubtedly the will to live and the will to die also influence the dying trajectory:

> One young man, recently a father, was told directly that his physical condition offered no hope of living more than a few additional months. Ten years and many operations later, he explained his pulling through as due to his intense desire to know his child.

Sometimes the will to live may be successful only for a brief period:

> The mother of a law student had an extremely serious heart attack two weeks before her daughter was to take the bar exam; the young woman telephoned the hospital (it was in a city 1500 miles away) each day to learn that her mother was still alive and would apparently live another day. The woman took the exam, then flew to see her mother, who died the day she arrived. When she was telling me about the experience, the lawyer felt certain that her mother willed herself to stay alive until the exam was over—knowing that, had she died sooner, her daughter would have come to her funeral rather than have taken the bar exam.

There's no way, with our present knowledge, to "prove" that the young man lived because he wanted to know his child or that the older woman held on to help her daughter through the exam period. After all, others have had equal reason to continue to live but haven't succeeded. Perhaps I believe these stories because I want to believe them. I don't know.

Some evidence suggests that the extent to which people are in control of their environments and their selves is a major factor in their will to live and in how long they live. Recall that hopelessness and helplessness are often proposed as the feelings that precipitate suicide. It would seem quite possible that the same feelings would lead to premature death, which can be interpreted as a kind of suicide or self-destructiveness.

The term *learned helplessness* is used to refer to an emotion and related behavior that occur when people believe that there is nothing they can do to avoid punishment or to obtain satisfaction. Such individuals anticipate that, no matter what they do, the situation will not change. This condition can readily lead to depression. Robert Kastenbaum, a highly creative scholar whose work on death dates back over 20 years, and his wife, Beatrice (1971), have suggested the concept of learned *hopelessness,* in which people come to have little faith in the possibility of the system ever changing. It is to avoid these feelings of helplessness and hopelessness that many physicians prefer that their patients not learn that they are terminally ill. They believe that after hope dies, the patient dies.

How can learned helplessness and hopelessness be reversed? I would suggest, based on my reading and experience, that these feelings are produced not from a lack of knowledge that you will die, but from an inability to make relevant decisions or remain in control of your behavior and functioning. Therefore, it would seem very possible that an accurate knowledge of the significance of your health condition would enable you to feel less helpless, especially if you are brought into the decision-making process.

Also influencing your dying trajectory are your personality and your social relationships. One very significant and sophisticated study developed an approach, based on careful analysis of the patient's health in relationship to the extensive statistics available on cancer patients to determine the probable life expectancy of different cancer patients. The authors then monitored the patients to see whether they lived longer or died sooner than expected. Their conclusions were intriguing:

> *Longer survivals* are associated with patients who have good relationships with others and who manage to preserve a reasonable degree of intimacy with family and friends until the very last. They ask for and receive much medical and emotional support. As a rule, they accept the reality of serious illness, but still do not believe that death is inevitable. . . . They are seldom deeply depressed but may voice resentment about various aspects of their treatment and illness. Whatever anger is displayed . . . does not alienate others but commands their attention. They may be afraid of dying alone and untended, so they refuse to let others pull away without taking care of their needs.
>
> *Shorter survivals* occur in patients who report poor social relationships, starting with early separations from their family of origin, and continuing

Theodore Lownik Library
Illinois Benedictine College
Illinois 60532

> throughout life. Sometimes they have diagnosed psychiatric disorders, but almost as often talk about repeated mutually destructive relationships with people through the years. At times, they have considered suicide. Now, when treatment fails, depression deepens, and they become highly pessimistic. . . . They want to die—a finding that often reflects more conflict than acceptance. [Weisman & Worden, 1975, p. 71]

A recent article in *Science* began by describing numerous studies that seemed to show a connection between expressing anger "toward not only their disease but their doctors" (Holden, 1978, p. 1364) and living longer, as well as between denial, repression, despair, and limited supportive relationships and living more briefly. The author presented alternative physiological and biochemical explanations of how these correlations might be effected—giving full consideration to the possibility of the placebo effect. She also explored the alternative that the research was faulty and that, in fact, there are no psychological or social predictors of cancer or cancer deaths. Her overall evidence, however, appeared to support the idea that life expectancy is affected by these psychosocial variables (Holden, 1978).

More recently, a study of women dying of breast cancer confirmed these results. Those who lived longest not only were more demanding of their physicians and less satisfied with their treatment, but also were rated as less well-adjusted, more anxious, and more hostile (Derogatis, Abeloff, & Melisaratos, 1979).

Leo Durocher, the well-known baseball player and manager, once stated that "nice guys finish last." Apparently "nice guys" die first, since those who live longer appear to be able to ask for help, to make demands, and to express resentment, *but* they do it in a way that "does not alienate others but commands their attention." Most probably, people who are too "nice" don't make the demands on others that they really require to have their health needs satisfied; at the same time, some people who seem "nice" are probably depressed and suppressing their underlying anger.

DYING BEGINS

Dying begins. For me, my dying begins when I learn that I have a condition that will eventually cause my death. For you, my dying begins when you learn that I have this condition. For the physician or for others, my dying starts when they learn that I have this condition. In an objective sense, my dying occurs at the time that the condition causing my death becomes irreversible—regardless of whether anyone knew it or not.

MY DYING BEGINS FOR ME

Some people never learn that they are dying. They are homicide or accident victims; they die from an initial massive coronary; they die from a progressive disease that has been misdiagnosed; or they have been sufficiently sheltered from knowledge of their real condition so that death is not anticipated. By the time they die, however, most people undoubtedly know what is happening. Many people have figured out that they are going to die about the same time the physician comes to that conclusion, and some certainly realize it even before the physician does.

Given the many ways of learning that you are dying, how many people die without knowing what's happening? The answer is, as best we can tell, not very many. In our Los Angeles study of 434 adults, over 80% answered yes to the question "Do you think a person dying of cancer probably senses he's dying anyway, without being told?" Interestingly enough, 20% of the men, but only 7% of the women, responded negatively to this item (Kalish & Reynolds, 1976).

Studies conducted with dying patients also indicate that most are aware. One investigator, using careful personal observations, noted that nearly half of the patients diagnosed as terminally ill overtly mentioned being aware of their prognosis; another sizable group avoided speaking of their future or used only vague terms. Only 5% appeared confident of recovery and 8% hoped for partial recovery (Hinton, 1972). Kübler-Ross (1970) reports that only three out of 200 dying persons were unaware of their true state at the end of their lives.

One large British research project interviewed the next of kin of several hundred persons who had died fairly recently. It found that numerous factors contributed to the awareness that the dying person and the next of kin had of the imminence of death. For example, a diagnosis of terminal cancer was more easily kept from a patient than other diagnoses, and the longer the individual was bedridden, the higher the probability that the patient and the next of kin knew of the prognosis (Cartwright, Hockey, & Anderson, 1973).

Similarly, physicians, when asked which patients they would inform that they were dying, were much more likely to tell a 55-year-old businessman of the nature of his condition than a 35-year-old mother of young children who did not seem aware of her death—although the doctors agreed almost unanimously that they would tell the woman's husband. If an elderly widower asked "This won't kill me, doctor, will it?", most doctors said they would deny to the patient that he was dying or else pass off his remark as a joke (Cartwright et al. 1973).

These findings point up the impossibility of responding to the question "Do people know when they are dying?" without some indication of the person's position on the dying trajectory. The closer to death someone is, the more likely that person is to be aware of her condition. It is similarly difficult to say when in the living-dying interval people should be told they are dying. You might contend that such knowledge needs to be provided as soon as the physician can make a diagnosis, or you might believe that a dying person need not be informed until his condition interferes with normal functioning, or until hospitalization is required, or until shortly before the death, or. . . .

In spite of all the ways in which people can learn that they are dying, we don't really know how most people do, in fact, learn. This is an obvious area for research, but working out a procedure to conduct the research will be exceedingly difficult. We might well find that the individual comes to this understanding only through a combination of sources and a period during which the initial hypothesis "I am dying" is tested out.

Another interesting point is just when do I define myself as dying (Kastenbaum, 1977)? To some extent, this occurs when I give up hope, but the situation is more complex. I can know that I will never recover from an illness, yet still not define myself as dying. Perhaps I will hold off from admitting that I'm dying until my activities are restricted or until I'm hospitalized or until my anxiety builds up. I am not denying my condition, but I am denying the "objective" definition of it. Once I define myself as dying or once you define me as dying, our perceptions are altered; these alterations are likely to influence our behavior, and these behavior changes, in turn, may influence my death trajectory. Your defining me as dying before I accept the definition may lead to some tension between us. It is like the story of the patient who is recovering from surgery but whose physician informs the patient's family that she has died. As the physician leaves the room, the woman raises herself onto her elbows and begins to protest, but her husband gently guides her back to a lying position: "Please dear, the physician knows best." Physicians are not beyond error, and they can misperceive a patient's condition or will to live. If you try to move me out of life before I am ready, I may submissively accept your definition of me, but I may also reject it and become angry with you.

LEARNING I'M DYING

How do I learn I am dying? The ways are numerous.

1. *Directly from a health professional*. Most frequently the physician will inform the patient of the prognosis, although how the doctor communicates the news will vary. The doctor may be gentle or abrupt, lengthy or brief, encouraging of questions and expressions of feeling or not. When the physician tells me that I am dying, I may not incorporate what I'm told. Perhaps the awareness will surface later or perhaps I will need to "learn" that I'm dying in another way—at a later time or in a less threatening setting. Occasionally the dying person learns from another health professional, perhaps a nurse or the hospital chaplain, but this is much less common.

2. *Indirectly from a health professional*. Standing outside the hospital room, the physician and the family members are discussing the person who is dying a few feet away from their conversation. Of course they talk only in whispers, but the sounds frequently carry amazingly well. At the end of the conversation, they enter the room in forced jovial spirits to offer encouragement to the patient. One older woman dying of cancer told her one confidante, her son, that "whenever I close my eyes, the nurse and my children seem to assume that I'm unable to hear anything."

3. *Directly or indirectly from people other than health professionals*. Family members and, very occasionally, friends will directly inform a patient of the prognosis. Also common, I believe, is the kind of indirect informing process described above. Once in a great while, another patient provides the information, usually inadvertently.

4. *Changes in the behavior of others*. The anecdote that best exemplifies this describes the ill man who, each morning, asked his nurse "How am I today, nurse?" And each morning the woman answered "You're fine—you'll be out of here in no time." Finally, one morning, the nurse read on the patient's chart that he was getting worse and probably terminally ill. The patient again asked "How am I today, nurse?" And she answered, "I'm sorry, but we're not allowed to give out that information. You will have to ask your physician."

Other changes in the behavior of friends, family members, and hospital staff also provide clues. Visits either increase or decrease noticeably; a brother from 1500 miles away "just happens" to have a business trip to the area and stops in; people who had been cheerful before suddenly seem to have been crying a great deal; conversation becomes stilted; planning for the summer vacation receives no response; the chaplain comes in to talk about religious views and immortality; body language and voices either become tense or show obviously false attempts at being casual and relaxed.

5. *Changes in medical care procedures*. Sometimes a significant change in medical-care procedures implies that the prognosis has also changed. For example, if planned surgery is cancelled, does that mean that you don't need the surgery because you'll get well without it—or that you're beyond the help of surgery? You're being sent to a room with a much sicker roommate: does that mean that you're also much sicker? The physician doesn't visit you as often; you're given sedatives more freely; a new physician has appeared and seems to be taking over from your personal physician. As you consider each of these stages, you will realize that they must be interpreted, since none of them is very clear in meaning. That's exactly the difficulty: a hospital patient is often not told, and, when told, not always honestly, the meaning of what's going on. Therefore, the patient is free to project the greatest hopes or wildest fears.

6. *Self-diagnosis*. Many patients read and talk to others a great deal about their own condition. In a melange of confusion, ignorance, and distortion there often is a fair amount of valid understanding. And even if the self-diagnosis is inaccurate, the degree to which the person accepts it and acts accordingly is extremely important. One young woman whose terminal diagnosis had been withheld from her learned it from an article describing her symptoms in *Reader's Digest.*

Part of self-diagnosis inevitably comes from the signals within the body. Pain and discomfort increase; psychomotor functioning diminishes; sedatives must become stronger in order to work properly. The fatally ill person often senses the changes within his or her own body and recognizes the future is brief.

In a Finnish study, 100 cancer patients were interviewed about their illness; in addition, their case records were examined and their physicians and appropriate nurses were also interviewed. The investigators determined that in 40% of the cases, the diagnosis had been spontaneously revealed to the patient by the physician; although almost all of these admitted to fear and anxiety on hearing the diagnosis, a great majority appeared satisfied with having been told with such frankness. Another 29% were told their diagnosis in response to direct questions, and they were unanimous in approving their physician's openness. An additional 6% had not asked the physician nor been told, but knew that they had cancer. The remaining 24% (the status of one patient could not be determined) had not asked their physician about their illness, had not been informed by the physician, and presumably did not know its nature, although some were aware that they had some form of tumor (Achté & Vauhkonen, 1971). These figures would obviously differ in different facilities and with different kinds of illnesses, but they present at least some initial data.

AWARENESS CONTEXTS

For some people, of course, awareness is irrelevant: people who die suddenly and unexpectedly; those who are confused or comatose; those whose conditions don't offer obvious cues and whose family and health caretakers can actually isolate them from knowing; those who are too young or severely retarded. But for most people, there is a period during which they can grasp the idea that the prognosis is or may be terminal.

In one of the first books of the "death awareness" movement, two medical sociologists (Glaser and Strauss, 1965) described the results of their intensive studies of death-awareness contexts. Their work has really not been improved upon since. The contexts that they described were *closed awareness, suspicion awareness, mutual pretense,* and *open awareness.*

CLOSED AWARENESS CONTEXT

Often an attempt is made to keep the patient from knowing of the terminal diagnosis. In some instances, the physician enters into a conspiracy with family members to withhold the information; occasionally he or she acts without talking to the family, or there are no family members to involve. Of course, the closer the individual is to death, the more likely he or she is to be aware that death is imminent. The communications from others, the signals from within the body, and the changing medical-care procedures become much too clear to ignore or deny.

Glaser and Strauss offer five reasons that contribute to the existence of the closed-awareness context. First, most persons lack the experience to recognize the signs of impending death. Second, physicians often do not inform patients directly of their terminal condition. Third, family members also find reasons to keep the prognosis secret. Fourth, "hospitals are admirably arranged, both by accident and by design, to hide medical information from patients" (1965, p. 31). Fifth, the patient normally has no "allies" that serve as advocates to obtain or transmit the information.

The task of keeping patients from learning they are going to die is immense. The staff, sometimes in conjunction with the family, need to develop a fictional future biography for the patient and must simultaneously engage the patient's trust while they are, in fact, lying (Glaser & Strauss, 1965). Everyone then enters into the game—except that the patient doesn't know it's a game. Over a period of time, of course, the fictional future biography must be revised. Frequently, the patient eventually learns that the biography is inaccurate; the patient may also learn that the biography was a lie from the start, and this knowledge may well mar future relationships between the patient and those who had participated in the deceit.

> Jack Kaplan was diagnosed as having terminal intestinal cancer and was expected to live 10–12 months. The course of his illness was such that while he had to remain home and would be in increasing pain and discomfort, he would be able to do a lot of things around the house. Since he was still a relatively young man, not quite 40, and had two elementary-school-age children, his wife and his physician decided not to say anything about his prognosis until the illness became incapacitating. Nor were the children informed, except to be told that their father had a serious illness and might not get better for at least a year.
>
> Jack accepted their story, went faithfully for his treatments, which were not fully explained to him, and remained optimistic about recovery. As time went on and his condition worsened, he became anxious and began to question his wife about his health. In order to maintain the conspiracy of silence, she avoided his questions, but this merely served to increase his anxiety and his questioning. His wife found it so difficult to be with him that she began to avoid him, which again made Jack more anxious and also angry. Some arguments began, and Jack even suggested marriage counseling, which, when his wife rejected the idea, increased his anger.
>
> Talks with the physician were no more helpful, since, although he was reassuring, he also began to avoid Jack. Jack became depressed and began to retreat from both his family and the physician. After about seven months, his condition worsened and he was taken to the hospital where he went downhill extremely quickly and died three days later without having regained consciousness.
>
> Jack's wife was extremely angry with the physician and blamed him for not telling Jack or having her tell Jack the truth. The physician was told about her anger and insisted that not informing Jack had been her idea. Mrs. Kaplan was depressed for many months after her husband's death and never forgave the doctor.
>
> The core of Emily Kaplan's anger did not arise from her husband's medical treatment or even his rapid decline, since she never considered the possibility that his anxiety and depression might have hastened his death. Her

> own words express her feelings best: "I had only a few months left with Jack, and we could have made those good months. We could have been close and talked and had some good times with the kids. We could even have planned the children's future. Instead, I ended up cut off from my husband, and he died furious with me. My children will remember their father as an angry man instead of a loving man, and they may think of me as a distant wife instead of the loving wife I was."

This anecdote was selected to prove my point. Not all closed awareness situations turn out this badly. In some instances, the dying person and others can communicate easily and warmly, while avoiding thoughts of the horse on the dining-room table. But often they can't. And, after all, as a friend said to me some years ago "It's my life and my death and my suffering, and it's not up to the physician or even to my husband to decide whether or not I want to know about dying. If I don't want to know, I'll find some way to tell them. Their task is to be competent, loving, and honest, not over-protective and deceitful."

Occasionally the closed awareness cuts in the other direction: the dying person, perhaps in collusion with family members, purposely does not give information to the physician. Family members often try their best to persuade the patient to seek medical help, but the dying person remains adamant (Cartwright, Hockey, & Anderson, 1973).

SUSPICION AWARENESS CONTEXT

When the clues become too strong to overlook, a patient may become suspicious that her condition is more serious than she had been told. Then a sparring match may begin. The patient tries to find out how sick she is, while simultaneously not wishing to find out that death is predicted. Sometimes the patient barricades herself against the ultimate knowledge by trying to get information first from people who are less official and whose judgments are less "final"—for example, first from an aide or chaplain, then from a nurse, and finally, if all the others imply that she is dying, from the physician.

When the health caretakers and the family are conspiring to keep the patient from learning the truth, the patient still has some options to gain information. The most obvious is to ask a direct question—with the expectation, not of being told the truth, but of finding clues to the truth in the voice and body language of the person queried (Glaser & Strauss, 1965). Another possibility is for a patient to tell his physician or spouse that he is dying and then wait to see the response. A third is to press for information about the future and also about the illness and to watch both explicit statements and what is not made explicit.

In response to the third approach the staff may try to be as honest as possible without telling the patient the truth. They may deflect questions by saying "We're all dying," or "This treatment is taking a little longer than we had hoped, but you'll be all right," or "You're going to get worse before you get better." (This latter statement was described to me by Dr. Avery Weisman, a psychoanalyst whose contributions to working with the dying are outstanding, as a particularly clever and also particularly dishonest approach. It has the effect of predicting all possibilities and, when believed, will encourage the patient to stop asking questions.)

Why are so many people reluctant to let a dying person know his prognosis? Many physicians and others claim that people give up hope when they learn they are going to die and that this loss of hope will make their final living-dying interval miserable and may actually hasten their death. Such knowledge is often claimed to precipitate "going to pieces" or becoming virtually psychotic. Also, the time of death, and even the inevitability of death, is rarely 100% predictable. Therefore, to tell someone she is dying when there is even the slightest chance for changing the direction of the trajectory is seen as being unfair or dishonest. In addition, both family members and health caretakers are often uncomfortable in confronting the deaths of others. In order to avoid their own pain and sense of failure, they try to create a situation in which the imminence of death can be ignored.

MUTUAL PRETENSE CONTEXT

Not infrequently both the patient and others in the social environment know that the patient is dying, but they pretend otherwise (Glaser & Strauss, 1965). Since the patient and the hospital staff are part of one system and the patient and his or her family are part of another system, the patient often maintains mutual pretense in both systems. Sometimes the mutual pretense is only with the family; it may be part of a conspiracy between the patient and the hospital to keep the family from knowing what is taking place.

Again a kind of game is established. Perhaps the patient has indicated unwillingness to talk about death; perhaps the staff has made apparent its reluctance to be open about the diagnosis. In either event, both parties agree to a set of implicit rules, based on not making the dying circumstances explicit. Although no research is available, my observations are that the desire to play the game comes most often from the staff, who parry questions from the patient in such ways as to communicate their desire to avoid discussion of the approaching death.

The staff—excluding the physician—might respond to my comment by reminding me that it is the physician's task to inform the patient and the family and not normally the staff's prerogative. They would be correct. Informally, nurses can find a way to communicate to a patient. Increasingly, nurses are doing so formally, but tradition and many hospital regulations leave it to the physician. In fact, about three-fourths of the respondents in one study stated that it was the responsibility of the physician to inform the dying person; only one respondent in six designated a family member (Kalish & Reynolds, 1976). With the present realities of the patient/health-care-staff system, it seems that breaking through the mutual pretense will need to be the responsibility either of the physician or of others who will put pressure on the physician to delegate this aspect of the traditional medical role.

One additional difficulty inherent in mutual pretense is that each party to the game only assumes that the other party knows. While, in fact, the patient may be suspicious, but not certain, of a diagnosis, the communication pattern established between him and the hospital may assume the patient's equal knowledge. Or, conversely, the patient may have come to believe that death is a certainty, while the truth is that the condition can be alleviated. Patients may misinterpret the numerous cues into a terminal diagnosis, then, feeling cut off from honest responses from both family and medical staff, they become anxious and depressed. Their anxieties and mistrust may even cause them to ignore the signs that signify that they are healthy and attend only to what reinforces their belief that they are dying.

When the mutual pretense game is played with family members, it often reduces the amount of support and care that would otherwise be possible. Both the dying person and family members have the "horse on the dining-room table" all the time, but their inability or unwillingness to discuss the horse leaves them limited to matters that may not be as important. This is exacerbated by the family's inability to know for certain exactly what the patient does know. They, therefore, don't really know whether the patient is fully aware of her condition or whether her avoidance of the topic is an attempt to protect them, while they are doing their best to protect her.

Mutual pretense may have advantages for friends and family who are not extremely close to the dying person. There is no need for people who have never had a close relationship to the dying person to begin to talk with her about death (Glaser & Strauss, 1965). However, for those who have intimate relationships, mutual pretense can provide extreme stress.

OPEN AWARENESS

Most people agree that the optimum situation is when the dying person knows he is dying, others in his environment know he is dying, and they can relate to each other through this knowledge. Studies consistently show that people believe a dying person has a right to know; the same studies also show that each individual is very likely to wish to be informed himself. Thus in the Los Angeles study, a substantial majority of all four ethnic groups (Black, Japanese American, Mexican American, and Anglo-American) felt that dying persons, in general, deserved to learn their prognosis, while an even more substantial majority of each group wished themselves to be informed. Apparently we are more confident of our own strength than of the strength of others (Kalish & Reynolds, 1976).

The majority of research and opinion articles also support the right of the dying person to be informed (Koenig, 1969).

How is the dying person to be informed? To some extent, the answers are obvious: with gentleness, with tact, with honesty. But there are further considerations. Avery Weisman (1972) suggests that when a patient asks whether she is going to die, she may really be asking her physician (or nurse or spouse) not to abandon her. It isn't necessary to sit down as soon as the terminal diagnosis is evident and present all the information directly. This can even be a cold way of doing it, a way to say to the patient "Here, I've done everything I can for you. Now you can go off and die and don't bother me."

Instead, the physician can tell the patient enough to enable the patient to ask direct questions that would lead to a full diagnosis and prognosis. That is, the doctor may say something like "From what the tests show, your condition is extremely serious." Or "It appears that you have a malignancy." The words, of course, should not be too technical for the patient to grasp. Armed with this information, the patient may probe for elaboration and clarification, and the physician should normally respond to each question honestly and without avoiding the intent of the patient's question.

Frequently the patient will not press for complete information during the first discussion with the physician. It might be enough for her to know that her condition is "extremely serious" or that she has a malignancy. Her concern may then be to know what treatment is recommended or whether she will be suffering pain. It may take a week or more to digest the meaning of this intrusion into her life. Only at the next visit with the physician will she ask more about what will happen. If the doctor hasn't put her off, the patient will feel free to ask more when she is ready.

Sometimes patients are given full information before they are ready, because no one, including physicians, can always understand the level of a patient's readiness to hear without denial. Many physicians have reported patients, who had been fully informed, returning two weeks later asking why they were losing weight or having pain, and then becoming angry that the physician hadn't told them the severity of their condition the first time—even though they had been told.

In spite of these problems, the open-awareness context provides many advantages to the dying person, to family members and friends, and to the health caretakers:

- "the patient [has] an opportunity to close his life in accordance with his own ideas about proper dying" (Glaser & Strauss, 1965, p. 103);
- the dying person is often able to complete some plans and projects, to make arrangements for survivors, and to participate in decisions concerning funeral and burial;
- there is the opportunity to reminisce, to talk with people who have been important, to end life conscious of what life has been;

- open awareness permits greater understanding of what is going on within his body and of what the medical staff members are doing to him.

All in all, it is easier to die when people you love and care for can talk with you freely about what is taking place, even if there is a great deal of pain and sadness in the discussions. Family members can show their grief openly, and love can be expressed openly, since it is amazing how often we neglect to tell those we love most how much we love them. Somehow, in the face of death, telling them that we love them becomes easier.

> My 81-year-old aunt was extremely ill and had been for two years; the indications were that she would probably not live for many more weeks. My home was 800 miles away, but I was able to get to visit her and my uncle for a couple of days. It bothered me to see her hooked into a machine that held her life; the ugly wig she had worn during the past couple of years had been discarded, and there were only a few wisps of hair left, but at least they were hers; her teeth had been placed in the drawer by her bed since she couldn't take solid food, and at this point she was not concerned about how she looked.
>
> My uncle and I were in her room, talking with her as she moved in and out of awareness. He was standing at the foot of the bed, and I was sitting next to her, holding her hand. He began to talk to her about coming to visit me, as soon as she could get up and around again, probably next summer. I noticed that she tuned his comments out. Then I found a pretext to get him out of the room.
>
> When we were alone, I stood up and kissed her. I'd like to say that it was easy, but it really wasn't. I told her that I loved her, and I realized that I had never said that to her before, hadn't even thought about it, hadn't even consciously thought that I loved her. I just . . . loved her.
>
> Then I said, "Bea, I have to leave now. I may never see you again, and I want you to know how much I love you." Her eyes were closed and she was breathing strangely, but she winced at my words, and I became frightened that I'd said too much, so I hesitated. "Well, I hope that I'll see you again, but I might not." And I left.
>
> She died before I could visit again, and I always wondered whether I should have said what I did, but it seemed important to say it. Even if it pained her to hear me, she knew it was true, and she had not shrunk from painful situations before. It had been easy for me over many years to talk and write about death and dying, but it was very difficult for me to be in the situation where someone I loved was dying. I did what I have told other people to do, and it wasn't at all natural—I had to force myself. But when I heard, three weeks later, that she had died, I considered myself fortunate to have had the chance to be with her before she died and to have been both caring and honest.

In some ways, open awareness makes dying more troubled. The patient may ask in anguish "Why me?" He may need to make some decisions about his own future in terms of following treatment plans; she may find that other people feel her pain so deeply that they cannot be with her.

It isn't that "good people" advocate open awareness and the inept or frightened or rigid counsel pretense or closed awareness. I can only say that both my own observations and those of people I most trust advocate open awareness for most patients under most conditions. Inevitably, each individual must be considered according to his or her unique self and situation.

MIDDLE KNOWLEDGE

"Somewhere between open knowledge of death and its utter repudiation is an area of uncertain certainty called 'middle knowledge' " (Weisman, 1972, p. 65). Like many powerful feelings, those feelings that say "I am dying" are not immediately integrated into our selves. We vascillate between accepting and denying, between full awareness and believing it can't possibly be. Not to me. "Patients seem to know and want to know, yet they often talk as if they did not know and did not want to be reminded of what they have been told" (Weisman, 1972, p. 66).

Weisman is making the point that awareness is not an all-or-none concept. We are aware and not aware. Recall your last exam or job interview or the last occasion in which you believed you were entering a committed intimate relationship. Did you feel, as you left the exam room, the interviewer's desk, or your "intimate's" presence, that things were settled? Probably not. If your experience was like the experiences of most of us, you had moments when you felt the job was yours, moments when you felt that you really did poorly, and moments when you told yourself it didn't really matter. You weave in and out of certainty. And this middle knowledge is what people often feel regarding their deaths.

As time goes on, living with the awareness of death may become easier, although we don't know for certain. Weisman (1972) believes that middle knowledge is especially likely to occur at certain significant transition points, like setbacks or sudden losses of capacity.

The topic of awareness contexts and communicating with the dying will recur frequently in this book. It remains one of the most critical matters in the care of the dying, and it seems to be one of the greatest sources of difficulty for health caretakers and family members. Regardless of what we believe we should do, doing it appropriately looms as a troublesome task.

10

NEEDS AND STAGES

"It wasn't until I learned that I was going to die that I really began to live." Have you ever had the experience of leaving a house or a community that you loved in the belief that you would never return? If so, do you recall your thinking as you parted? Perhaps you looked around in an especially loving way; maybe you carefully made note of each important item in the house or attended to all the things you had noticed before and many you hadn't as you walked or drove around the community.

When you recognize that life is finite and that your life is very likely to end in a relatively brief and relatively predictable time, you begin to notice things that you have never noticed previously. You also begin to consider the uses of your time differently than you had, since time takes on new meanings—or perhaps intensifies older meanings. Your situation has changed, but you are still you.

LABELED "DYING"

At some point in the dying trajectory, the individual is regarded as "dying." The label does not necessarily get applied all at once, nor do all important persons use it at the same time. Sometimes, for example, people don't agree on a prognosis, or one or more individuals retain hope of recovery long after the others have given up. But eventually everyone concerned applies the label.

By the time this occurs, the dying person may welcome it as an opportunity to stop fighting for life, to eliminate some of the discomforting and exhausting treatments, to fall back into passivity. Frequently the individual is both tired and weak, does not feel well, and may be ready to die. It is not unheard of for someone to remain alive not because he or she truly wishes to, but because some member of the family is not ready for death to occur.

Also, once a person is labelled dying, certain freedoms are granted. In some hospitals, visiting hours become more flexible, and occasionally children, who are otherwise forbidden from seeing the patient, are spirited up back staircases. Patient complaints may be responded to, and patient irritability may be ignored. Family and friends become more solicitous; people from the past, especially close relatives who live some distance away, make a significant effort to visit. If not in a hospital, recently forbidden foods, tobacco, alcoholic beverages may be returned, since "it doesn't make much difference now."

Along with the prerogatives, however, come some intensified problems. There is a definite tendency for us, the not-yet-dying, to isolate ourselves from the imminently dying. Their dying impinges on our consciousness, cuts through our denial, and is often painful in many ways, the more so if we love them. Therefore, many dying persons receive fewer visits from friends and family after the label is applied.

Health professionals also may reduce their visits, partly for the same reasons as the family members and partly because they view their own skills as best utilized for patients who can still recover. Despite pronouncements to the contrary, medical training focuses on cure more than on care, and physicians often underestimate the importance of their presence for someone even after the label of dying has been applied.

The well-known sociologist, Talcott Parsons, has outlined expectations for the *sick role:* (1) the sick person is expected to avoid situations and behavior that will make the condition worse; (2) he or she needs to accept the idea that help is required; (3) the patient must desire to get better; and (4) the help that is sought should be technically competent (Mechanic, 1968). Despite its limitations, especially with regard to chronic illness, the model is useful, but look what happens to these expectations when the label changes from sick to dying: (1) the person is still expected to avoid making the condition worse, but the importance of doing so has changed; (2) help is still required, but the nature of the help changes too in many instances; (3) the desire to get better may become irrelevant, *or* it may be more relevant than ever, since being labelled dying does not mean that death is inevitable—it merely means that someone believes that death is inevitable; and (4) the kinds of competence required have changed, at least in many instances. Since most dying people have previously been sick people, it can happen that a patient continues to perceive himself or herself as sick, while others have already applied the dying label and, therefore, have different expectations. This conflict in role perception is very likely to lead to high levels of stress for everyone, especially for the patient.

BECOMING A NON-PERSON

The labelling process can transform the dying person into a non-person—not officially, of course, but in the eyes of the hospital staff and even, to some extent, in the eyes of family and friends. You can discuss non-persons even while they are present, because non-persons are incapable of hearing. Not that these things are done on purpose or with malice; they just happen.

Also, non-persons don't remind us as much of our own eventual fate. The dying process and death of another inevitably reminds us that we are also mortal. Becker (1973) has described the powerful fear of decay and vulnerability that each of us feels, and it is felt especially in the face of death. If we can only depersonalize the dying person, then we are less likely to have to deal with the obvious: the state that person is in is the state I will be in eventually. I don't want to be helpless or hopeless, vulnerable or at the mercy of powers beyond my power to control . . . like this dying person. By making the dying person a non-person, I don't need to contemplate such terrible possibilities. At least, I can postpone them a little longer. Even if Becker's theories exaggerate what most people actually experience, I believe some of the process commonly occurs.

SOCIAL VALUE OF THE DYING

What makes a particular life valuable? Of course, the rhetoric is that all lives are valuable, probably equally valuable, but is that true for you? Is it true for most people? I don't think so. Most of us, I believe, place a higher value on those persons who represent certain valued characteristics. What are some of these values?

First, people in our society place a great deal of emphasis on the future; we believe in deferring present gratifications for the future—in planning for the future and not simply living in the moment. People often claim that ours is a youth-centered society. I don't agree, but I do believe it is a future-payoff-centered society. If we believe that youth offer a future payoff, we will place them in the limelight too. As part of this future-centeredness, we value a person who appears likely to make a substantial future contribution to the society and, to some extent, to himself or herself.

Second, we value people who are presently productive and achieving. The productivity can be financial or creative, or it can involve the production of useful services. Although we also respect past productivity, we seem to place much more emphasis on present and future achievements.

Third, we respect people who are liked by others, who have many friends.

Fourth, we respond to physical attractiveness and sexuality, which are personified by the young and the healthy.

Fifth, we admire knowledge, and we may be especially responsive to scientific and technological knowledge.

Sixth, influence and power certainly receive respect.

Seventh, we like people who can enjoy life, if their enjoyment does not violate our sense of ethics and morality.

Eighth, we like people who make us feel good, who don't make us feel guilty.

Ninth, we value persons who do the "right things" in life, however we may define those. Certainly people who get into knife fights, who drive while drunk, who attempt suicide are not people we value. We may understand the psychological or social dynamics that made them who they are, but they aren't people we normally respect.

Examine these nine criteria, or whatever other criteria you wish to include, with an individual who is dying in mind. There isn't much about the dying person to be valued; if the dying person is elderly, his or her social value has probably been low for some time.

The death of a highly valued person makes a greater impression on the health caretakers than that of someone with little value. An elderly wino, who has been in and out of the hospital for various causes for several years, is brought in dead; he has no known family. His death is not likely to upset the hospital staff. But the 25-year-old mother who has fought a valiant battle with leukemia and finally succumbs will cause grief for everyone (Glaser & Strauss, 1964). Unlike the elderly man, the young mother is at least valued for being productive (being a mother), for the physical attractiveness and sexuality of youth, and for having done the "right" things in life.

THE NEEDS OF THE DYING

What are the needs of the dying? The question is no more difficult—nor any easier—than the question, what are the needs of people? Given the latter query, you would probably respond in one of two ways. You might say that individual differences are so great that no one answer is possible; or you might outline some broad areas of needs—perhaps adding that great individual differences exist. But these two answers apply as well to the dying, who, despite the labelling, are presently living individuals; the difference between them and others is that their lives are influenced by the presumed imminence of their deaths.

When we consider the needs of the dying, we often think in terms of what can be done to facilitate "death with dignity" or a "good death." Perhaps we first need to recognize that, "if the dying die with a degree of nobility, it will be mostly their doing in doing their own dying" (Ramsey, 1975, p. 82). We can help create the conditions in which an individual can live with dignity until death, but we can't *give* death with dignity.

And people who live in dignity are people who are living as much as possible the way they wish to live. Therefore, "death with dignity" or a "good death" is what Avery Weisman has termed an "appropriate death," which is dying—or, more properly, living the end of life—as much as possible the way the individual wishes. If providing the conditions to permit an appropriate death is the overall goal, what are the specific needs that must be satisfied to bring this about?

There are a number of systems that classify psychological needs, but the hierarchy of needs developed by humanistic psychologist Abraham Maslow is one of the best known, and I will apply it here to the dying person. Maslow's system of needs assumes that the more basic need must be reasonably well-satisfied before the next higher need can receive attention (1955), but I won't make the same assumptions. Instead, I'll just address myself to his five need categories: physiological needs, safety and security needs, love and belonging needs, esteem and self-esteem needs, and self-actualization needs.

PHYSIOLOGICAL NEEDS

We all require food, air, temperature regulation, sleep, the avoidance of pain, and the opportunity for elimination. The dying are no different from the rest of us in requiring these things, except that the way they express their needs and the actions that must be taken to satisfy the needs may be different. Although there is nothing about being in the living-dying interval per se that influences any of the needs, given health conditions can affect the extent of the need and the method for its satisfaction. Thus, certain illnesses may make breathing difficult, so the dying person may require some help in breathing, but *not because* of dying. Similarly, diet is affected by one's health condition, so that appetite is likely to diminish with illness. Dying persons often eat less or are put on special diets, but again, not because they are dying. Knowing that someone is dying gives us only the slightest hint about what changes will occur in the nature of, intensity of, or satisfaction of physiological needs.

Nor is pain avoidance an exception, but fear of pain is so great and is so frequently associated with dying and death that it requires special mention. After concern over bringing grief to family members and being unable to help one's dependents, fear of pain during dying was the greatest concern in our Los Angeles survey (Kalish & Reynolds, 1976), and it was similarly second or third greatest (of seven) concerns in two related studies (Diggory & Rothman, 1961; Shneidman, 1971).

Dying is often uncomfortable and certainly can be painful—sometimes horribly painful—but, as indicated above, it is, not dying per se that produces the pain, but the condition causing the dying. Pain is often much more severe in health problems that don't result in death. The classical study of the painfulness of dying was reported by Dr. William Osler, a famous physician, in 1904. He stated "I have careful reports of about 500 death-beds, studied particularly with reference to the modes of death and the sensations of dying . . . 90 suffered bodily pain of one sort or another. . . ." (p. 19). Although the causes of death have changed enough since Osler's time that there might be increased pain during dying, the use of analgesics and improved medical techniques should diminish substantially the proportion of individuals who suffer moderate or great pain in dying. Of course, pain is so subjective that what constitutes "moderate or great pain" is open to considerable disagreement.

SAFETY AND SECURITY NEEDS

"If a patient asks, 'What do I have?' he usually means, 'Can I count on you?" (Weisman, 1972, p. 19). A dying person has as much need as anyone else—perhaps more need—to feel safe and secure. Of course, the causes of feeling unsafe and insecure may be different. An individual who knows his or her death is imminent is both more and less vulnerable. Diminished strength and health, the frequent need to turn decisions and responsibilities over to others, the imminent loss of experiencing and of loved ones make the dying more vulnerable. Yet they are less vulnerable because whatever does occur won't continue for long; in addition, they are free of many of society's restrictive demands.

There seem to be two major sources of the dying's feelings of insecurity: lack of trust in the health caretaking operations and fear of abandonment. Do you trust these virtual strangers—the physicians, nurses, aides, orderlies, dieticians, x-ray technicians, hospital administrators—and the health sciences, in general, to be responsible for what happens to you? Although part of the problem is simply whether you like them, it is more a question of trust—perhaps even of faith. This doesn't mean that you must believe that they will keep you alive indefinitely. Rather, it means that you trust them to give you appropriate care as long as you live under their guidance. If you are skeptical of the physician's knowledge of medicine or fear that the nurse will give you the wrong medication or wonder whether the diagnosis is really accurate, you will not feel safe and secure.

The other aspect of the need for safety and security is the feeling that you can indeed count on your physician to care for you and on your family and friends not to abandon you. Close your eyes and imagine yourself at a party where each person is blindfolded, has his or her hands tied back, and is led around the room in what is sometimes called "a trust walk." Now it is your turn. Just as some unknown guest begins to guide you around the room, you hear someone shout "Oh, my God!" You hear a flurry of movement; the door slams; and there you are. Is it a joke? No, it doesn't seem to be.

Being abandoned is very frightening. The lyrics of one song about death say "Teach me to die, hold on to my hand" (*Teach Me to Die* by Deanne Edwards). We are unprotected when we are abandoned. This is difficult enough under normal conditions, when we have full strength and capabilities, but it is worse, much worse, when we don't.

What does the feeling of abandonment cause? First of all, fear. I am abandoned—I am alone—I am lonely—no one will help me—no one cares. Second, it causes us to feel vulnerable, open to attack, unprotected.

Third, we often feel that we no longer have any control of what is happening. If we don't know what's going on and if others come in to look at us, make strange clucking noises, then disappear, how secure can we feel? We have no control over what happens, and we are likely to have no knowledge about what is going on when we are abandoned. Blindfolded, in the apartment, unable to use our hands, we are just *there,* waiting for whatever fate wills.

Fourth, we are angry when we are abandoned. It isn't fair. Why did all of you leave me? Frustration often leads to aggression, that is, to anger, among other reactions. And perhaps, fifth, abandonment leads to guilt. What have I done to be abandoned? If only I hadn't done . . . or said . . . or been. . . .

When we are dying, it is very easy to feel abandoned. Other people go on about their business; visits become fewer and fewer; the world goes on without you. How can that be? How can everything and everyone act as though nothing is happening *when I am dying!* Philip Wylie describes this in *Opus 21*, an autobiographical novel, in which he spends a very brief period in New York City—having been misdiagnosed as dying of cancer. For that one day the world has changed for him, but not for everyone else. He feels very alone. It is not that people have actually left him, but he feels alone nonetheless.

Carrying one step further the concept of the need of the dying for safety and security, Avery Weisman proposes that a dying person needs *safe conduct* (1977): cautious and prudent behavior and guidance through peril and the unknown. (It does *not* mean playing it safe.) Although clinical medical treatment can contribute to the patient's safe conduct, compassion and skill in human relationships are also required. Weisman believes that, if the professional health caretakers cannot offer adequate safe conduct, they should transfer responsibility for this task to others.

LOVE AND BELONGING NEEDS

There is no such thing as being too sick or too near death to need love. It is possible to be so uncomfortable or so confused that you can't respond to love, or it is possible to be embarrassed by love. And it is also possible that knowing your death will lead to the loss of loved ones is so painful that you avoid offers of love. But dying a lonely death—abandoned, without love, without anyone who cares—is often seen as the worst kind of death.

Love can come from many quarters, not only from family members and close friends. Sometimes a physician, nurse, other hospital staff member, or other health worker can express true concern and caring; a visit from a clergyman, a telephone call from a cousin across the country, or even the expressed fondness of a dog or cat can all provide a sense of being loved. Sometimes the dying person will need to reminisce about the former love of people who have died or are not available for other reasons. Reminiscing can be very helpful and satisfying for people of any age and health status, and it may be especially so for the dying—particularly for the elderly dying. It enables people to focus on times that were deeply satisfying, to remember themselves as whole and healthy, and to see their own histories as cohesive and meaningful.

ESTEEM AND SELF-ESTEEM NEEDS

Your esteem for me and my esteem for myself are based, to some extent, on past, present, and future accomplishments, on the degree to which I believe I am a "good human being," on how much others appear to like me, and—certainly in this society—on my competence and autonomy. As the dying process develops, I may become increasingly incapacitated, helpless, and dependent, and, consequently, an increasing burden and financial drain on those I love. My need for esteem is unchanged, but my opportunities to have it satisfied have diminished. I may even welcome the thought of death because only death will remove me from this unwelcome situation.

As infants, we were taught to be in control of our bodies and our selves. As very young children, we were proud of our ability to walk, to use the toilet properly, to eat by ourselves, to catch a ball. Our self-esteem depended in large measure on how well we could do these and similar things. We esteemed our control of self and our increasing independence and autonomy.

Now try to imagine being in a situation where your eating schedule and bedtimes are regulated by someone else, where you cannot decide whether you are going to walk or run, where your body will not follow instructions so that when you try to raise your arm above your head, your foot goes up instead.

When you feel vulnerable and the world and your future are unpredictable, you are likely to be frightened and unable to function effectively. You do not feel competent, and your environment is perceived as unfriendly and threatening. Everything works against your self-esteem. When you feel competent and in reasonable control, you can anticipate the future and feel confident about your ability to cope with it; consequently, the environment seems friendly and nonthreatening. You are not frightened, and you are able to function effectively.

Look what happens during the dying process. More and more decisions are turned over to other people. If you are hospitalized or bedridden, some decisions are based on institutional policy and some are made for the convenience of others. Fatigue, pain, discomfort, and weakness require that others do things or make decisions that you could previously have done or decided for yourself. Physical strength and sexual activity, both symbols of competence, diminish greatly.

Other kinds of control also become more difficult. One of the most upsetting changes that some very sick people suffer is loss of sphincter control. Not only does this produce unpleasant odors and make social contacts more difficult, but it is also understandably perceived as a regression to childish, even infantile, behavior. Its arrival at a time when other kinds of competence and control are also diminishing makes its effect particularly distressing.

In the dying process, everything seems to conspire to leave you vulnerable, helpless, and without control or capabilities. Your body is not obeying you; sedatives and lack of stimulation leave you somewhat confused; people in your environment are making decisions for you, even some you could make yourself, without even getting your participation; pain and discomfort take up so much of your time, energy, and attention that you have trouble directing your efforts toward anything that doesn't immediately involve you. In effect, you aren't treated as competent; you don't feel competent; in some ways, you are no longer as competent as you were.

Also, knowing that you will be dead in the foreseeable future means that you must anticipate not merely diminishing competence and control, but irreversible loss of competence and control. For some dying persons, it is the awareness of impending losses even more than previous losses that is so distressing.

Furthermore, it doesn't make much difference who you were previously. If you were once great and powerful, you will probably receive some extra attention, but you still will have little control or competence. The fact that you wrote a great novel, discovered a gold mine in Nevada, owned a factory employing thousands of people, or coached a championship team is of little importance.

How can the dying try to retain self-esteem? One way might be to reminisce about events that enhanced self-esteem. Also important are accomplishments in the present that lead to self-esteem. For the very ill, an accomplishment can be something as simple as walking across the room; for a healthier person, it might be a satisfying discussion with a friend or some work-related achievement. More fortunate persons are able to finish significant projects during their last months and weeks, so that the close of their lives resembles earlier stages and they do not confront the sorts of situations that lead to diminished self-esteem.

SELF-ACTUALIZATION NEEDS

Dying does not mean that development stops. In fact, some people seem to use the crisis of death to facilitate their personal growth. The dying person has little time to procrastinate and stall; if change is going to occur, it must occur very soon—immediately! This awareness can lead to rapid growth. Two case studies are representative of what can happen.

The first concerns a man who had a long history of psychotic behavior, including seven years in a state mental hospital, with severe delusions and hallucinations and paranoid ideation. Some years after leaving the hospital, he was able to work hard enough to maintain himself in the community, to give support to a troubled friend, and to maintain some relationship with his family. However, many of his symptoms remained. At that point, he was diagnosed as having terminal cancer, although his prognosis predicted many months of life. His psychotic symptoms and the acute tension with which he had been living virtually disappeared and did not return for the last two years of his life (Smith, 1975).

The second case study, describing the personal growth of a dying woman who was the focus of intensive research, led its authors to conclude that the end of life may be the impetus for resolving problems, establishing closer relationships, and even becoming more productive. Additionally, the authors noted that, over the course of time, the dying woman found her physiological needs increasingly important and her need for esteem much less so. When breathing is difficult and physical strength diminishes, more energy must be expended in satisfying physiological needs and less is left to satisfy esteem or self-actualization. Thus, as Maslow predicted, when needs lower down on the hierarchy are not satisfied, those higher are also frustrated (Zinker & Fink, 1966).

STAGES OF DYING

- A middle-aged man walks into the hospital clutching a paperback book; tomorrow morning he will have exploratory surgery for a possible cancer.
- A young poet, knowing he is to die within approximately two years, arranges for his remaining time to be filmed; in the film, he comments bitterly that his anger about dying was discounted by a nurse who told him that he was "in the *anger* stage."
- In a small, California resort town, 3000 people jam the local auditorium to hear a thin, middle-aged female psychiatrist talk about dying.

There is little doubt that the most familiar name associated with death and dying is that of the Swiss-born psychiatrist, Elisabeth Kübler-Ross. Her book, *On Death and Dying,* and her innumerable lectures, workshops, and films have been a powerful force to raise the general consciousness of people about the meaning of death and the concerns of the dying. Ross's major theoretical contribution has been the development of five stages of dying, and these deserve a careful examination.

Her first stage in the dying process is *denial and isolation*. Almost all patients, she points out, make use of denial both early in their awareness of their dying and from time to time later. It is not only a familiar but frequently a healthy response to a highly stressful situation; it acts as a time buffer to protect the individual from the shock of what is now faced.

Later in the dying process, people may use the defense mechanism of isolation: "the removal of the emotional aspects of an idea or thought they were originally associated with, permitting retention of the memory without its original emotional charge" (Goldenberg, 1977, p. 180). Although a kind of denial, isolation permits the patient to "talk about his health and his illness, his mortality and his immortality as if they were twin brothers permitted to exist side by side, thus facing death and still maintaining hope" (Kübler-Ross, 1969, p. 37).

Following denial and isolation, the dying person arrives at the stage of *anger,* which includes rage, envy, and resentment. If denial said "It can't be me," anger asks "Why me?" Family members and health caretakers find the stage of anger very difficult, since the anger is likely to flare up for a variety of reasons, not all of them overtly associated with the person's health.

Sometimes the anger is expressed directly through shouting; other times its expression is indirect, through complaints about the care; still other times its expression takes the form of bitterness about not being around to enjoy next summer or about having been abandoned by God. Since hospital staff prefer to operate a smooth-running institution, they may resent anger and either ignore the patient or respond in punitive or defensive ways. Although this resentment is understandable, the reasons for the dying person's anger are also understandable, and, after all, it isn't the staff person who is going to die shortly.

Bargaining is the third stage. The patient attempts to postpone the death or reduce the pain or have some extra strength. "Most bargains are made with God and are usually kept a secret . . ." (Kübler-Ross, 1969, p.74). When I was an undergraduate, a professor told us that he had been drowning and had promised God that, if he lived, he would become a devout Catholic; he was saved, and he fulfilled his part of the bargain. Extremely few individuals, of course, find their offer to bargain so successful.

When it becomes obvious that bargaining is not going to work, the dying person enters the stage of *depression.* Denial is no longer possible to sustain; anger has dissipated; bargaining has failed. Death is recognized to be inevitable, and the feelings of loss become overwhelming. Depression has been defined as "an emotional state characterized by despondency, guilt, feelings of unworthiness, and loss of both appetite and sexual desire" (Goldenberg, 1977, p. 586). We have all experienced some degree of sadness or depression when losses have occurred. We feel heavy, lack the desire to be involved, wish to avoid activity, often feel sorry for ourselves. Even though we know that our "down" mood won't last, we may feel too lethargic to do very much.

Depression doesn't last forever; eventually the dying person works through the acute sense of loss, finishes mourning for himself or herself, and arrives at the stage of *acceptance.* Acceptance need not be a happy stage: Ross describes it as being "almost void of feelings" (1960, p. 100). The dying person has now become extensively disengaged from most of what goes on in the world. Now is the time to be stirred up—it is the time to be left alone. Energy may be low, and only a few people are still welcome visitors. Like the person about to retire who has lost interest in the job, while finding increasing interest in retirement activities, the dying person is losing interest in this world and may find increasing interest in the existence still to come—however that existence is defined. For those who do not believe in a future existence, the new engagement can be with sleep and rest, with cessation of pain, or with reminiscence.

The person who has accepted death is no longer fearful; time can now be used for whatever is both possible and desired, since the anxiety of handling denial, anger, or depression is no longer incapacitating. This stage, according to Kübler-Ross, is the desired goal of dying persons.

THE SIGNIFICANCE OF KÜBLER-ROSS'S STAGES

Ross's book appeared at just the right time: people, especially those who had been caring for the dying, were ready to read something about death and dying—especially something that would help them make sense of the process. *On Death and Dying* did just that: "Many people have felt remarkably better after becoming acquainted with the stage theory of dying. Anxiety and lack of cognitive structure are replaced by the security of knowledge" (Kastenbaum, 1975, p. 40).

However, in some ways the book made too much sense. That is, the stages were so appealing that many people, especially nurses, who recognized that Dr. Kübler-Ross understood their problems, accepted them as gospel. They regarded the stages as a natural progression through which virtually everyone passed; patients who did not pass through the stages and did not arrive at the acceptance stage prior to death, were sometimes considered to have failed in their tasks. This may seem strange, but it occurred. A nurse would become angry with a patient who "regressed" from depression to anger; a patient would question why he or she was so long "in the anger stage."

Several questions have emerged: first, are these stages actually a natural progression? Second, does virtually everyone pass through them? Third, are these the only significant emotional responses that people have during the dying process? Fourth, is it emotionally adaptive to pass through the stages? Fifth, should some therapeutic intervention be offered to help people pass through the stages and arrive at acceptance?

In a review of the research evidence several years ago, one study concluded that the data showed that Ross's stages were not a natural progression and did not occur in a majority of instances (Schulz & Aderman, 1974). Objections have come from non-researchers as well. Based on his extensive work with dying persons, Shneidman (1973) stated that he observed alternation between acceptance and denial, rather than a unidirectional movement through five stages.

In my view, the consensus of opinion is that the answer to each of the first three questions I asked above is no. Different people die in different ways and experience a variety of feelings and emotions during the process: hope, fear, curiosity, envy, apathy, relief, even anticipation. And they appear to move back and forth from mood to mood; sometimes the moods follow each other in short order; other times two moods are present in the dying person simultaneously.

The answers to the last two questions I asked are more complex. For some people and under some circumstances, acceptance of death is certainly the way to an appropriate death. For others, this is not the case. Perhaps anger, even fury, is the most appropriate way to die: what a mockery death is; how destructive it is; how absurd it is—there is nothing good about death, at least about *my* death, and I have no intention of being peaceful or submissive or accepting. Two quotations seem appropriate, the first from Ecclesiastes 9:3 and the second from Dylan Thomas:

> This is the root of the evil in all that happens under the sun, that one fate comes to all. Therefore, men's minds are filled with evil and there is madness in their hearts while they live, for they know that afterward—they are off to the dead!

> Do not go gentle into that good night
> Old age should burn and rave at close of day
> Rage, rage against the dying of the light

In other words, death is so horrible that the only proper response is to be angry about dying. Is this the best way to die? That depends on the individual. Of course, dying peacefully and with acceptance is easier on the hospital staff and on family members and friends. It is a unique nurse or physician who is able to remain untouched by an angry dying patient—perhaps in part because the anger is often addressed directly to the medical treatment. How much more pleasant it is (although not without pain) to encounter someone who is no longer angry or blaming.

Sometimes the reason for not accepting death is quite different. Cornelius Ryan, a writer and historian, who was dying of cancer, found that the medications he was taking were not only distorting his appearance but affecting his thought processes so that he couldn't write. Rather than exchange his writing competence for pain-free time, he stated "I shall try never to feel peaceful and pain-free again. . . . These symptoms . . . may be quite closely linked to death. . . . Fast-paced mental activity and constant pain are now my criteria for being well" (*Newsweek*, 1979, p. 100). The decision to accept death and die without pain may give way to higher priorities.

The fifth question concerns therapeutic intervention to move people through the five stages. There seems little doubt that this would be a misuse of therapy. Two of the purposes of most therapy are to enable people to feel better about themselves and to make choices for themselves. If in this process, they move from denial through the next three stages to acceptance, that's fine; if they don't that is all right also. What does become dangerous, however, is to assume that progressing through the five stages is *the* best procedure for all, or even for most, people, and then to apply some program, no matter how well-meaning, to manipulate them through the stages.

Another matter is also important: we do not want to depersonalize dying people by placing them in a rigid system of classification and labelling them in terms of a category. To say literally or symbolically "Oh, I understand you, because you are in the anger stage" is to remove individuality from the dying person. It is comparable to the teaching physician who takes his students to visit a patient with pancreatic cancer and says "Now here is a pancreatic cancer." Not true. Here is a human being who has pancreatic cancer. The difference is more than theoretical, since we respond to people and things according to the labels we assign them.

The evidence is far from all in. We don't know how "most people should die." Therefore, my own belief is that we are better off following Weisman's admonition to help people die appropriate deaths—to die as much as possible the way they want to die, rather than according to a preestablished scheme.

THE DENIAL OF DYING

Denial is one of the major protective psychological mechanisms that enable people to cope with the flood of feelings that occur when the reality of death or dying becomes too great. In Chapter 4, I discussed the denial of death; earlier in this chapter, I touched on Ross's stage of denial; here I would like to amplify my discussion of the denial of dying.

Dying persons can deny the existence of information or they can reinterpret the meaning of the information to avoid its implications. One well-known author (Weisman, 1972) has proposed three degrees of denial. The first is the denial of facts; this is exemplified by an individual who, told by his or her physician that a scheduled operation is for cancer, subsequently believes that its purpose is to excise a benign tumor. Another example would be a person who, given a diagnosis by his or her physician of terminal cancer, asks on the doctor's next visit why he or she is experiencing stomach pain.

The second degree of denial is denial of implications. In this case, the patient acknowledges the disease but denies that it will end in death. A woman with intense pain radiating down the left side of her body insists that it doesn't hurt much, that she will be fine; a man observing a growing lump that is becoming increasingly painful and sensitive attributes it to a bruise he received months earlier.

The third degree is the denial of extinction. This form, not applicable to persons whose deeply felt religious beliefs include some form of immortality or continuity, is limited to people who accept a diagnosis and its implications but still talk and behave as though they were going to live through the ordeal (Weisman, 1972).

Another psychiatrist described two kinds of denial: adaptive and brittle. Brittle denial, which seems to cover the first two of Weisman's degrees of denial, is accompanied by observable anxiety and agitation. Often the individual will reject any attempts to improve his or her psychological or social functioning in the situation. Adaptive denial occurs when an individual, aware of the diagnosis and its implications, makes the decision not to dwell on this aspect of life but to emphasize strengths and opportunities. These individuals welcome help and support. This form of healthy denial may actually prolong life, since it exhibits a formidable will to live (Hyland, 1978).

We can deny the deaths of others in the same way that we deny our own dying and death. The following are excerpts from a brief statement that I wrote following the death of a friend:

> My first reaction after hanging up [after having heard of Don's death] and after a few moments of being with myself, was to send Don's wife a note. Somehow I could not do it—an overwhelming feeling kept pressing me to acknowledge, that, perhaps, a mistake had been made, and that such a note would only bring embarrassment or confusion. It took me a week to write this note. My next feeling was that I should send Don a note, telling him how sorry I was about . . . I wasn't sure about what. My selves watched each other struggle with this impossible thought, with only a thrust of reality that kept me from composing "Dear Don, I am sorry to hear that . . . but you will, of course, be . . . if there is anything . . . please. . . ." This feeling remained for several days.
>
> Then the arithmetic. If Don is 55 and I am . . . , then my youngest child will be . . . when I am 55, which means . . . , while my oldest will be . . . or about ready to . . . and the middle. . . .
>
> And finally the attempts to pull back from the view of my own termination. What had Don done to deserve to die? What was he doing that I was not doing, so that his death did not mean I was also mortal? Did he elicit the wrath of God? Did he violate the laws of good health? Perhaps he neglected an annual physical or consumed too much butter or bourbon or bacon or. . . . [Kalish, 1972].*

Don wasn't even a very close friend of mine, although I liked him and we did occasionally see each other socially and had done some work together. The denial process that I went through began with the denial of Don's death and ended with the denial of my own mortality. In between there was a fleeting interval when I contemplated the meaning of my own death; then I retreated into denial.

Often, when we are with someone who is dying, we feel a virtual

*From "Special Memorial . . ." by R. A. Kalish. In *The Gerontologist*, *12*, 4, 1972 (Winter). Reprinted by permission of author.

compulsion to tell her how well she looks, to tell him that we know he will soon be up and around again. This occurs not as a denial that they are dying, but from awkwardness about how to respond. We rationalize our behavior and say we do not want to make them feel uncomfortable, but the truth is that we are the ones who are uneasy.

If you haven't had the experience of denying that someone was dying, you might understand it better by recalling some related situation you have experienced. For example, can you remember the process you went through when an intimate relationship of yours was broken by the other person's leaving? Did you ever fail an examination that you had been positive you had passed easily? Have you ever lost a job you believed was secure? Denial is a familiar response in each of these situations.

Denial of death—your own or someone else's—can be either adaptive and helpful or maladaptive and disjunctive; it can even be both at the same time. Denial may be used to avoid the destructive impact of shock by postponing for a time the necessity of dealing with the idea of death. And it may function to keep a person from coping with intense feelings of anger and hurt, feelings that interfere with other kinds of behavior because they are too intense to stifle completely. It is not that denial is "good" or "bad"; an evaluation of its adaptive qualities must be done on an individual basis.

There is the temptation to support the denial of someone else because his or her pain causes us pain; our encouragement of the denial permits (or requires) that the pain not be displayed. Conversely, there is the temptation to press through denial, as we become impatient with other people's reluctance to accept reality:

> Sometimes the denial in the family is its only defense to help it get through the crisis, to give it time to integrate an unhappy truth. I didn't want to talk about Jean's impending death. I didn't want to admit he was dying. I couldn't. I preferred denial. Some of the doctors didn't understand and therefore didn't allow it [Paulay, 1977–78, p. 175].

Perhaps it was necessary for the physicians to have Ms. Paulay cease denying—perhaps not. It is impossible to make that determination without knowing a great deal more about the circumstances. What is apparent is that denial can serve an important function.

Be careful, however: not every instance in which someone denies a fear of death or avoids a death-related situation or refuses to accept the idea that death is inevitable is an example of the psychological mechanism of denial. There is a tendency to believe people when they say they are afraid of death but to accuse them of denying when they say they are unafraid. That may, indeed, be the case, but not in all instances. Fear of death, in a given situation, may be low or fairly well worked through; a person may avoid a death-related situation because other matters have higher priority; someone may refuse to accept a diagnosis of terminal illness for reasons that have nothing to do with unconscious dynamics.

THE TASKS OF THE DYING

Like everyone else, dying persons want to accomplish certain tasks. And, like everyone else's tasks, theirs may involve deeply personal considerations. Sometimes the tasks concern ongoing relationships; sometimes they require anticipating future needs. The main tasks of the dying seem to be completing unfinished business, dealing with medical-care needs, allocating time and energy resources, arranging for what happens after death, coping with losses, and encountering the mysteries of death itself. The latter two have been discussed extensively in this book. I will spend the next few pages on the first four of the tasks.

COMPLETING UNFINISHED BUSINESS

One of the major tasks of the dying is to deal with unfinished business. For example, this may refer to:

- calling your sister in Portland; you had an argument with her 27 years ago and you haven't spoken to her since;
- finishing the sweater you were knitting for your grandson;
- thanking the young nurse who had been particularly nice to you when your treatments were so painful;
- making certain that your store's books are available and that all records are up-to-date, so that your successor can take over without confusion;
- telling your children that you love them;
- making certain that your bankbooks and insurance policies are readily accessible;
- knowing that your fourth grandchild was born healthy.

As death approaches, many unfinished tasks recede in importance, although you would need to know a person very well to predict which tasks will remain prominent and which will diminish in importance. Sometimes preparing for death means "letting go" psychologically of people and of the responsibilities that you had maintained during your life. A young mother, for example, may be deeply concerned about her children's future, and she will not feel easy until she is assured that they will be properly cared for after her death.

A common error at this juncture is to discount the strength of feelings dying people have tied up in unfinished business. It is often much easier to help a person complete a task than to persuade her or him that the task is no longer important. We all face each moment the possibility that we will not be alive the next moment to complete a particular task, but the probability that we will not be alive is so small that we simultaneously ignore it and deny it. For the person well advanced in the living/dying interval, the probability is much greater, and the pressure of time, therefore, is much greater. You have many things you wish to do in the next few days, months, years—in your lifetime. Although right now you are required to make some decisions and eliminate some options, you expect to have time to do most of what you wish. The person who faces his or her own death and probable decline before death does not have the range of options that you have, and he or she confronts the task of deciding what can be accomplished and what must be left behind.

DEALING WITH MEDICAL CARE NEEDS

Not all people facing their deaths have changing medical-care needs, and not all persons whose medical care needs are changing significantly are dying, but the connection is still obvious. Sometimes the fatally ill person prefers to leave medical decisions to others, but other times he or she wishes to take a more active role in the way medical care is obtained. This obviously requires that the individual have some understanding of the medical diagnosis and prognosis, the meaning of various kinds of treatment, and the kinds of people and facilities that can provide the care.

When the medical-care decisions are made by others, the dying person is likely to become a passive participant in the care plan—following instructions (although not infrequently with considerable passive resistance) and doing what is required. There is considerable encouragement today to make the patient an active participant.

A dying cancer patient, for example, may decide to forego cobalt treatment, with its secondary effects of hair loss, nausea, and extreme fatigue, in exchange for an earlier death with less discomfort. Another patient may choose to live her last few weeks at home, even though this choice probably means that death will occur sooner.

> A well-known psychologist had had a severe heart attack and was informed by his physician that the only chance he had for a long life was to reduce his activity level, to stop all smoking and drinking, to eliminate sexual activity, and to change his eating habits. Rather than give up what he had enjoyed so much, he decided to live much as he had been living and to accept death when it came. He died of a second coronary about two years later, but the two years were enjoyable and fulfilling. More important, he died an appropriate death, that is, he died as he wished to die: while engaged in the excitement of a vigorous life.

ALLOCATING TIME AND ENERGY RESOURCES

When time and energy no longer seem infinite, people have to make choices. When people were asked how they wished to spend their last six months, their responses were highly variable (see Table 10-1). Of course, most of the people interviewed had never actually faced their own deaths, and it is difficult to know whether what they claimed would be what they would actually do under the circumstances.

TABLE 10-1. Responses of 434 Greater Los Angeles Residents Concerning Specific Plans and Preparations They Have Made for Their Own Death

	Percentage Answering Yes								
	Ethnicity				*Age*			*Sex*	
Questions: Have you	*Black American*	*Japanese American*	*Mexican American*	*"Anglo" American*	*20–39*	*40–59*	*60+*	*Men*	*Women*
taken out life insurance?	84*	70	52	65	61	76	66	73	63
made out a will?	22	21	12	36	10	22	39	26	19
made funeral arrangements?	13	11	8	14	3	11	24	13	10
paid for or are you now paying for a cemetery plot?	22	26	12	25	7	17	44	20	22
seriously talked with anyone about your . . . death?	27	16	33	37	28	28	29	28	28
arranged for someone to handle your affairs?	24	17	25	42	13	44	44	26	28

*Numbers are percentages.

From *Death and Ethnicity: A Psychocultural Study*, by R. A. Kalish and D. K. Reynolds. Copyright 1976. Reprinted by permission.

Major factors in how remaining time is spent are the nature and course of the illness. A person dying from a slow-acting cancer, which brings increasing fatigue and debilitation, allocates his or her time and energy very differently from the psychologist described above. And this brings us back to unfinished business. The pressure of certain unfinished tasks may be so great that the dying person will fight off death until a particular task is completed. Nevertheless, the illness eventually takes command, and death will occur in the face of the most powerful desire to continue.

ARRANGING FOR AFTER DEATH

If you died before you finished reading this sentence, what would happen to your body? Your possessions? Your survivors? Are the things that would happen what you would like to have happen? If you haven't made any preparations for your own death, you are not alone. Table 10-1 shows that, except for having bought life insurance, most people have not made specific arrangements for their deaths; even most older people have not gotten around to making out a will or arranging for someone to handle their affairs.

Life insurance is the most familiar preparation made for death. In 1976, a national survey found that 90% of families with both husband and wife present had some insurance; 80% of all adult men and 65% of all adult women were insured. Even among those 65 years of age and older, 68% of the men and 55% of the women carried life insurance. These figures are similar to the data reported in Table 10-1. The total amount of life insurance in force in 1978 was $2.9 trillion! Almost as many women carry life insurance as men. However, in spite of these statistics, the average coverage in 1978 was $40,800 per insured family (American Council of Life Insurance, 1979). Even allowing for the distortions of an inflationary economy, this amount of money would not keep a family going for very long.

A totally different kind of preparation for death is arranging to donate an organ—a kidney, or the cornea of an eye, for example—to someone else. Only 3% of the respondents in the Los Angeles study had made such preparations (Kalish & Reynolds, 1976), and the topic did not elicit a great deal of interest. Nonetheless, many people do make out and carry with them official cards stipulating that, in the event of their death, their body can be used for transplants or donated to a medical school to be used for instructional or research purposes.

Why bother making advance arrangements? Several answers are obvious. First, it allows what happens after your death to be as much as possible the way you want it to be; if you don't make arrangements, someone else—perhaps someone assigned by the courts—will. Second, it frees your family of the tasks so that they can deal unencumbered with their grief; they will still have ample practical matters to concern them. Third, it avoids having your estate, even if it is very small, tied up in courts for many months or longer; the better job you do in setting things up, the more quickly all matters will be settled. Fourth, if you have dependent children, you can assure them of the best living arrangement and care in the event one *or both* parents die.

One answer is less obvious. If you can arrange for what will happen when you die and if you can discuss this with persons who are important to you, you will begin to establish an open-awareness system. These individuals will know that you are capable of discussing your own death, and they will be more likely to be open with you when your death is actually imminent. Furthermore, they will feel satisfied that they are carrying out your wishes concerning your funeral, disposal of your body, and disposal of property, and this certainly will reduce the chance of tension and arguments among your survivors. Conversely, you can learn their preferences and perhaps alter some of your plans accordingly.

Why, then, do so many people never get around to making preparations? Financial costs are so low that lack of money can't explain the figures in Table 10-1; the effort required isn't great either. Some individuals, of course, have neither dependents nor possessions, so they may not feel any pressure to make arrangements. Others assume that because they are young and healthy, they are not going to die soon enough to worry about.

But there is still another reason, one that borders on superstition but is common even among individuals who aren't afraid to walk under ladders or to plan activities on Friday the 13th. If I make out a will or make funeral arrangements, I am admitting that I am going to die; therefore, I will die. If I don't make out a will and don't make funeral arrangements, I am not going to die. And the less I think about death, the less likely I am to die. Very few people will admit that their thoughts run along those lines, but my own observations are that such "logic" is more common than usually recognized.

Obviously many people do go to lawyers to set up wills, estates, and trusts. After all, there is good evidence that our greatest concern about dying is its consequences for our survivors. Therefore, once material possessions accumulate or a family develops, each adult begins to think of the others involved in his or her life.

Ironically, when a person does get around to seeing a lawyer, he or she is likely to find the word *death* avoided. Thomas Shaffer, a lawyer and law professor, reports several ways in which lawyers avoid bringing death directly into conversation, even if the entire purpose of a conversation is to prepare for death. They (1) use evasion and denial and change the subject; (2) employ raucous humor concerning death-related matters; and (3) save discussion of what happens when death occurs for the end of the allocated time, then shift the topic back to financial assets and family members as quickly as possible. They are also likely to remove the topic of children from any discussion (Shaffer, 1970). Shaffer also mentions that parents exhibit great stress when asked with whom their children should live if both parents die or are incapacitated. Disposing of money, furniture, and jewelry arouses the emotions less than dealing with the possibility that the children you love may lose you.

In our country we are no longer familiar with death, since professionals, rather than family and neighbors, perform the activities relating to death. Death, like most significant events in modern nations, is entangled in a web of bureaucracy. Death certificates, death records, wills, trusts, life insurance, health insurance, burial insurance, social security, pension and retirement plans, distribution of body parts—these are only some of the wheels that are set in motion when a person dies. In pioneer times, a person died, was buried in a wood coffin, had a funeral ceremony, and his death was recorded in the family Bible. No longer.

The tasks that face the dying person are considerable, and the psychological stresses and physical limitations that are present may render the accomplishment of these tasks even more difficult. It's useful to make some advance preparations, especially concerning some practical matters, so that your strength and resources can be applied to what is personally significant: being with those you care for, completing plans and projects, meditating or praying, reminiscing and trying to see your life in perspective, participating in activities that you particularly enjoy and that your health will permit.

11

THE PROCESS OF DYING: A LIFE-SPAN PERSPECTIVE

An infant dying of cancer, a child dying of cancer, an adolescent dying of cancer. A young adult suffering a fatal heart attack, a middle-aged adult suffering a fatal heart attack, an elderly adult suffering a fatal heart attack. Your reaction to each of these deaths is influenced by both the cause of death and the age of the dying person. One death seems somehow more appropriate than another; one strikes you as being easier to accept than another. Try to project yourself into each of these individuals: you are the child dying of cancer or the elderly person dying from a massive coronary. The malady is now in progress—it is happening to you. How do you feel in each age category? Does it matter whether you are child or adult? Or are you concerned entirely with the nature of the disease?

Although the process of dying is influenced by innumerable factors, only one of which is age, age enters into many of the other considerations. For example, the conditions from which persons die are related to age; the kinds of treatment recommended may be related to age; responses from health-care professionals may differ as a function of the age of the dying person; the meaning of one's own dying is not the same across the life span.

WHAT WE DIE FROM

Causes of dying change over the life span. Slightly over 1% of newborn infants died in 1977, and their deaths were recorded as *infant mortality,* although we know that that statistic can be further categorized as genetic abnormalities, prenatal infarctions, damage to the fetus as a result of toxins, drugs, and oxygen deprivation, and a variety of still-unknown causes (Carlin, 1977). As age increases, death rates drop, and death rates for children are extremely low. Deaths from "childhood diseases," such as measles, whooping cough, scarlet fever, and diphtheria, which occurred frequently at the turn of the century, have virtually vanished (*Information Please Almanac,* 1979). Although cancers and other illnesses do cause a few deaths in children, accidents are the major killers at this stage of the life span.

In the 15–24-year-old age group, the three leading causes of death are accidents, homicides, and suicides. Cancer is the fourth most common cause of death—followed by heart disease, pneumonia and influenza, and stroke. The rate of deaths from accidents decreases in the 25–44-year-old category, but the rates of all other causes of death increase. The death rates from various diseases increase much faster than the death rate from homicides and suicides.

By middle age, heart problems are overwhelmingly the major cause of death for men, while cancer is the primary cause of death for women. The second most frequent killer is cancer for men, heart attacks for women. Strokes rank third for both men and women. For women, cirrhosis of the liver, accidents, diabetes, and pneumonia/influenza are the next leading causes of death; for men, the sequence is accidents, cirrhosis, suicide, and pneumonia/influenza. Among the elderly, heart disease is the major killer, although it has been diminishing in recent years. Cancer and stroke rank second and third for men and third and second for women. Then come pneumonia/influenza, accidents, and diabetes for men; for women the order of the last two is reversed. As people get older, their deaths are more frequently caused by chronic than by acute conditions, accidents, homicides, suicides, or other causes of sudden death (*U.S. Fact Book,* 1977).

The nature of accidental deaths also changes over the life span. The number of motor-vehicle deaths rises from childhood to the late teens and early 20s, then decreases before slowly rising again in late middle age. Falls, on the other hand, cause few deaths for women and a much higher rate for men until the mid-50s, when the rate for both sexes rises rapidly; then, in the 65-and-over age group, falls become the major cause of accidental deaths. The percentage of all deaths that are accidental deaths and the percentage of accidental deaths that are motor-vehicle deaths rise from birth to the late teens, then decline through the rest of the life span (*Metropolitan Life Insurance Company, Statistical Bulletin,* July–September, 1978). This decline is caused by an increase in non-accidental causes of death, rather than by a decrease in accidental deaths.

THE DYING CHILD

Presumably infants and extremely young children do not understand the concepts of death and dying. If they are ill, they may sense that something is wrong, because of the way they feel or because of the way people are acting. They may become anxious or fearful in response to the anxieties or fears of others. Or their fear may occur when they are taken away from home to a strange hospital or faced with painful treatments. But these are matters that arise from being sick, not from dying per se. An otherwise healthy infant with a broken arm might experience more disruptive medical treatments than an infant of the same age in the beginning stages of leukemia.

AWARENESS AND COMMUNICATION

When children are still very young—2, 3, or 4 years old—their perceptions of what is happening to them are a direct reflection of their parents' behavior. If they are confident that they are not being abandoned by their parents, children can cope amazingly well with pain and unpleasant treatments (Easson, 1974). Before children can grasp the concept of their own deaths, even at a simple level, they must have (1) a concept of their own unique separateness, of not being a part of the parents; (2) a sense of continuity of time—past, present, and future; and (3) an ability to fantasize change in their physical selves (Easson, 1974). This means not that they are unafraid when they are dying but that their fears are in response to the reactions of others, rather than to their own dying.

Eventually, perhaps around the age of 8, children do understand that their "physical being" may cease to exist. They also have begun to comprehend the medical jargon that they hear from parents and health caretakers. Now they can become afraid of death itself (Easson, 1974).

However, some children have enough comprehension of what dying means and what is happening to them to develop this fear before 8. A group of medical investigators working with terminally ill children contended that those as young as 4 or 5 were aware of the consequences of their diseases and their imminent deaths, although many of their parents tried to shield them from the knowledge. Even younger children displayed concern about separation, disfigurement, and pain (Binger, Ablin, Feuerstein, Kushner, Zoger, & Mikkelsen, 1969).

A number of observers have commented that young children do not ask questions about their own dying (for example, Richmond & Waisman, 1955). Although such statements are correct, there are several possible interpretations of this behavior. One is simply that the child does not comprehend what is happening. However, it is also possible that the child is aware that something extremely serious is going on, which might lead to death, but doesn't ask because either he or she doesn't wish to know more or assumes that the all-powerful adults will bring back her or his health. A third possibility is that the significant adults in the child's social milieu have communicated to the child that questions would be troublesome, so that the child is protecting the adults. When parents, physicians, or nurses continue to tell a child that "everything will be all right," the child may feel that questioning would be challenging the authority of adults. Since the support of these adults is so important, the child is reluctant to risk alienating them by probing with unwanted questions.

One investigator worked with 64 children between the ages of 6 and 10. Some had been diagnosed as having chronic illnesses that would lead to death; some had chronic diseases with good prognoses; and others either had brief illnesses or were not ill at all. The fatally ill children showed much greater general anxiety and much greater anxiety related to death, mutilation, and loneliness than the other children, including the other chronically ill children (Waechter, 1971). A later study found essentially the same relationship (Spinetta, Rigler, & Karon, 1973). This suggests that these children were somewhat aware of their condition; they may even have had a realistic knowledge that they were going to die. An alternative explanation, although one that does not necessarily rule out the previous interpretation, is that their anxiety reflected the greater anxiety that their parents and the hospital staff exhibited in their presence. As adults, in general, become better able to be honest with children, the anxiety of both children and adults may diminish.

Another author makes an even stronger case that children have knowledge of their prognoses. This author worked with a group of children, primarily between the ages of 3 and 9, all of whom, the author believed, came to comprehend the state of their health. Some of the signs she noted were preoccupation with death and disease, marked fear of wasting time, avoidance of any discussion of the future, death imagery in their play and art work, and preoccupation that things be done immediately. The author concluded that all children eventually came to an understanding of death as "mutilating experiences, bringing in their wake separation and loss of identity. Death . . . is a final and irreversible fact of life" (Bluebond-Langner, 1977, p. 60), although children obviously expressed their feelings in less sophisticated terms. Apparently children who are terminally ill do not understand death, at least their own death, as indicated by the stages proposed by Nagy in 1948 (see Chapter 7); rather, they attain a much more sophisticated awareness than has usually been assumed.

The same author, Dr. Bluebond-Langner, has suggested five stages of understanding that dying children go through, almost regardless of age:

1. becomes aware that the illness is "serious";
2. learns the names of drugs and side effects;
3. learns purposes of treatments and procedures;
4. experiences the disease as a series of relapses and remissions;
5. experiences the disease as a series of relapses and remissions that will eventually cease with the advent of death (Bluebond-Langner, 1977).

As the children go through these five stages of acquisition of knowledge, they also go through five coordinated stages of self-perception:

1. seriously ill,
2. seriously ill, but will get better,
3. always ill, but will get better,
4. always ill and will never get better,
5. dying (Bluebond-Langner, 1977).

For each stage to occur, certain conditions must be met. For example, the child does not move to stage five until he or she learns that another child has died. Neither age nor intellectual ability has much to do with the progression from stage one to stage five. Rather, the child must have gone through appropriate experiences: had the condition for a while, visited the hospital, and lost friends of the same approximate age and with the same illness (Bluebond-Langner, 1977). This author's conclusions, based on her research with leukemic children, are still controversial, since they contradict other opinion and research. I personally believe that most of her work will be confirmed by others who study the self-awareness of dying children.

The arguments about whether or not children should be informed of their terminal prognoses are similar to those advanced for other age groups (for example, Share, 1972). In one study of leukemic children, the authors came to believe that avoiding a child's questions about his or her illness served to increase distress and anxiety; conversely, "Relevant information in response to specific questions from the dying child provided relief and reassurance to that child" (Townes & Wold, 1977, p. 140).

Most of the previous discussion has concerned children who spend all or much of their time in hospitals, but many dying children live at home and pursue fairly normal lives for extended periods, and this circumstance often changes if and how they learn about their illness. One child first learned that she was leukemic from a schoolmate who blurted out that she knew about her friend's illness (Toch, 1977). Others have learned through playmates as well as through the stage whispers of well-meaning adults. It is impossible to control the entire social environment.

When all is said and done, we still know that some children want to know more about their conditions, some want not to know any more than they do, and all want to learn at a pace that they can control. In serving the needs of the child, we must be sensitive to what each individual child is communicating to us. This requires that we not impose our desires upon the child—that is, that we not inadvertently communicate to a child that *we* want to protect *ourselves* from having to cope with her or his emotional and physical pain. At the same time, we should not lose sight of the importance for the child of an emotionally supportive social environment.

REACTIONS OF DYING CHILDREN

Generally, the feelings children express about their own dying and death are the same as those expressed by people of other ages: guilt, fear, anxiety, anger, denial. Some children regress to behavior that they had previously outgrown. So do some adults. Because their cognitive development is not yet complete, however, children may interpret their impending deaths in somewhat different fashions.

One interpretation children make is that their death is a punishment for having been "bad." Although adults may feel this way also (see Chapter 3), their intellectual understanding casts a different light on the feeling. Eight-year-olds, for example, are at a stage in their lives when they believe "there is a logical, inevitable planned sequence to events" (Easson, 1974, p. 26). Therefore, having a fatal illness can only be understood as a dreadful punishment for a dreadful transgression. Since all children misbehave in some fashion, the opportunity for projection is always available (Easson, 1974).

The course of the illness is also an obvious factor in determining a child's feelings. Being unable to play with friends, undergoing unpleasant treatments, observing the strain on the family, encountering the ambivalence of brothers and sisters—all can occur during the duration of a fatal illness. Children become cognizant of being different, but don't know how to cope with this. Resentment builds as treatments become more complex and the opportunities for normal living become more limited (Toch, 1977).

Separation fears, death fears and anxieties, and mutilation fears are reported with considerable consistency in studies of dying children (Morrissey, 1965; Natterson & Knudson, 1960). These feelings, of course, occur at all ages, and it is difficult to know how much they are reactions to treatment, hospitalization, pain, and the fears and anxieties displayed by others and how much they are generated directly by the knowledge of impending death.

The importance of understanding the sources of these fears extends beyond intellectual curiosity. If children are fearful of their actual death, it might be appropriate to respond by permitting them greater freedom to discuss their fears in an open awareness context. On the other hand, if the fears are based on a lack of understanding of the treatment procedures or on perceptions of the anxieties of others, we can attempt to deal with these matters directly. In either instance, the fear of abandonment and separation is likely to occur, and the child's anxieties can be partially assuaged both by verbal reassurance and by tangible proof that caring adults will continue to be available.

The concept of mutilation, mentioned several times, requires further explanation. There are two causes of mutilation fears. First, death itself is a kind of mutilation, a destruction of the physical body. The awareness that the body will deteriorate during the dying process is frightening: it indicates loss of control and a changing self. I will no longer be a whole person, but only part of a person. The comparable awareness of the body's decay after death is also very upsetting to some people, although many children may not know that the body decays.

Second, the effects of the illness or of medical treatments may be seen as mutilation. One adolescent had lost her hair through radiation treatment for cancer and had been wearing a poorly fitting wig. When her wig was replaced with a more attractive one, she no longer felt so self-conscious nor was she as concerned about how her friends viewed her. She felt much better about herself after that (Schowalter, 1977).

THE DYING ADOLESCENT

What little has been written about the dying adolescent has not added anything meaningful to what has already been discussed in this and previous chapters. Many teenagers are placed on hospital pediatrics wards and are, therefore, treated along with younger children. Sometimes they are involved in helping to care for the younger children, and this offers them some meaningful activity during their illness.

Adolescents are assumed, probably justifiably, to be extremely self-conscious about their physical appearance and deeply concerned about what others think of them. They are just beginning to establish their independence from parents and their own identity. They have begun to look forward to the end of their schooling and the beginning of what some of them see as "their real life." Of course, death changes this. Although I can't point to research or the experiences of people who care for dying adolescents, I would assume that adolescents approach their death much as most adults do.

There is one exception: teenagers have only begun to live their lives, and they are very likely to feel cheated out of what they had taken for granted would be theirs. I would hypothesize that adolescents, like young adults—especially young adults with new families or new careers—would be very angry to learn they were going to die before having had adequate opportunity to live. Because adolescents are more likely than other age groups to die from accidents, suicides, and homicides, their deaths usually occur quickly and unexpectedly. This means that the dying process for teenagers is usually very brief. Therefore, adolescents do not share some of the concerns other dying persons do.

For this very reason, the dying adolescent is in a uniquely different situation. Physicians and nurses seldom have had much experience with the age group; medical and other professional literature says little about the psychological state of the dying adolescent; and so many adults find teenagers to be mysteries, in general, that a dying teenager would be considered particularly troublesome. On the one hand, they are categorized as children in the hospital facility; on the other hand, they have an adult's comprehension of what is happening to them. This is obviously a topic that requires a great deal more attention.

YOUTH AND THE MIDDLE-AGED

Most of the literature about the dying is specifically about children and the elderly or about everybody else lumped together. Because I've discussed the "everybody-else" category in previous chapters, here I will examine a number of concerns that appear to be specific for adults of various age groups.

First, as mentioned before, as one grows older, the causes of death and, consequently, the processes of dying change. When deaths from heart, stroke, and cancer replace deaths from accidents, homicides, and suicides, the time that the dying person has to plan for his or her own death increases. This permits spending time with family members, talking about one's own imminent death, winding up plans and projects, and making preparations for survivors.

What I die from determines to an appreciable extent the pain, discomfort, financial cost, awareness of self, and cognitive competence that I experience during the dying process. The person dying from cancer may have weeks, months, or sometimes years to continue working, being with people, completing old and even generating new tasks, traveling, or reading. In this case it isn't age per se that influences the dying process; rather, the causes of death typical of different ages lead to different dying processes.

Second, older people are at a unique point in their careers. By 50 or 55, most people can predict reasonably well their future work lives. Future promotions and work projects, for example, are rather predictable. At this time many people begin to look to sources outside of work for satisfaction. It is not so much that people are planning for retirement, although I believe that that does occur in a preliminary fashion, but that the challenges of major new gains from work diminish. Certainly, this is not true for everyone. Some people, like women returning to the work force, enter new careers at this age. And, of course, others still find excitement and new opportunity in their careers. At this point, however, satisfaction from one's work usually comes from doing the job well, rather than from exploring new territory. Consequently, when people this age find they are dying, they feel that they are losing what they have, not what they might yet attain.

Third, the older I am when I die, the less likely I am to feel that I am dying "ahead of time." To die at 35 is to be cheated out of what I believe life promised me; if I die at 55, I will still feel cheated, but less so.

WHEN THE ELDERLY DIE

To discuss the dying of older persons is, for the most part, to continue examining the topics of the two previous sections. The major factor is not the age of the dying person, but the condition causing death. There is no need to repeat previous discussions. Here we will look at matters that affect the elderly with greater frequency than other age groups.

First, the death of an elderly person is considered by the community to be less tragic than other deaths (for example, Kalish & Reynolds, 1976). Therefore, the social value of the remaining life of the older person diminishes, and he or she is likely to receive less attention and fewer life-sustaining measures than younger people. The investment of time, energy, money, and personal affect in the remaining time of a dying older person is often seen to produce little reward.

Second, because it is assumed that an older person will die soon of some illness—if not the present one—the impetus for keeping the person alive or even for providing optimum care is less.

Third, many older persons reside in long-term-care institutions during their dying process, especially during the early phases prior to hospitalization. This has obvious implications for the kinds of family contact that occur during this period and for the extent of professional medical attention.

Fourth, because more older persons than non-elderly are confused or comatose during the period leading up to death, they receive a different kind of care. Communication is more difficult or impossible. They are already functioning as non-persons in many ways, and they may even engender resentment from those who are required to care for them, because the demanding nature of their illness is not compensated for by a reciprocal human relationship.

Fifth, an extremely high proportion of older persons, especially older women, enter the living/dying interval without a spouse to help in their care. Some of them also do not have children, brothers, or sisters who are capable and willing to participate in their care. Consequently, they may die without the ongoing love and attention that are, at least potentially, available to those with families. They are also less likely to have an advocate to intercede on their behalf with health or social agency staff.

Sixth, an older person frequently has reviewed his or her life; this reminiscing over an extended period of time helps to integrate the person's entire life (Butler, 1963). When an older person realizes that the living/dying interval has begun, the pressure to review his or her life increases. On the one hand, doing so may make death easier; on the other hand, impending death may encourage the effort. Butler adds an important point qualifying his suggestion that reminiscing may make death more acceptable: "I do not intend to imply that a 'serene and dignified acceptance of death' is necessarily appropriate, noble, or to be valued. Those who die screaming may be expressing a rage that is as fitting as dignity" (Butler, 1963, in Neugarten, 1965, p. 494).

All of the foregoing suggest that the conditions in which older people die are more isolated and lonely than those in which younger persons die. Sometimes we seem to justify the deaths of older people: we remind ourselves of how ill they were; we suggest that somehow they're to blame for their deaths; we insist that they had nothing more to live for anyway.

Although the elderly appear better able to cope with dying and death, they may still struggle to maintain life. Their struggle probably receives less support than the efforts of younger people. I would hypothesize that one of the reasons older people die sooner than expected is that, having lost support from others, they find themselves with less sense of being cared for and being cared about. "The terminally aged may be as helpless as a child, but they seldom arouse tenderness" (Weisman, 1972, p. 144). Eventually they tire and simply give up life.

DYING IN INSTITUTIONS AND RETIREMENT COMMUNITIES

What happens to older people when they die in institutions or retirement communities? Although they are less likely to have access to their adult children in both settings, in the retirement communities, at least, they are very likely to receive support from friends who reside near them. And if the facility is church-related, there may be a sense of connection with their faith. Both settings serve constantly to remind older people of their mortality, because they frequently see other residents become ill and die.

Sometimes this constant exposure makes the elderly come to accept their own deaths more easily. For example, the author of one incisive study of a retirement community concluded that its residents accepted impending death in a matter-of-fact fashion and were not preoccupied with dying.

Many elderly persons (in the general community, as well as in retirement communities) are ready to die but, because they have an obligation to care for a husband or a sister, they feel useful to someone else, and this feeling makes their lives meaningful. A woman in her 90s stated "I'd like to live as old as I am useful. And after that, I'm willing to go" (Marshall, 1975); another, when asked how long she would like to live, answered "[Until] I'm no use to my sister any longer" (Marshall, 1975).

Nursing homes are, of course, very different from retirement communities. In fact, about their only similarity is a population of older persons, and, even then, the average age in a nursing home is usually at least ten years older than in a retirement community. Although only about 5% of persons over age 65 are in any kind of long-term-care institution at any time, a much higher percentage—probably around 25%—are in a nursing home at some time in their lives (Kastenbaum & Candy, 1973).

When an older person enters a nursing home, he or she and the staff are both aware that it is likely to be the person's last residence. In a way then, the dying process begins there, regardless of the condition of the person's health. Residents may seek confirmation from the staff and from within themselves that they do indeed have a future, that is, that death is not near. Without this confirmation their feelings of hope wane. They find themselves bargaining for postponement of death—an endeavor for which the resident may or may not receive encouragement and support from the staff (Gustafson, 1973).

Several studies have examined the effects of relocation on the health and longevity of elderly nursing-home patients. Although the results have been somewhat in conflict, the general conclusions reached were that older residents who were in poor health were likely to die sooner as a result of relocating, even if the move improved their living conditions. If residents are to be moved, it is important to provide them with as much preparation for the move and as much information about the new facilities as possible. Moving from one residence to another is stressful for everyone, even for those who choose to move, and elderly nursing-home patients who are already in very poor health and confused are likely to find the move especially stressful. This may well account for the increase in deaths (Rowland, 1977).

WHEN DYING IS ALL RIGHT

There comes a time, especially for older persons, when dying is all right. To use the expression suggested by Marshall (1980), there comes a time when dying is "legitimated," a point at which death is neither too soon nor too late. Marshall proposes five situations in which death is considered preferable:

First, when one is unable to be active;

Second, when one is unable to be useful;

Third, when one becomes a burden because of physical infirmity or social dependency;

Fourth, when one loses one's mental faculties;

Fifth, when one has progressively deteriorating physical health and concomitant physical discomfort.

Each of us depends on our system of values to decide if we would want to live in each of the five situations. Of course, a hypothetical decision might well be contradicted when a real decision has to be made. Although a person of any age might have to make these choices, they are more likely to fall to an older person.

Each of the five cases exemplifies a situation which runs counter to the general values of our society and its criteria for a full life. We place great stress in our society on autonomy and independence, on competence, comfort, activity and involvement, health, growth and the possibility of growth. When any one of these becomes impossible, the potential for enjoying the kind of life that we have been brought up to value diminishes greatly. Not all societies are concerned if the elderly must be cared for; not all societies believe that being useful is the criterion for a worthwhile life—but our society does. Another culture might consider death preferable to bringing intense shame to the family, to being captured in battle, to being entered by an evil spirit.

If you work with the elderly and want them to choose life, rather than death, when faced with any of the above five situations, you have three alternative approaches. First, you can try to help the older person believe that death is still worse than any of the situations. Second, you can try to help the older person believe that the situation itself really isn't so bad. And third, you can try to change the circumstances of the situation, if possible, so that the older person does, for example, remain active or useful.

Since you, too, will have to make decisions, based on your own values, about when life is worthwhile, you should begin reflecting on the subject now. Once you reach your own conclusions, however, you must be doubly careful not to impose or project them upon someone else.

Perhaps it would be most appropriate to close this chapter with the words of someone who was dying. The writer was a 13-year-old boy dying from leukemia, and the excerpt is from a letter that he wrote to physicians and nurses:

> I am dying. . . . No one likes to talk about such things. In fact, no one likes to talk about much at all. . . . I am the one who is dying. I know you feel insecure, don't know what to say, don't know what to do. But please believe me, if you care, you can't go wrong. Just admit that you care. This is what we search for. We may ask for whys and wherefores, but we really don't want answers. Don't run away. Wait. All I want to know is that there will be someone to hold my hand when I need it. I'm afraid. . . . I've never died before. . . .*

*Quoted in Christopher News Notes, #206, "Let's Talk About Death," undated. Reprinted by permission of the *Cadillac Evening News*, Cadillac, Michigan.

PART 3
GRIEF AND BEREAVEMENT

*El Funeral de Mi Tia Elena**

I have recently returned from a trip to a small town in northern Mexico, where I attended the funeral of my maternal aunt, my Tia Elena. My purpose in giving this descriptive account is to relate my experiences and sentiments as a Mexican American to a Mexican funeral.

Tia Elena was in her late 50s when she died, the mother of three boys and one girl, ranging in age from 19 to 29. Her dying was prolonged and painful, but I will describe that later, in keeping with the way I learned of the circumstances.

ARRIVAL IN MEXICO

I left Los Angeles International Airport Tuesday evening and flew directly to Tucson. From there I was driven to the small town . . . where my aunt had lived most of her life and where she was to be buried. My thoughts were engaged by my aunt and her children, but they also encompassed my other relatives, some of whom I had never seen and others whom I would see for the first time in many years. . . . I had already been cautioned by other relatives here in the States, "Mexican funerals are much different than the ones here. They are longer and more of an emotional strain."

As is customary in Mexico, a wake was held prior to the burial. In most deaths, the body is brought to the home of the deceased for viewing by relatives and friends for a period of 24 hours. In this instance, however, the wake was held in the home of my Uncle Jaime, my Tia's oldest brother. This occurred because my aunt had expressed her wishes to be buried in her small hometown, where she had lived most of her life and where her parents are buried, rather than . . . where she had resided with her husband and children for the previous ten years. . . .

I arrived at my Uncle Jaime's home the morning before the burial and a few hours before my aunt's body was to arrive for the wake. I noticed that

*Adapted from "The Funeral of My Aunt Elena," in *A Funeral in Mexico: Description and Analysis*, by P. Osuna and D. K. Reynolds. In *Omega*, 1970, *1*. Reprinted by permission of Baywood Publishing Company.

the immediate family was not yet present, but that my Tia Laura (Uncle Jaime's wife) and a few relatives and friends of my deceased aunt (all female) were there, and were all dressed traditionally in black mourning clothes. I had worn a navy blue dress for the trip, but I also made sure I had packed a black dress, just in case. . . . My relatives later assured me when I asked, that the navy blue dress I was wearing was perfectly appropriate, explaining that since I was from "the other side" (U.S.A.), I was not expected to follow strict customs. I remained in the navy blue dress for that day and wore the black one the following day for the burial service.

PREPARING THE WAKE

Preparations for the wake were well under way. The living room furniture had been rearranged. All the tables, chairs, and couches had been placed along these walls, while the area along the fourth wall was occupied by a piano upon which the floral wreaths were to be arranged. Two chrome stands upon which the casket would be set were in the center of the room.

Women were busy taking care of last-minute arrangements. Most of my Tia's friends and relatives were in the kitchen helping to prepare the food that would be eaten during the wake. A few women were busy setting up more chairs in the living room, while two others were dusting the four tall silver candlesticks borrowed from the town's casket maker. These would be placed alongside the four corners of the casket.

Although I don't recall ever making the decision to participate in the arrangements, I soon found myself helping place large white candles into the silver holders; these would be lit the moment the body arrived and would remain burning until the end of the wake. I did what seemed natural and what I felt was part of my duty as a member of the bereaved family and a Latin woman. My Tia's four sisters were present at this time, but they did not help with these menial tasks, nor were they expected to do so, since it was implicitly assumed that their sorrow was greater than that of the other women and, therefore, they should be absolved of these duties.

During this time there was a constant flow of people entering and leaving the house. Most of them were neighbors who were coming to bring some food or to offer their assistance. . . . It was not unusual for neighbors to come and offer their condolences to my aunt's four sisters, and to take the opportunity for saying hello and briefly [to] catch up on what had occurred over the years since they had last met.

Approximately an hour or so before the body arrived, a few men started coming to the house. They were my Tia's two brothers and a few of her nephews. Like the rest of the people, the nephews would first go over to their four aunts and uncles and offer their condolences and then mingle with the rest of the people.

The general trend of conversation centered around the cause of my Tia's death and the shock it had been. The immediate family had only learned of the gravity of my aunt's illness on the day before she died, while other relatives were unsuspecting of her condition until her death was announced. . . .

THE WAKE BEGINS

Emotions were beginning to mount as the hour approached for the arrival of the body. I was in the kitchen conversing with some of my relatives when someone came into the room announcing, "Ya llego." ("She's here.") Immediately everyone went into the living room. . . .

One by one, my Tia's four children entered the room. They were greeted by their aunts, uncles, cousins and other relatives. Soon they started asking for my uncle, my Tia's husband, and were told by one of the sons that he was too upset to come over now. No one questioned or criticized my uncle's behavior. The sound of muffled crying and voices saying, "I'm so sorry," seemed to echo through the rooms.

Within minutes the house began to fill with even more people. Several of them were friends and ex-business acquaintances of my widowed uncle. The men, including my Tia's three sons, were not dressed in black. They were, however, all dressed in suits and, perhaps the only sign of mourning apparel was an occasional black tie.

I recall leaving the living room and going into the kitchen with one of my cousins. When I returned to the living room a few minutes later, the casket was being placed on the chrome stand in the center of the room. It was smoky gray in color with silver handles. The casket, made in the United States, had been selected in Guadalajara by my Tia's four children. As I approached the casket, I noticed two of my aunts dusting it off.

There was a man standing near the casket whom I assumed was the driver of the private hearse. He was talking with Tia Laura, and then he slowly opened the lid of the casket. The casket was lined in white satin and there was a glass cover shielding the body. He then unscrewed the frame of the glass cover so that Tia Laura could reposition the body which had slid down a little toward the foot of the casket. . . .

The body, which had been embalmed in Guadalajara, was covered by a white satin shroud, and according to custom, only the face could be seen. After the corpse had been repositioned, the glass cover was put in place again, and thereafter never removed. Only that part of the casket lid covering the upper half of the body was left opened. On the closed part of the casket a wreath was placed with a banner reading, "From your loving children and husband. . . ."

Almost everyone present in the room went past the casket to view the body. The women often cried softly while the men were more restrained. Afterwards, they gathered in small groups in the living room and exchanged comments.

Frequently, I heard remarks concerning what a shock her death was, how fast the cancer had caused her death, or how almost unrecognizable she looked. Inevitably, nearly everyone at one time or another commented on their last living experience with my Tia. . . .

MY UNCLE ARRIVES

A short time later, my Tia's husband arrived. Again, everyone came to him and paid their condolences. Emotions seemed to rise again and some of my aunts and relatives started to cry when they saw my uncle. Uncle Jaime then took my Tia's husband into the dining room and gave him a small glass of straight liquor.

The people then began to settle themselves in various rooms. A handful stayed in the living room while nearly all the older men went into the dining room, where they remained throughout most of the wake. A few of my aunts went into one of the three bedrooms with other women who were consoling them. The majority of the women went into the kitchen and took charge of serving coffee and food. When I entered the kitchen, there was a group of women sitting around the table with my Tia's children, while Tia Laura was giving the driver of the hearse something to eat.

Conversation centered around finding out as much as possible about my Tia's illness. "What had the doctors said?" "Had she suffered?" Other questions were directed to the circumstances surrounding her last moments in the hospital. "Had she known she had cancer?" "Did she know she was dying?" For the next few hours my Tia's four children sat at the kitchen table, surrounded by relatives, answering such questions.

My Tia's husband spent most of the time in the dining room with the other men. Once in a while, he entered the kitchen, but when he did, all conversation regarding my Tia's illness, death and funeral arrangements stopped so as not to upset him further. Since I did not spend much time in the dining room, I have no information as to the topics of the men's conversation. They did, however, seem to be spending a great deal of time talking, eating and drinking. Unlike the women, the men drank mostly liquor, which was provided by Uncle Jaime. The liquor included everything from tequila to cognac to Johnny Walker. Although there was quite a bit of heavy drinking, no one seemed to lose control.

In the course of the time I spent in the kitchen, I learned many things regarding my Tia's sickness and death. I found out that she never confided to anyone in the family that she knew she was going to die. It was not until after her death that her children were informed by the nun who had nursed her in the hospital, that my Tia had confided in her and had made requests for funeral arrangements. She had also asked for the last rites, five days before her death. As my cousin so aptly put it, "All that time we tried so hard to keep the fact that she was going to die a secret from her and instead of us fooling her, she ended up fooling us." There had even been times when her pain had been so great that she had had to ask her son to leave her bedside, so that he would not become aware of her agony.

Another point of interest, which was revealed in the talk in the kitchen, was that the immediate family, after leaving Guadalajara, stopped off at their home . . . where they awaited the arrival of the casket. While the family waited, neighbors and friends dropped in to pay their condolences and await the casket, too. Late that afternoon, when the casket finally arrived, the family opened the casket for viewing upon the request of the neighbors. This allowed those people who were unable to attend the burial the opportunity for a last farewell. At that time, the immediate family accompanied by neighbors and a few friends kept an all-night vigil. The following morning the family left with the casket for the place of burial.

At different intervals throughout the course of the wake, friends and relatives would go into the living room and view the body. They would sit or stand by the casket for as long as they desired. Usually there was a member of my Tia's family already present since it is the responsibility of family members to see . . . that the body is never left unattended. During the twenty-four hours that the body was present in my uncle's home, it was never left alone. On various occasions, I, too, walked into the living room, not always to view the body but just to sit by the casket. I found this very comforting since it gave me an opportunity to withdraw from social interaction and spend as much time as I wished reminiscing on past experiences with my Tia.

THE ROSARY

Later that evening the priest arrived at my uncle's home and said the Rosary. This event took place in the living room and was attended mostly by women. However, I did notice three or four men in the back of the room. After the Rosary, the priest was invited to dinner, and as was the case with the driver of the hearse, he promptly accepted.

As the early hours of the morning approached, people became less tense and more relaxed. There was even a moment when someone started telling jokes in the kitchen, but this was quickly criticized and discontinued. The trend of conversation drifted from things connected with my Tia's illness or death to more general topics. People who had not seen each other, perhaps in many years, began recounting past experiences.

By this time most of the friends had already gone, and only family members remained. My Tia's husband had left also and did not return even for the Requiem Mass or for the burial. My Tia's four children took this opportunity to slip out and get a few hours of sleep. For this my cousins were criticized by some of the relatives who remained in the house.

It was felt that they should at least have taken turns standing guard over the body as is customary; the fact that they were very tired was no excuse because it was their duty to watch the body. This criticism was made despite the fact that one of my Tia's sisters had remained in the living room all night watching over the body until the casket was removed for burial.

THE DAY OF BURIAL

For the day of the burial all preparations were made exactly as my Tia had requested. Neighbors, friends and relatives began to gather again at my uncle's home. Again, the women were all dressed in black but this time they wore mantillas. As soon as the immediate family arrived, the atmosphere again became tense and strained, for this was the sign that the end of the wake was . . . near. Once again people walked past to view the body and once more many tears were shed. I saw my two uncles' eyes filled with tears as they both took one last look at their younger sister.

The floral wreaths sent by families, friends and business acquaintances had been removed so that they could be placed in the church and at the grave site. Then the casket was taken to the church in the fashion my Tia had requested.

She did not want her body to be taken to the church in a hearse but instead asked that the casket be carried on men's shoulders down the streets of her hometown. Tia Elena did not care to have a pompous, lavish funeral even though economically she could have well afforded one. Hers was a well-to-do family, even by North American standards. She had explicitly stated that she preferred to be buried as her father and mother had been, in a simple, humble manner.

The nine men stood ready to carry the heavy casket. They included my Tia's sons, nephews and son-in-law. As the men walked out of my uncle's home and on to the street, I heard the bells of the church tolling in the distance. Men, women and children came out of their homes and stood in their doorways as the procession slowly passed. Most of the young men walked behind the casket while a few women walked along the sidewalk to the church. The other people followed in cars.

When we arrived at the church, the men carried the casket inside. In the church the priest dressed in black vestments was waiting to say Requiem Mass. The immediate family sat in the front pews of the church near the casket. The other women generally sat a few rows behind the immediate family while the men sat in the back of the church. During the mass the casket remained closed.

After mass the priest came down the altar to the casket. He walked around the casket twice, first sprinkling it with holy water and then incensing it. Finishing this, the priest nodded to the pall bearers. This was their cue that the religious ceremony had ended and that they were to remove the body.

By the time the people filed out of the church, the body had already been placed in a white hearse. From there the body was taken to the cemetery. The procession to the cemetery was somewhat different. The hearse led the way . . . but this time a group of men both young and old followed along on foot. No women joined this group, instead they followed behind in cars.

THE INTERMENT

By the time I reached the cemetery, the casket had already been placed by the grave. My Tia's open grave was completely visible. It was approximately six feet deep, eight feet long and four feet wide. The lower half of the grave had been lined with bricks while the upper half was unlined. The grave had been dug to accommodate two coffins. One space would be occupied by my Tia's coffin and the remaining space will be given to the next person in the family who dies and wishes to be buried in that town. The grave site is located near other family graves.

After everyone had arrived at the grave site the casket was once again opened. My Tia's three sons stood near the casket and walked over to view the body for the last time. Then my Tia's youngest son, 19 years old, bent over and kissed the coffin. Her two other sons only paused briefly. They were followed by three of my aunts. For me this was the most emotionally draining time of the entire service. My tears were now flowing as were those of the others; they were, however, tears for the living, not for the dead.

The casket was then closed and lowered with straps into the grave. Everyone stood watching while two workmen placed wooden boards over the brick-lined portion of the grave. A workman then proceeded to step down into the grave. Then another workman handed him one pail of cement after another until he had completely sealed off the lower portion of the grave. Finishing this, the workmen left and were soon followed by the immediate family and other relatives.

The next evening, as I was flying back to Los Angeles, I thought about the intimacy with death that had been expressed in the wake and in the funeral and burial ceremonies. Emotions were expressed honestly and without embarrassment, yet the life-oriented tasks of eating, drinking and relating to other people went on.

12

THE GRIEVING PROCESS

Anything that you have, you can lose; anything you are attached to, you can be separated from; anything you love can be taken away from you. Yet, if you really have nothing to lose, you have nothing.

There are numerous kinds of losses that each of us suffers, and there is no way we can avoid loss in our lives. Consider your own life and ask yourself how often you have lost each of the following:

- ○ a parent, brother or sister, spouse, or child through death;
- ○ a familiar relationship with a spouse, parent, or child through divorce;
- ○ a job that you either liked or had become attached to;
- ○ a familiar neighborhood;
- ○ a home you either liked or had become attached to;
- ○ some physical capacity, such as the ability to walk or to hear;
- ○ a pet, through death or other cause;
- ○ faith in or respect for an important system of religious, moral or political beliefs;
- ○ something you owned that was important to you, such as a wedding ring, a car you loved, or a family heirloom;
- ○ membership in a group that was important to you, such as a social club or a group of close friends;
- ○ anything else that really mattered to you.

There are other kinds of losses: the loss of a wonderful dream for the future, carried by so many young and some not-so-young; the loss of innocence, when, for example, a child first learns that the world can be cruel or adults malevolent; the loss of sexual virginity; the loss of respect for someone previously idolized. Each of these losses can lead to bereavement, grief, and mourning.

Bereavement is a state involving loss. In fact, to *bereave* means "to take away from, to rob, to dispossess." Although the term usually implies that the loss produces unhappiness, this is not essential to its meaning: my father, to whom I am very close, dies, and I am bereaved; my mother, whom I have not seen in 15 years, dies, and I am also bereaved—perhaps equally so in the strict definition. In both instances, I have had something taken away from me, although the value of that something differs greatly.

Grief refers to the sorrow, anger, guilt, and confusion that can arise when you have suffered a loss or are bereaved. It seems fair to say that you can't grieve without being bereaved, but you can be bereaved and not grieve. Although the process of grieving is necessary to full recovery from a significant loss, grieving itself means pain and suffering.

Mourning is the overt expression of grief and bereavement. The ways in which we mourn are heavily influenced by our culture; we may dress in black or in white, attend funerals or say prayers at home, drink and laugh at the wake or take tranquilizers and cry at the funeral.

THE NATURE OF GRIEF AND ITS PAIN

"The pain of grief is just as much a part of life as the joy of love; it is, perhaps, the price we pay for love, the cost of commitment" (Parkes, 1972, pp. 5–6).

> I always emphasize to my clients that they only do what they choose to do. When they say they don't have any choice, I point out that they have a choice, but that the alternative is too unappealing to be considered. One young man was telling me of the pain he was suffering because of the death of his father, and he challenged me by saying that he hadn't wanted his father to die and he hadn't wanted the pain of his grief. I asked him why his father's death pained him so much, and he responded by saying that he had loved his father. I then suggested that he could have avoided the pain by not loving his father. He was quickly aware that the love he had for his father was well worth the suffering he was experiencing. Realizing that he had made a choice and that his choice was a good one, he felt less unhappy and much more willing to accept the pain and survive it. [Reprinted by permission of John Enright.]

Human beings are not the only form of animal life to suffer grief. Other animals, especially primates, also grieve when loss occurs, especially when an infant dies or when captivity separates them from companions or mates (Averill, 1968). Although the evidence for grief in animals other than primates is limited, some individuals report observing similar behavior in dogs and even birds. "The loss of a mate by one of these birds (jackdaws and geese) typically occasions frantic searching and calling. If this is unsuccessful in reuniting the pair, a period of depressed activity may ensue, including a loss of sexual interest in potential new partners" (Averill, 1968, p. 732).

STAGES OF NORMAL GRIEF

Stages of grief, like stages of dying, have frequently been described in the literature about death. Many people have applied Elisabeth Kübler-Ross's five stages of dying to the process of grieving as well, and this application can serve as a useful framework. I personally prefer other stage theories of grieving. Averill, for example, proposes three stages of grieving: shock, despair, and recovery. British psychiatrist Colin Parkes suggests four: numbness, pining, depression, and recovery.

In comparing these theories, one sees that the last two are almost identical, except that Averill encompasses Parkes' two stages of pining and depression in the one stage of despair. Kübler-Ross's denial stage is comparable to the first stages described by Averill and Parkes; she has no stage similar to Parkes' pining, but her stages of anger and depression are counterparts of despair and depression; her final stage of acceptance is the equivalent of recovery. So the three theories parallel one another.

In reviewing these theories one should keep in mind that the stages of grieving are not invariable or even, necessarily, adaptive. Perhaps it is most useful to heed Parkes' (1972) reminder that grief is a process and that what is observed early in the process of grieving differs from what is seen later. There is also a strong tendency to underestimate the time it takes to move from the initial shock of death to moderate recovery. People, of course, return to what appears to a casual observer to be normal functioning in a few days, but the pangs of grief continue for weeks and months, although with diminishing frequency and intensity. A reminder of the dead person or simply a period where the level of general stress is high may produce a wave of grief one, two, or several years later. Certainly it takes at least one year for a reasonable recovery in most instances, and a two-year period is not unusual (a time period also proposed by Weiss, 1975, for recovery from divorce). In some ways an important loss always remains with us.

NORMAL RESPONSES TO THE DEATH OF SOMEONE LOVED

Undoubtedly Erich Lindemann's 1944 article on the symptomatology of grief is the single most influential piece of writing on the topic. Basing his comments on interviews and psychotherapy with over 100 bereaved persons who had lost family members in a catastrophic restaurant fire, the psychiatrist developed careful descriptions of normal and pathological grieving reactions.

There are an immense number of possible responses to the death of a loved person that are all part of the normal grieving process. For the most part, the period of grieving enables the bereaved person to deal with the intense feelings that follow the death; sometimes the feelings are so intense and so unusual for the person that she or he worries about being "crazy."

One set of symptoms common to all the people whom Lindemann interviewed included "sensations of somatic distress occurring in waves lasting from twenty minutes to an hour at a time, a feeling of tightness in the throat, choking with shortness of breath, need for sighing, and an empty feeling in the abdomen, lack of muscular power and an intense subjective distress described as tension or mental pain" (1944, p. 187). Parkes (1972) refers to this constellation of reactions as "pangs" and indicates that they are the single most characteristic response to grief. Adding sobbing and crying to Lindemann's description, Parkes says these pangs begin shortly after the death—a few hours or a few days later—and last from a few days to about two weeks. Over time, the pangs occur less frequently, until eventually they are expressed only when there is an anniversary or other reminder of the death.

In instances in which grief pangs do not occur right away, the bereaved frequently feel numb; that is, they perceive themselves as being without appropriate feelings and sometimes without any feelings at all (Parkes, 1972). The numbness is not continuous; strong feelings will sometimes interrupt, and it tends to pass within a few days. In effect, it appears to be the counterpart of a state of shock after an accident. Persons falling from mountains describe a similar state (Noyes & Kletti, 1972), which is characterized by a sense of unreality and lack of feelings.

Other symptoms have also been mentioned (Lindemann, 1944; Parkes, 1972): deep sighing, lack of physical strength, restless and aimless hyperactivity, loss of appetite, preoccupation with thoughts of the dead person, and loss of interest in activities, people, or things that had previously given pleasure and enjoyment. (It is worth mentioning that, although Lindemann and Parkes are not describing identical occurrences, their descriptions are sufficiently similar to have warranted integration for this discussion.)

DEPRESSION, SADNESS, SORROW

Everything we know about grief indicates that sadness and sorrow that may be intense enough to be considered depression are among the most familiar characteristics of grieving. The death of a loved person is an objective loss, and we are sad when we lose what we love. The grandfather of bereavement research, sociologist Thomas Eliot (1955), described this sorrow as "inevitable but not insurmountable."

We anticipate that people who are grieving will behave in ways that we might consider pathological under other circumstances (Averill, 1968). Numerous investigators have found that widows and widowers describe many more depressive symptoms than do people in carefully selected non-bereaved comparison groups (for example, Maddison & Viola, 1968; Parkes & Brown, 1972). One study found that 35 % of a group of 109 widows and widowers who were evaluated one month after bereavement displayed symptoms similar to those of depressed psychiatric patients. The only real difference between those who were very depressed and those who were not was that fewer of the former had children to whom they felt close living nearby. The investigators proposed that this group's lack of access to emotional support from their children had contributed to their depression (Clayton, Halikas, & Maurice, 1972). Not having children available and no longer having the companionship of a spouse, these individuals may have become lonely and isolated.

A follow-up study with the same persons a year later produced additional interesting results. At that time only 16 (17 %) of the 92 participants located were considered depressed; 12 (15 %) of the depressed widows and widowers had been depressed a year earlier, and 4 who previously had seemed healthy had become depressed. On the other hand, 24 of the 36 persons who had been depressed after the first month of bereavement and 52 of the 56 persons who had not been depressed were not depressed a year later. The depressed group also reported a high incidence of dizziness, blurred vision, chest pains, and poor general health. These findings confirm the results of other studies (for example, Bornstein, Clayton, Halikas, Maurice, & Robins, 1973).

At the end of the study, the authors make an extremely important point: ". . . grief is not a model for psychotic depression. Although some of our patients had depressive symptoms, none could be called psychotic at 13 months. . . . The normal depression of widowhood . . . is . . . different from clinical affective" emotional disorder (Bornstein et al., 1973, p. 566).

DENIAL

When death occurs suddenly and unexpectedly—and even in some other circumstances—the response of close family members may be denial. Sometimes this denial is so radical that the survivors do not believe that the person is actually dead. More often, however, their feelings are split, knowing the person is dead yet not able to believe it. You continue to make plans which implicitly assume the person is still alive; you think, for example, as you drive home from work, how nice it will be to discuss your exciting new development program with—and then reality intrudes.

Denial may take other forms. Someone will maintain a child's room just as it was when he or she died. A widower, for example, will continue to say "we" even though only one person is now involved. It's difficult to know exactly how much each of these actions depends on denial and how much on other factors, but denial is normally at least partially involved.

SEARCHING

Part of the process of pining is what has been referred to as the "search for the lost object." In the case of death, of course, the lost object is the deceased person. " 'I can't help looking for him everywhere . . . I walk around searching for him . . . I felt that if I could have come somewhere I could have found him' " (Parkes, 1972, p. 44).

This is a restless kind of searching, accompanied by preoccupation with thoughts of the dead person. Part of this is a perceptual sensitization so that others seem to look like the dead person, and varied events constantly recall general or specific memories of him or her. Sometimes grieving persons turn over specific past events in their minds, perhaps in an attempt to hold on to the person who died.

As might be expected, dreams of the dead person are not uncommon, but more significant are experiences in which the survivor feels the dead person is actually present. Although this topic was mentioned in Chapter 6, it merits attention here also. A familiar experience for bereaved persons, and one that sometimes occurs months and years after the death, is sensing the presence of the dead individual. "Just as I was falling asleep, I looked over to his side of the bed, and I know I saw him. I shook my head and looked again, but he had disappeared. It was like a dream, but it wasn't a dream." Or "Every evening, after dinner, we would sit and have a cup of tea together. I still sit in that chair and have tea, and sometimes I just know he's in his chair and having a cup with me. Once I even smelled his pipe, even though I had thrown those things out long ago, and I hear his voice in my head. Of course, I know all this sounds crazy."

These experiences can be understood as part of searching for or trying to contact the dead person. When one recent widow told her young children that their father had died, they took his clothes out of the closet and curled up under them. And my own experience is relevant here.

> When I was a junior in college, I wrote a short story about a young man who had gone to the cemetery to visit his father's grave. He had never been there before, but he felt sure he could find the grave without instructions. In effect, he believed he would have some form of mystic guidance. However, he never found the grave, and it was a deeply moving experience for him.

The odd thing is that I don't really know today whether I was writing about my own personal experience or not. I don't think I ever tried to visit my father's grave (his body was transported 500 miles from the city where we then lived to the place where he had been born), but I'm not completely certain that I didn't make the attempt. This is a graphic example of the search for the dead person and the confusion it creates.

RELIEF

Mingled with other emotions after a death are often feelings of relief. Now it's over. Now I don't have to wonder when he will die or whether she will be in pain. Now I don't have to look at him, lying in the hospital and suffering—and suffer myself as I do. Now I don't have to spend hours every day, changing the bedding and cleaning up. Now I don't have to wake up two or three times every night to respond to her call bell.

Some of the relief comes from being relieved of the caretaking responsibilities and from no longer having to watch someone who is dearly loved suffer and die. Some of the relief comes from the return to familiar routines. The dying process often requires that old and preferred routines be discarded for new ones. Death offers the possibility of returning to the earlier ways of living: a dutiful daughter, who left her job to care for her mother, can now return to work; a grandson, who came home every day after school to attend to his grandfather, can now play instead; a husband and three children can now have dinners with their wife/mother, who no longer needs to visit the hospital after work every day.

Relief comes also from a new sense of freedom—although it may have a considerable admixture of guilt. Since any relationship presents some restrictions, becoming freed of that relationship offers new options in life. I very much love my mother, father, sister, brother, spouse, son, daughter, but, if that person were not around, how much freedom I could have! Sometimes a person's death gives one freer access to money, work, better social position, or even to people. The death of a monarch, for example, permits the next in line to assume the throne; the death of a father permits a son to take over the family business; the death of a woman permits her husband, whom she was divorcing, to return home to the task of parenting his young children.

Relief, of course, like other emotions evoked by a death, occurs in conjunction with a variety of feelings, such as guilt, anger, and "emptiness." Consider the implications for guilt, for example, in the situations described in the previous paragraph.

GUILT

Another common emotion evoked by bereavement is guilt. Because this feeling is painful, it, in turn, elicits anger directed toward the dead person, who is the source of guilt. But being angry with someone who is dead is obviously unfair and inappropriate, so the anger engenders still more guilt. The guilt arises from a number of sources. Most familiar is the

"If only I had . . . " syndrome: If only I had kept him from driving that car; if only I had not permitted them to operate on her; if only I had been a better parent; if only I had been more attentive while she was alive; if only I had. . . . That is, guilt can arise from feeling that you could have done something to prevent the death and that you did not treat the person right while he or she was alive.

People trying to comfort bereaved persons can respond by saying, for example, "There is nothing you could have done" or "She/he would understand." Often, of course, this kind of affirmation is less important than simply listening and indicating that you understand and like the bereaved person.

An excellent example of guilt arising from the feeling that one could have prevented a death—and of a double-bind situation—may be the case of a person recovering from a serious heart attack. Let's say the heart patient, a man, has returned to near-normal functioning but has been put on a fairly strict regimen in which he has to watch his diet, eliminate smoking, keep sexual activity moderate (no one has ever figured out exactly how to interpret that admonition), exercise moderately, and avoid stress. If the heart patient does not stick to his regimen, what is his wife to do? If she tries to control his diet and presses him to work less and exercise more, she may be inducing him to circumvent her or she may be causing an increase in stress. Conversely, if she permits him to continue as he is doing, she is permitting life-threatening practices. If her husband then has a second major coronary and dies, the wife can find justification for her guilt in whatever she had attempted to do. (This example is drawn from Schoenberg & Stichman, 1974.)

Sometimes the guilt arises from having had unconscious (or even conscious) death wishes directed toward the dead person. Now that she or he is really dead, there is some implicit sense that you caused the death, or, at the very least, that your wishes were evil.

> An attractive young woman married a very close and extremely wealthy friend of her father's when she was 22 and he was 42. Within a few years, she became restless in the marriage and left her husband, whom she angrily accused of being insensitive to her feelings and of maintaining other sexual relationships, and he eventually sued for divorce. By the time the suit had begun, she was seeing a man her own age, a graduate student in history. Her husband was debating whether or not to settle the divorce suit out of court, when his sports car rear-ended a medium-sized truck and he died before reaching the hospital. His wife, now an extremely wealthy widow, remarried shortly after.

In this story, virtually a Cinderella story, one matter is omitted: given her anger with her husband before his death, the wife felt tremendous guilt for her death wishes and was never happy in her new marriage.

The above events are all true, other than some minor changes caused by my own uncertain memory, except for one: I don't have the vaguest idea whether the wife felt guilty or not. The one time I visited her and her new husband, she seemed gloriously happy, but she and I were not close friends and she would certainly never have confided any guilt feelings to me. Since I don't know the real ending, I made up my own. You can do the same.

The above example suggests a further source of guilt: benefitting from someone's death in some fashion. For example, your uncle, whom you cared for deeply, died and left you a large inheritance. You are simultaneously pleased and sad over his death. Or you received a promotion at work when your supervisor died; you feel guilty because you are glad that he is no longer preventing your move up in the company.

Death wishes need not be as potentially obvious as in the case of the young woman I described above. No important relationship is entirely positive, and few or none are entirely negative. Therefore, every death produces both gain and loss. Think for a while of the person you love most in the world. You may imagine that, if that person died, you would never stop grieving. Yet, think of some of the freedoms that the death of that person would offer: freedom to leave where you are and go elsewhere, freedom from having to adjust to someone else's eating and sleeping patterns, freedom to have social or sexual relationships with people that are now forbidden to you, freedom to dress or drive or speak in ways you now feel uncomfortable in doing. These kinds of feelings and tensions do not mean that the relationship is not good, but that no relationship is entirely satisfactory. You can play out the opposite scene with someone you dislike intensely, perhaps learning—if nothing else—that it is important to you to have someone you dislike so much. When someone important to us dies, our grief is a strange, often unexpected, mixture of many feelings, among which are frequently guilt and anger.

The final source of guilt that I'll examine here is survival itself. In some instances, survivors feel guilty for having survived. Survival guilt has been noted with people who have lived through active combat or the Nazi holocaust or the Hiroshima and Nagasaki atomic bombings. Survival guilt caused them to ask "Why did I deserve to survive?" Those who lived felt fortunate, but at the same time they felt that, in some fashion, their lives were paid for by other people's deaths. A middle-aged woman recalls her childhood in a Nazi concentration camp. Prisoners were lined up and counted off by fives; on any day all the number threes, or perhaps the fours, were marched off to extermination in the gas chambers. Had this woman been a "three" on the wrong day, someone else would have lived, and she would have died. A soldier who fought in Italy in World War II still wonders why he survived hand-to-hand combat when so many men with young children were killed.

ANGER

Parkes (1972) reports that most of the British widows he interviewed admitted strong feelings of anger at some time during the first years after the deaths of their husbands. This anger, related to restlessness, tension, and a rigidly controlled impulsiveness, was expressed in comments like "My nerves are on edge" or "I feel all in a turmoil inside."

Why did the widows feel anger, when they were still alive? Part of their anger probably came from guilt, as I explained earlier. However, another major source probably was the sense of having been abandoned. The bereaved implicitly feel that persons who have died did so on purpose—to make them feel bad or to cause them to fend for themselves. A grieving person recognizes consciously that this isn't true; nevertheless, it is a way of expressing anger over having been left.

Bowlby, in describing the process that infants go through when separated from their mothers, cites the stages as (1) protest, (2) despair, and (3) apathy (1961). The anger that a grieving person feels is comparable to the protest expressed by the infant. After all, both feel abandoned; both are suffering from separation. As an example, when an elderly woman was told by her daughter that her son-in-law was going to die of cancer soon, she sat down abruptly, shook her head mournfully, and cried out "Oh, that this should happen to me!" In a way, of course, she was being self-centered, since her son-in-law was about to die, her daughter was about to be widowed, and her grandchildren were about to become fatherless. On the other hand, her cry was very human and understandable: she was expressing her own protest and anger.

Anger is frequently displaced. The older woman mentioned above was not so much expressing anger with her son-in-law as expressing a generalized, undirected anger, comparable to Bowlby's protest. But victims of displaced anger are common, and they often are not aware of what is happening. (Similar reactions occur during the period following a divorce.) The grieving person may direct his or her anger at others who are around and who are often trying to be helpful. Also, anger is often directed at God, at the medical profession in general, at a particular hospital or physician, or at others who might possibly have had some responsibility. And, of course, the dead people themselves can become lightning rods for the anger and can be accused of not having taken adequate precautions or not having "tried hard enough." "Widows often seem to regard the pain of grieving as an unjust punishment and to feel angry with the presumed author. The death is personalized as something that has been done to them and they seek for someone to blame. . . . God and the doctors came in for a lot of angry criticism since both were seen as having power over life and death" (Parkes, 1972, p. 81). Others also become scapegoats: family members, employers, funeral directors.

There are other possible sources of anger that tend to be overlooked: fatigue, poor diet, reduced life space, all of which lead to lower resistance to stress. During both the period prior to the death and the days following it, many grieving persons don't eat and sleep well. Frequently the death follows a period of intense caretaking, which absorbed most of the person's time and energy. We would all become irritable under those conditions, even without having suffered a loss through death. Therefore, it may be important to differentiate irritability and anger: the former attributable to general tension and poor health habits, the latter being a function of the loss.

MAKING SENSE OF THE WORLD

A common occurrence during the grieving period is to go over, again and again, all the events that led up to the death. This can become a virtual preoccupation with some individuals, but almost all of us partake of it to some extent. In the days and weeks after the death, the closest family members will share experiences with each other—sometimes providing new information and insights into the person who died, sometimes reminiscing over familiar experiences.

Each person offers his or her own piece of the puzzle of death. "When I saw him last Saturday, he looked as though he were rallying." "Yes, but the next morning, the nurse told me he had had a bad night." "Do you think it might have had something to do with his sister's illness?" "I doubt it, but I heard from an aide that he fell going to the bathroom that morning." "That explains that bruise on his elbow." "No wonder he told me that he was angry because he couldn't seem to do anything right." And so it goes, the attempt to understand why someone who was rallying on Saturday was dead on Wednesday.

When a death is caused by an accident or a disaster, the effort to make sense of it is pursued more vigorously. As added pieces of news come trickling in, they are integrated into the puzzle. The bereaved want to put the death into a perspective that they can understand—divine intervention, a curse from a neighboring tribe, or a logical sequence of cause and effect, or whatever it may be.

In no case has this effort been more evident than in the constant review of the death of President John F. Kennedy. Although some two decades have passed since his assassination, the events leading up to the killing are regularly dragged into public view. The presumed issues—whether or not there was a conspiracy and, if so, whether it was from the political left or the political right—strike me as of little importance today. Rather, we are still trying to make sense of the entire event. That the death was the act of one unstable man working alone strikes many people as impossible. How could such an absurd set of circumstances destroy such a powerful man? It is easier to believe that an intricate conspiracy by the CIA or by the Communist Party was the basis for the killing.

Eventually each of us finds an adequate "story of the dying and death"—of John Kennedy or of our father or of a friend. Versions of the death may differ—whether the physician really did all she could to save the patient, whether Aunt Bella showed up frequently at the hospital or not, whether the operation succeeded or didn't quite succeed, whether father was ready to die or would have lived longer if possible—but each person's version satisfies him, and that version, with slight modifications, becomes the official version for the teller.

The vestiges of grief, however, remain much longer than a few years, probably forever. A 50-year-old biologist came in for therapy following a very upsetting divorce proceeding. During the fourteenth session, she began to speak for the first time about her father, who had died nearly 30 years earlier; within a few minutes, the client was sobbing deeply, as she recalled the pain of losing her father. It wasn't that she had refrained from appropriate grieving at the time her father had died; rather the grief was so great that there was still more that needed expression.

The stages of dying eventually end, but the stages of grieving do not. Even full recovery does not mean that all sense of loss, all sense of sadness and deprivation, all sense of anger and guilt have ended. Nor, as Victor Marshall has pointed out, should we wish this to be the case (personal communication, 1979).

"THE BROKEN HEART"

The metaphor of the broken heart is an old one, but it appears that the metaphor may have a strong basis in reality. A British study of 4500 widowers over the age of 54 found a major increase in their death rate in the six months following bereavement, after which it dropped back to expected levels (Young, Benjamin, & Wallis, 1963). When a further analysis was made of the causes of death, a very high proportion was due to heart disease (Parkes, Benjamin, & Fitzgerald, 1969).

Many other studies have documented significant increases in illness and in death following bereavement. One comprehensive review of numerous such investigations supports the existence of the relationship, largely for the six or so months after the death (Rowland, 1977). This appears to be true not only for widows, but for parents, brothers, and sisters as well (Rees & Lutkins, 1967). The responses of infants and very young children to separation may offer some explanation of this phenomenon. Many years ago, it was observed that children who had been placed in institutions both had a high rate of illness and underwent a pattern of protest followed by despair and then by apathy (Bowlby, 1961; Ribble, 1943). As the children became apathetic, they appeared to give up, and many became sick. The symptoms were termed *marasmus*, but the condition was somewhat different from that normally defined by the medical term. This syndrome was believed to be a response to separation, and concern about separation was termed *separation anxiety*.

Despair and apathy might be seen as paralleling Parkes' stages of pining and depression, while the pattern of protest, despair, and apathy could be viewed as paralleling the stage of denial, anger, bargaining, depression, and acceptance. (The latter supposition would put a considerably different light on the idea that acceptance is adaptive in a positive sense; it implies that acceptance is adaptive only in the sense of adapting to the inevitable but certainly not to encouraging the optimum enjoyment of life. This matter deserves closer consideration.)

Parkes, who is often cited in these pages, had worked closely with Bowlby, whose work on separation has made a tremendous impact on the field of infant and child development. In pursuing the work with adults, Parkes found, as have subsequent researchers, the previously mentioned increase in physical problems, including health problems leading to death (Maddison & Viola, 1968; Parkes, 1964, 1972; Reese & Lutkins, 1967).

Later work comparing non-elderly widows with comparable married women demonstrated that the widows had many more symptoms, including nervousness, depression, fear of "going crazy," persisting fears, nightmares, insomnia, reduced work capacity, and fatigue. All of these had been considered typical symptoms of grieving, but these widows also complained of headaches, dizziness, fainting spells, skin rashes, indigestion, vomiting, palpitations, chest pains, and other physical symptoms (Maddison & Viola, 1968).

What produces these physical symptoms? One obvious explanation is that the fatigue, poor diet, irregular habits, and social restrictions that are often experienced by persons caring for the dying and by others who are deeply concerned, may reduce the body's ability to protect itself from disease and to recover from disease, once it occurs. There is also the possibility that the depression and hopelessness that often accompany bereavement have a direct effect on body chemistry that alters its resistance to disease. Schulz (1978) has combined these two ideas and called them the "desolation effect."

OTHER RESULTS OF "THE BROKEN HEART"

Increased illness rates are noted shortly after bereavement, and the studies of death following loss have been restricted to a fairly brief period. However, other possible consequences of bereavement take longer to emerge. For example, numerous studies have investigated the possible relationships between bereavement and mental hospitalization, suicide, and illegal behavior. Despite some conflicting results, the weight of the evidence would seem to support correlation between bereavement and these events.

It isn't, however, sufficient to establish the relationships. One must ask if early childhood bereavement influences later psychiatric problems and if recent bereavement influences psychiatric problems in general. One review article cites six studies that found schizophrenic patients had a higher than anticipated rate of childhood bereavement and five studies that showed no such relationship (Bendiksen & Fulton, 1975). One of the better known of the former class of studies, conducted some 40 years ago, determined that schizophrenic patients were more likely to have lost either a brother or a sister than patients of other psychiatric classifications or than people in the community (Rosenzweig & Bray, 1943). Other studies have shown that the death of a parent in childhood is predictive of later institutionalization (Barry, 1949; Parkes, 1964; Stein & Susser, 1969).

One group of investigators provided an interesting variation on the usual study of the incidence of early bereavements among psychiatric patients. Using a participant group of over 400 hospitalized patients, they found not only a much higher than expected rate of early parental deaths but more such deaths occurring in the first five years of life than in the second, and more in the second five years than in the third (Archibald, Bell, Miller, & Tuddenham, 1962). In other words, the parents of hospitalized patients were more likely to have died early in the life of the individuals than the parents in the general population. This obviously suggests that the loss of a parent during the first few years of life is a more distressing factor for later development than a subsequent death. Although the specific kind of parent-child relationship may vary and although the specific nature of the emotional disturbance may vary, the essential relationship is found with considerable consistency. Sometimes the immediate response to a death and subsequent behavior appear to be pathological. As Freud has said "Melancholia instead of a state of grief develops in some people, whom we consequently suspect of a morbid pathological disposition" (1917, 1959, p. 153). The features that Freud observed in these individuals included dejection, loss of interest in the outside world, loss of capacity to love, lowered activity level, poor self-concept, and a "delusional expectation of punishment" (1917, 1959, p. 153). According to Freud, most of these are the same symptoms found in normal grief; it is poor self-concept, which includes self-recriminations and a feeling of worthlessness, that accounts for the pathology. This suggests that the sense of loss, rather than involving the dead person, is actually involving the individual himself or herself. "In grief the world becomes poor and empty; in melancholia it is the ego itself" (Freud, 1917, 1959, p. 155).

Some fifty years later, when Parkes (1972) compared the experiences, feelings, and behavior of bereaved psychiatric patients with widows displaying normal grief, he found the former group expressed their grief over a longer period of time and took longer to begin to express grief. In addition, there was only one symptom that was not shared by both psychiatric patients and widows with normal expression of grief: the patients had markedly more ideas of guilt and self-reproach. This would appear to be a direct confirmation of Freud's earlier formulation.

The data from studies investigating the relationship between early bereavement and illegal behavior show comparable findings. An earlier study described a series of cases of juvenile delinquents whose behavior appeared to have been a direct outcome of their bereavement (Shoor & Speed, 1963). Later, other investigators analyzed data from a large sample and concluded that childhood bereavement was predictive of individuals who would be convicted of illegal offenses by their early 20s (Markusen & Fulton, 1971).

Suicides seem to follow a similar pattern. A British research group found that having experienced parental loss as a child did not appear to predict later suicides (Bunch, Barraclough, Nelson, & Sainsbury, 1971a), but recent loss of a parent was related to suicide (Bunch, Barraclough, Nelson, & Sainsbury, 1971b).

The obvious results of coping inadequately with loss include a longer duration of grieving, which means more psychological suffering, more health problems, poorer social relationships, less effective work capacity, and generally lowered satisfaction in life. Some bereaved spouses may remain withdrawn, perhaps not leaving their homes except when they have to; others continue to be preoccupied with thoughts and images of the dead person; still others throw themselves into work or into a project, but remain tense and have a lower resistance to stress. Each of these responses has been noted in numerous instances and some have been confirmed by research.

CAUSES OF "THE BROKEN HEART"

What personal characteristics or experiences lead to poor responses in grieving? An early separation or loss that was never adequately mourned may be one. The person would suffer from the recent death and from the intense feelings about the earlier death that are revived by the subsequent one.

Sometimes an individual delays expression of grief. This may occur because the grief is so overwhelming that the person's ego-defense system protects him from the emotion or because the immediate demands for effective functioning are so great that the bereaved person cannot remove attention from getting things done.

Lindemann (1944) describes a teenage girl whose parents and boyfriend all died in the Coconut Grove fire; while recuperating from her own burns for ten weeks following the deaths, she was cheerful and displayed no signs of distress. Only then did she begin to express her normal grief. In this instance, the delay may have been adaptive—allowing the girl to survive a highly stressful period. In other instances, in which delays are considerably longer or the grief is never expressed, the individuals pay a high price in later emotional and health difficulties.

Sometimes the "broken heart" syndrome can be explained most effectively in terms of an increase in detrimental health practices. Studying a small number of bereaved family members in Scotland, one researcher found a high proportion of those who had used either liquor or cigarettes prior to the death had increased their usage significantly afterwards (Levy & Sclare, 1976). Substantially increased usage of liquor and sedatives was also found to occur among non-elderly widows in the more comprehensive research of Glick, Weiss, and Parkes (1974). The implications of these practices for physical health are obvious, but there has not been research that shows direct links between these practices and ill health for widows.

Parkes (1972) described three patterns of grieving among widows. One group became severely disturbed right after bereavement and remained disturbed for about two months; by the third month they were only mildly upset. The second group showed only moderate disturbance initially, then a week later became intensely upset, and subsequently recovered more rapidly than the others. The third group showed little or no emotion until toward the end of the first month after the death and did not show intense emotion until around two months later. Parkes concluded that grieving can be postponed but not altogether avoided. However, the postponement takes its toll; members of the group that postponed grief longest had more physical and emotional problems one year later than did people in the other groups.

In a recent study, 68 widows and widowers were interviewed first shortly after bereavement and then a year later. The persons who were having the most difficulty in coping with their loss a year later were those from lower socioeconomic backgrounds, persons whose spouse had died after a very short illness with little warning of death, and those who also had had another life crisis during that time (Parkes, 1975). Compared to younger people, older people in England are both less likely to see a physician following a death and less likely to receive sedatives and other medications. It appears probably that they cope better with the death (Cartwright et al., 1973).

One source proposes that certain characteristics of some kinds of death make it more difficult for the bereaved to resolve their grief. These include:

- suicides or deaths caused by self-neglect or carelessness;
- untimely deaths—for example, deaths of young people, of people just married, or people on the verge of some significant achievement;
- deaths that required the bereaved person to care for the dying individual in ways that proved to be distressing to the former;
- deaths for which the bereaved person has a basis for believing he or she was partly or fully responsible—for example, a child drowning in the family swimming pool, the deceased woman whose husband had insisted her symptoms were "only psychosomatic";
- homicides;
- unconfirmed deaths where no body is available to be buried;
- other sudden and unexpected deaths, in addition to those cited above;
- deaths that are so painful, prolonged, and drawn-out that the survivors have become impatient for the death to occur (Simpson, 1979).

Traditionally, guidelines have indicated how to behave following a death. Wakes, funerals, and a variety of other rituals and ceremonies all took place without much decision. Today, more choice is offered, including the possibility of not performing any rituals, participating in any ceremonies, or changing one's everyday behavior at all. Whereas the vastly increased number of options certainly increases personal freedom, it also may make grieving more stressful. And this stress may be exacerbated by the lack of a system of meaningful, cohesive religious beliefs (Gorer, 1967; Parkes, 1972).

In summarizing the evidence, Parkes describes the "typical" high risk spouse.

> [She is] a young widow with children living at home and no close relatives nearby. She would be a timid, clinging person who had reacted badly to separation in the past and had a previous history of depressive illness. Closely bound up with her husband in an over-reliant or ambivalent relationship, she would not have prepared herself for his unexpected and untimely death. Cultural and familial tradition would prevent her from expressing the feelings that then threatened to emerge. Other stresses occurring before or after the bereavement—such as loss of income, changes of home, and difficulties with children—would increase her burden. [Parkes, 1972, p. 147]

ANNIVERSARY REACTIONS AND RELATED OCCURRENCES

For some people certain dates have a death-related significance. Thus, Christmas, which is presumed a time of happiness, intensifies unhappiness and depression in some individuals, and is a season of suicides as well as of pleasure. Some fascinating research has shown that people are more likely to die after such occasions as Christmas and Yom Kippur and their own birthdays than before (Phillips & Feldman, 1973). One study showed that five times as many people die in the three months following their birthday as in the three months preceding that occasion (Kunz & Summers, 1979–80). Although the figures somewhat exaggerate the actual situation, the results are certainly provocative. It seems as though some people exert their will to live until a certain important event takes place, then they permit themselves to die.

More specifically, the term *anniversary reaction* refers to a significant change in behavior or feelings on the anniversary of a death. I personally have no doubt that this occurs, since I have both experienced it and observed it in people close to me. Research supports my views. One study, for example, showed that 100% of 16 bereaved persons who had been classified previously as depressed and over 60% of 76 people who were not so classified described either a mild or a severe reaction on the anniversary of their spouse's death (Bornstein & Clayton, 1972). Another project found evidence that suicides are more likely to take place within 30 days of the anniversary of a parent's death than would be expected by chance (Bunch & Barraclough, 1971).

The term *anniversary reaction* has another use, which is close enough to the first definition to be confusing. When an individual attains the age at which one of his or her parents died, there is a higher than chance occurrence of various signs of distress. Thus, mental hospital admissions occur more frequently to persons at or near the age when a parent died than would normally be assumed (Hilgard & Newman, 1959). Similarly, there is evidence that admissions increase when a person's oldest child becomes the same age that the person was when his or her parent died. That is, if your mother died when you were 12, it will be somewhat more likely than would happen by chance that you will be admitted to a psychiatric hospital when your oldest child reaches 12 (Hilgard & Newman, 1961). In effect, the disturbance apparently results from a reestablishment of conditions similar to those at the time of the original death: now I am the parent, and my child is me, and a parent dies when the child turns 12.

I need to add that research does not always support the idea that psychiatric hospitalization is related to anniversary reactions. Furthermore, the chances of any one individual being hospitalized or committing suicide on a significant date are extremely small; they are only slightly higher than the likelihood either would occur on any other date. However, the increase in depression on anniversaries and on other significant dates appears beyond dispute.

We are all affected by loss at one time or another, and therefore we have all experienced some kind of grief. Frequently we do not respond as we would have anticipated; sometimes we are not even aware that what we are doing or how we are feeling has been affected by grief. And, although when and how we mourn are greatly influenced by our culture, I would doubt if there is any culture that does not recognize and make allowance for grief in some form.

13

BEREAVEMENT ROLES AND RITUALS

Do you feel grief in the same way that I feel grief? We probably can't ever answer that question, since words are such inadequate approximations of the reality of feelings, but we can respond to the question, Do you express bereavement in the same way that I do? The answer is probably not. The expression of bereavement depends so much on previous experiences, on roles and relationships, on the kinds of support one has, and on the nature of the death itself that even though two people may attempt to follow similar mourning rituals, they are likely to be quite different in their expression of their bereavement.

Although all people who are bereaved do share a common experience and certain similar feelings and behavior, their bereavement and the way they mourn vary considerably as a function of sex, age, income, and available support systems.

THE LOSSES OF ROLES AND RELATIONSHIPS

The meaning of a person's death for the survivors includes not only the loss of someone to whom they are deeply attached, but the loss of someone who performed meaningful roles in their lives. A father might be despised by two of his four school-age children, but his death is still a significant loss in their lives; a woman might be resented and ignored by her husband, but her death will leave large gaps in his life.

Since elderly people perform fewer important roles in the lives of others than younger persons, their deaths are less disruptive of the social fabric: fewer tasks must be taken over by others. The elderly are also more isolated and have a generally lower social value (see Chapter 11 for a more complete discussion). These cultural factors conspire to reduce the grief felt when an older person dies—a matter confirmed by studies in which their deaths are viewed as less tragic than the deaths of persons of other ages (for example, Kalish & Reynolds, 1976; Kastenbaum & Aisenberg, 1972).

However, since younger people are not expected to die, there is often no prior planning for their deaths. Neither the Chicago White Sox nor CBS has a plan to replace its regular shortstop or television series star in the event of death. (*Chico and the Man,* a television program, immediately went off the air when its star committed suicide.) Similarly, stores, factories, and government agencies don't have plans to replace various personnel. However, with extremely few exceptions, the death of one person, even an important person, would not spell disaster for any of these enterprises. Small businesses, creative enterprises, and other endeavors with one or two key persons would, of course, be exceptions. Even political organizations and government can continue to function after the death of an office-holder, since there is normally some process to select a replacement. At the national level, we have been able to survive the sudden deaths of seven presidents because a system of replacement existed, although only recently have we developed a system for replacing the vice-president.

Families, however, are more like small businesses or partnerships, in which the death of a key person might have disastrous results. There is normally no formal resolution of this difficulty, although ancient Jewish law provides the levirate, a custom which encourages the dead husband's brother to marry the widow. In this instance, the motive is not to care for the widow but to provide the lineage with children, preferably sons, in the name of the brother (Cross, 1958). A study of 85 cultures around the world showed that a majority of them had some form of levirate marriage (or its opposite, sororate), although rarely requiring it (Murdock, 1949).

The usual response in our culture to replacing a parent who has died is the emergence of an informal network of other family members and friends. The grandmother helps with some cooking; an uncle serves as an occasional surrogate father, especially for the boys; an older woman cousin provides some instruction for the girls. And inevitably the remaining parent takes over some of the tasks and responsibilities of the dead spouse. When people move around a great deal or do not maintain family ties, this network is less effective.

Replacing the lost relationship of the dead spouse and parent is probably more difficult than replacing the lost roles. If the father has died, the mother can usually find some way to have money, although often not as much as previously; if the mother has died, the father can find someone to take care of the house and the children. Often today, since traditional roles are viewed more flexibly, the mother is totally capable of earning sufficient income, while the father has the ability to care for the house and children.

When one parent dies, the other parent has multiple new responsibilities, which can interfere with his or her grieving. Children need to be cared for; arrangements must be made for future income; legal arrangements may be necessary (for example, transferring title to a house to a widow, changing names on bank accounts); and decisions concerning moving, schooling, and related matters must be made. Given all these demands, the grieving person may find no time to express his or her own grief, especially after the first burst of community and family help has been spent.

One woman phrased this with poignance. "You hold the kids when they cry, but there was no one to hold me when I cried." Sometimes there isn't even opportunity to cry. The needs of a grieving spouse for a loan or for a friend to make a meal are easily understood; the need for someone to stay with the person's children while he or she takes off alone for the weekend is often not recognized.

One study found that women suffering the death of a husband or a child, had more difficulty than men in working through their grief and took longer to do so (Evans, 1975). This may reflect a greater willingness on the part of women to express grief or a greater dependence on the relationship that has been lost. Since the study participants tended to be women from more traditional home backgrounds, they may not have had work or organizational involvements as the men had, to compensate for the loss.

Because in our society adults function as couples, in many communities a single person may have difficulty developing social relationships. Since most singles' and single-parents' groups are concerned with the divorced and the never-married, widows and widowers frequently have trouble in finding responsive friends. Thus, the companion role provided by the spouse is also difficult to replace.

However, it is probably the loss of the caring relationship (even if the couple fought a great deal and seemed ready to separate) that takes its greatest toll on the survivor. Someone to talk to, to sleep with, to hold and to be held by, to be familiar with your habits and likes and dislikes, to share experiences with, to share tasks with—these are the components that are missing after a spouse dies.

In many marriages, of course, the wife and husband did not talk to each other, often didn't sleep with each other and very seldom made love, did not hold each other, or share very much with each other. Yet there is still a bonding or attachment that occurs. I use the metaphor of a large spider web, with many strands of differing strength. Death cuts the web down the middle, severing almost all the strands (the sense that the dead person is still in some kind of contact or communication or is waiting in a subsequent existence suggests that two or three strands still exist). The cutting of each strand is painful, and cutting all the strands is immensely painful. As time goes on, the surviving spouse will often see the severed strands, with the ends just hanging there limply and unconnected, and this association will serve to revive the pain.

Frequently the dead person and the severed relationship are idealized. "Don't speak ill of the dead" is a familiar expression, one to which many adhere. Troubles and tensions are forgotten, repressed, or ignored, and the dead person is recalled as a paragon of virtues. This position is encouraged not only by close friends and relatives, but by the eulogy at the funeral and by society in general. Parkes (1972) interviewed the family members of widows to try to determine the extent to which the women were idealizing their deceased husbands. However, he had to give up the task because it engendered resentment among the research participants.

It's not unusual for the pain to be so great that the survivor expresses a desire to avoid any such strong attachment in the future. The fear that a new intimacy will also end in death is too great to permit. Nonetheless, replacement relationships do occur, although, as a very wise friend of mine said, "No relationship is ever really replaced; every relationship is unique." So it isn't, strictly speaking, a replacement, but rather a relationship that offers some of the same qualities and responds to some of the same needs and role requirements.

At the turn of the century, it was common for a young wife to die in childbirth or succumb to illness or epidemic and leave her husband with relatively young children. He would eventually remarry, and his second wife was, not infrequently, a considerably younger woman. Today the situation has changed. It is more likely that the father will die and his role will need replacing. Since the average widow loses her husband when she is 56 years old, their children are probably at least in their teens. The surviving widow has fewer chances to remarry, if that happens to be her choice, because there are fewer available men older than she, and there is the well-known tendency of men to marry younger women. However, even today about 20% of children in the United States will lose one parent before age 16 (Simpson, 1979). Because of the high divorce rate, new attention is being paid to women who return to singlehood during their middle years, and this concern will benefit middle-aged and elderly widows.

Exacerbating the usual process of grieving is what Kastenbaum (1969) has termed *bereavement overload.* This concept can be understood in two different ways. First, the death of one person leads to many losses; for example, the death of a young father means that his children have lost someone to whom they were deeply attached; it is also possible that they will now see less of their mother, who will need to work; changes in the financial situation may require that they leave their home, move to another neighborhood, enter another school, and reside too far from their old friends to play with them. Thus, a father's death sets into motion a series of related losses.

The second, and original, use of the term refers to the frequency with which someone, most often an older person, will suffer several significant deaths in a brief period of time. A 60-year-old woman may lose her husband, her brother, and her mother within a period of 18 months. Before she has time to recover from one major loss, she is caught up in another, and, if one bereavement is not adequately mourned, a subsequent death is probably much more difficult to work through. In a sense, the entire country suffered bereavement overload with the deaths of John Kennedy, Robert Kennedy, and Martin Luther King within a relatively brief period. After such experiences, it takes an unusually long time before people are willing to relax again and to trust leaders not to abandon them. The fears for the life of Ted Kennedy may be interpreted in terms of this inability to relax and trust.

WIDOWS AND WIDOWERS

There are presently about 11 million widows in the United States who are not remarried—roughly one of every eight women 14 years of age or older; there are only some 2 million widowers in the United States— about one in every 40 males (*Metropolitan Life Insurance Statistical Bulletin,* September, 1977). Three explanations probably account for the discrepancy: first, women live longer than men; second, women marry men older than themselves; third, widowers are much more likely to remarry than widows (Bequaert, 1976).

The fact that women outlive men is often presented as a basis for the advantages of being a woman, but even that is questionable. Wives tend to nurse their husbands through the final illness, arrange for a funeral and burial, and then have to work out a way to live a number of years without the valuable support of a spouse. Their income is often severely diminished at that point, and their age frequently makes it difficult to enter the job market, unless they already have a work history. The number of men available for dating or remarriage is also limited, in particular for older women in our society.

So widows tend to socialize with other women; some of them are previous friends who are still married, but many of them are also widows. Obviously some widows maintain friendships with both members of a couple, but there is a strong tendency for couples to participate socially with other couples. In one study, 38% of the widows stated that they had a less active social life than before the death of their husbands, but 43% claimed to have perceived no change, and 12% even had a more extensive social life (Lopata, 1973).

When older women lose their husbands, they often move into a "society of widows," that is, a group of other widows who have developed friendships over a period of time (now that older divorced women are increasingly familiar, I would assume that this "society" is extended to them as well). Younger women have more difficulty in finding widowed age peers, and their divorced friends and acquaintances can be insensitive to the feelings of widows. (Divorced people tend to joke about ex-spouses, which can make widows extremely uncomfortable.)

Widows themselves give three reasons for strains in their relationships with married women. First, they feel that being a widow is like being a fifth wheel; second, they believe other women are jealous when their husbands are around widows; and third, they have had the experience of being propositioned by the husbands of their friends. Although these views are not held by a majority of widows, they represent the experiences of some (Lopata, 1973).

Those women who do develop satisfactory friendships tend to have more formal education, a reasonable income, and "the physical and psychic energy needed to initiate change" (Lopata, 1973, p. 216). Since these are likely to be characteristics related to many kinds of success for both women and men, it would seem that people who do things better and have more resources continue to do things better and get more resources.

In addition to the difficulties of coping with their grief and maintaining friendships, widows suffer the additional problems of stigmatization (Parkes, 1972). The taboo of death appears to rub off on the widow, and she can be treated much as funeral directors are treated. In some societies, widows are approached as unclean, and among the Agutainos of Polawan, they must announce themselves as they approach others, since to see them is to court one's own death (Cochrane, 1936). We don't ostracize widows in our society, but we often don't know what to say to someone who has recently lost a spouse, and we are more comfortable when we can avoid people to whom we have trouble talking.

That widows and widowers are deprived is evident. Each has lost someone important, even if the previous relationship was far from ideal. During the relationship, a network of close associations and shared experiences developed over a period—often a lengthy period—of time. Prior to the marriage was a courtship period when this association began and received its initial testing; mourning is like the courtship period in reverse, as the widow or widower begins the process of reducing emotional involvement or attachment in the relationship with the dead spouse (Marris, 1975). Often, perhaps usually, some sense of attachment, of connectedness, continues indefinitely.

In focusing on the problems of bereavement, the practical problems of widows and widowers can easily be overlooked. A 45-year-old widow with three school-age children and a 65-year-old widow with grown, self-sufficient children obviously have very different practical problems. The same is true of men, except that widowers with children are considered to need a woman's help, and they are more likely to be aided by women (mothers-in-law and sisters-in-law are especially supportive); widows may require financial aid, and much of their help comes from brothers-in-law. Also, while widowers receive relatively more help from family and friends, widows are more likely to seek help from social workers, physicians, or others (Glick, Weiss, & Parkes, 1974). Clergy, however, probably provide more support to both widows and widowers than any of the other groups does.

Many people in the helping professions underestimate the importance of financial problems and overestimate the importance of emotional stresses. In one study a group of widows overwhelmingly agreed that financial knowledge was the most important way to help women prepare for widowhood (Barrett, 1978). Another study found that 71% of the husbands of over 1,700 women widowed before they were elderly had not made out wills; in these cases the average family income dropped to only slightly more than half of what it had been before the husband died (Nuckols, 1973). Having to cope simultaneously with the emotional pain of the death and the practical changes in financial status can be an inordinately great task.

Discussing financial matters when death is not pressing anticipates this difficulty. Yet, because denial often operates, people frequently feel that talking about money and death is either in poor taste or in some magical fashion will cause a death to occur. One young woman, whose husband was dying of cancer, said that she rejected his attempts to discuss money as a part of her own denial that he was dying.

At least in one study, widowers under age 45 seemed to weather their losses more successfully than widows of comparable age, even though they were more concerned about managing household and child-care tasks. Men were more confident that they would recover from their loss, were less fearful of "nervous breakdowns," exhibited less general anxiety, and fared better during the funeral and burial (Glick, Weiss, & Parkes, 1974). These authors distinguished *social recovery* from what I would term *emotional recovery*. While acknowledging that men advanced considerably more quickly in the former—reestablishing social and sexual relationships faster and often getting married sooner (which may be viewed either as a sign of emotional adequacy, an indication of emotional neediness, or evidence of having repressed grief), the authors believed the men's emotional recovery proceeded at the same pace, or a slightly slower one, than the widows' (Glick, Weiss, & Parkes, 1974).

When (and if) remarriage does occur, it is more likely to be with someone else whose spouse has died than with a divorced or never-married person. To some extent, this undoubtedly reflects age differences—widows and widowers are generally older than most people in either of the other groups—but it probably also reflects the understanding that these people have of each other. A wife who cherishes the memory of her dead husband can accept her new husband's continued attachment to his deceased wife; a divorced woman will not have shared the same experience and may be less patient with his fond reminiscences.

THE MEANING TO SURVIVORS OF SPECIFIC KINDS OF DEATH

Each type of death produces its own consequences. These derive in part from the nature of the cause of death and the care the dying required. The survivors of death from suicide, for example, probably had various emotional problems with the deceased before his or her death and almost certainly suffered guilt after the death. At the same time they probably spent no time in attending to the physical care of the dying person since the death was sudden. The death of someone in an automobile accident usually has involved no prior emotional distress related to the cause of death (unless she or he was a reckless driver), relatively little time in physical care, in most instances, and a psychological reaction quite different from the reaction to a suicide. If, however, a death occurs from a slowly degenerating neural condition, living with and caring for the dying will have been very different for the bereaved and will probably produce a different reaction when death arrives.

THE DEATH OF A SISTER OR BROTHER

Since children are still often assumed to be innocent of knowledge of death, family deaths are often kept from them. Yet, there is good evidence to believe that these deaths affect them in many ways. Exploratory observations of the reactions of children to their mother's miscarriage (Cain, Erickson, Fast, & Vaughan, 1964), the death of a sibling (Cain, Fast, & Erickson, 1964), or the death of an identical twin indicate that these deaths do affect the children, almost regardless of their age. If, indeed, the child is too young to know that a death has occurred, he or she is still likely to be aware of some stress and disruption. Later it might become evident to the child that the stress was an earlier death.

The effect of a sibling death is, I believe, greatly underestimated, even if the brother or sister died before the birth of the present child. In fact, there have been some studies of "substitute" or "replacement" children (Cain & Cain, 1964). One young woman I knew slightly had been conceived about two months after the death of another child in the family, and she was even given the name of the dead child. When she told me about this, as an adult, she admitted that she was never sure of who she was. Am I myself? Or am I the girl who died? Who is Janet Farr? And she also wondered whether the love she received from her parents was for her or for her dead sister. Although you might think she was just being foolish, hers is not a unique response.

After the death of a child, parents are likely to be anxious about their next child, and this may take the form of being overprotective. "It is not unusual for parents to find themselves watching their sleeping child and envisioning how they are going to react if they should find this child dead, too" (Szybist, n.d., p. 18). Getting pregnant again as quickly as possible is not a way to heal grief (nor is getting a new dog for a child right after the death of his or her beloved pet a good way to heal that grief); decisions need to be made on the basis of wanting or not wanting another child for its own sake.

THE DEATH OF A PARENT FOLLOWING DIVORCE

In spite of the prevalence of divorce in this country and the accompanying numbers of children brought up in single-parent or stepfamily homes, we usually think of an intact family when we contemplate the effects of the death of a parent upon a child.

One book, however, has described two other common family situations in which children find themselves coping with the death of a parent. In the first and probably more frequent situation, the death of a divorced parent occurs—usually a father whose children are living with their mother and, perhaps, with her new husband. Normally when a parent dies, the children can find solace with the surviving parent, but this is not always the case when the parents are divorced. The surviving parent may be estranged from or antagonistic to the dead ex-spouse, and, even though she may be willing to comfort the children and listen to their grief, she often does not share their sorrow (Visher & Visher, 1979).

In the second situation, the children are living with one parent, again presumably the mother, and her new husband. Perhaps the children have developed a real sense of this being their family, and the stepparent performs the parental role in many ways. Then the mother dies, and the children normally move to live with their father. Obviously this will often be an excellent solution, but there are also situations in which the noncustodial parent is not prepared for such an undertaking. Perhaps he has remarried and established a new household with children, and the addition of his children, while acceptable for weekends or a month in the summer, can be highly disruptive on a permanent basis. At the same time, the children have not only lost their mother, but are often separated from others whom they have come to view as their family (Visher & Visher, 1979).

Nor should grandparents be forgotten. In a stepfamily, all children often share all grandparents. When the biological parent dies and the children relocate to live with their other parent, they may lose all contact with their stepgrandparents. In fact, there is no longer any official family tie. Conversely, when the biological parent not living with the children dies, the former spouse may not be eager to maintain contact with her ex-in-laws, and once again the children may lose contact with their grandparents.

SUDDEN INFANT DEATH SYNDROME

One particular kind of death can be especially cruel: the sudden infant death syndrome, also known as SIDS or crib death. This syndrome, widely discussed today, refers to an infant death that occurs without warning, without—at least at present—known cause, and without any known history of health problems; it also occurs quickly, so that parents may leave their infant after an early evening feeding and return, four hours later or sometimes even ten minutes later, to find their baby dead.

There are an estimated 10,000 sudden infant deaths a year in the United States—comprising about 10% of all deaths in the first year of life. Most of these deaths occur to infants between 3 weeks and 5 months of age, to babies whose birth weight is low, and to those from low-income families (Bergman, Pomeroy, & Beckwith, 1969).

Although the cause has not been determined, many causes have been eliminated. Crib deaths are *not* caused by birth control pills or fluoridated water, since the condition was reported for many years before either of these technological developments; they are *not* the result of suffocating, vomiting, choking, breast-feeding, or bottle-feeding; sudden infant death is *not* a hereditary condition. And the fact that the deaths can occur in as brief a time as five minutes eliminates a host of other diseases (Anonymous, 1972; Szybist, n.d.).

Although sudden infant deaths do occur to the infants of parents of all ages and from all kinds of living conditions, there are some circumstances in which the deaths occur more frequently. For example, relatively more deaths occur during the winter months; sudden infant deaths are more frequent when the mother is young, non-White, and living in a crowded home; and, as mentioned above, they occur more often to people from lower income groups (even when race is controlled as a predictive factor) (Illinois Department of Public Health, 1978).

Since an apparently healthy child dies suddenly, the parents feel extremely guilty. The mother and father, under tremendous stress because of the death, sometimes turn to blame each other. Father blames mother for being careless, for not having noticed that the baby had a cold or that the blanket was over the child's head; mother blames father for not wanting to leave the television set to check on the baby, for not wishing to move out of the city to the cleaner air of the country. And each, of course, feels that he or she must have done something wrong or the baby would still be alive. Their speculations range from having bad genes to being an incompetent parent.

To make matters worse, other family members, friends, and neighbors are also likely to blame the parents, overtly or implicitly. "I knew she shouldn't have married him, his brother being retarded and all that." "I hear they use marijuana in the evening, and they are probably so out of it, they didn't hear the baby cry." "I wonder if she did let him suffocate—I heard her saying that she wasn't sure she wanted a third baby." Also, especially in the past, the police, suspecting child abuse, sometimes questioned the parents as possible offenders rather than providing support to deeply grieving people (Halpern, 1972).

Occasionally either a babysitter, who might have been with the child at that time, or an older sibling, who had expressed some resentment of the baby, gets blamed. Since siblings almost always have mixed feelings about a new baby, they feel very guilty, even if they never came near the infant, and later absolution from their parents does not completely remove the guilt (Halpern, 1972).

Since newspapers and other media have been carrying accounts of crib deaths and since the National Foundation for Sudden Infant Death, Inc. (1501 Broadway, New York, New York, 10036) has been providing services to crib-death parents, these parents now have emotional support available.

Nonetheless, parents may still feel "toxic." One mother stated that for two years after her infant died, she was not able to hold a baby for fear that she would cause that baby's death also. A letter written to a crib-death research project exemplifies the guilt a parent feels.

> When I went to bed that night, I put her in bed with me because she was fussing. When I woke up and found her, I got out of bed and carried her around with me for I don't know how long before I realized that she was really gone. . . . I told everyone I had smothered her sometime during the night. The doctor, the nurses at the hospital, and the ambulance driver said she had never smothered. If I could only believe that. . . . I still can't convince myself that it [a disease] was the cause of her death. [Bergman et al., 1969, p. 103]

Crib deaths are only a modest statistic in the number of infant and child deaths that occur each year but the levels of distress they cause are dramatic.

THE CULTURAL MILIEU

Bereavement and mourning are directly affected by one's culture; grief is indirectly affected by it. Thus, the situations in which you are bereaved are culturally defined. If I live in a society with strong extended family networks, I might be bereaved by the death of a second cousin or my mother's brother's father-in-law. If I live in a society based on strong nuclear family attachments, such deaths would not necessarily be the basis for bereavement, although I might still feel bereaved if I happen particularly to care for the person. For example, among the Trobriand Islanders in the South Pacific, only the losses of maternal kin are sources of bereavement; the loss of either paternal kin or even one's spouse is not considered as profound (Volkart & Michael, 1957). A spouse, however, is allowed to grieve because of her or his sadness.

Similarly, if I lived in a society with a very high fetal- and infant-mortality rate, I might not be considered bereaved if my fourth child were stillborn; in nations with very low infant mortality, I would be bereaved. Or, when a ruler dies in office, the entire country, sometimes much of the rest of the world, enters a state of bereavement; the loss is defined for people by their culture or by their government.

DEFINING THE TIME OF BEREAVEMENT

Bereavement is not always culturally defined as occurring at the time of a death. Among the Kotas of South India, an initial funeral is held shortly after a man dies, but his spirit does not leave for the afterworld until a second funeral is conducted; this latter funeral is held once a year for all persons who have died since the previous community funeral. If a widow becomes pregnant before the second funeral—and she is likely to try to do so—the child takes the name, clan, and property of the dead husband (Mandelbaum, 1959). Thus, to some extent, the widow does not become bereaved at the time of the death. Although this implies that the way she mourns will be affected by the community's definition of bereavement, she may, in fact, still suffer as intense grief at her husband's death as a widow in Minneapolis, Osaka, or Kiev would.

Another situation in which bereavement did not accompany death was reported by Robert Lifton (1967) in his study of the *hibakusha*, the survivors of the atomic blasts at Hiroshima and Nagasaki. These persons were so numbed by their experience that they did not express bereavement. They were too numb to feel the grief that they knew was expected of them, and they even felt guilt and shame that they were not expressing the kind of grief that such immense losses normally elicit.

Bereavement can also precede clinical death. In Chapter 2, I discussed social death, which can lead to a type of bereavement. However it is possible to feel the loss of someone you love considerably before their death, even without having it lead to social death. A 35-year-old nurse was told that her father was going to die of cancer in about six months; she later said that she felt more bereaved at that moment than she ever felt later. She brought her father to her home and cared for him there, with the support of her husband. She and her father enjoyed their time together, and they even valued the occasions when they just held each other's hand and cried. After seven months, he slipped into a coma and died three days later. When I interviewed her, about a year after his death, she told me "I never cried when he died—I think I'd finished with crying by that time. I was relieved that it was over for both of us."

Bereavement, grief, and mourning before a person's death has been called "anticipatory bereavement" or "anticipatory grief" (Lindemann, 1944). Although there is some controversy over aspects of anticipatory grief, the evidence indicates (a) that it occurs, (b) that it leads to greater calm and acceptance of the ensuing death (Fulton and Fulton, 1971), and (c) that it permits the bereaved person to regain full capacity for effective functioning and subsequent happiness more rapidly (Glick, Weiss, & Parkes, 1974).

Anticipatory grief has its dangers. For example, if the mourning period prior to the actual death is extremely successful, that is, if the person finishes grieving, what is the basis for continuing the relationship? After all, the dying person is still alive, yet mourning has been completed. It has been suggested that the bereaved persons may abandon the dying person if they complete mourning before death occurs (Fulton & Fulton, 1971). Also, the significance of the funeral is diminished, since its function as a way to permit the expression of grief and family solidarity has already been superseded by the previous grieving. This may be a particular problem with the death of the elderly, especially the very old and the institutionalized, for whom there have been years of anticipatory grieving in some instances, and whose death therefore makes relatively little impact (Fulton & Fulton, 1971).

Evidence supports the above description. One study, which followed 68 widows and widowers under the age of 45, found that the opportunity for anticipatory grieving diminished the likelihood for psychological difficulties 13 months after the death (Parkes, 1975). A subsequent study examined the experiences and behavior of 80 widows, also approximately one year after their husbands' deaths. Younger widows, those 45 years of age or less, reported much less distress when they had had at least six days of warning of their husbands' deaths. For middle-aged and older widows an anticipatory period seemed to make little or no difference; however, results in this study were not totally consistent (Ball, 1976–77). Finally, a third study found that parents of dying children were more accepting of their loss when there had been time for anticipatory grieving (Binger, Ablin, Feuerstein, Kushner, Zoger, & Mikkelsen, 1969).

The expected length of mourning is also culturally influenced, although obviously an individual's grief is also a determining factor. Table 13-1 shows some cultural norms for bereavement. Each person was asked how long before a person of his or her approximate age, sex, and ethnic group should wait before doing each of the things listed in the table. Note that appropriate mourning is not an all-or-nothing matter; people think certain apects of mourning should last longer than others.

Mourning need not ever completely cease. On the anniversary of a death, Jews have a *Jahrzeit,* when candles are lit and special prayers may be offered; this occurs for the rest of the lives of the survivors in many instances. Many other societies have designated a lengthy mourning period.

CULTURAL EFFECTS ON GRIEF

Culture affects grief less directly than it affects bereavement and mourning practices. Some cultures encourage the expression of emotions during grieving, while others do not. It's possible that the encouragement of such expression serves to intensify the underlying feelings, since we know from other sources that attitudes not only influence behavior but are directly influenced by behavior; that is, we do something and then develop attitudes or feelings as the result of doing it. Therefore, if I cry at a funeral because it is expected of me, my crying may well lead to feelings of grief that are likely, in turn, to produce more crying.

Cultures also influence the kinds of attachments that we develop, and grief occurs when we lose a relationship in which the attachments are strong. When many people are equally important in someone's life, the death of one of those persons is not likely to cause immense grief; how-

TABLE 13-1. Responses of 434 Persons in the Greater Los Angeles Area Regarding the Length of Time Following a Death of Spouse before It Would Be Appropriate for a Person of Respondent's Age, Sex, and Ethnicity to Do Each of the Indicated Actions

	Percent of Black Americans	*Percent of Japanese Americans*	*Percent of Mexican Americans*	*Percent of "Anglo" Americans*
To remarry				
Unimportant to wait	34	14	22	26
1 week–6 months	15	3	1	23
1 year	25	30	38	34
2 years +	11	26	20	11
Other (including never/depends)	16	28	19	7
To stop wearing black				
Unimportant to wait	62	42	52	53
1 day–4 months	24	26	11	31
6 months +	11	21	35	6
Other/depends	4	11	3	11
To return to his/her place of employment				
Unimportant to wait	39	22	27	47
1 day–1 week	39	28	37	35
1 month +	17	35	27	9
Other/depends	6	16	9	10
To start going out with other men/women				
Unimportant to wait	30	17	17	25
1 week–1 month	14	8	4	9
6 months	24	22	22	29
1 year +	11	34	40	21
Other/depends	21	19	18	17

From *Death and Ethnicity: A Psychocultural Study,* by R. A. Kalish and D. K. Reynolds. Copyright 1976. Reprinted by permission.

ever, when only a few people are very important in one's life, the death of one of them will probably lead to grief and suffering. We can at least speculate, then, that our system of nuclear families makes each individual in our system more important, so that the death of one will bring greater grief, but to fewer people.

FORMS OF MOURNING

The cultural differences in mourning are considerable. They range from *suttee,* the Hindu practice of burning a dead man's widow to enhance his memory and his family's prestige (which, incidentally, was optional) (Kroeber, 1948) to wearing a black armband for a year following the death to having a ceremonial meal.

These variations occur for all aspects of mourning. They "may last for days, weeks, or years; they may require abstentions from communication concerning the deceased, or they may enjoin public proclamation. The emotions of the bereaved may be publicly displayed in weeping and wailing, suppressed with stoic resolve, or camouflaged behind the mask of some other affect, for example, with smiling and laughter" (Averill, 1968, p. 722).

Washing and cleanliness are rituals frequently associated with mourning; sometimes anyone who has touched a dead body is expected to be cleansed with water (Frazer & Gaster, 1959). Celibacy for the survivors, especially the surviving spouse, may also be required. In our society, we seem to have a strange mixture of feelings about sexual behavior following the death of a spouse. On the one hand, "proper" respect is defined in part as abstention from sexual behavior for a time; on the other hand, widows often report being propositioned by men who claim to assume that, having been cut off from a sexual relationship with their husbands, these women are in need of sex and must be provided for.

The anthropological literature is filled with descriptions of mourning behavior, and there are reviews of these studies in reference sources as well (for example, Frazer & Gaster, 1959). When you read these, it is important to avoid finding the customs of other societies "cute" or "strange"; they need to be understood in terms of the entire societal milieu, not taken out of context as we tend to do. After all, think how strange our relative lack of ritualized mourning behavior would seem to persons from other cultures. It probably appears that we do not respect our dead relatives, since once the funeral is over, little or nothing is expected from the survivors. The differences among ethnic communities in the United States, as shown in Table 13-1, are good evidence of this. Consider the opinions that the family-oriented communities (Japanese-American and Mexican-American) and the individually-oriented communities (Black-American and "Anglo" American) must have of each other's customs of gravesite visits (Kalish & Reynolds, 1976) (see Table 13-2).

FUNERALS

Because anthropologists and historians have paid so much attention to funerals and burial rites, we have a rich literature of these death-associated rituals throughout the world. Once again there is the tendency to find the customs of other people either strange and funny or strange and admirable. Within the proper context, the customs of most other people make excellent sense, but this volume does not permit the opportunity to describe these contexts.

One major cultural difference involves what happens to the body. In our society most people are interred in caskets under the earth or in mausoleums. Some people are cremated; among these, most are content to

TABLE 13-2. Responses of 434 Persons in the Greater Los Angeles Area to Questions Concerning Visiting the Gravesite of a Spouse

	Percent of Black Americans	*Percent of Japanese Americans*	*Percent of Mexican Americans*	*Percent of "Anglo" Americans*
What do you feel is the fewest number of times he/she would visit his/her spouse's grave during the first year—not counting the burial service?				
Unimportant to do	39	7	11	35
1–2 times	32	18	19	11
3–5 times	16	18	12	18
6 + times	13	58	59	35
(Don't know, etc.)	(11)	(6)	(3)	(19)
What do you feel is the fewest number of times he/she should visit his/her spouse's grave during the fifth year after the death?				
Unimportant to do	52	8	20	43
1–2 times	30	47	39	35
3–5 times	9	16	22	15
6 + times	10	30	18	6
(Don't know, etc.)	(14)	(6)	(4)	(22)

From *Death and Ethnicity: A Psychocultural Study,* by R. A. Kalish and D. K. Reynolds. Copyright 1976. Reprinted by permission.

have their ashes scattered in the garden of the crematorium, but again there are those with other plans, such as having their ashes taken to places of special significance: "I arranged for an airplane to drop Mom's ashes in Hawaii over Haleakala, where Dad's ashes are also. That has been their plan since I can remember—it was the place that they both loved best."

In some countries, such as Nepal, bodies are not cremated in private but are burned in public. When we visited Katmandu in 1963, we noticed a funeral pyre on a small barge adjacent to the shore of a river. When the body on the pyre was burning, we seemed to be the only ones to notice. The Nepalese either considered it not worth their attention or were too polite to pay attention.

Water burial is also common, although limited in our culture to persons who have died at sea. Tibetans can choose among earth burial, cremation, water burial, or "air burial." In the last-named, the body is left exposed to be eaten by vultures or dogs or to decompose. These four methods of disposal derive from the Tibetan view that, because the universe is composed of these four elements (certainly similar to early Western thought), the body should return to one of them (Habenstein & Lamers, 1960). Each of these modes of disposing of the body is accompanied by its own unique rituals; for example, prior to air burial the body is ceremonially cut apart. Also, each kind of burial is used relatively more often for certain kinds of persons than for other kinds; water burial is used for beggars, lepers, babies, and the poor, while cremation is usually reserved for high lamas (Habenstein & Lamers, 1960).

Lavish funerals and prestigious burial sites have long been used to indicate wealth and status (consider where Washington, Jefferson, Lincoln, Grant, Roosevelt, and Kennedy are buried). Conversely, people who have had relatively little during their lives may be given lavish funerals to provide them at their deaths with what they were not able to have during their lives.

In the United States, about 9% of deaths result in cremation (Howard Raether, executive director, National Funeral Directors Association, personal communication, 1979). In most of these cases there is first a funeral with the body present. Public services that include a viewing of the body preceding the service and a committal at wherever the body is buried still represent over 75% of all deaths (Raether & Slater, 1974), although different communities and different parts of the country vary in this practice.

At one time, funeral attendance, ritual mourning, and cemetery visits were routine. Not so anymore. A seminary professor noted that fewer than half the students in his class, most of whom planned to join the clergy, had ever attended a funeral (Raether & Slater, 1974). Among Los Angeles residents, 42% of those between 20 and 39 had not attended a funeral in the previous two years, and an additional 51% had attended fewer than three. More surprising, more than one-fourth of those 60 and over had not been to a funeral in two years, and another 36% had not been to more than three (Kalish & Reynolds, 1976).

In summing up the meaning of a funeral, one article proposes that "a funeral becomes that experience in which a person can face the reality of what has happened, let memory become a part of the process of grieving, and, in the experience, express honest feelings, accept the community support that is freely proffered, and attempt to place the death in a context of meaning acceptable to the individual experiencing the trauma of separation" (Raether & Slater, 1977 p. 237). The same authors distinguish five phases in the funeral and burial experience: (1) the removal of the body or the separation of the dead from the living; (2) the visitation period—attending a wake or a scripture service, or sitting shiva; (3) the funeral rite itself; (4) the procession from the place where the funeral is held to the place of burial or disposal of the body; and (5) the committal of the body to, in the case of our culture, the earth (Raether & Slater, 1977).

THE CONTROVERSY OVER FUNERALS

Funeral directors and their supporters contend that the funeral itself provides a kind of closure to the relationship with the dead person and that this is especially true when there is an open casket. The "anti-funeralists" disagree heartily, arguing that the funeral directors are only trying to make more money and that the embalmer's art is grotesque. The verdict of the bereaved is also split. Parkes (1972) found that about half the widows he interviewed were upset by seeing their husband's body at the funeral, while the other half felt their last view was helpful. One limitation, of course, is that the embalmed body is only *relatively* lifelike: the pallor still indicates that it is a corpse, not a person. (Of course, if it looked completely lifelike, other stresses might ensue.) Embalming does not preserve the body indefinitely, as often assumed, but it does preserve the body through the funeral and for a period thereafter (Simpson, 1979).

Objections to funerals are similar to objections to other rituals, such as weddings. One frequent complaint is that funeral directors use dubious selling practices; a second is that today's elaborate funerals are too expensive and that people who can't really afford them are manipulated into having them; third, some people say that funerals should be simple, plain, and concerned with religious beliefs and support for the bereaved, but that today's funerals concentrate on lavish caskets and motorcades. The same complaints are levelled against car salespersons and people who have expensive weddings or bar mitzvahs, but the anger directed at morticians is more intense. This anger arises in part because the bereaved are such highly vulnerable consumers that exploitation is easily accomplished and partly because many of the death-related angers and anxieties are readily displaced onto funeral directors.

Obviously, one way to avoid the exploitation that can occur when bereavement makes one vulnerable is to make funeral arrangements in advance. Among the adults interviewed in Los Angeles, only 3% of those 39 years of age and under had made such arrangements, and only 24% of those 60 and over had done so (Kalish & Reynolds, 1976). There are two ways to make such arrangements. One is directly with a funeral home, which can record the kind of funeral you wish, with the assurance that you can get it at the recognized price when the time comes. The alternative is through a Memorial Society, a loosely associated group of local organizations that contract with one of more local mortuaries to get funerals at the lowest possible price. Members, who join for life by paying a very small amount for themselves and their families, select the funeral home they wish and the funeral they wish (that is, the point on the plain-to-lavish continuum), and they fill out a form so indicating, which is their arrangement with the mortuary. In effect, membership signifies that the person wishes a modest and inexpensive funeral and burial; the extent to which clergy and others are involved must be settled separately.

Does viewing the embalmed body at the funeral help heal the survivors' grief or is it destructive to that process? Does the funeral help provide a sense of closure, a feeling that the death has actually occurred, or is it of little use in this regard? Is it appropriate or inappropriate to spend money on a funeral, money they could have used for more immediate needs in life? Answers to these questions depend so much on individual circumstances and good evidence is so scanty that I personally believe we need to consider our own value systems rather than pretend to any objective information.

Perhaps my own personal experiences may illustrate the complexity of just one of these issues. The first time I attended a funeral of someone I loved, I was disturbed by the cosmetic job that presumed to make him look "just like he did when he was alive." The embalmer not only could not overcome the ravages of cancer, but I resented the waxy appearance. Some 30 years later, I attended a funeral with a closed casket that was positioned between the mourners and the pulpit, and I found myself resenting the absence of the person within the casket. I was obviously angry because I felt that the empty box did not represent the person I loved. Of course, the box was not empty, but it felt empty to me. I wanted the dead person to be there, and, if he couldn't be there, I wanted something that appeared more like him than a covered container. Thus in one instance I was upset because the body was on view and in the other I was upset because it wasn't.

The process of dying and the process of grieving are both extremely complex matters, and policy decisions need to be made on the basis of the best available information. But we need to know when we make a decision based on sound information and when our decision reflects feelings, beliefs, or implicit values. Grieving has only begun at the time of the funeral, and it continues for many months. The grief expressed at a funeral represents only a small portion of the grief a person will express. Therefore, we need to take care that we neither overestimate nor underestimate the significance of this ceremony.

PART

4
CARING RELATIONSHIPS

*Notes on Eleanor**

These extracts are from the journal of Marcy Adamski, written when she was a volunteer with Shanti, an organization that provides free psychological and social services to dying persons. Ms. Adamski is presently a counselor and consultant working with the dying.

October 31

Went to visit Eleanor. She had just spoken to her daughter on the telephone and was quite angry because her daughter didn't seem to take her illness seriously. Eleanor told her that she was afraid to go to sleep at night because she was frightened she wouldn't wake up. The daughter took this statement lightly. Eleanor feels she should call at least once a week. She repeated that she was terrified of death. I want to talk to her more about this.

November 7

Spent an hour with Eleanor today. When I walked in, I was startled by her appearance. She was lying back in her bed, eyes shut, and looked very pale. For one fleeting moment I thought she had died—that no one had noticed and I would be the one to discover her.

She opened her eyes and smiled, but I sensed that her mood was very down. She looked weary and agitated. I did not offer solutions, just tried to share her sadness.

Eleanor: "It's hard to be here. When a person's family just dumps them and they don't call or visit, then a person is all alone. My eyes are out of focus from the medicine, my intestines are bad, and my bladder gives me trouble. My back and legs hurt so much. And I was up all night. I'm afraid to go to sleep. I think I won't wake up."

Marcy: "Are you afraid you will die in your sleep?"

Eleanor: "No, I wish I would."

Marcy: "Then what are you afraid of?"

*"Notes on Eleanor," by M. Adamski. Copyright © 1980 by Marcella Adamski. Reprinted by permission of author.

Eleanor: "It would be a bother for people to have to find me. I've seen a lot of dead people."

Then she changed the subject abruptly. She did not want to go on and seemed annoyed at my questioning. She again expressed annoyance with her son for not telephoning. Then she complained that she could not see to dial his number. I told her how to have the operator make the connection and that I would help her print his number on a large card. She became quite vexed. "You young people think everything is so easy just because you can handle it."

I wondered whether or not to stay, but in retrospect I realize that she needed to express her anger and disappointment toward her son, to displace it onto me. I found myself just being silent and listening, repeating back and expressing empathy. At times I thought I should change my tack and cheer her up, but later I recalled that, last week, when I had felt depressed, I hadn't wanted to be cheered up.

Eleanor felt there is nothing to live for. Her body is worn out, her family has put her away. "My mother was an invalid. I cared for her, and she died at 54. Look at me—90! I didn't think it would be like this—would be this hard. Life is terrible."

November 14

Stopped by to see Eleanor. She was in a rage. Sitting up in bed in great agitation. "Everything is miserable and don't tell me it isn't!" She brought up her father and how he acted in certain situations. I asked her to pretend he was right here. What would he say? "Get out of bed!" And what would you say back? "I can't—I'm sick."

"I worked hard all my life. I wish I never gave so much to others—that's why my body is all worn out. What do you get for it?" She was angry and depressed. I wanted to go, feeling that even my accepting her emotions was annoying. It was like being on top of the deck of a ship being tossed about by a ferocious storm.

November 20

Saw Eleanor. She was less in turmoil. In fact, she smiled a great deal. She wished her son would visit. Since she can't see well enough to write, I offered to write for her. She was delighted. She dreamed that the nursing home was her own childhood home and she would get into trouble if she didn't keep the rules.

December 2

Eleanor died last night at 9:15 p.m.

I had arrived at the convalescent home yesterday at 2:00 p.m. to talk with her about her views on what it was like to be old and to face death. She had wanted to share her ideas with me. I went to her room, but the bed was empty. I looked in the room at the end of the hall and saw Eleanor's roommate standing by the bed of a very old and ill woman. I asked where Eleanor was. "There!" I was so stunned and disbelieving that it was really Eleanor that I checked the identification band on her wrist. Even then I thought it was another Mrs. Barrett.

Her features were drastically changed. She had suffered a massive stroke, but she could still hear and understand. I realized she was dying and asked if her son had been sent for. He had been notified but wasn't certain he could come. I also wanted to telephone Virginia, her old friend, to be with her, so I asked where Eleanor's address book was. They opened a closet in the room. All her things had been stacked in boxes. I felt infuriated that she was already dead to them and all was made ready to "ship her out." We found the address book, and I called Virginia.

Virginia hadn't come to visit Eleanor because of the Thanksgiving holidays and because she had a touch of flu. I reflected how abandoned Eleanor must have felt over the holidays, and I also felt guilty that I hadn't come to see her in a week. Virginia was reluctant to come—she would need to break a dinner engagement—but I pressed her and she acquiesced.

After Virginia had been there a while, she wanted to leave. She said her own kind of good-by: "I'll be back." She was not able to say a real good-by. Several other people, aides, an assistant administrator, a couple of nurses, came in and spoke about her as if she were already dead. They referred to her physical condition, her appearance, and how close to death she appeared—even though she was still sporadically conscious. I wanted to shove them out of hearing distance. Yet I realized that it was their way of coping—mine too.

The doctor came, and I left. When he came out, I ran after him and told him only that I was Eleanor's friend. Although I had always thought of him as unexpressive and unemotional, we walked down the corridor with his arm around my waist and mine around his. Eleanor could die at any moment. The medication would also make her sleepy. (I pondered the trade-off of reduction of pain and loss of consciousness.) He told me that he thought Eleanor would die 20 years ago. "You don't know when, you just don't know."

A nurse came in and, as we talked, she told me of her own bouts with cancer. Another woman dropped by and all three of us talked. When Eleanor's roommate came back, she told me of her life. I held her hand and Eleanor's. Finally all the visitors had left. It was like being in the center of a great drama. Another nurse, who had always seemed so calm and imposing, told me about her own concerns. She had been depressed a few days earlier and didn't know why. Then she realized it was her birthday: 58. Her father had died when he was 58.

Finally, aside from the nurse dropping by from time to time, I was completely alone with Eleanor. It was dark outside. With each breath there was a deep growling sound. Like someone drowning. I wondered if I was prepared to spend the night. I decided yes. I wondered whether (and hoped) her son would arrive in time. If I wasn't there, no one would be there. The nurse was only able to drop by to see if she was still alive. She had no time to be with her. My cat was hungry. I was missing my women's group. I wondered if my friend had called. What does all this loving get you, Eleanor? You are indeed alone after giving a lifetime for others. What *was* I doing there? How *did* I get into this? What was going on inside of Eleanor? Struggle? Nothingness? Was there something I should say into her ear? Get better? Don't die? Die? I only held her hand. Stroked her head, kissed her. I began to meditate. Feeling empty, I called on Jesus, Buddha, and everyone else I could think of. There was only this—an old old lady dying. What *am* I doing here? I would rather be holding the hand of the man I love than the hand of a dying woman. But I was here. And there was no other place to be. No one was waiting for me but my cat. I thought of how Eleanor was afraid of dying but how much she wanted death.

I went out for a cup of coffee. Came back in 15 minutes. I needed to get away. Her breathing changed a little. Pulling in more air. Deeper sighs. I knew a certain fear but chose not to be afraid. When I looked back at Eleanor, her eyes were half opened—staring at nothing I could see. Breath—pause—breath—longer pause.

"Eleanor, you are dying." I stroked her head and in front of my wide peering gaze, she died.

I went to tell the nurse, who checked her pulse, then closed her eyes. They called the morgue. Her son hadn't arrived. Eleanor's face was changing rapidly. Death was setting in. The spirit was gone. Eleanor was dead. But not over.

14

CARING RELATIONSHIPS IN HEALTH SETTINGS

As the death-awareness movement has become more visible and gained supporters, increasing numbers of people have begun to participate in paid or volunteer work with the dying and the bereaved. Some of these persons initiate their own involvement: a hospital chaplain asks to be referred to patients who are dying; a woman volunteers to work with a group like Compassionate Friends; a psychologist teaches professional and student morticians about relating effectively to the bereaved.

We are all survivors of the deaths of others. We are all individuals who will someday die. Consequently, the insights we gain from those who work, or otherwise relate in a structured fashion, with the dying and the bereaved are insights we can readily apply to our own lives.

Perhaps a close friend or family member has died. Perhaps you have had occasion to believe that you were going to die in the foreseeable future. Perhaps you have been told of the sudden, unexpected death of a person you cared about. If you have experienced any of these events, you will understand the sensitivity needed to work with the dying and the bereaved.

PROBLEMS OF RELATING

A decade ago, I might have written that it was almost impossible to find people who would work with dying persons. Although that is no longer true, it does not mean that working in a death-related capacity has become easy. A number of reasons for this appear likely.

First, the future of dying people is a particularly limited one; we are reluctant to invest a lot of our time and energy when an individual will not be around to relate to or be productive in any fashion. Their social value becomes less. And many people desire to work only with individuals who have a potentially promising future. The dying are disengaging; others are disengaging from them. The impetus to care for and to care about them diminishes.

Second, dying people remind us that we also will not live forever. They remind us that we, like they, are transient, impermanent, subject to decay and death. Many of us don't like the reminder and don't want to work in a setting in which we are constantly reminded of our mortality.

Third, when we begin to think about our own mortality and transiency, we are also required thereby to consider the ephemeral quality of what we accomplish. The novel we write, the educational program we develop, the sales campaign we devise, the computer software we create, the fine wood cabinet we design—none of these will last forever.

Fourth, death is loss, and we don't like to have to encounter a series of losses. It is bad enough that we must suffer the pain from the inevitable losses of people we love; we don't want to add to our pain by developing new relationships with people we know are going to die.

Fifth, the dying remind us that we cannot truly control our environment. Two weeks before writing this, I fell while playing with some energetic children and seriously bruised my left arm and hand. The physician thought I might have a hairline fracture, and I had to wear a cast and a sling for several days. The immediate consequences of the incident were extremely limited, but the event reminded me of the suddenness with which life can change, the absurdity of an event that comes unexpectedly from nowhere and can wipe out life or deprive life of some of its most basic satisfactions. I thought a great deal about the changeability, the absurdity, the chance-like quality of so much of life, and I felt relieved that my pain had been so slight and my incapacitation had been so brief. Work with people who are dying is a constant reminder that change, absurdity, and chance are always potential occurrences in our lives. It is easier to ignore dying and death and to pretend to ourselves that we are really in charge of everything.

Sixth, dying people often look peculiar, talk strangely, have an unpleasant odor, and are not able to offer some of the normal amenities of normal relationships. This is especially true during the later stages of some diseases.

Nevertheless, despite these and other reasons for not working with dying persons, many individuals make the conscious choice to devote at least a part of their working time to the dying. Their own interests and experiences are sufficient to overcome the negative pressures. Some people may even be attracted to work in an area whose many negative qualities discourage the service of others.

Sometimes a person will put so much effort into working with the dying and their survivors that the stresses resulting from these continued and intense relationships become too great, and the person must retreat. This is accomplished either psychologically by reducing the sense of personal involvement and caring or physically by leaving the situation altogether. I once asked Lawrence LeShan what he had learned as a full-time psychotherapist on what was probably the first project offering mental-health services to non-elderly, terminally ill patients. His response was significant: "In the future, I would never spend more than 25% of my time with such relationships." Constant intense involvement with people who will shortly die can be too stressful.

HEALTH-CARE PROFESSIONALS

Most, although not all, dying persons require some form of health care from some kind of health professional in some sort of health facility. This might be, for example, medication administered by a physician in a hospital or blood pressure taken by a nurse in a nursing home. It could even be acupuncture at home done by a friend trained in this technique (although this might stretch the terms *care, professional,* and *facility* somewhat).

In the eyes of the community, the most powerful and undoubtedly the most prominent member of the health-care team is the physician. I once described today's physician as a contemporary priest: she or he is considered the gatekeeper to the rewards of today's religion (long and healthy life on earth), just as the traditional priest was the gatekeeper to the rewards of traditional religion (access to a life after death with God). Unfortunately, since each of us sees others die, we know that the new "priest" fails in keeping us alive forever; the traditional priest's promises of life everlasting could never be verified by those still alive (Kalish, 1980).

From all that I can determine, most physicians perceive their role to be that of producing a cure so that a patient can return to normal activities, or at least to near-normal activities. The fact that doctors cannot accomplish this for the dying patient is a source of conflict for many physicians. If they continue to treat a dying person, they are applying their costly skills and training to a situation that might better be handled by others; if they do not continue to treat the dying person, then they feel they have failed to fulfill the patient's expectations. Furthermore, if physicians identify with every dying patient, they are likely to suffer emotional exhaustion or else find themselves withdrawing psychologically; conversely, if they do not have any emotional involvement with dying patients, they may communicate an unfeeling quality at the very time that the patients need to relate to a health professional with feelings.

If physicians define their task as providing cure, improvement, or at least maintenance levels of functioning for a patient, then they are inevitably going to fail with each dying person; if, on the other hand, they define their task as assuaging physical and psychological suffering and increasing physical and psychological satisfactions, they may perceive themselves as succeeding, even if the patient is dying.

Too often physicians make impossible demands of themselves, then react maladaptively to the situation. Three frequent maladaptive responses are anger, denial, and depression/resignation (Garfield, 1978). A physician may actually exhibit anger toward a patient, usually in indirect ways, if the patient does not respond as the physician feels he or she should. The anger may take the form of avoiding the patient. This avoidance can, in turn, intensify a patient's fears of abandonment by significant persons. Or the anger may be manifest in a tense voice or a brittle touch. Physicians also displace their anger onto other hospital staff members, the patient's family, or even their own family and friends.

Physicians may also use the mechanism of denial to avoid confronting the inevitability of the death of a particular patient. They may deny the death by turning their attention to other activities, more demanding patients, or personal obligations (Artiss & Levine, 1973); or denial may occur by a refusal to treat patients who cannot possibly recover—accomplished by transferring them to other facilities or to other health-care professionals (Garfield, 1978).

Some physicians become depressed, and depression can be understood as anger turned inward. "I have known physicians who, for years, via a sheer act of will, fought off incipient depression only to succumb finally to the cumulative emotional impact of patient deaths" (Garfield, 1978, p. 107). Some such physicians turn to their informal social network of other physicians for understanding and support; others get the help they need from their spouses; a relatively few seek professional help, usually from psychotherapists. Others respond by withdrawal, somatic problems, or chronic depressed behavior, which often interferes with their ability to work.

Physicians are human—a platitude that is ignored both by patients, who want them to perform miracles, and by the physicians themselves, who may unconsciously expect themselves to be able to perform the same miracles. Sometimes the frustrations of their final inability to keep a person alive burst through in angry humor—one example being the physician who became angry with the paperwork that confronted him. "The doctor agonized, 'Here a human died and I must fill out *cards*' " (Reynolds & Kalish, 1974, p. 149).

Although physicians have the final authority about medical decisions in health institutions, it is nurses and aides who have the greater power in terms of day-to-day patient care. When a patient is hospitalized, his or her physician may appear for a few minutes four or five days a week; the nurse is within a few feet of the patient for 40 hours a week. Often the nurse develops a closer relationship to the patient than the physician does, especially if the hospital stay is a long one or if the patient returns to the hospital on several occasions. If my own observations are accurate, nurses were the first group of people to become interested in the topics of death and dying; even now, nurses, more than other vocational groups, have sought additional knowledge—through reading, conferences, workshops, educational films—about death and dying. Moreover, the professional literature is filled with articles and books discussing nurse/dying-patient relationships. In some institutions, especially long-term care facilities, it is aides rather than nurses or physicians who provide the most personal care for dying persons. And, in individual instances, a hospital chaplain or social worker will prove to be most attentive. However, for the most part, nurses and physicians appear to perform the most important roles in health-care settings.

HEALTH-CARE FACILITIES

Most deaths in the United States and Canada occur in hospitals; a smaller number occur in other institutions, such as nursing homes, mental hospitals and board-and-care facilities. In hospitals, patients usually come and go fairly quickly, so that interactions among patients tend to be limited to those who share the same room. The death of a patient may upset that person's roommate, and occasionally may upset hospital staff, but rarely will it affect the other patients.

However, in settings where patients reside for longer periods, such as nursing homes, Veterans Administration facilities, and hospital units for the chronically ill, the death of one patient may have a profound effect on other patients. Patients get to know each other, share experiences, meet family members, and support each other when troubles arise. As in any other institution—college dorms, prisons, military bases—friendships can become very close. Often, when a resident dies, especially a resident who had lived in the facility for some time, there is great sorrow among the others.

Some of the larger institutions have special wards set aside for patients who are extremely ill and expected to die shortly. One such facility was referred to by both patients and staff as "Death Valley" (Kastenbaum, 1967); another was alternately called "the morgue" and "the dumping ground" (Reynolds & Kalish, 1974). Patients who are transferred to these wards without adequate explanation may assume, sometimes incorrectly, that the transfer signifies that they are terminally ill. When one patient returned from "Death Valley" to his previous ward in a geriatric hospital, several of his wardmates were astounded to see him—literally viewing him as someone returned from the dead.

When death does occur in hospitals or other institutions, an attempt is usually made to remove the body without the other patients noticing. Sometimes, frequently in a pediatric facility, the other patients are told that the missing patient had been transferred to another unit. However, patients are often familiar enough with hospital practice to understand that *transferred* means "died." In order to remove a body unobtrusively, one hospital aide may engage the deceased's roommates in conversation—drawing their attention away from the bed where the corpse is lying—while other staff members place the body on a gurney and draw it away. Another ploy is for a nurse to come up to the bed of the dead person, say "Time for your x-ray," then, with the help of an aide, place the body on a gurney and continue talking as if the person were still alive (Sudnow, 1967).

One part of preparing a body for removal is "wrapping." "The procedure essentially involves the complete removal of the . . . clothing . . . jewelry, and the folding of a heavy gauge muslin sheet completely around the body, pinning it down the front with large safety pins . . ." (Sudnow, 1967, p. 70). Other preparations follow, including a rapid cleaning of the body, crossing the hands and feet and binding them together, placing gauze pads over the eyes, and of course, removing all medical equipment that might have been used previously to sustain life (Sudnow, 1967).

Where the body is then taken depends on a number of factors. For example, some bodies will have immediate autopsies; some will go to the hospital morgue, waiting for a pick-up from the funeral home; a few will be taken to facilities where they will be used as donors for some form of organ transplant.

DYING IN A HOSPITAL VERSUS DYING AT HOME

Where do people die? Some die in their own homes, either because their deaths occur suddenly and unexpectedly or because they had planned to spend their last days and weeks at home. Others die in the community, again because their deaths occur without warning, from an accident or an unexpected coronary, for example. Many die in long-term care institutions. A very few die in hospices or under a hospice-care program. But most people in the United States, Canada, England, and most European nations die in hospitals (Hinton, 1979; Lerner, 1970).

As health care has become more effective and health-care institutions have become more efficient, increasing numbers of people have sought the best facilities possible to help them recover from their illnesses. Even when their conditions are no longer remediable, they tend to remain in hospitals, where professional staff is readily available, where medical equipment is at hand, and where the technology of medicine is at its best.

Hospitals offer other advantages for dying persons and their families. The demands of caring for someone at home often requires physical space, which may be in short supply; access to someone who will operate medical equipment, administer medicine, or monitor health conditions; and people to render care 24 hours a day. When any of these is unavailable at home, some form of hospital or institutional care may be necessary.

In addition, we have become accustomed to giving medical care priority over personal or spiritual care. The hospital is presumably the most effective and efficient place for the physical body to receive care, although it may not offer an optimum environment for retaining autonomy or for enjoying intimate personal relationships. Thus, although most people will state that they would prefer to die at home (Kalish & Reynolds, 1976), the assumption is often made that the hospital is the "proper" place to die.

What are the factors that determine where a person dies?

First, and perhaps most obvious, is the condition that is leading to death. Some conditions require hospital treatment in order to reduce pain and discomfort or avoid contagion; other conditions do not require medical or professional care or else lead so quickly to death that there is no opportunity for such care. Also some diseases lead to such repugnant changes in appearance or odors that family members who have a low tolerance for them would have great difficulty dealing with the unpleasant circumstances.

A second factor is the availability of caretakers outside of an institution or hospital and their attitudes toward caring for a dying person. In a British study, only 25% of persons who lived alone died in their own homes; 59% died in hospitals. Conversely, 47% of those with living spouses and 49% of those who lived with younger relatives (regardless of whether they were with a spouse) died at home; the comparable figures for hospital deaths were 46% and 41%, respectively. Since married men are more likely to die at home than married women, it would appear that wives are more likely to care for dying husbands than the converse (Cartwright et al., 1973). It isn't enough, however, to have a spouse or live with younger relatives; these people must be willing to undergo the demanding routines often required in the care of dying persons.

Finances are a third factor. In some situations, hospital care is less expensive; in other situations, home care is less expensive. When insurance or Medicare or Medicaid will cover most hospital bills but relatively few incurred at home, the dying may choose hospital care to avoid immense financial costs. Sometimes, because family members provide care at home or the person doesn't need extra care at home, considerable money is saved by remaining home. The determination of financial cost is largely a function of what expenses will be covered by private insurance or governmental health-care programs.

Fourth is the competency of the available institutions. If a particular hospital is well reputed or the patient or family members have had good prior experiences with it, they are more likely to trust its care.

A fifth possible factor is age, insofar as older people are more likely to die in nursing homes and other non-hospital institutions, while younger people are most likely to die in hospitals (most probably because of the kinds of conditions that cause their deaths). From age 55 on, the proportion of all deaths that occur in British hospitals remains the same; 12% of persons 85 years of age and older will die in other institutions, and deaths at home will diminish accordingly (Cartwright et al., 1973).

Over and above all demographic factors are personal preferences. Some individuals greatly prefer being at home, where they have familiar surroundings, fewer restrictive rules and regulations, greater autonomy, more access to family and friends, and more opportunity for individual choice. On the other hand, some persons are concerned about limited space in the home, about disturbing or burdening the lives of family members, or about altering the nature of previous role relationships (for example, being cared for by their children), and will choose a hospital or other institution.

People are also concerned about whether returning home may mean that emergency treatment will not be available when necessary or that ongoing treatment may be curtailed—thus increasing distress or reducing probable life expectancy. For many dying persons, the opportunity to die at home is well worth the loss of a few days of life; others will remain in the hospital in order to hold on to life as long as possible.

Since a hospital or other institution is still perceived as the "natural" place to die, many people don't even consider the alternative of dying at home. The physician is often the appropriate person to propose this alternative, but he or she may be reluctant to interfere in family dynamics. This seems to be an issue that the dying person and his or her family should be able to resolve, although the former may fear to bring the matter up, dreading rejection or—even worse—irritated acceptance if his or her preference is to die at home. It is useful to have an understanding in advance.

THE HOSPICE PROGRAM

Discussing the relative merits of institutional care versus home care implies that these are the only alternatives for the dying. However, this isn't the case: the hospice program combines institutional care and home care and adds a dimension of its own. This innovative and humanistic program for the care of the terminally ill patient, launched in its present form in England in 1967, has spread rapidly throughout Europe and North America.

The term *hospice* originally described a waiting place for travelers, primarily the pilgrims during the Middle Ages. Later, hospices were established for the incurably ill, the destitute, parentless children, and the elderly, while the acutely sick were admitted to hospitals. Then, in the nineteenth and twentieth centuries, a Catholic religious order developed hospices for dying persons, to "welcome those whom no one else wanted to care for and give them the promise that this welcome would last as long as the need existed" (Saunders, 1977, p. 160).

This was the model used by Cicely Saunders, the British physician who developed St. Christopher's Hospice, itself the model for the present hospice movement. Since hospice services are not requested until the individual and his or her physicians believe that further treatment and cure are no longer possible, the hospice program differs considerably from general hospital care, although many of its principles could readily be incorporated into hospital programs. These principles are:

1. Patients and their family members should be seen as a unit, and "nothing we do as caregivers should serve to separate someone who is dying from his or her family" (Woodson, 1978, p. 378); this requires a fully open system for visitors of all ages.
2. The program needs to begin from the moment of admission to the hospice; at St. Christopher's, for example, patients are greeted as they enter, whether by ambulance or on foot, and are personally guided—normally with their family members—to their beds.
3. All possible efforts should be extended to keep patients at home as long as they wish, while at the same time giving these outpatients the assurance that they have priority in entering the in-patient service when necessary.
4. The family, assisted by volunteers and trained staff, should receive home health-care aid. They learn how to provide medical care at home for the patient and how to help the patient and each other through psychological and social stress.
5. Pain can be controlled by understanding the basis of pain—the extent to which it is physical, psychological, social, or spiritual—and by treating it before it begins; the knowledge that one's pain can and will be controlled reduces stress and tension, and leads, consequently, to the reduction of the pain itself; the administration of a successful pain-management program requires knowledge of both the biochemical impact of drugs and the psychosocial condition of the patient (Woodson, 1978).

Because of its extensive home-health and home-care programs and its use of volunteers, the hospice can handle a large number of patients during the course of a year. It also is less expensive than hospital care. St. Christopher's, when it had only 60 beds (it now has about 70), was still able to accept 550 admissions a year with a median length of stay of only ten days (Saunders, 1977). This brief time period is due to both the excellent home-care programs and the high death rate of patients.

The hospice movement in North America has differed somewhat from its European counterpart. Here, the hospice usually consists initially of an out-patient service with some back-up beds available in a local hospital and does not include its own physical plant. This, I suspect, will mean that the program will be more closely linked with traditional medical institutions and that most in-patient service will be provided by existing hospitals, rather than by free-standing institutions. The hospice team will provide out-patient and family-support services, along with some in-patient programs.

Perhaps the most innovative aspect of the hospice movement is the change in attitude it has effected. The attitude toward a dying person has changed from "There is nothing more we can do to help," to "We need to provide the best human care possible." Although some health-care professionals have always espoused this latter view, hospitals and other institutions have not always incorporated it into practice.

Although studies of hospices are now in progress, relatively few have been completed. One study has compared a small number (34) of cancer patients at St. Christopher's with a similar number of comparable patients who died elsewhere. The results are illuminating:

1. The hospice patients were more mobile.
2. The hospice patients rated their physical pain as less severe, but this was not due to more drug-caused confusion.
3. Spouses of hospice patients reported both less anxiety and fewer somatic symptoms.
4. Spouses of hospice patients spent more time visiting; more time talking to staff, other patients, and other visitors; and more time helping care for the patient.
5. Because patients at the hospice perceived physicians and nurses as less busy, they found them more accessible.
6. Very few hospice patients were reported by their families as upset by the deaths of other patients.
7. Seventy-eight percent of the patients' families regarded St. Christopher's as being like a family; 11% of the matched non-hospice families felt that way about the institutions where their dying family members were (Parkes, 1975).

Another investigation compared the emotional state, attitudes toward illness, and opinions of care of cancer patients in a hospice with those in two other settings: an acute hospital and a long-term care facility. Hospice patients were found to be less anxious and less depressed; the general open awareness context of the hospice received substantial approval; and the hospice staff and treatment program were better received than those of the other institutions (Hinton, 1979). Although these studies are few, they do suggest that a substantial number of persons prefer hospice programs.

Nonetheless, there are some limitations to hospices. First, many health professionals oppose segregating the dying from other patients. They believe that this kind of labeling is harmful: being in a *place for the dying* exacts a toll of unnecessary anxiety. Second, hospice care is not appropriate for everyone: some deaths do not permit hospice care; some health conditions require equipment or treatment not available in hospices; some persons will find the program unsuited to their personal needs.

The advantage of the hospice program is not that it solves the problem of where to die, but that it offers another significant choice, which itself includes alternative models. The National Hospice Organization is located at 765 Prospect Street, New Haven, Connecticut 06511.

TREATMENT FOR THE DYING: SOME SPECIAL SITUATIONS

Over the centuries, many treatments have been prescribed for the critically ill to restore them to partial or even full levels of functioning.

Some of these, like bloodletting, have been discontinued; others, like prayer, are still used, normally either in association with medical treatment or after such treatment is no longer productive; still others, like the visualization methods (see p. 272) for reducing cancer sites, are new and still experimental, although not usually acceptable to physicians and other credentialed health professionals. Sometimes, of course, the treatment attempts not to cure the disease but to diminish its pain, discomfort, and incapacitation. The hospice program attempts this last-named; so does the treatment of giving LSD and marijuana to the dying.

TWO MEDICALLY ACCEPTED TREATMENT PROCEDURES—AND THEIR PROBLEMS

The most familiar approach to treating people who are dying is to utilize what is termed *the medical model.* People are essentially biological organisms, and, when they are dying, something has gone wrong with their biology or chemistry; by altering the biology or chemistry (virtually always to be accomplished by a person with recognized credentials and license), their death trajectory can frequently be reversed.

Sometimes this approach doesn't work because the disease is too far advanced, recuperative powers are too limited, or medical science does not have sufficient knowledge or power. On other occasions, however, the medical model doesn't work because the treatment is so demanding, so painful, so incapacitating, or otherwise so distasteful that the patient selects to die rather than continue treatment. Thus, a patient may need to choose between certain death from cancer within six to nine months or an operation that, while offering a reasonable chance of increasing life expectancy to several years, may not succeed and, if successful, would still leave the patient without the ability to walk.

One medically accepted procedure for critically ill cancer patients is radiation treatment. Sometimes the treatment is given in the hope of destroying enough cancer cells to permit a lengthy future life, with reasonable or even good health. In other instances, radiation is recommended in order to slow down the spread of the cancer, but it is recognized that dying can only be postponed.

Radiation treatment has significant side effects, ranging from extreme fatigue to vomiting to hair loss. One woman described her life with this procedure as "one week of post- reatment sickness, one week of slow recovery, and one week of health, before I have to take the next treatment." She finally chose to stop the treatment and lived an almost-normal life for about as long as had been predicted with radiation therapy. Another woman became so embarrassed by her baldness that she refused to wear a wig and isolated herself from everyone she knew.

An obvious question emerges: has anyone attempted to develop psychological and social supports for people who are undergoing difficult treatments for life-threatening illnesses? Such support is not unknown, but it also is not routine. Family, friends, and neighbors assist, but relatively little psychosocial help is offered through the formal channels of health institutions, and psychotherapists and counselors in private practice have rarely had experience with such patients and may be resistant to treating them.

A second example of a medically accepted treatment for survival is machine dependency. Many individuals remain alive only because some kind of machine has been placed in their bodies (such as a pacemaker) or can be temporarily used as part of their bodies. Chronic hemodialysis, a treatment for kidney failure, is probably one of the more dramatic and most frequently discussed of all forms of such treatment. The patient normally goes to a center twice a week to be dialyzed: the blood is shunted from his or her body through a machine that first cleanses it of impurities—the task that the kidneys normally accomplish—and then returns it to the body.

There is no question that these machines prolong life, since patients will die fairly soon if they do not arrive for their dialysis. The treatment includes some dietary and related restrictions and some care requirements; it even may have some severe side effects; however, the greatest difficulty in the treatment is probably learning to live with the dialyzer (Abram, 1977). An intense relationship between the person and the machine may develop since the treatment demands some 30 hours a week of "intimacy." Some dialysis patients see themselves as having been brought back from the dead; many have fantasies of being part machine, part person (Abram, 1977). A very new procedure, still in an experimental stage, permits the kidney patient almost complete freedom from the present dialysis process and its dietary restrictions.

There are other problems: failing health, deteriorating body image, loss of previous family status, sexual impotence, increasing dependence on others, and financial stress arising from job difficulties and treatment costs. Furthermore, the death rate from cardiovascular and other medical problems runs at least 5% per year (Abram, 1976). No wonder that dialysis patients often talk about suicide: one study of nearly 3500 patients found that approximately one in 20 had died from some form of self-destructive behavior; either they committed suicide or they decided to withdraw from the program and not follow medical requirements (Abram, Moore, & Westervelt, 1971).

Psychological support services for dialysis patients and their spouses (whose suffering should not be underestimated) is limited. In some instances, physicians have even expressed their feelings that patients find such programs upsetting and recommended that the programs should be cancelled (Abram, 1977). I know personally of one instance, some years ago, when the physician in charge of a dialysis unit ordered nurses to discourage any contact between spouses of patients for fear that they would upset each other and, thereby, upset the patients.

Is life worth living if one is machine-dependent or debilitated by the side effects of various treatments? This is a value judgment, of course, that can be made only by each individual for himself or herself. More understanding of the psychological stresses attached to these treatment procedures and more services to help patients and family members handle these stresses could undoubtedly reduce many of the problems.

TWO MEDICALLY CONTROVERSIAL TREATMENT PROCEDURES—AND THEIR PROBLEMS

The mainstream of Western medicine regards many health-treatment programs as inappropriate, unproven, or even peculiar. These include treatment of cancer by laetrile, faith-healing, acupuncture, and meditation. Each of these treatments has its adherents and its detractors, even within the medical profession; some, like laetrile, are new; others, like acupuncture and faith-healing, have a long history, although not necessarily in Western culture.

Another controversial health-treatment program that claims to be effective, especially in healing cancer patients who have been given up as terminally ill by their physicians, is the combined imagery, relaxation, and psychotherapy program developed by physician Carl Simonton (Simonton, Matthews-Simonton, & Creighton, 1978). The Simonton approach requires that cancer patients accept responsibility for having cancer; that is, they are told that they have, perhaps unconsciously, caused their cancer, and, therefore, they also have the power to get rid of the cancer. Part of the treatment is to develop visual imagery of the site of the cancer—to see it in the mind's eye in either literal or metaphoric terms—then to visualize healthy cells attacking and destroying the cancerous cells. It is easy to see that this approach takes the control of the illness away from the physician and places it directly in the hands of the patient. It says, in effect, that whether you live or die is completely up to you; you have the power; use it. The treatment also includes relaxation techniques and appropriate traditional medical regimens.

Simonton and his followers have claimed an extremely high rate of success—especially considering that they work primarily with patients diagnosed as having terminal cancer. Of 159 patients whom they treated, 63 were alive an average of two years after treatment began, and those who died had lived over 20 months from the time treatment was initiated. The life expectancy of these patients had previously been approximately one year, so even those who died far outlived their prognoses. Equally important, the activity level of the patients was considerably greater than had been anticipated (Simonton et al., 1978).

The explanation that Simonton offers for the success of his process combines psychological knowledge with biomedical and clinical medical information. The mere diagnosis of cancer is stress-producing and simultaneously causes depression; it often leads to hopelessness and helplessness (the syndrome frequently cited as occurring when people commit suicide). A diagnosis of cancer is perceived to be equivalent to a verdict of death; dying quietly and bravely seems to be the optimum scenario available.

The Simonton approach undoubtedly marshalls whatever will to live exists, and the patient's belief that he or she has power or can succeed where his or her physician has failed may certainly reduce depression and promote health and well-being in a variety of ways. On the other hand, the emphasis on being responsible for one's own illness may induce immense guilt, anxiety, and stress for the patient who is not recovering or at least remaining stable, and this could exacerbate the health problem and turn the last months of life into a period of depression and tension (Rosenbaum, 1978). Simonton explains that there are times when people have decided that they are ready to die and that such patients should be given support in their decision (Simonton et al., 1978). The possibility that cancer deaths may occur regardless of acceptance of responsibility, desire to live, and adherence to the treatment program is less effectively discussed.

It seems possible to explain Simonton's results without depending on his specific techniques, at least until someone conducts research using both control groups and varied experimental conditions. (An example of the latter would be to compare patients using all Simonton's techniques with those using all except visual imagery.) Such an explanation might hypothesize that high psychological stress, perhaps loss-related stress, induces biochemical changes in the human body that encourage the growth and spread of cancerous cells. Patients who are diagnosed as having cancer feel powerless to do anything about it and also fear its outcome; these feelings increase stress and, thereby, increase the spread of the disease. Perhaps the stress-induced changes inhibit or interfere with the body's natural defenses, its immunological system, so that the individual is no longer as capable of destroying the destructive cells.

For many cancer patients, the Simonton approach enhances the sense of power and self-sufficiency—thus reducing feelings of psychological stress and perhaps restoring the body's defenses. Instead of concentrating on losses, people focus on what they have. In some fashion and for some persons, this process encourages the growth of healthy cells and thus blocks the spread of cancer. This oversimplified explanation does not contradict Simonton's models, but it does suggest that Simonton's specific techniques would not be necessary for success. Instead, a variety of self-healing approaches would be equally likely to lead to health. Another way of looking at this would be that the Simonton method has a powerful placebo effect (Holden, 1978); however, that assumption introduces the possibility of reducing all non-biochemical treatments of any disease to a placebo effect.

In fact, many people have regained health by methods that do not fit the specific techniques. I personally know several people who have experienced such recovery—perhaps you do also. One woman reduced the size of a cancer-infested area by 50% during a three-month period; the only change in her life during that period had been a deep devotion to meditation and relaxation exercises. Although she eventually died from the cancer, she outlived the predictions of her life expectancy by many months. A middle-aged man I know visited a faith healer, who was also a personal friend; after several sessions over a period of weeks, his diagnosed cancer disappeared altogether. These two examples could be explained by the model described in the previous paragraphs.

An illness, of course, exists in a body that has a history and that contains a brain, and it is not at all farfetched to assume that the history and the brain activities will influence other parts of the body in ways we cannot presently understand. There are still several basic questions that must be asked about the effectiveness of Simonton's techniques and comparable healing programs:

> First, do they work? True, many people claim to have been cured by these programs, but I don't know of any systematic research conducted by anyone who was not an advocate in the first place.
>
> Second, if they do work, why do they work? Does taking responsibility for one's own illness cause these techniques to work? Are we responsible for our own cancers? Do the visual imagery techniques really lead to the death of cancer cells? If so, by what process?
>
> Third, if Simonton's method does work, are its techniques the only ones that would work, or would meditation or prayer or faith healing or psychotherapy work just as well? Or better? Or better for some persons?
>
> Fourth, if these healing programs do work, can they be used for people dying of other causes such as heart attacks, strokes, and respiratory diseases?
>
> Finally, are there any hazardous side effects?

One of the obvious implications of assuming that no one dies of cancer without wanting to, either consciously or unconsciously, is to conclude that no ones dies of anything without wanting to, either consciously or unconsciously. Therefore, if you only wanted to do so strongly enough, you could live forever, but, because you don't want to, you don't. The logical conclusion of the Simonton method might be that we are on the threshold of eliminating death from the world, at least for true believers. This conclusion strikes me as a return to a very naive level of denial of the reality of death. Nevertheless, whatever your own personal beliefs, the Simonton techniques and reported successes are very provocative to the contemplation of the interaction of psychological, social, and medical aspects of living and dying.

A second controversial procedure used with the dying is directed more at helping people through the living-dying interval than at producing a cure. This is the use of lysergic acid diethylamide, or LSD, as a treatment. The LSD is administered only under careful supervision, and a professional psychotherapist or comparable person is available to the patient throughout the experience. In addition, there is ample preliminary discussion concerning what might happen and some subsequent discussion as to what did occur. Therefore, it is possible that the positive effects of LSD are due not so much to its direct chemical action, as to the extensive caring relationships surrounding its administration.

How does LSD help patients in the living-dying interval? Dying patients report that, through their psychedelic experiences, they experience "the importance of accepting, surrendering, and relinquishing" (Grof & Halifax, 1977, p. 52), as well as a sense of unity or oneness with the infinite or cosmos. The boundaries of the self and of consciousness become blurred, and transpersonal experiences, such as out-of-body experiences or space and time travel, are not uncommon. "In the extreme form the individual consciousness seems to encompass the totality of existence and identify with that of the universal mind" (Grof & Halifax, 1977, p. 56).

If you look back at these past few sentences, you will realize that LSD seems to have the effect of reducing the distinctions between life and death, between this world and other worlds, between body and spirit. It may, in fact, enable some people to face their own deaths more peacefully because they have the sense of having already experienced what death may be, and the experiences have not been distressing. Death becomes not an end, not extinction, but a shift to a form or level of being that is not altogether different from what has already been experienced (Grof & Halifax, 1977).

LSD appears also to reduce pain, perhaps by increasing a sense of well-being and relaxation or perhaps through some more direct biochemical means. Both the reduction in pain and the improved sense of well-being permit the living-dying interval to be more fulfilling—more open to the enjoyment of the company of other people and to the accomplishment of final tasks. It must be emphasized that LSD does not reduce pain, as some drugs do, by clouding consciousness and reducing awareness. Rather, it improves awareness and permits the cognitive powers of the individual to be more active and alert. Use of the drug does not encourage hiding from death or denying it but allows patients to cope with their dying more effectively (Pahnke, 1969). It should be mentioned, of course, that LSD is not given on a continuing basis; one or two experiences appear to have a very powerful effect.

In one study that examined the effects of LSD on 50 cancer patients, 18 patients had greatly reduced physical and emotional stress after the treatment; another 18 improved moderately; and only four persons showed any detrimental effects. The study, however, had some methodological limitations: the patients were also receiving psychotherapy; ratings were made by people who were aware of what was going on; and there was no control group (Grof, Pahnke, Kurland, & Goodman, 1971). The same five questions that I asked about the Simonton and similar methods should be asked here too. Over a decade ago, Dr. Cicely Saunders, the founder of the hospice movement, mentioned to me that her patients at St. Christopher's Hospice improved as a result of being well treated in the hospice setting as much as any patients did who were part of expensive and elaborate LSD or psychotherapy programs.

The issues raised again are behavioral, medical, and spiritual. Does the experience with LSD add something over and above good medical and personal care? At present we can only question. The answers, however, may take us far beyond the health care of the dying into the realms of mystical experience, the nature of humankind, and the limits of sensory reality.

Because there is a lengthy history of quackery among persons promising miraculous cures for cancer and other diseases and because of the immense cost in both money and unneeded suffering, caution is necessary in accepting claims of cures, even from reputable persons. What is required is carefully conducted and controlled studies that are planned so that the biases of the experimenters are unable to influence their results.

The caring relationships discussed in this chapter have all concerned the dying person, not the survivors. Relatively little has been done in any formal setting for family members of the dying or of the recently dead, and health settings are frequently inappropriate places for such support. However, some discussion of the bereaved will be included in the next chapter.

15

CARING RELATIONSHIPS: MENTAL HEALTH AND EDUCATION

Not all care for the dying takes place in health facilities, nor is it accomplished by trained health-care personnel. In fact, if we think of caring in its broadest sense, most caring for the dying and the bereaved occurs in homes, churches, social and mental health agencies, and elsewhere in the community.

There are three major types of death-related services. The first includes mental health and social service programs: counseling and psychotherapy, crisis intervention, support groups, social services, and religious/spiritual guidance. The second grouping comprises technical and financial services: legal counseling for wills and trusts, funerals and burials, and other financial and legal services. The third group covers death education: credit and non-credit courses, public school programs, workshops, media, books, conferences, and the literature and other services provided by relevant organizations.

The audience for these three kinds of service is numerous and varied. Obviously it includes the dying and the bereaved. It also includes people responsible for caring for a dying family member. Then there are the numerous professionals and volunteers whose work brings them into contact with death and dying. The rest of the audience is the rest of us, those for whom death and dying are not immediately pressing matters, but who can benefit from greater understanding of the meaning of death and the process of dying.

Obviously there are no rigid boundaries separating these people. A funeral director, in offering technical advice, inevitably becomes both a crisis-intervention worker and a death educator; a professor teaching an undergraduate course on death and loss is inevitably drawn into providing emotional support for a student whose mother has just died; a cleric, while providing emotional support for a recent widow, may also discuss funeral arrangements and financial matters with her.

MENTAL HEALTH AND SOCIAL SERVICES

The stresses that accompany dying and death are intense. This is true for the person who is dying, for family members and friends, and for people in the health-related professions. At one time or another, all of these individuals may need emotional support services for themselves.

PSYCHOTHERAPY AND COUNSELING WITH THE DYING

I could make the case that all psychotherapy involves death-related issues. That is, I believe that dealing with our own feelings about loss, finitude, mortality, immortality, death, and dying is an ongoing process that is never fully resolved, although its priority ebbs and flows across time. Therefore, a patient's concern with mortality is one factor in any psychotherapeutic relationship.

More to the present point is the use of psychotherapy with dying persons. A dying person will enter therapy for a variety of reasons, any one of which may be particularly stressful. First, since dying is really a phase of living, persons who are dying still have most or all their usual conflicts and anxieties. Of course, some may have receded in importance because dying has taken precedence: anxieties about work and achievement *may* diminish; conflicts with grown children *may* be resolved; financial problems *may* now seem unimportant. Conversely, any one of these sources of stress may actually increase in importance and intensity because impending death places a boundary on the opportunity to resolve the problem.

Second, there are significant stresses imposed on many dying persons by their physical suffering, the losses already experienced, and the anticipation of additional losses.

Third, a dying person's will to live may have so diminished that he or she is failing more rapidly than necessary.

Fourth, fear of death may be limiting the individual's ability to make good use of the time remaining. Stress may derive less from the idea of loss of self than from unfinished tasks and unresolved relationships—leading to a sense of despair that forms a cloud over everything else in the patient's life.

There are numerous difficulties in providing psychotherapy to dying persons, the most obvious one being that the traditional 50-minute hour in the therapist's office may be impossible, either because the patient cannot get there or because sitting for nearly an hour (contrary to stereotypes, most psychotherapists do not have couches in their offices) is uncomfortable. On the other hand, there is no sacred rule that psychotherapy must be performed for 50-minute sessions sitting in offices; perhaps 20 minutes by a hospital bed would be just as significant.

Other difficulties may arise from a psychotherapist's social and psychological beliefs. As I mentioned in the previous chapter, a psychotherapist may perceive a dying person's social value to be reduced. A second source of difficulty in treating the dying may be that the therapist is reminded and upset by the spectre of her own death. Third, some therapists, particularly psychoanalysts, are reluctant to begin therapy with a patient who will not be able to continue in the relationship for an extended period. Fourth, to the extent that a psychotherapist maintains a pathology model of psychotherapy, work with dying persons may be counterproductive: the dying person may have neither the time nor the energy to deal with a lifetime of memories, events, and relationships that have contributed to an emotional pathology. Rather, he may need to focus on the meaning of the past, to become involved in the meaning of the present, and to cope with a limited future.

LeShan, whose writing on this topic dates back over 20 years, has emphasized that most psychotherapy with dying persons should focus neither on mental pathology nor on preparation for death. Instead, the therapeutic issues are finding areas of personal strength and preparing for remaining life (LeShan, 1969b).

Patients who lack the will to live, who feel despair, may have long histories of such feelings, which often incorporate low self-esteem. The physical pain and discomfort of dying, the loss of supportive persons, and the recognition of finitude often conspire to intensify despair. If the meaning of life was questionable when the person was healthy and involved with work, community, activities, accomplishments, family, and friends, it is likely to be even more dubious when these supports (and distractions) are no longer available.

Those persons who were not fully engaged each day of their lives, but spent most days planning for a nebulous future, now find that they will not have that future and that they have wasted what they did have—time. "'I always lived as if there were only tomorrow and yesterday. Today didn't exist'" (LeShan, 1969b, pp. 38–39).

However, even individuals who have maintained the will to live and who have lived fully in the present may need to reexamine their values and bases for meaning as they face death. Most of us put considerable value on long-term relationships, the development of competency in our work, and effective interactions with our physical and social environments, and psychotherapy has traditionally focused on enabling people to accomplish these goals more successfully. For the dying person, however, external accomplishments are often impossible, and the focus often needs to be on internal and personal growth (LeShan, 1969b). It becomes the process and satisfaction of growing and not the notion, "I have grown to a preestablished point," that is of therapeutic value.

The very fact that therapy is taking place provides some sense of potential growth. "There can be great value . . . in . . . someone's believing in him enough to . . . work to help him toward greater self-understanding and inner growth at a time when he cannot 'repay' by a long period of adequate functioning. . . . Life no longer . . . seems to have the quality of something that is fading away, but takes on new meaning and validity" (LeShan & LeShan, 1961, p. 318). If the dying person can understand that the worth of a person's life is not in accomplishments, but in one's humanity and self, then not having reached the achievement goals established years earlier will seem less important, and the dying person can get on with the task of living in whatever time is left. The reduced stress and anxiety and the increased desire for inner growth may even serve to mobilize the life force and reverse the downhill path of the illness (LeShan, 1969a).

A caring relationship does not have to offer formal psychotherapy in order to have a psychotherapeutic effect. Or, putting it another way, much of the psychotherapeutic effect of any relationship occurs because of its human caring qualities. Thus, the concerned physician, the attentive nurse, the interested chaplain may all contribute to a substantial therapeutic effect, even though their procedures are much different than that of the psychotherapist.

PSYCHOTHERAPY AND COUNSELING WITH THE BEREAVED

Bereaved persons suffer their grief not only in the period shortly following a death, but from early in the living-dying interval until years, even decades, after the death. Since virtually all adults eventually suffer significant losses, all psychotherapy, in a sense, includes psychotherapy for the bereaved. However, I would differentiate four stages of bereavement, each of which calls for somewhat different kinds of therapeutic support.

The first stage occurs during the living-dying interval. Emotional stress is high and, often, unrelenting; the demands of caretaking may lead to fatigue, poor diet, and lack of recreation and social relationships. A good, relaxed dinner, a weekend away, or a movie may be more valuable than any kind of psychotherapy at this point. Psychotherapy might be helpful in enabling the individual to improve the relationship with the dying person, if there are still tensions; to handle his or her feelings of guilt and any unresolved, distressing aspects of the relationship; to deal with impending loss and possible loneliness; to be able to take responsibility as required and turn over responsibility to others as appropriate; to recognize his or her own limitations and to accept them; and to begin an engagement in what life will be after the death occurs. Over and above all else, these people who have begun to grieve but are not yet technically bereaved may need someone to whom they can express feelings of anger, frustration, fear, and hope.

Psychotherapy during the second stage, at the time of death, is most likely to be a kind of crisis intervention; there may be an understanding that the therapeutic relationship will need to continue for some time. Feelings are likely to be intense; moods will come and go quickly; depression will be constant, underlying all else. Psychotherapy can offer catharsis, an opportunity to reminisce and simultaneously to begin to become future-oriented, a time to explore what the loss means and is likely to mean and to continue work begun in the first stage.

For some bereaved persons, the third stage, during the weeks following the death, is often still filled with acute grief and intense mourning; others display little grief. For the latter, therapy might be used to help them begin active mourning, to permit the expression of feelings, although some of these individuals have worked through their loss in ways that are not evident to others. Probably those who need therapy the most are those who have neither grieved overtly nor worked through their feelings of grief in other ways: those who insist on being "brave" and "going on as though nothing ever happened."

And, finally, psychotherapy may be called for to help individuals who, even years after the loss, have not successfully completed their grieving. This includes more people than is, I believe, normally assumed. One psychiatrist has developed what he terms *re-grief therapy* to work with such persons. The goals of re-grief therapy are to help the individual understand why she or he has not finished grieving and, then, to "complete it in the present, to experience and to express the emotions generated by his loss" (Volkan, Cilluffo, & Sarvay, 1975, p. 191). For some reasons, the bereaved individual is unable to let go of the person who has died, and Volkan and his associates focus the psychotherapy both on "letting go" and differentiating the therapy client from the person who has died, since there is a tendency to obscure the distinctions between the self and the dead person (Volkan, 1970). Sometimes this identification is accomplished by keeping some possession or other object associated with the dead person to form a linkage. The linking object has intense emotional connotations for the therapy client, and the client must deal with these feelings (Volkan et al., 1975). This is not the only form of psychotherapy appropriate for people who have not overcome their grief but it is the only one I know of that has been developed specifically for this one task.

Another therapeutic approach to facilitate expression of grief is to have the client talk directly to a fantasized image of the dead person. This can be done in the therapy session, where it may be particularly powerful, or at home or anywhere, for that matter. The client will turn to an empty chair, perhaps visualize the dead person, and say what he or she had not said while the person was still alive. This may include expressions of love, of anger, of desire for absolution of guilt, of sadness at the loss of the relationship. Talking *to* instead of talking *about* is very likely to elicit strong feelings.

One familiar source of social and emotional support for troubled persons (and for those who are not troubled) is the self-help group, directed either by an outside professional or by a group member. Widows have used this kind of program, and the results from one research study have shown it to be quite effective. Some 70 widows who responded to a request in a local newspaper participated in a group program for seven weeks; three kinds of groups had been established: self-help, confidant (where women were encouraged to develop a confidant relationship with another woman in the group), and conciousness-raising, and each woman was assigned randomly to one group. After the program, the women, when compared to control-group participants, indicated higher self-esteem, greater optimism concerning their future physical health, and more ability to feel and express the intensity of their grief. They also found themselves less predisposed to remarry. A follow-up, conducted several months later, showed that most of these changes had endured. This project suggests that such groups can be very helpful—an important finding because, while the costs in money and time were modest, the results showed the process to be valuable (Barrett, 1978).

There are times, especially at the start of grieving, just after the death has occurred or around the time of the funeral, when the intensity of sorrow is so great that many persons resort to tranquilizers and alcohol. Physicians are likely to prescribe tranquilizers fairly freely at that time. Respondents in the Los Angeles study were very likely to expect others to take tranquilizers during a wake or funeral (40–50% of the Blacks, Mexican Americans, and Whites) and fairly likely to expect others to drink during those occasions (20–40% of the same three ethnic communities) (Kalish & Reynolds, 1976). Confirming these results was a study of widows and widowers: about one-third had used tranquilizers in the years since their spouse's death and nearly one-third had used sleeping medicine; there was no indication of the extent of overlap (Bornstein et al., 1973).

Some people have expressed concern that frequent use of tranquilizers will impede the normal grieving process, and there is some controversy about whether they should be used at all at this point. I personally believe that our feelings, especially our loss-connected feelings, catch up with us one way or another, at one time or another. When they are not permitted expression at the time they initially occur, they may return to haunt us later. For most of us, our psychological processes of denial and repression serve to protect us from emotional pain, and perhaps the use of drugs is indeed counterindicated.

OTHER SUPPORT SERVICES

So far my discussion has concentrated on the more formal psychotherapeutic approach to mental-health support services, but therapy is not required in most situations. Even when it is desirable, it may be impractical. A frequent alternative to therapy is crisis intervention, which has as its goal the reduction of crisis-caused stress and the development of improved coping strategies, perhaps in tandem with better utilization of community support networks. Crisis intervention may involve counseling and therapy, either individually or with the family, but it need not. The use of crisis intervention assumes that, if the individual can be aided through the stress of the crisis situation, he or she will be able to function independently and effectively afterwards; conversely, if the emotional support is not provided, the situational stress may evolve into long-term distress. A middle-aged woman, for example, who has just been diagnosed as having cancer that is probably terminal, is obviously facing a crisis, as is her family. Improved understanding of her condition and its probable course, planning how to keep her involved in family matters rather than ostracizing her through social death (Oppenheimer, 1967), and discussing the family members' fears, anxieties, and angers are a few of the areas that might be covered in crisis intervention.

In one study, 60 terminally ill cancer patients were asked about the kinds of services that they wanted. They mentioned help with (1) financial problems, which arose frequently from high medical costs and reduced income; (2) illness-related matters, such as concern about pain, loss of strength and energy, long confinements to home and hospital, and trouble with medical tests and procedures; (3) changes in social and sexual relationships; (4) difficulties at the hospital, including erratic nursing attention, inadequate information about their condition, impersonal treatment; and (5) handling emotional problems, including anxiety, depression, hostility, and suicidal ideation (Koenig, 1968).

Some of these patient concerns may have arisen because of particular treatment in the hospital at which the study was done, but others are probably quite general. The study was geared to social workers, and all the help described can be provided by trained social workers, but these and other support services for the dying and a wide array of support services for the bereaved can also be administered by nurses, physicians, chaplains, clergy, and—in some instances—funeral directors.

Social workers, psychologists, and all of the above except funeral directors are most likely to be available only during the first stage of grief, that which occurs before the person dies. The physician and the nurse attend primarily to the dying person, and the family member is normally only given emotional support indirectly as a part of the medical service. The chaplain and the social worker or psychologist are also most likely to provide services for the dying person, although they are more likely to be aware of the emotional needs of the family members. Sometimes a chaplain or a staff social worker or psychologist will make an appointment to see a grieving family member after the death has occurred or at particularly stressful times during the living-dying interval.

The role of the minister, priest, or rabbi is unique, since this person is likely to have an ongoing relationship with the family, and her or his presence provides someone who has known both the dead person and the family members for some years. (Interestingly enough, because of their extensive social and community activities, many funeral directors have personal relationships with their clients.) Since we tend to endow clergy with healing powers, they are often encouraged to provide informal supportive therapy. Sometimes this may develop into a more formalized, continuing therapeutic relationship.

What kinds of training do these people have for offering therapy and supportive services? The clinical social worker and the clinical psychologist usually had both training and supervised experience in therapy as part of their graduate work, although it cannot be taken for granted that either the course work or the supervised experience ever so much as touched obliquely on death-related matters. Nurses are much less likely to have had any training in therapy, but they are very likely to have some formal background—a course, a workshop—on death and loss. Clergy and chaplains are increasingly likely to have had some formal course work in their graduate education on working with the dying and the bereaved; they also are likely to have been active in developing special programs and workshops; and many have had course work and supervised experience in pastoral counseling, which is a form of clinical psychotherapy.

Of the above vocational groups, the least likely to have had formal training in either counseling or psychological relationships with the dying or the bereaved are the physicians and the funeral directors. Although they are both highly skilled and officially licensed for their own disciplines and although they both have extensive contact with death, neither their required training nor traditional definitions of their roles encourage them to become proficient with these psychological skills. That many have chosen to gain such competence anyway and that some training programs now include counseling materials testify to the interest of numerous individual physicians and funeral directors.

TECHNICAL AND FINANCIAL SERVICES

Providing information and counseling about technical and financial matters can lead to the development of caring relationships. Funeral directors and physicians, for example, both of whom are experts in their technology, are in a position to provide considerable psychological benefit to the people whose lives they touch, if they can include with their technological skills some significant human sensitivity.

This, of course, must be done without sacrificing those very skills. A funeral director who is warm, sensitive, caring—and sloppy—may be appreciated for this humanity, but is not likely to get much business. A physician who is loving, attentive, concerned—and lacking medical knowledge—is certainly not providing what her or his professional role requires.

FINANCIAL SERVICES

Who develops relationships with the dying and the bereaved that are based on technical and financial service? Certainly lawyers do—they make out wills, are responsible for distributing assets after the death, and consult on keeping inheritance and estate taxes low. Trust officers, working for banks, may be in contact with their clients, when the latter are dying, to offer assurance, to clarify the intent of the clients regarding the use of the estate, to learn more about their health. After the death, the trust officers are supposed to carry out the terms of the estate—to distribute and invest money as was indicated. These persons are, therefore, extremely important to the well being of the survivors, since they hold the family purse strings. Although the relationship between trust officer and bereaved person is likely to center on finances, the trust officer is still part of a caring relationship, even though the caring is largely caring for the use of money.

The financial problems of the dying and the bereaved are probably among the sources of stress most ignored by practitioners in care-giving fields. To some extent, this is because the care-givers are more oriented to psychological, social, and medical aspects of care; to some extent, it occurs because these people usually cannot do anything about the financial situation.

The cost of dying can be immense, and it is not unusual to have these expenses wipe out the entire estate of the dying person and then make inroads into the assets of the survivors. The patient is encouraged to seek the best possible medical help, to rest and not to worry about costs, and to concentrate on getting better, yet the dying person is well aware that the longer the illness lasts, the more expensive it will be. This is an inducement either to get better quickly or to die quickly; if the former appears impossible, the latter may have to suffice.

If the dying person has been working, the income will eventually stop, and this provides additional stress. "I don't want to be a burden to my family" is one of the most familiar phrases expressed by both the elderly and the dying, and not being a financial burden is high on most persons' lists.

There are indirect costs associated with dying and death that are often not anticipated. For example, assume that a middle-aged father dies, leaving his wife to care for teenage children. Unless the estate is fairly large, income will probably diminish, in spite of Social Security survivor benefits; also, costs of maintaining a home with a single working parent tend to go up; then there are many funeral and burial costs. In addition, there may be unexpected estate taxes; selling the family home may not only reduce the standard of living, but add moving costs, and it may also produce a surprisingly high capital gains tax on the inflated home value.

Grieving survivors often take precipitous actions that they may later regret: they sell a home they should keep; they move to a new community when they should remain where they are; they try to turn their assets into cash or they try to turn their cash into income-producing assets when they should have avoided immediate change. The issue is not the specific action taken but the fact that action taken under duress may be inappropriate. Both dying persons and bereaved persons could frequently benefit from financial counseling, especially if provided in a warm, supportive fashion.

THE ROLE OF FUNERAL DIRECTOR

Is the funeral director a mental-health professional? Certainly not in the technical sense of the term, although he or she is a professional whose work involves mental health in a very direct fashion. First and foremost, the funeral director is a highly skilled person, part professional, part business executive and part technician, whose task it is to remove the bodies of dead persons from the social milieu of the living. He or she is expected to do this in accordance with health regulations, business regulations and ethics, religious rituals and ceremonies, and personal sensitivity.

It is partly this mixture of roles that produces trouble for the funeral director. His role as a professional who works with the dead has simultaneously a taboo quality and a service orientation; his role as a business executive permits him to seek not just payment for services but financial profit for his organization. But some people feel that to earn money and make a profit from death is profane (physicians and clergy sometimes find the same reaction toward their dual roles as service providers and business executives), and they resent, sometimes without realizing it, the funeral director for his or her earning capacity.

Funeral directors appear to come under attack in three ways. First, they become a source of humor, which may well be a way in which people handle their anxiety concerning death. An old radio character, Digger O'Dell, speaking in a very somber, somewhat quavering voice, would say "Well, it's time to leave now—I'll be *shovel*ing along." Or "I would be the last one to let you down."

The second basis for attack is financial. Half the respondents in a national survey stated that they perceived funeral directors as combining professional and business services, and fewer than one-fourth viewed them only as businesspersons or as having a lower status than businesspersons (Fulton, 1963, 1965). This uneasy position has made them the objects of frequent criticism for dubious financial practices. Since funeral directors are working with (or selling to) a highly vulnerable group of people, they are expected to be much more ethical and less profit-oriented than, for example, car repair services or the oil industry. Both of these businesses have also come under criticism for exploiting the public, but the criticism directed toward them has been considerably less angry than that hurled at funeral directors. Again, I suspect that much of this strong emotional attack arises from the association of the funeral director with death, a role that makes many people very uncomfortable. Nonetheless, there have been considerable attempts to document their exploitation (Federal Trade Commission, 1978; Harmer, 1963; Mitford, 1963). There is suggestion that exploitation tends to come more from larger, more bureaucratic funeral homes than from those that are integrated into the community (Pine, 1975).

Third, some individuals believe that funeral directors aid in the denial of the reality of death, partly through their tendency to avoid using words like *death* in their discussions with the bereaved and partly through their embalming practices, which prettify the body. However, because many of the major critics of these forms of death avoidance do not attend funerals, reject the idea of open-casket ceremonies, and prefer non-traditional services, it is difficult to know who is doing the denying—or whether these kinds of denial are necessarily negative.

When people are asked directly to describe their reactions to a particular funeral that they helped arrange, almost all express high regard for the funeral director. This is true for both clergy and members of their congregations (Kalish & Goldberg, 1978, 1979–1980). Nonetheless, there are obviously enough incidents that anger people and enough desire for simpler, less costly funerals to lead to the development of memorial societies, in which arrangements are made at any time during a person's life for a funeral and burial (Fulton, 1963, 1965).

In recent years, some funeral directors have attempted to move into new territory and act as grief counselors as well. This attempt to extend their role, which represents a formalization of something they already did informally, has caused controversy, even within the profession, and relatively little has been done to provide appropriate training to pursue this task. An alternative, proposed by the funeral directors themselves, is to have trained professionals in the community to work in liaison with funeral directors in providing mental health services and to encourage the formation of the Widow-to-Widow program or similar programs (Steele, 1975), which I will discuss in the next chapter.

DEATH EDUCATION

In 1977, the first issue of a new journal appeared. The name of the journal was *Death Education*. In 1978, the first annual meeting of a new national organization (established in about 1975) was held in Washington, D.C. The name of the organization was the Forum for Death Education and

Counseling. The new journal was the second in its field; it followed the first, *Omega*, by eight years; the new organization was also the second of its kind; the first, an organization centered in the Philadelphia area and called Ars Moriendi, had been founded several years earlier.

Does the emergence of this interest mean we are going to have specialists called death educators and death counselors, just as we have specialists called sex educators or health educators and sex therapists or health psychologists? The answer appears to be yes. However, it is not a new field that is emerging but a new specialization for a number of familiar fields.

CONTENTS OF DEATH EDUCATION PROGRAMS

Death education is simply what its name implies: an educational process in which a learner receives some form of understanding about death. The student of death education may be (1) personally concerned because of some early experience in life that has never been completely resolved; (2) personally concerned because of some present experience, such as the illness or death of a family member; (3) involved with death or dying because of work or because of a volunteer service project; or (4) interested in learning more about death and dying to better understand what death means or to develop a more satisfying philosophy of death.

Death education can take a variety of forms:

- a credit course in a graduate or undergraduate college program;
- a special project in a high school class;
- a seminar in a professional school: medical, nursing, seminary, social work, mortuary sciences;
- a series, for example, of Tuesday evening lectures in a Presbyterian church; a series of Sunday morning, preservice discussions in a Unitarian church; a discussion group for the recently bereaved in a Catholic church;
- a single presentation at a senior center;
- a book, magazine article, newspaper story, or television or radio program or series;
- a weekend university-sponsored, continuing education workshop taken for credit;
- an informal discussion with the physician-father of one of the pupils in a fifth-grade class;
- an in-service program for nurses, chaplains, funeral directors, journalists, physicians, hospital aides, nursing-home administrators, mental-health professionals, clergy.

Death education programs are just as varied in format, length, interest, numbers of students, cost, and everything else as any other kind of education. They are also just as helpful, disturbing, growth-producing, anxiety-creating, and generally productive as any other educational program, although the nature of the topics covered is likely to make them a little more upsetting than a course on nutrition or one on nursing-home cost accounting.

The format of a specific educational program is as varied as the format of any topic covered in educational programs. Thus, a discussion of death on *Mister Rogers' Neighborhood* (Sharapan, 1977) is just as much death education as a credit university course; a class period discussing death themes in Melville's novels or in Hesse or Kafka is just as much death education as a class period spent discussing improved hospice programming. Educational needs are served by consciousness-raising as much as by learning facts.

Some people believe that proper death education must be directed to reducing death anxieties and improving sensitivity to the feelings of persons undergoing death-related experiences; others seem to think that only an increase in factual knowledge is appropriate death education. The answer, I feel, does not lie in between but encompasses both. If you are reading this book in conjunction with a course, you may be using class time to discuss feelings and experiences about death and dying and reading time to increase your information on the topics. In any event, both learning information through reading and listening and learning new feelings and attitudes through planned experiences are educational.

Death education programs can be oriented toward a variety of topics or disciplines: medicine, nursing, or general health care; theology, religion, or pastoral care; fiction, drama, or poetry; psychology, psychiatry, or psychotherapy; sociology, anthropology, or social work; art, music, or dance; history, philosophy, or ethics; or any combination of the above.

Furthermore, death education can focus on death, the process of dying, grief and bereavement, or caring relationships (the four major sections of this book), or equally on all of the above. Since most death education has been directed toward persons who work with the dying, it has emphasized the process of dying and caring relationships, rather than the meaning of death or the nature of grief (Kastenbaum, 1977). This emphasis may have been taken too far: "For some in fact, the dying process is taken to be identical to the whole concern with death" (Kastenbaum, 1977, p. 90).

Kastenbaum (1977) expresses an additional concern about death education in an article titled "We Covered Death Today": "One can deny death by accepting its commonalities and correlates with safer, more familiar experience. Death becomes a course title and number. It is a topic on the syllabus. It is a certain time or space allotment in the media. In effect, death is set alongside everything else that reassures us through its ongoing, routine nature. This tamed version of death education makes one think of a Disneyworld attraction as contrasted with the tang and danger of a true adventure" (Kastenbaum, 1977, p. 91).

EVALUATION OF DEATH EDUCATION PROGRAMS

Does death education work? This can only be answered, of course, in terms of what we want it to accomplish. We can evaluate a particular death education program on the basis of whether the participants (1) learned factual information, (2) became more aware of their own feelings about their own dying and death, (3) became better able to develop relationships with the dying and the grieving, (4) reduced their personal death fears and anxieties, (5) were better able to understand death themes in literature, music, or art, (6) had greater appreciation of philosophic treatments of death, or (7) were more capable of developing death education or counseling programs themselves.

Several studies have looked at changes in death attitudes as a result of participation in death education programs. In one typical study, 39 students from university health education classes were selected to receive the death education instructional materials and 40 to receive regular health education materials. Two death attitude scales were administered to all students both before and after the courses. The experimental group changed more in the expected direction, that is, toward favorable death attitudes, than did the control group. The conclusion, therefore, was reached that the death education course had changed death attitudes (Watts, 1977). A more cautious interpretation could be that the students in the class learned what attitudes were considered to be "better" and responded in terms of those attitudes.

In a later study, involving a larger number of students, death attitudes of students in a death education class were compared with those of students in an introductory psychology class. This time, the death education students displayed less fear of the death and dying of others (based on Collett & Lester, 1969), but did not indicate significant changes in attitudes toward their own deaths or dying. In addition, a number of other measurements of death attitudes showed some small differences with no discernible meaningful pattern (Leviton & Fretz, 1978–1979). In a third study comparing two eight-hour workshops, one using an experiential approach and the other, a didactic approach, some slight additional changes seemed produced by the experiential approach. These changes were indicated on one of the two scales administered; the other gave no advantage to the experiential approach (Durlak, 1978–1979).

A final study is worthy of note because of the honesty of the investigators. This one again compared college students in a death education course with a control group; it found that the only significant difference in changes between the two groups was that the students taking the course thought a great deal more about their deaths than those who didn't take the course (Knott & Prull, 1976).

In summary, research results for establishing attitude changes through death education courses are erratic and of limited validity. This, however, is also true of attempts to change other kinds of attitudes through courses and workshops. It is probably best to assume that death education can provide useful information, induce a kind of consciousness-raising, encourage an evaluation of one's own views, sensitize students to what others are feeling, and provide a generally useful framework for thinking about death and the process of dying. To expect a death education course also to reduce death fears and anxieties is probably asking too much of a relatively brief educational experience.

ANOTHER KIND OF EVALUATION

Well-controlled, carefully planned and conducted studies provide one kind of evaluation. Another kind of evaluation, which should not be overlooked, is the keen, incisive insight of a knowledgeable person. One such insight is physician Michael Simpson's warning about death and dying courses, some of which are "undoubtedly valuable, and undertaken by sensitive, responsible, and talented teachers. Others are produced by self-seeking exhibitionists" (1979, p. 5). "Most of the leaders of the [death awareness] movement have been relatively restrained in seeking to avoid the development of strong personality cults, though there are one or two pop gurus who work the tear-stained lecture circuit especially assiduously and attract the Death Groupies" (Simpson, 1979, p. 6).

Another author, long involved in the study of death and loss, once quipped to me "In death you can make a good living" (Fulton, personal communication, 1973). Neither he nor I object to anyone making a good living, but we, like Simpson and many others, are sensitive to the exploitation of the death, dying, and grief of vulnerable persons, done in the guise of service. Persons who are dying or bereaved are especially vulnerable, and their vulnerability can lead to their victimization by exploitative persons who promote themselves as death educators or death counselors. Part of functioning as a death educator is maintaining a high standard of personal and professional ethics.

16

CARING ORGANIZATIONS, CARING PEOPLE, AND CARING FOR YOURSELF

Most caring relationships occur not in hospitals or therapists' offices or classrooms, but in the community and the home. Their participants are not health professionals or volunteers or social workers or educators, but friends, relatives, neighbors, and people who are understanding because of their own experiences. In the final chapter of this book, I want to discuss two more kinds of caring relationships. First, I want to describe some organizations that have enabled non-professionals in the community to offer support to others in the community who are troubled; second, I want to touch on several matters that concern each of us in our own personal relationships with the dying and the bereaved.

CARING RELATIONSHIPS THROUGH ORGANIZATIONS

Innumerable organizations have been created to provide caring relationships for people who are concerned with death, the process of dying, or grief. Some of these organizations are directed by professionals, while others depend primarily on voluntary staffing and leadership. Some are national organizations with local chapters or are informally linked with comparable organizations; others are strictly local. Some have highly varied programs; others restrict themselves to a single issue. Some are funded by local government; others operate, usually with very limited funding, from private donations.

Although there are many organizations that merit discussion, I have needed to limit myself to only a few. I've picked four that have had national visibility: suicide prevention centers, Make Today Count, Compassionate Friends, and Shanti. Each of these depends heavily on volunteers, but their aims, programs, and procedures differ considerably.

SUICIDE PREVENTION CENTERS

Probably the best-known of these organizations is the suicide prevention center. The primary purpose of the various SPCs across the country is to develop a telephone-response system to permit people contemplating suicide to call in and receive information, personal support, and a kind of quasi-psychotherapy. Suicide prevention centers also offer community education programs and may be affiliated with other community services at the local level. Some of these centers have followed the lead of the Los Angeles center, the first one established in North America, by conducting research, developing new program ideas, and trying to influence local and national policy (for example, suicide prevention centers in the San Francisco Bay area have been trying to have higher barriers installed on the Golden Gate Bridge, where suicide leaps are frequent). In addition, these centers attempt to increase national consciousness about the problems of suicide and may also provide individual counseling for persons attempting suicide or relatives of persons who have committed or attempted suicide. Most centers, however, do not have extensive facilities, and they must be content with providing telephone help, some community education, and, frequently, referrals for persons whose needs go beyond their ability to provide services.

Individual suicide prevention centers are autonomous, linked together through membership in the American Association of Suicidology and through regional associations, which are often informal. Their source of funding varies, but much of it comes through city, state, and county mental health funds, and they are likely to be city or county agencies.

Do suicide prevention centers reduce suicides and suicide attempts? That question has been debated by those within and outside the field. The answer is uncertain. Most people who call in to SPCs are not considered likely candidates for a suicide attempt (Lester & Lester, 1971); many are lonely and depressed, seeking a friendly voice; some are chronic callers; others want information about helping a friend or relative who appears likely to make a suicide attempt or who has already done so.

That SPCs prevent some suicides is virtually certain. That they keep the suicide rate from going up is much less so. However, they provide other resources: they offer a system of aid for many isolated, depressed persons; they help people understand the dynamics of suicide, and, consequently, become better able to help a friend or relative who has made a suicide attempt; they have changed the attitudes toward people who attempt or commit suicide; and they have made mental health professionals aware of the need for suicide prevention.

One issue that inevitably emerges in a discussion of suicide prevention is whether people who wish to die should be prevented from taking their own lives. I can answer this very clearly for myself: usually the question is moot—people who want to die will not contact suicide prevention centers; they will find a way to die. However, if I knew someone was contemplating suicide, I would try to determine the reasons for the decision. Since the desire to commit suicide may be based on factors that can be changed, I would attempt to learn what in the life of the individual led to these feelings of helplessness and hopelessness and to determine if there were any way of altering these factors, so that the person might choose life rather than death. The "right to commit" suicide is a fascinating topic for discussion, but its practical applications are limited.

MAKE TODAY COUNT

Orville Kelly's experiences as he coped with his diagnosis of cancer and a limited life expectancy persuaded him to reach out to others who were living with the same sword of Damocles overhead. Thus in mid-1973 a group of 18 people met—the group included patients, family members of patients, and professionals—and launched Make Today Count in order to meet with others with whom they could talk and share their problems. The meeting was described by the wire services, carried to newspapers all over the country, and Orville Kelly and Make Today Count became the focal point for a national organization. Kelly died of his cancer in 1980, having outlived his prognosis, but his death did not halt the organization, and today there are chapters all over the country.

The purpose of the organization is to bring together people who are either suffering from cancer or who are closely related to someone who is. They meet, exchange experiences, provide social and emotional support, offer encouragement, and try to make each day matter. The psychological difficulties suffered by cancer patients are not always recognized. "Many patients experience deep emotional problems centering on loss of sex appeal or rejection after a scarring operation for certain types of cancer, or on loss of hair or disfigurement from radiation therapy" (Kelly, 1978, p. 65). These, of course, are only two of many such problems. "It isn't possible to solve all of these problems, but bringing them out in the open and discussing them seems to help. Just knowing that others face some of the same problems relieves the anxieties of many patients and family members" (Kelly, 1978, p. 65).

Make Today Count is an example of an organization begun not by professional caretakers or professional organizers but by those individuals most affected. Chapters are fairly autonomous, and funding needs are minimal, since there are no paid local leaders and national office expenses are extremely modest; local programming requires only that people get together to serve their own purposes. Individual chapters are begun by clergy and physicians, as well as by patients and family members, and meetings are usually held in homes and churches. The present address of their headquarters is 218 South Sixth Street, Burlington, Iowa 52601.

COMPASSIONATE FRIENDS

Like Make Today Count, Compassionate Friends is an informal operation with over 150 chapters throughout the United States. Chapters also exist in Canada, as well as in England, where the organization began in 1969. Chapters are begun by bereaved parents; finances are minimal—voluntary contributions rather than dues cover costs; meetings are held in public buildings and churches; work at both local and national levels is accomplished mostly by volunteers. The major difference between the two organizations is their membership: participants in Make Today Count are themselves facing death or facing the death of someone they love; participants in Compassionate Friends are parents who have already experienced the death of a child.

The aims of Compassionate Friends are to (1) offer support and friendship to sorrowing parents, (2) listen with understanding and provide "telephone friends," (3) come together with others once a month, (4) offer information about the process of grieving, and (5) provide contact and friendship with other bereaved parents who have lived through the experience and are finding hope and strength in their lives. Perhaps the group's orientation is best expressed in a statement from its brochure: "Many bereaved parents do have the need for more understanding, more hope, more knowledge, or more comfort than the people around them provide. Sometimes a conversation, a book, or a professional presentation may assist healing and give new insight and understanding about a particular question or concern. In trying to help bereaved parents cope with their loss, Compassionate Friends does not focus morbidly on death and thus only rekindle unhappy feelings. We do acknowledge the pain that is a part of loving. We have loved, therefore, we grieve. We are willing to share someone's sorrow."

(The information for these paragraphs comes from the brochure of this organization and was confirmed at their national headquarters. For more information, write Compassionate Friends, National Headquarters, P.O. Box 1347, Oak Brook, Illinois 60521.)

SHANTI

The Shanti Project provides the services of carefully selected, trained volunteers—who have had either relevant professional training or personal experience in coping with death and dying—for anyone dealing with a life-threatening illness. Launched in early 1975, the organization is more like a suicide prevention center than like either Make Today Count or Compassionate Friends. Shanti services are normally provided by a single individual, occasionally with help from others, to a single person or family. Although experiences are shared, this is not the core of the program, as it is with Make Today Count and Compassionate Friends. Rather, the Shanti volunteer functions as a friend: offering information, running errands, holding the patient's hand, talking, listening, responding, or simply caring.

In addition to requests for information, Shanti receives four other basic kinds of requests for service. First, patients request personal counseling, companionship, or emotional support from a volunteer; their request may be specific—to learn how to relax or tell others of the imminent death—or it may be general—for example, to ask the volunteer for comfort and friendship or just to "be there." Second, there are requests for volunteers to spend time with a member of a patient's family or with the entire family. Dying persons often recognize that their family members need as much or more help than they themselves, and it is not unusual for the dying to ask help for another.

Third, people request help after the death of someone close to them. And, fourth, Shanti receives calls from people who work with the dying outside of an institutional setting. This may be a private-duty nurse who has been caring for a dying person, a teacher working with a terminally ill child, or a clergyman who has been providing support for a member of his congregation.

Shanti volunteers do not function on a regular schedule; instead they develop appropriate kinds of time to be with the person who contacts them. This may mean a five-minute telephone call to the hospital room or an all-night vigil. Funding for Shanti comes primarily from private sources, although federal money has supported some limited projects. This private money includes foundation grants, individual donations, and occasional bequests from people who had deeply appreciated their services. (Information for these paragraphs comes from a personal discussion with Dr. Charles Garfield, founder and presently chairperson of the Shanti Board of Trustees. The present mailing address is 106 Evergreen Lane, Berkeley, California 94705.)

These four organizations represent a small sampling from the great diversity of organizations whose goals are helping people intimately concerned with dying and death. Other groups have developed for parents whose children have heart defects, parents whose children have died from Sudden Infant Death Syndrome, patients and spouses of patients who have suffered major heart disorders, women who have had a breast removed because of cancer, families of persons who have suffered severe brain damage, children who are themselves terminally ill, women and men who have recently lost a spouse through death, and persons who are themselves cancer victims.

These organizations often have to struggle to continue to function, sometimes because they cannot find adequate funds and other times because of inadequate leadership or planning. The organizations come and go—perhaps aided by newspaper coverage or harmed by the loss of the individual who worked hardest. Nonetheless, I find the dynamic quality of such groups to be a very healthy sign. They display a willingness of people to take time to help others, and they also indicate the ability of those who are dying or who have suffered the loss of someone else to do something for themselves. Rather than sitting back passively waiting for someone else to plan and develop a program, the people who are closest to a problem are developing the program themselves, and the caregivers receive payment in personal satisfaction.

GUIDELINES FOR CARING RELATIONSHIPS

When all is said and done, the most important relationships for the dying and the grieving are going to be with those persons to whom they have been closest all along. You may or may not have a professional relationship that involves dying and death, but you are very likely to have many such personal relationships. What then can you do to make these relationships better, both for you and for others?

WORKING ON YOURSELF

First, you can be more conscious of what is going on. Perhaps this is why you are reading this book right now. We have hundreds of years of experience in relating to dying persons, thousands of pages of writing, tens of thousands of experienced persons, and millions of personal experiences. There is no need, as Kastenbaum has succinctly phrased it, "to re-invent the square wheel."

Second, you can probe your own assumptions and expectations to try to understand how you developed your views. To what extent are you drawing from one or two personal experiences? To what extent are you biased by your own prejudices—for example, toward the elderly, toward physicians, toward funeral directors, toward cancer? To what extent are your psychological defenses propelling you toward your present beliefs: your own denial, your own fears and anxieties, your own projection?

Third, you can be honest with yourself about what you are willing to give to the dying or bereaved; otherwise, you will find it difficult to be honest with them. Are you offering an intimate relationship or an occasional visit? Will you really "keep in touch," or do you say that just as an excuse to get away? Do you actually want that person living with you during the living-dying interval, or do you find yourself resenting the guilt that pressed you to make the offer? So often, when we do things we don't want to do for someone, that person ends up suffering.

Fourth, try to understand your own feelings about death and dying. Your own anxieties and denial can limit your competence in relating to others, although I personally disagree with the claim that no one can work with dying persons until his or her own death fears have been worked through. That is like saying that no clergy should ever doubt his or her religious beliefs or that no psychologist should ever practice until he or she has left all his or her peculiarities behind. I believe that you can provide good emotional support to a friend or family member, even though you still have strong anxieties about death or, for example, feel uneasy about embracing someone with cancer. Perhaps the best approach is to acknowledge your anxieties or discomfort to that person. Obviously, it's useful to have as few anxieties as possible impinging on you and to have insight into the sources of your stress, but we can't postpone caring relationships until we have perfected our adjustment or our personal growth.

Fifth, be willing just to be there, without doing anything. Even be willing not to be there. Too many of us feel that, unless we are doing something active, something "positive," we aren't being effective. There are things you are not going to be able to do: you are not going to be able to take the pain of a loss away from other people. It is their pain, and they will suffer it. With both the dying and the grieving, your presence is sometimes more important than your "doing something." A close friend of mine, who was mourning a loss that had actually occurred sometime earlier, became angry with me and ordered me to leave her house; it was late at night, and I told her that I wasn't going to leave but would go into the den and sleep on the couch there. About one hour later, much calmed, she came in and woke me up; we had coffee together and talked for several hours more. In that situation I took a risk—that leaving her presence and not leaving the house was what would be most helpful to her. My behavior turned out to have been appropriate, although, obviously, it doesn't always work out that way. What my action "said" was, in effect "I care for you and will respect your desire to have privacy from me, but I will continue to make myself available when you wish it."

Sixth, be aware of your energy levels and avoid exhaustion and burn-out. If you don't eat, sleep, or have any leisure for an extended period, you may find your ability to care for someone diminished. You need to know yourself, but, since the stress of a close relationship to someone dying may alter your capabilities without your realizing it, you may also have to be alert to what your friends and family are telling you.

One author has proposed six reasons that staff in hospitals choose to work with the dying and has suggested that each of these reasons brings its own unique forms of stress. I suspect that the reasons are also largely applicable to people who wish to be with the dying. The reasons: (1) accident or convenience, (2) a desire to do the "in thing" or to affiliate with a charismatic leader, (3) intellectual appeal and a desire for mastery over pain and death, (4) a sense of "calling," (5) previous personal experience, and (6) a suspicion that one might someday develop the disease one is treating (Vachon, 1978). I'm not certain whether I agree that there are only six reasons—in fact, I think the above list contains not six but nine different reasons. However, I believe that Vachon's overall point is very important: because work with the dying is stressful, attention must be paid to the possibility of emotional exhaustion or burn-out if effective personal and professional services are going to be provided to dying persons and their families.

BEING WITH THE DYING AND THE GRIEVING

Psychologist Lawrence LeShan described to me two kinds of roles people who relate to the dying play. The first is that of a mechanic, who helps the person die, and the second is that of a gardener, who helps the person live in whatever time is left. Most of us see ourselves as gardeners, but we too readily become mechanics and, consequently, emphasize the wrong things.

Dying people bring their own strengths to their predicaments, but they are often not permitted to use their strength. "It's not the patient's illness or dying that produces upset, but the insanity of those around him who deny reality" (LeShan, personal communication). LeShan makes the case a little stronger than I would, but I certainly agree in principle. The dying person receives so many mixed messages, finds so many people who are not honest (and eventually doesn't know which ones are honest), that personal strength is dissipated just in dealing with the anxiety caused by these uncertainties.

Chaplain Walter Johnson, a Presbyterian clergyman serving at a hospital near San Francisco, described to me an equation that sums up LeShan's statements in a different way:

Truth minus love = brutality
Love minus truth = sentimentality
Truth plus love = healing relationship

Over and over again, dying and grieving persons indicate that they fear being abandoned. Thus, one of the most important aspects of a caring relationship is to reduce this fear. But this must be done in a realistic fashion. First, you need to be reasonably—not precisely, just reasonably—clear about the kind and amount of aid you are offering: daily visits? weekly visits? home care during the living-dying interval? Of course the nature of your help can change, but, if it does, it must be explained reasonably clearly. Second, you should live up to your offer. As much as the dying person may wish to hear that you will visit frequently, it is probably more important to be able to count on whatever you have offered to do—even if it's less than might have been wished.

You can abandon a person by not being there physically. You can also be there physically, but be far away psychologically. Of course, when you are suffering yourself, from depression and impending loss, you may spend some of your visiting time immersed in your own fantasies. Sick people understand that as well as healthy people. But the greater distress occurs when you isolate yourself from the dying person by hiding behind a barrier of pretense. Usually, as I have emphasized in this volume, an open-awareness context is most valuable for caring relationships. That way you can talk or just be together silently without being anxious lest you give away "the secret."

This does not require that you or anyone inform the dying person specifically that he or she is dying. And it certainly doesn't permit you or anyone to offer a timetable for death. Elisabeth Kübler-Ross (1974) encourages letting the patient know that the condition is serious, then permitting the patient to digest this information and bring up the subjects of death and dying when he wishes. If someone believes you care and are open to talking about what is important, that person will bring up dying when he is ready.

Dying people—and, to a lesser extent, those who are grieving—are very vulnerable to others, and they are likely to be willing to pay a high price to keep from being abandoned. If they feel that you might leave them if they tried to talk about death, they probably won't talk about death; if they feel you might leave them if they complained about hospital care or medical care, they will probably avoid such discussion. Your presence, as friend or hospital worker or physician, is more important than airing these ideas or grievances; dying people are in a good position to evaluate other people and then respond in terms of their own survival.

This includes bedside conversions, whether the debate concerns God, afterlife, politics, life-style changes, or the relative merits of community college or a university. The dying person, in order to keep you from leaving, might even totally distort her views. I've often wondered how many deathbed religious conversions were founded on a desire to have one's clergyman present and approving.

Of course, you can disagree with someone who is dying, even become angry with that person, as long as you make it clear that your disagreement or anger will not cause you to leave and remain away. There is no reason why you shouldn't offer your religious views or beliefs about life after death, as long as the price of your company is not agreement with your views.

None of this discussion should be interpreted as meaning that psychological and social care is so important that medical care is unimportant. Medical procedures, medication, surgery, home care—all should be of the highest quality possible. You might even function as an advocate for the dying person or the bereaved individual to get improved physical care.

Similarly, because practical arrangements may worry a dying person, your assistance may entail helping with these arrangements. Knowing that a "proper" funeral has been arranged, that a favorite cousin will receive the topaz earrings, that the children's college has been taken care of, that a caring nurse will be given a token gift, that the credit-card bills have been paid—all these and countless other tasks may weigh heavily on a dying person, who is unable to do them herself. Caring for that person may mean feeding the cat or emptying the garbage or picking up a suit at the cleaners.

The dying or the grieving person may wish to discuss his or her feelings, either about death or about any other topic. You can permit such discussion, but without causing the person to feel that your own needs are so tied up in "talking about death" that the conversation must be held *for you!* I've found dying people to be extremely solicitous of the feelings of those who visit them. If you want to talk about my dying, if that makes you happy and fulfills you, all right, I'll talk about it, although the truth is that I'm rather bored with talking about it.

All of which means that your major task in communication is to be sensitive to what the dying or grieving person is saying to you, to be aware of symbolic language, of body language, and of attempts to find out what you know and how you feel. Sometimes when a patient complains about the physician or the hospital or family members and friends, she is expressing a deeply felt grievance; sometimes the same words are indirectly expressing a displaced anger about dying. Similarly, some patients will become angry with fate or with God, but others are expressing the message "I don't want to die!" And it isn't unusual for dying persons to become angry with those who care for them—like the classroom teacher who harangues the students who are attending class about excessive absences. After all, you are there and provide an available scapegoat. It's helpful to be sensitive to the possibility that these sorts of situations may arise.

Fortunately, dying and grieving people, behind their distress, anger, and frustration, are really caring people—at least as caring as anyone else—and they are likely to care for you. If you do something foolish, misinterpret the meaning of what they are saying, forget to arrive on time, or inadvertantly make a silly statement, they are likely to be forgiving. If they realize that you care for them and that they can trust you, they will overlook all kinds of things they might not really like.

In addition, there are some specific things you can do to facilitate a caring relationship. For example, when you visit someone in a hospital, it can help if your face is on the same level as his face; so sit down to talk. And once you are sitting down, don't sneak quick looks at your watch when you think you aren't being observed; rather, state at the beginning that you can stay for ten minutes or only a couple of minutes or an hour or whatever. And while you are sitting down, don't be afraid to touch your friend's hand or face or to hold hands. Touch is a powerful tool in building a caring relationship. But also don't be reluctant to withdraw your hand if you sense that touching makes your friend uncomfortable.

It may also be helpful to encourage reminiscing. Ask the elderly widow to tell you about her husband, who has recently died. Ask the dying man to tell you about what it was like when he was young. Ask people to tell you about the things that they are proud of, about the times they enjoyed, about the people they liked, about the good things that have happened in their lives.

David Oliver, a sociologist now teaching in Kansas City, tells of visiting an elderly woman in a San Antonio nursing home. He had asked to be introduced to someone who was cognitively alert, who had lived in San Antonio for many years, and who had very few visitors. Oliver told the woman that he had recently moved to San Antonio, that he liked the city, and that he wanted to know more about it: would she tell him what San Antonio was like when she was young? He assumed that 30 to 40 minutes would exhaust both the woman and him. It was over 90 minutes later when the woman began to tire and Dave removed his third 30-minute tape. It had been an exhilarating experience. As Dave left, he said "I'll be back in a couple of months and see you then." Her response was, "I don't think I'll be here then." He hesitated at the door, then turned and said "That's possible, but I hope you will be here and, if you are, I will see you in two months." When he returned, two months later, the woman had died, but she had left her legacy both in Dave's experiences and on his tapes.

Reminiscing with people they love may be very valuable for the dying. It can be an attempt to make sense out of their personal histories, to try to recall why they as individuals mattered or made a difference, to put events and situations into perspective. When this is shared with someone they love, the events take on even more importance. And when the person they talk with also shared the experience they are reliving, the significance can become still greater (Kübler-Ross, 1974).

Nor do you have to be afraid of your own tears, if the experience touches you. The person who is dying can take care of you, or you can take care of each other. A caring relationship is not a one-way relationship—it is reciprocal, although each person gets something different. Chaplain Johnson, mentioned earlier, has offered some helpful words: "Don't cry for the future—cry for right now." There is enough pain and loss and fear happening at the moment to allow for many tears. And there is no need to be brave, put up a good front, or deny hope, when the tears are for the feelings and events of the moment. It hurts, physically and emotionally, right now. You can cry right now.

Don't expect people to follow a preestablished program to die in preestablished stages. Elisabeth Kübler-Ross herself has said "Patients do not necessarily follow a classical pattern from the stage of denial to . . . acceptance. Most of my patients have exhibited two or three stages simultaneously and these do not always occur in the same order" (1974, pp. 25–26). The right way to die is the way the person wants to die, and, if you are open and available, the person will probably let you know what that is. It's not your task to set up a stage time schedule or to be critical of people who don't die the way you want them to die.

CARING FOR PERSONS YOU LOVE

One of the most demanding, and often one of the most rewarding, relationships that you can enter is that of caring for someone you love who is dying. Most dying people receive a lot of physical and psychological care from family members. According to a British study described earlier, married persons received most of their help from spouses (30%) and from children (31%); those widowed or divorced received their support from children (40%) and children-in-law (16%); persons who had never married obtained help from brothers and sisters (24%) and other relatives and in-laws (31%) (Cartwright et al., 1973). The nature of the help received is shown in Table 16–1.

The person who provides the greatest amount of care is in a unique situation. Such caring is often a full-time job, and demands—ranging from changing the dying person's bedding, to giving a bath, to sitting silently and holding hands, to talking about funerals and cemeteries—may be made around the clock. As the person's condition worsens, the demands for attention and involvement increase. At this point, some people hire caretakers at home or transfer the dying to an acute hospital or long-term care facility; others, who want the dying to be able to die at home, face tasks that are continual, difficult, and emotionally draining.

TABLE 16–1. Nature of Help Given Dying Persons by Family and Other Roles

	Percent of Spouses	*Percent of Daughters*	*Percent of Sons*	*Percent of Other Relatives*	*Percent of Friends, Neighbors, Others*
Personal care	80	62	44	47	33
Nursing care	61	39	14	18	9
Night care	55	34	31	24	21
Social care	61	52	39	33	26
Financial care	n.a.	6	15	3	—
Housework	22[a]	50[a]	21	35	44
Total Number	289	341	218	553	441

SOURCE: From *Life before Death*, by A. Cartwright, L. Hockey and J. L. Anderson. Copyright 1973 by Routledge and Kegan Paul. Reprinted by permission.

NOTES: Based on 785 deaths in England.

Examples of personal care are washing, bathing, and taking the dying to the bathroom. Examples of nursing care include giving medicines and injections and massaging the patient. Examples of social care are reading to and writing letters for the dying.

[a]Not including persons who had previously done housework.

The major caretaker may come to resent her involvement, feel that others in the family are not helping enough or that the sacrifices made to provide the care—such as leaving a job, relocating from another community, or requiring younger children to become self-sufficient—are high prices to pay. Given that some tension and resentment might enter the relationship, the caretaker may end up feeling angry and, then, guilty over the anger and over the feeling that she could have done better.

On the other hand, this person has done more than any other. The caretaker, more than any other person, can feel, after the death has occurred, "I did everything I could have done." She becomes a kind of gatekeeper to the dying person and to information about the dying person. When the person's condition becomes truly incapacitating, those who wish to visit must make arrangements through this caretaker; people who call need to talk to the caretaker; friends who want to send their regards or check to see how everything is, do it through the caretaker.

One issue is usually overlooked: who is taking care of the caretaker? Is there enough sustenance from the caretaking role to provide the caretaker with a sense of well being? Are there others in her life who can provide the emotional support that is needed to endure both the physical fatigue and the emotional pain? Are there others also offering help to the dying person? (Table 16–1 would indicate that there often are.) Will there be material rewards after the death has occurred? If the illness is lengthy, is there a way for the caretaker to leave for an evening, a day, a two-week trip?

It's important, as we turn more and more attention to caring for persons who are dying and those who are grieving, that we don't ignore or turn into "villains" those who, either as professionals or as family members, are doing their best to provide physical and emotional care and support.

CARING WHEN DEATH OCCURS

The approach of death, whether at the hospital or in the home, tends to alter the caring procedures. Even in institutions, the psychosocial takes precedence over the medical at that point (Glaser & Strauss, 1968). Rules are bent and even broken. Children, too young to be permitted to visit, are smuggled up the back stairs; forbidden food, drink, or tobacco is provided. The hospital, however, does have practical matters to attend to: seeking autopsy permission when appropriate; anticipating the removal of the body without disturbing the other patients in the room; preparing the death certificate; and establishing the *death watch.*

THE DEATH WATCH

At the end of the death trajectory, the hospital staff (or, if the patient is at home, whoever is responsible for care) becomes deeply involved with providing comfort, reducing pain, and offering the human companionship that may be more important than anything else (Glaser & Strauss, 1968). When the family is not present and the death occurs in the hospital, the person attending these last hours will often need to report to the family how the death occurred; the extent to which they report accurately or attempt to make the family feel better about the final moments of dying is never fully known. Often, of course, the death occurs when no one is in attendance: "She just slipped away quietly during the night."

During the death watch, if the patient is alert, he or she may want to see certain members of the family or make a final attempt to reconcile an ancient feud or confess some earlier transgression in a last attempt to assuage guilt. Similarly, family members may wish to come for a final reunion or to make peace. However, as Kübler-Ross (1969) and others have pointed out, these last hours may be used by the dying person to see only those individuals who seem very important at the time, and it is possible that a cousin or a close friend may appear, only to be told that the dying person has found it impossible to visit with everyone.

Among many families, the death watch is a respected tradition, and at least one family member or friend will be with the dying person at all times. At times, several people will arrive, and, as death nears, many family members may wish to be in attendance. Although this may be a long-held and valued practice of these families, it is often contrary to hospital regulations and regarded as a threat to efficiency and decorum. The nursing staff will try to get most of the visitors to leave; if necessary they will complain that the behavior is disruptive to the other patients.

Although I don't wish at this time to thrust myself right in the middle of the conflict between the needs of the individual dying person and the institution's wish for quiet, I do want to note that we seem to make an implicit assumption that there is value to being in a quiet, peaceful environment when death occurs (Glaser & Strauss, 1968). This may be a valid assumption, but I certainly don't know the evidence for it. Obviously, for people with limited energy, too much stimulation may hasten death, but for some people for whom death is at hand, a certain amount of chaos, noise, and excitement might be desirable.

Although some families will establish a round-the-clock vigil, this is impractical or impossible for others, and the hospital staff will often urge family members to return home to sleep or to get some relief from the tension of being at the hospital. In these situations, however, the family is usually telephoned when death is imminent, so that they can be with their relative when death occurs.

The hospital staff faces a dilemma in these situations. If they telephone the family too soon and the patient recovers somewhat, the trip to the hospital with all its attendant tensions will have to be repeated. It is not unknown for a dying patient to rally three or four times and for the family to have rushed to the hospital for its farewells each time. As might be expected, the family members eventually become detached from the patient's death—a strange example of the boy who cried wolf. On the other hand, if the call is too late, the patient will be dead before the family arrives, and the family may feel guilty about having left the hospital or be angry with the staff for their poor timing.

AT THE MOMENT OF DEATH

Attending a person at the moment of death can be very distressing. Not only are the attending person's feelings about death and loss stress-provoking but the physical changes the body undergoes are also found upsetting (Glaser & Strauss, 1968). Therefore, it is important, even rewarding, to know that one's presence might have provided the deceased with comfort, with a feeling of not having been abandoned.

For the most part, neither fear nor pain appear to be present as death occurs. In our society, many, perhaps most, people are confused or comatose as they die, because of medication or of the effects of their illness. Some people still fight for life—they may feel they are leaving unfinished business, or, not reconciled to death, they do not want to die. Other deaths are, indeed, beautiful: the dying person has made peace with himself or herself and with others, has felt life to be fulfilling, and is ready for the release that comes with death.

And there may be visions. Lecturing in the early 1930s, Alfred Worcester (1940) noted the frequency of such reports in both earlier medical literature and in his own extensive experience as a physician:

> I found a patient propped up in bed, smoking a cigarette and reading the morning paper. He seemed to be normally convalescent after an appendectomy a week earlier. As I left his room the nurse stopped me to report that the patient had been talking to some visitor invisible to her, who he said was dressed in white. I went back to ask him about it. "Oh, it was only my sister," he answered casually and went on reading the newspaper. His sister had died previously, yet her presence seemed to him merely a natural fact. A few hours afterwards, without any other warning, his heart suddenly stopped beating. [p. 54]

The patient was not a particularly religious man nor was Dr. Worcester inclined to the mystical. The story is like many others reported by people during near-death experiences, on "successful" LSD trips, or during mystical or deeply religious experiences; it is also like incidents reported by persons who claim to have died and subsequently returned from death. Dr. Worcester did not presume to explain the cause, nor shall I. The possibilities range wide—from signals of impending death within the body to an encounter with actual ghosts or spirits to a shortage of oxygen in the brain. Your interpretation of these events, and the intensity with which you adhere to it, will say a great deal about your concepts both of subjective reality and of death and immortality.

ARS MORIENDI

Ars Moriendi. The art of dying. What is the art of dying? To die peacefully, accepting death? To die bravely? To die fighting death? In earlier times, people wrote books about how to die, because they believed that the way a person died was a measure of personal worth (Aries, 1974). In earlier times, people "departed easily, as if they were just moving into a new house" (Solzhenitsyn, 1969, p. 100). People were familiar with dying and death, and the possibility of death was never far away; it was neither frightening nor awesome (Aries, 1974). This no longer appears to be the case.

Styles of dying, like all styles, change with time. There have been times in the history of Western culture when, for example, the main concern of the dying person was to conduct himself or herself well during the dying process, since good behavior during this period would be rewarded by entry into heaven (Aries, 1974). At other times, the bedroom of the dying person would be visited, not only by the priest, but by friends, neighbors, family members, and even passersby; nor were children excluded from this event (Aries, 1974).

Preparation to die today seems to concentrate more on the survivors and on unfinished business on earth than on assuring passage to heaven. Since Vatican II, even the Roman Catholic sacrament for the sick, previously referred to as extreme unction, focuses more on grace and life than on expiation of sin, more on healing and less strictly on preparation for death.

Over the centuries, the perceived value of the art of dying has waxed and waned. In some eras, dying well was a significant measure of one's competence; at other times, such as our own, dying has virtually been taken out of the hands of the person to whom it is happening and invested in the health professionals. Now it seems that increasing numbers of people are taking dying and death back into their own hands. The title of a popular book, *Living Your Dying* (Keleman, 1974), testifies to this trend.

A friend suggested "End the book with a section on preparing for death." I thought about that. I could write about the practical matters of preparing for death: making financial arrangements, finishing wills, letting them know at work that you won't be back. Or I could write about the emotional considerations: understand what your death means to you, try to keep important "unfinished business" (that is, unresolved conflicts) with others to a minimum.

In some ways, this entire book encourages preparing for death. By reading and thinking about death, you inevitably begin, even if implicitly, your preparation for your own death. By ridding yourself of stereotypes of what dying is like, by differentiating the process of dying from the illness or condition from which you are dying and this, in turn, from the event of death, by giving thought to death and the process of dying, you can become better prepared for death.

In *The Christmas Carol,* Dickens wrote of Christmas Past, Christmas Present, and Christmas Yet-To-Come. I often think of each of us as consisting of past, present, and yet-to-come. Our past is our memories, for without memories we are nothing. Our present is our meanings, including relationships and tasks, for without these our present is simply empty movement through time and space. Our future is time and hope, for without time there is no future, and without hope, time has little value.

Preparing for death means immersing ourselves even more deeply in the past, present, and yet-to-come. In confronting death, we can enrich ourselves by our memories. This, of course, implies that our lives should be such as to bring us memories that will enrich us. We can enrich ourselves with our meanings—knowing that we have had meaning and that we still have meaning. And we can enrich ourselves with time, even though we realize that there is little time, but, then when all is said and done, time is all that any of us ever has.

A few years ago, a brief book appeared that outlined six styles of dying or of meeting death. Its author encouraged readers to select their own style of dying, and she emphasized that no one style is superior, in principle, to any other, although there may be one style that is superior for you (McCoy, 1974). I was drawn back to this book now because the author is really writing about how to live until death, not just about how to die. The six chapter titles and subtitles are direct quotations representing her six styles.* The comments are my interpretation.

Style One. *For everything there is a season. (An accepting life style that meets death as an inevitable part of creation.)* Death is natural, and I might as well accept it. I can blame it on fate, nature, evolution, or God's will, and I can accept it actively or with resignation, with relief or with distress, but it *will* happen, and accepting it makes the most sense.

Style Two. *Do not go gentle into that good night. (A defiant life style that rebels against death as a personal destroyer.)* Lots of things in life are inevitable, but that doesn't mean I have to wait and let them happen. I can be angry, even in a rage, when I feel cheated or when I feel something important is taken from me. It's not my task to make things easier for people who love me and take care of me. If they really love me, they will understand. Death has no right to take me, and I will fight it every step of the way.

Style Three. *Eat, drink, and be merry. (A sensuous life style that fears death as the denial of human meaning.)* Living fully is good, and death negates the possibility of living fully. I want to live today and worry about death only when I absolutely must. I delight in experiences, not just those that are hedonistic, but those that fulfill my spiritual needs as well. Eventually, when I can no longer postpone it, I may also delight in the anticipation of experiencing death, since it too is an experience.

Style Four. *No one ever died with warm feet. (A humorous life style that dances with death around the edges of ultimate mystery.)* The title is based on an

*From *To Die with Style!* by M. C. McCoy. Copyright 1974 by Abingdon Press. Reprinted by permission of Abingdon Press, Nashville, Tennessee.

anecdote: a theologian was thought to be dead. To make sure one person in the room encouraged another to feel the man's feet, since, he commented, no one ever died with warm feet. At that point, the theologian quipped "John Hus did," and then he lapsed back into himself and soon died. (John Hus was burned at the stake.) In a sense, if I can laugh at death, I can conquer death as it conquers me.

Style Five. *Good night, sweet prince. (A tragic life style that experiences death as always too soon.)* Life is so short that I cannot do all that I wish; death is tragic, poignant, as in the scene from *Hamlet* from which the quote is taken. The unfairness of life, in which some of us pile so many tragic events, is too great. I live and can enjoy life, but always against the backdrop of my eventual death. The comedy must eventually turn into tragedy.

Style Six. *Come now, greatest of feasts. (A questing life style that seeks to find in death the meaning of existence.)* It isn't that I will give up the search now for the meaning of life, but that I anticipate finding it for certain in death, or after death (after McCoy, 1974).

Each of these six styles emerges from the rest of our lives, just as preparing for death must emerge from the rest of our lives. We can accept, become angry, hide in living, be humorous, be tragic, or search for meaning. And we can do some of each.

For me, the best—and in some ways the only—preparation for death is to live each day and each year so that I will be able to look back with feelings of pleasure, satisfaction, and warmth. In essence, the best preparation for death requires that we make the best use of life.

REFERENCES

Abram, H. S. *The choice between dialysis and transplant: Psychosocial considerations.* Presentation at the Institute of Society, Ethics, and Life Sciences, Hastings Center, New York, 1976.

Abram, H. S. Survival by machine: The psychological stress of chronic hemodialysis. In R. H. Moos (Ed.), *Coping with physical illness.* New York: Plenum, 1977.

Abram, H. S., Moore, G. L., & Westervelt, F. B. Suicidal behavior in chronic dialysis patients. *American Journal of Psychiatry,* 1971, *127,* 1199–1204.

Achte, K. A., & Vauhkonen, M.-L. Cancer and the psyche. *Omega,* 1971, *2,* 46–56.

Alexander, I. E., & Adlerstein, A. M. Studies in the psychology of death. In H. P. David & J. C. Brenglemann (Eds.), *Perspectives in personality research.* New York: Springer, 1960.

Alexander, I. E., Colley, R. S., & Adlerstein, A. M. Is death a matter of indifference? *Journal of Psychology,* 1957, *43,* 277–283.

American Council of Life Insurance. *1979 life insurance fact book.* Washington, D.C.: Author, 1979.

Appleton, W. S. The blame of dying young. *American Journal of Psychoanalysis,* 1975, *35,* 377–381.

Archibald, H. C., Bell, D., Miller, C., & Tuddenham, R. D. Bereavement in childhood and adult psychiatric disturbance. *Psychosomatic Medicine,* 1962, *24,* 343–351.

Argyle, M., & Beit-Hallahmi, B. *The social psychology of religion.* London: Routledge & Kegan Paul, 1975.

Ariès, P. *Western attitudes toward death: From the Middle Ages to the present* (P. M. Ranum, Trans.). Baltimore: Johns Hopkins University Press, 1974.

Artiss, K., & Levine, A. Doctor-patient relations in severe illness. *New England Journal of Medicine,* 1973, *288,* 1210–1214.

Augustine, M. J., & Kalish, R. A. Religion, transcendence, and appropriate death. *Journal of Transpersonal Psychology,* 1975, *7,* 1–13.

Averill, J. R. Grief: Its nature and significance. *Psychological Bulletin,* 1968, *70,* 721–748.

Ball, J. F. Widow's grief: The impact of age and mode of death. *Omega,* 1976–77, *7,* 307–333.

Barber, T. X. Death by suggestion. *Psychosomatic Medicine,* 1961, *23,* 153–155.

Barrett, C. J. Effectiveness of widows' groups in facilitating change. *Journal of Consulting and Clinical Psychology,* 1978, *46,* 20–31. (a)

Barrett, C. J. *Strategies for preventing the stresses of widowhood.* Presentation at the Southwestern Psychological Association, New Orleans, 1978. Cited in a working document prepared by R. L. Taylor. (b)

Barry, H., Jr. Significance of maternal bereavement before the age of eight in psychiatric patients. *Archives of Neurology and Psychiatry,* 1949, *62,* 630–637.

Becker, E. *The denial of death.* New York: The Free Press, 1973.

Bellah, R. Transcendence on contemporary piety. In D. Cutler (Ed.), *The religious situation.* Boston: Beacon, 1969.

Beller, S., & Palmore, E. Longevity in Turkey. *Gerontologist,* 1974, *14,* 373–376.

Bendiksen, R., & Fulton, R. Death and the child: An anterospective test of the childhood bereavement and later behavior disorder hypothesis. *Omega,* 1975, *6,* 45–59.

Bengtson, V. L., Cuellar, J. B., & Ragan, P. K. Stratum contrasts and similarities in attitudes toward death. *Journal of Gerontology,* 1977, *32,* 76–88.

Bequaert, L. H. *Single women: Alone and together.* Boston: Beacon Press, 1976.

Bergman, A. B., Pomery, M. A., & Beckwith, B. The psychiatric toll of the sudden infant death syndrome. *GP,* December 1969, *40,* 99–105.

Bertman, S. L. The arts: A source of comfort and insight for children who are learning about death. *Omega,* 1979–80, *10,* 147–162.

Binger, C. M., Ablin, A. R., Feuerstein, R. C., Kushner, J. H., Zoger, S., & Mikkelsen, C. Childhood leukemia: Emotional impact on patient and family. *New England Journal of Medicine,* 1969, *280,* 414–418.

Blauner, R. Death and social structure. *Psychiatry,* 1966, *29,* 378–394.

Blauner, R. Personal communication.

Blazer, J. A. The relationship between meaning in life and fear of death. *Psychology,* 1973, *10,* 33–34.

Bluebond-Langner, M. Meanings of death to children. In H. Feifel (Ed.), *New meanings of death.* New York: McGraw-Hill, 1977.

Bornstein, P. E., & Clayton, P. J. The anniversary reaction. *Diseases of the Nervous System,* 1972, *33,* 470–472.

Bornstein, P. E., Clayton, P. J., Halikas, J. A., Maurice, W. L., & Robins, E. The depression of widowhood after thirteen months. *British Journal of Psychiatry,* 1973, *122,* 561–566.

Bowlby, J. Childhood mourning and its implications for psychiatry. *American Journal of Psychiatry,* 1961, *118,* 481–498.

Bowra, C. M. *The Greek experience.* New York: Mentor Books, 1957.

Brent, S. B. Puns, metaphors, and misunderstandings in a two-year-old's conception of death. *Omega,* 1977–78, *8,* 285–293.

Bromberg, W., & Schilder, P. Death and dying. *Psychoanalytic Review,* 1933, *20,* 133–185.

Bryer, K. B. The Amish way of death. *American Psychologist,* 1979, *34,* 255–261.

Bulka, R. P. Death in life—Talmudic and logotherapeutic affirmations. *Humanitas,* 1974, *10*(1), 33–41.

Bunch, J., & Barraclough, B. The influence of parental death anniversaries upon suicide dates. *British Journal of Psychiatry,* 1971, *118,* 621–626.

Bunch, J., Barraclough, B., Nelson, B., & Sainsbury, P. Early parental bereavement and suicide. *Social Psychiatry,* 1971, *6,* 200–202. (a)

Bunch, J., Barraclough, B., Nelson, B., & Sainsbury, P. Suicide following bereavement of parents. *Social Psychiatry,* 1971, *6,* 193–199. (b)

Butler, R. N. The life review: An interpretation of reminiscence in the aged. *Psychiatry, Journal for the Study of Interpersonal Processes,* 1963. Reprinted in B. L. Neugarten (Ed.), *Middle age and aging.* Chicago: University of Chicago Press, 1968.

Bytheway, W. R. Aspects of old age in age-specific mortality rates. In J. P. Carse & A. B. Dallery (Eds.), *Death and society.* New York: Harcourt Brace Jovanovich, 1977. (Originally published, 1970.)

Cain, A. C., & Cain, B. S. On replacing a child. *Journal of the American Academy of Child Psychiatry,* 1964, *3,* 443–456.

Cain, A. C., Erickson, M. E., Fast, I., & Vaughan, R. A. Children's disturbed reactions to their mother's miscarriage. *Psychosomatic Medicine*, 1964, *26*, 58–66.

Cain, A. C., Fast, I., & Erickson, M. E. Children's disturbed reactions to the death of a sibling. *American Journal of Orthopsychiatry*, 1964, *34*, 741–752.

Cannon, W. B. Voodoo death. *American Anthropologist*, 1942, *44*, 169–181.

Cantril, H. (Ed.). *Public opinion: 1935–1946*. Princeton: Princeton University Press, 1951.

Cappon, D. Attitudes on death. *Omega*, 1970, *1*, 103–108.

Carlin, J. E. The life of the malformed child. In E. M. Pattison (Ed.), *The experience of dying*. Englewood Cliffs, N.J.: Prentice-Hall, 1977.

Cartwright, A., Hockey, L., & Anderson, J. L. *Life before death*. London: Routledge & Kegan Paul, 1973.

Castaneda, C. *A separate reality: Further conversations with Don Juan*. New York: Pocket Books, 1972.

Choron, J. *Death and western thought*. New York: Collier, 1963.

Choron, J. *Modern man and mortality*. New York: Macmillan, 1964.

Clayton, P. J., Halikas, J. A., & Maurice, W. L. The depression of widowhood. *British Journal of Psychiatry*, 1972, *120*, 71–77.

Cochrane, A. L. A little widow is a dangerous thing. *International Journal of Psychoanalysis*, 1936, *17*, 494–509.

Collett, L. J., & Lester, D. The fear of death and the fear of dying. *The Journal of Psychology*, 1969, *72*, 179–181.

Comfort, A. Longer life by 1990? *New Scientist*, 1969, *11*, 549–551.

Cross, F. L. (Ed.). *Oxford dictionary of the Christian church*. London: Oxford University Press, 1958.

Cutter, F. Robert Seymour: A psycho-historical autopsy. *Omega*, 1971, *2*, 195–214.

Derogatis, L., Abeloff, M., & Melisaratos, N. Psychological coping mechanisms and survival time in metastatic breast cancer. *Journal of the American Medical Association*, 1979, *242* (4), 1504–1508.

Dickstein, L. S. Death concern: Measurement and correlates. *Psychological Reports*, 1972, *30*, 563–571.

Diggory, J. C., & Rothman, D. Z. Values destroyed by death. *Journal of Abnormal and Social Psychology*, 1961, *63*, 205–210.

Dore, R. P. *City life in Japan*. Berkeley & Los Angeles: University of California Press, 1958.

Dorpat, T. L., & Ripley, H. S. The relationship between attempted suicide and committed suicide. *Comprehensive Psychiatry*, 1967, *8*, 74–79.

Dublin, L. I. *Factbook on man from birth to death*. New York: Macmillan, 1951.

Durlak, J. A. Relationship between individual attitudes toward life and death. *Journal of Consulting and Clinical Psychology*, 1972, *38*, 463.

Durlak, J. A. Relationship between attitudes toward life and death among elderly women. *Development Psychology*, 1973, *8*, 146.

Durlak, J. A. Comparison between experiential and didactic methods of death education. *Omega*, 1978–79, *9*, 57–66.

Easson, W. M. Management of the dying child. *Journal of Clinical Child Psychology*, 1974, *3*(2), 25–27.

Edinger, E. Metaphysics and the unconscious. *Spring*, 1969, 101–128.

Eliot, T. D. Attitudes toward euthanasia. *Research Studies, State College of Washington*, 1947, *15*, 131–134.

Eliot, T. D. Bereavement: Inevitable but not insurmountable. In H. Becker & R. Hill (Eds.), *Family, marriage, and parenthood*. Boston: Heath, 1955.
Engel, G. Emotional stress and sudden death. *Psychology Today*, November 1977, *11*, 114; 118; 153–154.
Erikson, E. *Childhood and society* (2nd ed.). New York: Norton, 1963.
Ettinger, R. C. W. *The prospect of immortality*. New York: MacFadden, 1966.
Evans, J. C., Jr. *Impact of theological orientation on pastors' grief work therapy with grieving church members*. Unpublished doctoral dissertation, California School of Professional Psychology, Berkeley, 1975.
Farberow, N. L. Introduction. In N. L. Farberow (Ed.), *Taboo topics*. New York: Atherton Press, 1963.
Federal Trade Commission, Bureau of Consumer Protection. *Funeral industry practices*. Washington, D.C.: Author, 1978.
Feifel, H. Older persons look at death. *Geriatrics*, March 1956, *11*, 127–130.
Feifel, H. Attitudes toward death in some normal and mentally ill populations. In H. Feifel (Ed.), *The meaning of death*. New York: McGraw-Hill, 1959.
Feifel, H. Death. In N. L. Farberow (Ed.), *Taboo topics*. New York: Atherton Press, 1963.
Feifel, H., & Branscomb, A. B. Who's afraid of death? *Journal of Abnormal Psychology*, 1973, *81*, 282–288.
Feldman, M. J., & Hersen, M. Attitudes toward death in nightmare subjects. *Journal of Abnormal Psychology*, 1967, *72*, 421–425.
Fenichel, O. *The psychoanalytic theory of neuroses*. New York: Norton, 1945.
Fortier, M. K. *Dreams and preparation for death*. Unpublished doctoral dissertation, California School of Professional Psychology, Berkeley, 1972.
Frankl, V. E. *Man's search for meaning: An introduction to logotherapy*. New York: Washington Square Press, 1963.
Frazer, J. G., & Gaster, T. H. *The new Golden Bough*. New York: S. G. Phillips, 1959.
Freud, S. Thoughts for the times on war and death (J. Traviere, Trans.). In *Collected papers* (Vol. 4). New York: Basic Books, 1959. (Originally published, 1915.) (a)
Freud, S. Mourning and melancholia (J. Traviere, Trans.). In *Collected papers* (Vol. 4). New York: Basic Books, 1959. (Originally published, 1917.) (b)
Freud, S. *Beyond the pleasure principle* (J. Strachey, Trans.) New York: Liveright, 1950. (Originally published, 1920.)
Fulton, R. *The sacred and the secular: Attitudes of the American public toward death*. Milwaukee: Bulfin, 1963.
Fulton, R. The sacred and the secular: Attitudes of the American public toward death, funerals, and funeral directors. In R. Fulton (Ed.), *Death and identity*. New York: Wiley, 1965.
Fulton, R., & Fulton, J. A psychosocial aspect of terminal care: Anticipatory grief. *Omega*, 1971, *2*, 91–100.
Garfield, C. A. Ego functioning, fear of death, and altered states of consciousness. In C. A. Garfield (Ed.), *Rediscovery of the body*. New York: Dell, 1977.
Garfield, C. A. Elements of psychosocial oncology: Doctor-patient relationships in terminal illness. In C. A. Garfield (Ed.), *Psychosocial care of the dying patient*. New York: McGraw-Hill, 1978.
Garfield, C. A. The dying patient's concern with "life after death." In R. Kastenbaum (Ed.), *Between life and death*. New York: Springer, 1979.
Geer, J. H. The development of a scale to measure fear. *Behavior Research and Therapy*, 1965, *3*, 45–53.

Glaser, B. G., & Strauss, A. L. The social loss of dying patients. *American Journal of Nursing,* 1964, *64,* 119–121.

Glaser, B. G., & Strauss, A. L. *Awareness of dying.* Chicago: Aldine, 1965.

Glaser, B. G., & Strauss, A. L. *Time for dying.* Chicago: Aldine, 1968.

Glick, I. O., Weiss, R. S., & Parkes, C. M. *The first year of bereavement.* New York: Wiley, 1974.

Glock, C. Y., & Stark, R. *Religion and society in tension.* Chicago: Rand McNally, 1965.

Goldenberg, H. *Abnormal psychology: A social/community approach.* Monterey, Calif.: Brooks/Cole, 1977.

Golding, S. L., Atwood, G. E., & Goodman, R. A. Anxiety and two cognitive forms of resistance to the idea of death. *Psychological Reports,* 1966, *18,* 359–364.

Gorer, G. The pornography of death. In W. Phillips & P. Rahv (Eds.), *Modern writing.* New York: McGraw-Hill, 1959.

Gorer, G. *Death, grief, and mourning.* New York: Anchor Books, 1967.

Gottlieb, C. Modern art and death. In H. Feifel (Ed.), *The meaning of death.* New York: McGraw-Hill, 1959.

Greeley, A. M. *Sociology of the paranormal: A reconnaissance.* Beverly Hills, Calif.: Sage Publications, 1975.

Greenberger, E. Fantasies of women confronting death. *Journal of Consulting Psychology,* 1965, *29,* 252–260.

Grof, S., & Halifax, J. *The human encounter with death.* New York: Dutton, 1977.

Grof, S., Pahnke, W. N., Kurland, A. A., & Goodman, L. E. *LSD-assisted psychotherapy in patients with terminal cancer.* Presentation at the Fifth Symposium of the Foundation of Thanatology, New York, 1971. (Mimeograph)

Gustafson, E. Dying: The career of the nursing-home patient. *Journal of Health and Social Behavior,* 1973, *13,* 226–235.

Habenstein, R. W., & Lamers, W. M. *Funeral customs the world over.* Milwaukee: Bulfin, 1963.

Hackett, T. P., & Weisman, A. D. "Hexing" in modern medicine. *Proceedings of the Third World Congress of Psychiatry,* 1961, 1249–52.

Hall, G. S. Thanatophobia and immortality. *American Journal of Psychology,* 1915, *26,* 550–613.

Halpern, W. I. Some psychiatric sequelae to crib death. *American Journal of Psychiatry,* 1972, *129*(4), 58–62.

Handal, P. J. The relationship between subjective life expectancy, death anxiety, and general anxiety. *Journal of Clinical Psychology,* 1969, *25,* 39–42.

Handal, P. J., & Rychlak, J. F. Curvilinearity between dream content and death anxiety and the relationship of death anxiety to repression-sensitization. *Journal of Abnormal Psychology,* 1971, *77,* 11–16.

Harmer, R. M. *The high cost of dying.* New York: Crowell-Collier, 1963.

Haug, M. Aging and the right to terminate medical treatment. *Journal of Gerontology,* 1978, *33,* 586–591.

Hilgard, J. R., & Newman, M. F. Anniversaries in mental illness. *Psychiatry,* 1959, *22,* 113–121.

Hilgard, J. R., & Newman, M. F. Evidence for functional genesis in mental illness: Schizophrenia, depressive psychosis, and psychoneurosis. *Journal of Nervous and Mental Diseases,* 1961, *132,* 3–16.

Hinton, J. M. The physical and mental distress of the dying. *Quarterly Journal of Medicine,* 1963, *32,* 1–21.

Hinton, J. M. *Dying* (2nd ed.). Baltimore: Penguin, 1972.

Hinton, J. M. Comparison of places and policies for terminal care. *Lancet,* January 6, 1979, 8106, 29–32.

Holden, C. Cancer and the mind: How are they connected? *Science,* June 1978, *200,* 1363–1369.

Huber, P. S. Death and society among the Anggor of New Guinea. *Omega,* 1972, *3,* 233–243.

Hyland, J. M. *The role of denial in the patient with cancer.* Presentation at the Forum for Death Education and Counseling, Washington, D.C., 1978.

Illinois Department of Public Health, Sudden Infant Death Syndrome & Information and Counseling Project. *Sudden infant death.* Author, 1978.

Jackson, E. N. *Telling a child about death.* New York: Channel Press, 1965.

Jeffers, F. C., Nichols, C. R., & Eisdorfer, C. Attitudes of older persons toward death: A preliminary study. *Journal of Gerontology,* 1961, *16,* 53–56.

Jones, B. *Design for death.* London: Andre Deutsch, 1967.

Jones, E. *The life and work of Sigmund Freud.* New York: Basic Books, 1952.

Jung, C. G. The soul and death. In H. Feifel (Ed.), *The meaning of death.* New York: McGraw-Hill, 1959. (Originally published, 1934.)

Kalish, R. A. An approach to the study of death attitudes. *American Behavioral Scientist,* 1963, *6,* 68–70.

Kalish, R. A. A continuum of subjectively perceived death. *Gerontologist,* 1966, *6,* 73–76.

Kalish, R. A. Life and death: Dividing the indivisible. *Social Science and Medicine,* 1968, *2,* 249–259.

Kalish, R. A. Experiences of persons reprieved from death. In A. H. Kutscher (Ed.), *Death and bereavement.* Springfield, Ill.: Charles C Thomas, 1969.

Kalish, R. A. Non-medical interventions in life and death. *Social Science and Medicine,* 1970, *4,* 655–665.

Kalish, R. A. Sex and marital role differences in anticipation of age-produced dependency. *Journal of Genetic Psychology,* 1971, *119,* 53–62.

Kalish, R. A. Special memorial. . . . *Gerontologist,* 1972, *12,* 324.

Kalish, R. A. Dying and preparing for death: A view of families. In H. Feifel (Ed.), *New meanings of death.* New York: McGraw-Hill, 1977.

Kalish, R. A. Death educator as deacon. *Omega,* 1980–81, *11,* 75–85.

Kalish, R. A., & Goldberg, H. Clergy attitudes toward funeral directors. *Death Education,* 1978, *2,* 247–260.

Kalish, R. A., & Goldberg, H. Community attitudes toward funeral directors. *Omega,* 1979–80, *10,* 335–346.

Kalish, R. A., & Johnson, A. I. Value similarities and differences in three generations of women. *Journal of Marriage and the Family,* 1972, *34,* 49–54.

Kalish, R. A., & Reynolds, D. K. *Death and ethnicity: A psychocultural study.* Los Angeles: University of Southern California Press, 1976.

Kalish, R. A., Reynolds, D. K., & Farberow, N. L. Community attitudes toward suicide. *Community Mental Health Journal,* 1974, *10,* 301–308.

Kass, L. R. Death as an event: A commentary on Robert Morison. *Science,* 1971, *173,* 698–702.

Kastenbaum, R. J. Multiple perspectives on a geriatric "Death Valley." *Community Mental Health Journal,* 1967, *3,* 21–29. (a)

Kastenbaum, R. J. The mental life of dying geriatric patients. *The Gerontologist,* 1967, *7,* 97–100. (b)

Kastenbaum, R. J. The child's understanding of death: How does it develop? In E. A. Grollman (Ed.), *Explaining death to children.* Boston: Beacon Press, 1967. (c)

Kastenbaum, R. J. Death and bereavement in later life. In A. H. Kutscher (Ed.), *Death and bereavement.* Springfield, Ill.: Charles C Thomas, 1969.

Kastenbaum, R. J. Is death a life crisis? On the confrontation with death in theory and practice. In N. Datan & L. H. Ginsberg (Eds.), *Life-span developmental psychology: Normative life crises.* New York: Academic Press, 1975.

Kastenbaum, R. J. We covered death today. *Death Education,* 1977, *1,* 86–92.

Kastenbaum, R. J. *Death, society, and human experience.* St. Louis: Mosby, 1977.

Kastenbaum, R. J., & Aisenberg, R. B. *The psychology of death.* New York: Springer, 1972.

Kastenbaum, R. J., & Briscoe, L. The street corner: Laboratory for the study of life-threatening behavior. *Omega,* 1975, *6,* 33–44.

Kastenbaum, R. J., & Candy, S. E. The 4% fallacy: A methodological and empirical critique of extended care facility population statistics. *Aging and Human Development,* 1973, *4,* 15–22.

Kastenbaum, R. J., & Kastenbaum, B. S. Hope, survival, and the caring environment. In E. Palmore & F. C. Jeffers (Eds.), *Prediction of life span.* Lexington, Mass.: D. C. Heath, 1971.

Keleman, S. *Living your dying.* New York: Random House, 1974.

Kelly, O. E. Living with a life-threatening illness. In C. A. Garfield (Ed.), *Psychosocial care of the dying patient.* New York: McGraw-Hill, 1978.

Kimsey, L. R., Roberts, J. L., & Logan, D. L. Death, dying, and denial in the aged. *American Journal of Psychiatry,* 1972, *129,* 161–166.

Klein, M. A contribution to the theory of anxiety and guilt. *International Journal of Psychoanalysis,* 1948, *29,* 114–123.

Knott, J. E., & Prull, R. W. Death education: Accountable to whom? For what? *Omega,* 1976, *7,* 177–181.

Knutson, A. L. The definition and value of a new human life. *Social Science and Medicine,* 1967, *1,* 7–29.

Koenig, R. R. Fatal illness: A survey of social service needs. *Social Work,* 1968, *13,* 85–90.

Koenig, R. R. Anticipating death from cancer—physician and patient attitudes. *Michigan Medicine,* 1969, *68,* 899–905.

Koestenbaum, P. *The vitality of death.* Westport, Conn.: Greenwood Publishing Company, 1971.

Kogan, N., & Wallach, M. Age changes in values and attitudes. *Journal of Gerontology,* 1961, *16,* 272–280.

Kroeber, A. L. *Anthropology* (2nd ed.). New York: Harcourt, Brace, 1948.

Kübler-Ross, E. *On death and dying.* New York: Macmillan, 1969.

Kübler-Ross, E. *Questions and answers on death and dying.* New York: Macmillan, 1974.

Kübler-Ross, E. The languages of dying. *Journal of Clinical Child Psychology,* Summer 1974, *3,* 22–24.

Kübler-Ross, E. Introduction. In E. Kübler-Ross (Ed.), *Death: The final stage of growth.* Englewood Cliffs, N.J.: Prentice-Hall, 1975.

Kunz, P. R., & Summers, J. A time to die: A study of the relationship of birthdays to time of death. *Omega,* 1979–80, *10,* 281–290.

Langer, W. L. The black death. *Scientific American,* February 1964, *210,* 114–121.

Leaf, A. Getting old. *Scientific American,* September 1973, *229,* 44–53.

Lepp, I. *Death and its mysteries.* New York: Macmillan, 1968.

Lerner, M. When, why, and where people die. In O. G. Brim, H. E. Freeman, S. Levine, & N. A. Scotch (Eds.), *The dying patient.* New York: Russell Sage, 1970.

LeShan, L. Mobilizing the life force. *Annals of the New York Academy of Sciences,* 1969, *164,* 847–861. (a)

LeShan, L. Psychotherapy and the dying patient. In L. Pearson (Ed.), *Death and dying.* Cleveland: Case Western Reserve University Press, 1969. (b)

LeShan, L., & LeShan, E. Psychotherapy and the patient with a limited life span. *Psychiatry,* 1961, *24,* 318–323.

Lester, D. Experimental and correlational studies of the fear of death. *Psychological Bulletin,* 1967, *67,* 27–36.

Lester, G., & Lester, D. *Suicide: The gamble with death.* Englewood Cliffs, N.J.: Prentice-Hall, 1971.

Levinson, D. J. *The seasons of a man's life.* New York: Knopf, 1978.

Leviton, D., & Fretz, B. Effects of death education on fear of death and attitudes towards death and life. *Omega,* 1978–79, *3,* 267–277.

Levy, B., & Sclare, A. A study of bereavement in general practice. *Journal of the Royal College of General Practitioners,* 1976, *26,* 329–336.

Lifton, R. J. *Death in life: Survivors of Hiroshima.* New York: Random House, 1967.

Lifton, R. J. The sense of immortality: On death and the continuity of life. In H. Feifel (Ed.), *New meanings of death.* New York: McGraw-Hill, 1977.

Lifton, R. J., & Olson, E. *Living and dying.* New York: Praeger, 1974.

Lindemann, E. Symptomatology and management of acute grief. *American Journal of Psychiatry,* 1944, *101,* 141–148. Reprinted in R. Fulton (Ed.), *Death and identity.* New York: Wiley, 1965.

The longest war. *Newsweek,* June 11, 1979, p. 100.

Lopata, H. Z. *Widowhood in an American city.* Cambridge, Mass.: Schenkman, 1973.

Maddison, D., & Viola, A. The health of widows in the year following bereavement. *Journal of Psychosomatic Research,* 1968, *12,* 297–306.

Mandelbaum, D. G. Social uses of funeral rites. In H. Feifel (Ed.), *The meaning of death.* New York: McGraw-Hill, 1959.

Markusen, E., & Fulton, R. Childhood bereavement and behavioral disorders: A critical review. *Omega,* 1971, *2,* 107–117.

Marris, P. *Loss and change.* New York: Anchor Books, 1975.

Marshall, V. W. Socialization for impending death in a retirement village. *American Journal of Sociology,* 1975, *80,* 1124–1144.

Marshall, V. W. *Last chapters: A Sociology of aging and dying.* Monterey, Calif.: Brooks/Cole, 1980.

Marshall, V. W. Death, dying, and adjustment to death and dying. In D. Mangen & W. A. Peterson (Eds.), *Research instruments in social gerontology.* Minneapolis: University of Minnesota Press, in press.

Martin, D. S., & Wrightsman, L. The relationship between religious behavior and concern about death. *Journal of Social Psychology,* 1965, *65,* 317–323.

Maslow, A. H. *Religions, values, and peak experiences.* New York: Viking Press, 1970.

Maurer, A. The child's knowledge of non-existence. *Journal of Existential Psychiatry,* 1961, *2,* 193–212.

Maurer, A. Maturation of concepts of death. *British Journal of Medical Psychology,* 1966, *39,* 35–51.

Mazess, R. B., & Forman, S. H. Longevity and age by exaggeration in Vilcabamba, Ecuador. *Journal of Gerontology,* 1979, *34,* 94–98.

Mbiti, J. S. *African religions and philosophy.* Garden City, N.Y.: Anchor Books, 1970.
McClelland, D. The Harlequin complex. In R. White (Ed.), *The study of lives.* New York: Atherton Press, 1963.
McCoy, M. C. *To die with style!* Nashville: Abingdon Press, 1974.
Mechanic, D. *Medical sociology: A selective view.* New York: The Free Press, 1968.
Medvedev, Z. A. Caucasus and Altay longevity: A biological or social problem? *Gerontologist,* 1974, *14,* 381–387.
Menig-Peterson, C., & McCabe, A. Children talk about death. *Omega,* 1977–78, *8,* 305–317.
Meyers, D. W. The California Natural Death Act: A critical appraisal. *California State Bar Journal,* 1977, *52,* 326–331; 381–383.
Mitchell, M. E. *The child's attitude to death.* New York: Schocken, 1967.
Mitford, J. *The American way of death.* New York: Simon & Schuster, 1963.
Moody, R. A., Jr. *Life after life.* New York: Bantam Books, 1976.
Morgan, S. A., Buchanan, D., & Abram, H. S. Psychosocial aspects of hyaline membrane disease. *Psychosomatics,* 1976, *17*(3), 147–150.
Morrissey, J. R. A note on interviews with children facing imminent death. *Social Casework,* 1963, *44,* 343–345.
Moss, L. M., & Hamilton, D. F. Psychotherapy of the suicidal patient. In E. S. Shneidman & N. L. Farberow (Eds.), *Clues to suicide.* New York: McGraw-Hill, 1957.
Murdock, G. P. *Social structure.* New York: Macmillan, 1949.
Myers, G. C., & Soldo, B. J. Older Americans: Who are they? In R. A. Kalish (Ed.), *The later years: Social applications of gerontology.* Monterey, Calif.: Brooks/Cole, 1977.
Nagy, M. H. The child's theories concerning death. *Journal of Genetic Psychology,* 1948, *73,* 3–27.
National Council on the Aging. *The myth and reality of aging in America.* Washington, D.C.: Author, 1975.
Natterson, J. M., & Knudson, A. G. Observations concerning fear of death in fatally ill children and their mothers. *Psychosomatic Medicine,* 1960, *22,* 456–465.
Nelson, L. D., & Nelson, C. C. *Religion and death anxiety.* Presentation at the annual meeting of the Society for the Scientific Study of Religion, San Francisco, 1973.
Nelson, L. D., & Nelson, C. C. A factor analytic inquiry into the multidimensionality of death anxiety. *Omega,* 1975, *6,* 171–178.
Noss, J. B. *Man's religions* (4th ed.). New York: Macmillan, 1969.
Noyes, R., & Kletti, R. The experience of dying from falls. *Omega,* 1972, *3,* 45–52.
Noyes, R., & Kletti, R. Depersonalization in the face of life-threatening danger: An interpretation. *Omega,* 1976, *7,* 103–114.
Noyes, R., & Slymen, D. J. The subjective response to life-threatening danger. *Omega,* 1978–79, *9,* 313–321.
Nuckols, R. Widows study. JSAS *Catalog of Selected Documents in Psychology,* 1973, *3,* 9. Cited in a working document prepared by R. L. Taylor.
Oppenheimer, J. R. Use of crisis intervention in casework with the cancer patient and his family. *Social Work,* April 1967, *12,* 44–52.
Osis, K., & Haraldsson, E. *At the hour of death.* New York: Avon, 1977.
Osler, W. *Science and immortality.* Boston: Houghton Mifflin, 1904.
Pahnke, W. A. The psychedelic mystical experience in the human encounter with death. *Harvard Theological Review,* 1969, *62,* 1–32.

Parkes, C. M. The effects of bereavement on physical and mental health—a study of the medical records of widows. *British Medical Journal,* 1964, *2,* 274–279.

Parkes, C. M. *Bereavement.* New York: International Universities Press, 1972.

Parkes, C. M. Components of the reaction to the loss of a limb, spouse, or home. *Journal of Psychosomatic Research,* 1972, *16,* 343–349.

Parkes, C. M. *Evaluation of family care in terminal illness.* Alexander Ming Fisher lecture, Columbia University, New York, 1975. Reported in Saunders, 1977.

Parkes, C. M. Determinants of outcome following bereavement. *Omega,* 1975, *6,* 303–323.

Parkes, C. M., Benjamin, B., & Fitzgerald, R. G. Broken heart: A statistical study of increased mortality among widowers. *British Medical Journal,* 1969, *1,* 740–743.

Parkes, C. M., & Brown, R. Health after bereavement: A controlled study of young Boston widows and widowers. *Psychosomatic Medicine,* 1972, *34,* 449–461.

Parsons, T., & Lidz, V. Death in American society. In E. S. Schneidman (Ed.), *Essays in self-destruction.* New York: Science House, 1967.

Pattison, E. M. (Ed.). *The experience of dying.* Englewood Cliffs, N.J.: Prentice-Hall, 1977. (a)

Pattison, E. M. The dying experience—retrospective analysis. In E. M. Pattison (Ed.), *The experience of dying.* Englewood Cliffs, N.J.: Prentice-Hall, 1977. (b)

Paulay, D. Slow death: One survivor's experience. *Omega,* 1977–78, *8,* 173–179.

Phillips, D. P., & Feldman, K. A. A dip in deaths before ceremonial occasions: Some new relationships between social integration and mortality. *American Sociological Review,* 1973, *38,* 678–696.

Pine, V. R. The social context of disaster. In V. R. Pine (Ed.), *Responding to disaster.* Milwaukee: Bulfin, 1974.

Pine, V. R. *Caretaker of the dead: The American funeral director.* New York: Irvington, 1975.

Pollak, J. M. Correlates of death anxiety: A review of empirical studies. *Omega,* 1979–80, *10,* 97–121.

Portz, A. The child's sense of death. In A. Godin (Ed.), *Death and presence.* Brussels, Belgium: Lumen Vitae Press, 1972.

Raether, H. C., & Slater, R. C. *The funeral: Facing death as an experience of life.* Milwaukee: National Funeral Directors Association, 1974.

Raether, H. C., & Slater, R. C. Immediate postdeath activities in the United States. In H. Feifel (Ed.), *New meanings of death.* New York: McGraw-Hill, 1977.

Ramsey, P. The indignity of 'death with dignity.' In P. Steinfels & R. M. Veatch (Eds.), *Death inside out.* New York: Harper & Row, 1975.

Rees, W. D., & Lutkins, S. G. Mortality of bereavement. *British Medical Journal,* 1967, *4,* 13–16.

Reynolds, D. K., & Farberow, N. L. *Suicide: Inside and out.* Berkeley & Los Angeles: University of California Press, 1976.

Reynolds, D. K., & Kalish, R. A. Anticipation of futurity as a function of ethnicity and age. *Journal of Gerontology,* 1974, *29,* 224–231. (a)

Reynolds, D. K., & Kalish, R. A. The social ecology of dying: Observations of wards for the terminally ill. *Hospital and Community Psychiatry,* 1974, *25*(3), 147–152. (b)

Reynolds, D. K., & Kalish, R. A. Death rates, attitudes, and the ethnic press. *Ethnicity,* 1976, *3,* 305–316.

Rhudick, R. J., & Dibner, A. S. Age, personality, and health correlates of death concern in normal aged individuals. *Journal of Gerontology,* 1961, *16,* 44–49.

Ribble, M. A. *The rights of infants: Early psychological needs and their satisfaction.* New York: Columbia University Press, 1943.

Richmond, J. B., & Waisman, H. A. Psychologic aspects of management of children with malignant diseases. *American Journal of the Diseases of Children,* 1955, *89,* 42–47.

Richter, C. P. The phenomenon of unexplained sudden death in animals and man. In H. Feifel (Ed.), *The meaning of death.* New York: McGraw-Hill, 1959.

Riley, J. W., Jr. Unpublished research data. In M. Riley, A. Foner, & Associates (Eds.), *Aging and society: Vol. I: An inventory of research findings.* New York: Russell Sage, 1968.

Riley, J. W., Jr. What people think about death. In O. G. Brim, H. E. Freeman, S. Levine, & N. A. Scotch (Eds.), *The dying patient.* New York: Russell Sage, 1970.

Rosen, D. Suicide survivors: A follow-up study of persons who survived jumps from the Golden Gate and San Francisco Bay bridges. *Western Journal of Medicine,* 1975, *122,* 289–294.

Rosen, D. Suicide survivors: Psychotherapeutic implications of egocide. *Suicide and Life-Threatening Behavior,* 1976, *6,* 209–215.

Rosenbaum, E. H. Oncology/hematology and psychosocial support of the cancer patient. In C. A. Garfield (Ed.), *Psychosocial care of the dying patient.* New York: McGraw-Hill, 1978.

Rosenfeld, A. H. *New views on older lives.* Washington, D.C.: Government Printing Office, 1978.

Rosenzweig, S., & Bray, D. Sibling deaths in the anamneses of schizophrenic patients. *Archives of Neurology and Psychiatry,* 1943, *49,* 71–92.

Rothstein, S. H. *Aging awareness and personalization of death in the young and middle adult years.* Unpublished doctoral dissertation, University of Chicago, 1967.

Rowland, K. F. Environmental events predicting death for the elderly. *Psychological Bulletin,* 1977, *84,* 349–372.

Sabom, M. B., & Kreutziger, S. The experience of near death. *Death Education,* 1977, *1,* 195–203.

Saltus, R. Suicides climb among the young. *San Francisco Examiner and Chronicle,* Oct 21, 1979, p. 18.

Saunders, C. Dying they live: St. Christopher's Hospice. In H. Feifel (Ed.), *New meanings of death.* New York: McGraw-Hill, 1977.

Schoenberg, J., & Stichman, J. *How to survive your husband's heart attack.* New York: David McKay, 1974.

Schowalter, J. E. The adolescent with cancer. In E. M. Pattison (Ed.), *The experience of dying.* Englewood Cliffs, N.J.: Prentice-Hall, 1977.

Schulz, R. *The psychology of death, dying, and bereavement.* Reading, Mass.: Addison-Wesley, 1978.

Schulz, R., & Aderman, D. Clinical research and the stages of dying. *Omega,* 1974, *5,* 137–143.

Scott, C. A. Old age and death. *American Journal of Psychology,* 1896, *8,* 54–122.

Searles, H. F. Schizophrenia and the inevitability of death. *Psychiatric Quarterly,* 1961, *35,* 631–655.

Segal, H. Fear of death: Notes on the analysis of an old man. *International Journal of Psychoanalysis,* 1958, *39,* 178–181.

Shaffer, T. L. *Death, property, and lawyers.* New York: Dunellen, 1970.
Shaffer, T. L., & Rodes, R. E., Jr. Law for those who are to die. In H. Feifel (Ed.), *New meanings of death.* New York: McGraw-Hill, 1977.
Sharapan, H. "Mister Rogers' Neighborhood": Dealing with death on children's television series. *Death Education,* 1977, *1,* 131–136.
Share, L. Family communication in the crisis of a child's fatal illness: A literature review and analysis. *Omega,* 1972, *3,* 187–201.
Sharma, K. L., & Jain, U. C. Religiosity and fear of death in young and retired persons. *Indian Journal of Gerontology,* 1969, *1,* 110–114.
Sheehy, G. *Passages.* New York: Dutton, 1976.
Shneidman, E. S. The enemy. *Psychology Today,* August 1970, *4,* 37–41.
Shneidman, E. S. You and death. *Psychology Today,* 1971, *5,* 43*ff.*
Shneidman, E. S. On the deromanticization of death. *American Journal of Psychotherapy,* 1971, *25,* 4–17.
Shneidman, E. S. *Deaths of man.* New York: Quadrangle/New York Times, 1973.
Shoor, M., & Speed, M. H. Death, delinquency, and the mourning process. *Psychiatry Quarterly,* 1963, *37,* 540–548.
Siegman, A. Mimeograph, 1961.
Simmons, L. W. *The role of the aged in primitive society.* New Haven: Yale University Press, 1945.
Simonton, O. C., Matthews-Simonton, S., & Creighton, J. *Getting well again.* Los Angeles: Tarcher, 1978.
Simpson, M. A. *The facts of death.* Englewood Cliffs, N.J.: Prentice-Hall, 1979.
Smith, J. Q. The life and death of a schizophrenic. *Psychotherapy: Theory, Research, and Practice,* 1975, *12,* 2–7.
Solzhenitsyn, A. *Cancer ward.* New York: Farrar, Straus, and Giroux, 1969.
Some basic facts about SIDS. Washington, D.C.: Government Printing Office, 1972.
Spinetta, J. J. Communication patterns in families dealing with life-threatening illness. In O. J. Z. Sahler (Ed.), *The child and death.* St. Louis: Mosby, 1978.
Spinetta, J. J., Rigler, D., & Karon, M. Anxiety in the dying child. *Pediatrics,* 1973, *52,* 841–844.
Steele, D. W. *The funeral director's guide to designing and implementing programs for the widowed.* No city cited: National Funeral Directors Association, 1975.
Stein, Z., & Susser, M. Widowhood and mental illness. *British Journal of Preventive Social Medicine,* 1969, *23,* 106–110.
Stekel, W. *Conditions of nervous anxiety and their treatment.* New York: Liveright Publishing Co., 1949.
Strassman, H. D., Thaler, M., & Schein, E. H. A prisoner of war syndrome: Apathy as a reaction to severe stress. *American Journal of Psychiatry,* 1956, *112,* 998–1003.
Strauss, A. L., & Glaser, B. G. *Anguish.* Mill Valley, Calif.: Sociology Press, 1970.
Sudnow, D. *Passing on: The social organization of dying.* Englewood Cliffs, N.J.: Prentice-Hall, 1967.
Swenson, W. M. Attitudes toward death in an aged population. *Journal of Gerontology,* 1961, *16,* 49–52.
Szybist, C. *The subsequent child.* New York: National Foundation for Sudden Infant Death, n.d.
Templer, D. I. The construction and validation of a death anxiety scale. *Journal of General Psychology,* 1970, *82,* 165–177.

Templer, D. I. Death anxiety in religiously very involved persons. *Psychological Reports,* 1972, *31,* 361–362.

Templer, D. I., Ruff, C., & Frank, C. Death anxiety: Age, sex, and parental resemblance in diverse populations. *Developmental Psychology,* 1971, *4,* 108.

Thielicke, H. *Death and life.* Philadelphia: Fortress Press, 1970.

Tillich, P. *The theology of culture.* New York: Oxford University Press, 1959.

Toch, R. Cancer in the school-age child. In E. M. Pattison (Ed.), *The experience of dying.* Englewood Cliffs, N.J.: Prentice-Hall, 1977.

Townes, B. D., & Wold, D. A. Childhood leukemia. In E. M. Pattison (Ed.), *The experience of dying.* Englewood Cliffs, N.J.: Prentice-Hall, 1977.

Vachon, M. L. S. Motivation and stress experienced by staff working with the terminally ill. *Death Education,* 1978, *2,* 113–122.

Veatch, R. M. *Death, dying, and the biological revolution.* New Haven: Yale University Press, 1976.

Visher, E. B., & Visher, J. S. *Stepfamilies: A guide to working with stepparents and stepchildren.* New York: Brunner Mazel, 1979.

Volkan, V. D. Typical findings in pathological grief. *Psychiatric Quarterly,* 1970, *44,* 231–250.

Volkan, V. D., Cilluffo, A. F., & Sarvay, T. L., Jr. Re-grief therapy and the function of the linking object as a key to stimulate emotionality. In P. Olsen (Ed.), *Emotional flooding.* New York: Behavioral Publications, 1975.

Volkart, E. H., & Michael, S. T. Bereavement and mental health. In A. H. Leighton, J. A. Clausen, & R. N. Wilson (Eds.), *Explorations in social psychiatry.* New York: Basic Books, 1957.

Waechter, E. H. Children's awareness of fatal illness. *American Journal of Nursing,* 1971, *71,* 1168–1172.

Wahl, C. W. The fear of death. In H. Feifel (Ed.), *The meaning of death.* New York: McGraw-Hill, 1959.

Wass, H., Christian, M., Myers, J., & Murphy, M. Similarities and dissimilarities in attitudes toward death in a population of older persons. *Omega,* 1978–79, *9,* 337–354.

Watts, A. W. *The way of Zen.* New York: Pantheon, 1957.

Watts, P. R. Evaluation of death attitude change resulting from a death education instructional unit. *Death Education,* 1977, *1,* 187–193.

Weisman, A. D. *On dying and denying.* New York: Behavioral Publications, 1972.

Weisman, A. D., & Hackett, T. P. Predilection to death: Death and dying as a psychiatric problem. *Psychosomatic Medicine,* 1961, *23,* 232–256.

Weisman, A. D., & Kastenbaum, R. J. The psychological autopsy: A study of the terminal phase of life. *Community Mental Health Journal Monograph,* No. 4. New York: Behavioral Publications, 1968.

Weisman, A. D., & Worden, J. W. Psychosocial analysis of cancer deaths. *Omega,* 1975, *6,* 61–75.

Weiss, R. S. *Marital separation.* New York: Basic Books, 1975.

Wolfenstein, M. *Disaster: A psychological essay.* New York: The Free Press, 1957.

Woodruff, D. S. *Can you live to be 100?* New York: Chatham Square Press, 1977.

Woodson, R. Hospice care in terminal illness. In C. A. Garfield (Ed.), *Psychosocial care of the dying patient.* New York: McGraw-Hill, 1978.

Worcester, A. *The care of the aged, the dying and the dead* (2nd ed.). Springfield, Ill.: Charles C Thomas, 1961.

Yamamoto, J., Okonogi, K., Iwasaki, T., & Yoshimura, S. Mourning in Japan. *American Journal of Psychiatry,* 1969, *125,* 1660–1665.

Young, M., Benjamin, B., & Wallis, C. The mortality of widowers. *Lancet,* 1963, *2,* 454–456.

Zeligs, R. *Children's experience with death.* Springfield, Ill.: Charles C Thomas, 1974.

Zinker, J. C., & Fink, S. L. The possibility of psychological growth in a dying person. *Journal of General Psychology,* 1966, *74,* 185–199.

NAME INDEX

SUBJECT INDEX